OXFORD

Papua New Guinea
Lower Primary
DICTIONARY

Adapted by
Ken & Lesley Wing Jan

OXFORD
UNIVERSITY PRESS
AUSTRALIA & NEW ZEALAND

Oxford University Press is a department of the University of Oxford. It furthers the University's objective of excellence in research, scholarship, and education by publishing worldwide. Oxford is a registered trademark of Oxford University Press in the UK and in certain other countries.

Published in Australia by
Oxford University Press
Level 8,737 Bourke Street,Docklands,Victoria 3008,Australia

First published 2007
Reprinted 2007, 2009, 2011, 2012, 2013 (twice), 2014, 2016, 2019 (twice), 2021, 2023, 2024

This edition is adapted by Ken and Lesley Win Jan from the
Oxford Papua New Guinea: The Essential Primary Dictionary.

Papua New Guinea Lower Primary Dictionary

ISBN 978 0 19 556061 9

Printed in China by Golden Cup Printing Co. Ltd

Oxford University Press Australia & New Zealand is committed to sourcing paper responsibly.

Contents

Introduction iv

- How the dictionary is set out v
- How the information about each word is set out vi

Papua New Guinea Lower Primary Dictionary 1

Appendices 258

- Days of the week 258
- Months of the year 258
- Words that come from people's names 259
- Shapes 260
- Solid shapes 260
- Machines, science and technology 261
- Papua New Guinea 261
- Biological classification words 263
- My body: inside and out 263
- Abbreviations 263
- Map of Papua New Guinea 264

Introduction

Welcome to
Papua New Guinea Lower Primary Dictionary

By using this **dictionary** you should be able to find out new things about many of the words that you use including:

- their meanings (definitions);
- how they are used in sentences (part of speech);
- how they are said (pronunciation guide);
- how they are spelt; and
- other words that are related to them (Word Building).

At the end of the dictionary are the **appendices**. These are lists of words that are grouped together because they are similar in some way. Beside each word is a page number that will help you find more information about it.

To help you successfully use this dictionary, the information on the following pages should be very useful.

How the dictionary is set out

Alphabetical order

The words are arranged in alphabetical order. Down the side of each page is an alphabet strip to help you with the alphabetical order.

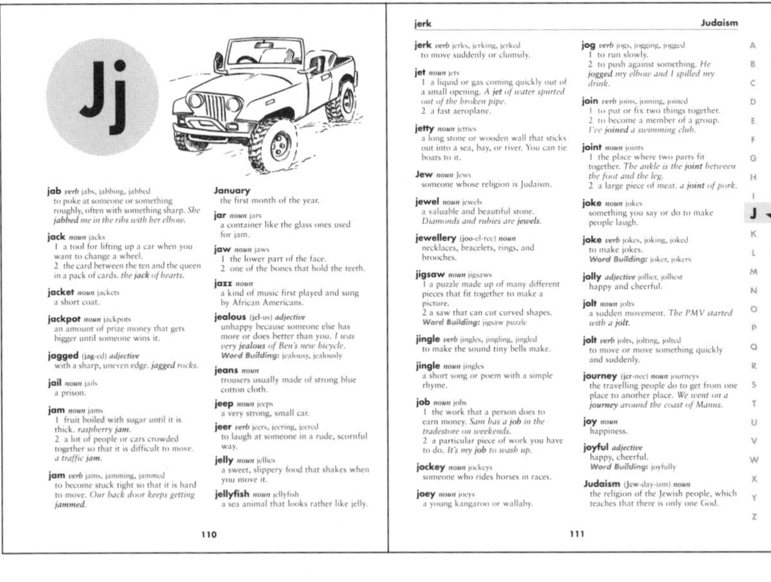

Jj

jab *verb* jabs, jabbing, jabbed
to poke at someone or something roughly, often with something sharp. *She* ***jabbed*** *me in the ribs with her elbow.*

jack *noun* jacks
1 a tool for lifting up a car when you want to change a wheel.
2 the card between the ten and the queen in a pack of cards. *the* ***jack*** *of hearts.*

jacket *noun* jackets
a short coat.

jackpot *noun* jackpots
an amount of prize money that gets bigger until someone wins it.

jagged (jag-ed) *adjective*
with a sharp, uneven edge. ***jagged*** *rocks.*

jail *noun* jails
a prison.

jam *noun* jams
1 fruit boiled with sugar until it is thick. *raspberry* ***jam.***
2 a lot of people or cars crowded together so that it is difficult to move. *a traffic* ***jam.***

jam *verb* jams, jamming, jammed
to become stuck tight so that it is hard to move. *Our back door keeps getting* ***jammed.***

January
the first month of the year.

jar *noun* jars
a container like the glass ones used for jam.

jaw *noun* jaws
1 the lower part of the face.
2 one of the bones that hold the teeth.

jazz *noun*
a kind of music first played and sung by African Americans.

jealous (jel-us) *adjective*
unhappy because someone else has more or does better than you. *I was very* ***jealous*** *of Ben's new bicycle.*
Word Building: jealousy, jealously

jeans *noun*
trousers usually made of strong blue cotton cloth.

jeep *noun* jeeps
a very strong, small car.

jeer *verb* jeers, jeering, jeered
to laugh at someone in a rude, scornful way.

jelly *noun* jellies
a sweet, slippery food that shakes when you move it.

jellyfish *noun* jellyfish
a sea animal that looks rather like jelly.

110

jerk — **Judaism**

jerk *verb* jerks, jerking, jerked
to move suddenly or clumsily.

jet *noun* jets
1 a liquid or gas coming quickly out of a small opening. *A* ***jet*** *of water spurted out of the broken pipe.*
2 a fast aeroplane.

jetty *noun* jetties
a long stone or wooden wall that sticks out into a sea, bay, or river. You can tie boats to it.

Jew *noun* Jews
someone whose religion is Judaism.

jewel *noun* jewels
a valuable and beautiful stone. *Diamonds and rubies are* ***jewels.***

jewellery (joo-el-ree) *noun*
necklaces, bracelets, rings, and brooches.

jigsaw *noun* jigsaws
1 a puzzle made up of many different pieces that fit together to make a picture.
2 a saw that can cut curved shapes.
Word Building: jigsaw puzzle

jingle *verb* jingles, jingling, jingled
to make the sound tiny bells make.

jingle *noun* jingles
a short song or poem with a simple rhyme.

job *noun* jobs
1 the work that a person does to earn money. *Sam has a* ***job*** *in the tradestore on weekends.*
2 a particular piece of work you have to do. *It's my* ***job*** *to wash up.*

jockey *noun* jockeys
someone who rides horses in races.

joey *noun* joeys
a young kangaroo or wallaby.

jog *verb* jogs, jogging, jogged
1 to run slowly.
2 to push against something. *He* ***jogged*** *my elbow and I spilled my drink.*

join *verb* joins, joining, joined
1 to put or fix two things together.
2 to become a member of a group. *I've* ***joined*** *a swimming club.*

joint *noun* joints
1 the place where two parts fit together. *The ankle is the* ***joint*** *between the foot and the leg.*
2 a large piece of meat. *a* ***joint*** *of pork.*

joke *noun* jokes
something you say or do to make people laugh.

joke *verb* jokes, joking, joked
to make jokes.
Word Building: joker, jokers

jolly *adjective* jollier, jolliest
happy and cheerful.

jolt *noun* jolts
a sudden movement. *The PMV started with a* ***jolt.***

jolt *verb* jolts, jolting, jolted
to move or move something quickly and suddenly.

journey (jer-nee) *noun* journeys
the travelling people do to get from one place to another place. *We went on a* ***journey*** *around the coast of Manus.*

joy *noun*
happiness.

joyful *adjective*
happy, cheerful.
Word Building: joyfully

Judaism (Jew-day-izm) *noun*
the religion of the Jewish people, which teaches that there is only one God.

A B C D E F G H I **J** K L M N O P Q R S T U V W X Y Z

111

An alphabet strip is on the outer side of this page.

This guide word is the last word on the page.

Guide words

At the top of each page there are two guide words. These help you work out which words will be on the page.

This guide word is the first word on the page.

cover — **creature**

cover *verb* covers, covering, covered
to put something over or around something else. *She* ***covered*** *him with a blanket.*

covering *noun* coverings
something which covers something else. *a* ***covering*** *of dust on the table.*

cow *noun* cows
a female animal kept by farmers for its milk.

coward *noun* cowards
someone who is afraid when they ought to be brave.

crab *noun* crabs
an animal with a shell, claws, and ten legs that lives in or near the sea.

crack *noun* cracks
1 a narrow gap or thin line where something is nearly broken. *There is a* ***crack*** *in this glass.*
2 a sudden loud noise. *a* ***crack*** *of thunder.*

crack *verb* cracks, cracking, cracked
1 to get or make a crack. *This mug is* ***cracked.*** *Be careful not to* ***crack*** *the glass.*
2 to make the sudden, sharp noise a dry twig makes when you break it.

crackle *verb* crackles, crackling, crackled
to make the cracking sounds burning wood makes.

craft *noun* crafts
a task which needs great skill; a skill. *Weaving is a* ***craft.***

crafty *adjective* craftier, craftiest
clever in a sly sort of way.
Word Building: craftily

cramp *noun* cramps
a pain you get in your arm, leg, or stomach when a muscle tightens.

cramp *verb* cramps, cramping, cramped
to keep in a very small space.

crane *noun* cranes
1 a machine for lifting heavy things.
2 a large bird with very long legs.

crash *noun* crashes
1 an accident in which a car, truck, train, or plane hits something.
2 the noise of something crashing. *I heard a loud* ***crash*** *as the tree fell.*

crash *verb* crashes, crashing, crashed
to hit something with a loud noise.

crate *noun* crates
a box for carrying bottles or other things.

crater *noun* craters
1 a round opening at the top of a volcano.
2 a round hole in the ground made by something falling.

crawl *verb* crawls, crawling, crawled
1 to move on your hands and knees. *Babies* ***crawl*** *before they can walk.*
2 to move slowly. *The car* ***crawled*** *along in the dark.*

crayfish *noun* crayfish
a hard-shelled animal that looks like a lobster. Some types live in the sea and others in fresh water.

crayon *noun* crayons
1 a stick of coloured wax used for drawing.
2 a coloured pencil.

crazy *adjective* crazier, craziest
likely to do strange or silly things.
Word Building: crazily

cream *noun*
the thick yellowish liquid that comes to the top of milk.

crease *verb* creases, creasing, creased
to make a line in something by folding or pressing on it.

create *verb* creates, creating, created
to make something no one else has made or can make.
Word Building: creation, creator

creature (kree-cher) *noun* creatures
any animal.

48

creek — **crouch**

creek *noun* creeks
a small river.

creep *verb* creeps, creeping, crept
1 to move along, keeping close to the ground. *We* ***crept*** *through the hole in the hedge.*
2 to move quietly or secretly. *We* ***crept*** *away and nobody saw us.*

crept *verb* see creep

crescent (kres-ent) *noun* crescents
something shaped in a curve like a new moon.

crest *noun* crests
1 the top of a hill or a wave.
2 a bunch of feathers on a bird's head.

crew *noun* crews
a group of people who work together on a boat or aeroplane.

cricket *noun*
1 a game played in a field by two teams with a ball, bats, and two wickets.
2 a brown insect like a grasshopper that makes a shrill sound by rubbing its wings together.

cried *verb* see cry

crime *noun* crimes
an activity such as stealing which is against the law.

criminal *noun* criminals
someone who has done something bad that is against the law.

crimson *noun, adjective*
a deep red colour.

cripple *verb* cripples, crippling, crippled
to hurt someone's legs so badly that they cannot walk. *She was* ***crippled*** *in an accident.*

crisp *adjective* crisper, crispest
1 very dry so that it breaks easily. *a* ***crisp*** *biscuit.*
2 firm and fresh. *a* ***crisp*** *apple.*

croak *verb* croaks, croaking, croaked
to make the hoarse sound a frog makes.

crocodile *noun* crocodiles
a large meat-eating reptile that lives in water and on land in some hot countries. It has short legs, a long body, and sharp teeth.

crook *noun* crooks
someone who cheats or robs people.

crooked *adjective*
not straight. ***crooked*** *teeth.*
Word Building: crookedly

crop *noun* crops
plants which are grown for food. *Taro and kaukau are* ***crops.***

cross *adjective* crosser, crossest
angry, in a bad temper.
Word Building: crossly

cross *noun* crosses
a mark like **x** or **+**.

cross *verb* crosses, crossing, crossed
1 to move across something. *Take care when you* ***cross*** *the road.*
2 to make a shape like a cross. ***Cross*** *your arms.*
to cross something out to put a line through it.

crossing *noun* crossings
a place where you can cross a road.

crouch *verb* crouches, crouching, crouched
to lean forwards and bend your knees so that your bottom is almost touching the ground.

A B **C** D E F G H I J K L M N O P Q R S T U V W X Y Z

49

How the information about each word is set out

Each word listed in the dictionary is called a **headword**. The information after each headword is called an **entry**.

The **entry** (information) about each listed word (**headword**) may be set out in the following way.

Pronunciation guide
This helps you work out how to say the word. The part in bold print is the part that you emphasise when you say the word.

Headword
The word that you look up is printed in green, bold print.

Part of speech
This tells you the work that the word usually does in a sentence.

operate (op-er-ate) *verb* operates, operating, operated
1 to work a machine or tool. *Can you operate a drill?*
2 to fix up a part of your body that is sick or hurt. This is done by a doctor who usually puts you to sleep for a short time and uses special tools to work on the body part.
Word Building: operation, operator
*The boy had an **operation** to fix his broken leg.*

Definition
This explains what the word means. Sometimes a word has more than one meaning so each meaning (definition) is given a number.

Sentence
Sometimes a sentence is written to help you understand the word's meaning and how it can be used.

Word Building
These are some examples of other words that can be built from the headword or other words that are related to it.

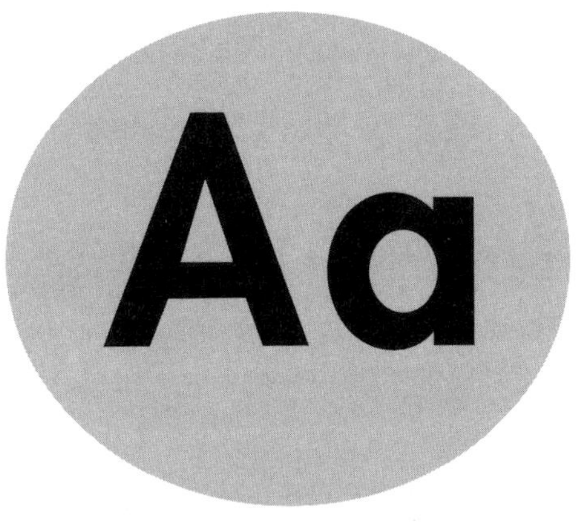

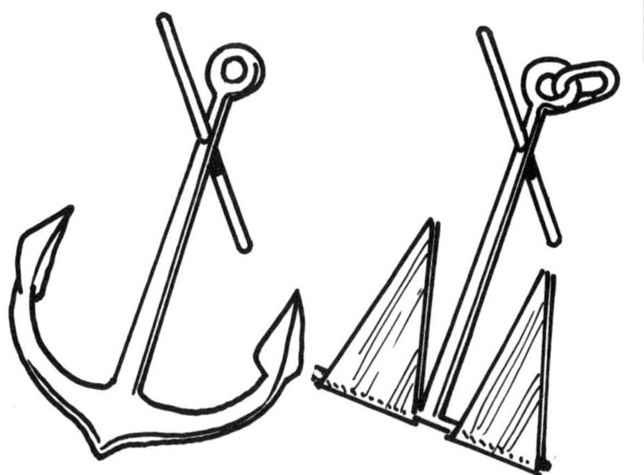

abandon *verb* abandons, abandoning, abandoned
1 to leave someone or something somewhere without intending ever to return to them. *People who* ***abandon*** *pets are cruel.*
2 to stop doing something before it is finished. *We* ***abandoned*** *our game when it started to rain.*

abbreviate (a-bree-vee-ate) *verb* abbreviates, abbreviating, abbreviated
to shorten a word or group of words.
Word Building: abbreviation
PTO is an ***abbreviation*** *of 'Please turn over'.*

abdomen *noun*
the part of the body below the chest which contains the stomach.

ability *noun* abilities
the power, skill, or opportunity to do something. *Owls have the* ***ability*** *to see in the dark.*

able *adjective* abler, ablest
if you are able to do something, you can do it. *Will you be* ***able*** *to go to the party?*

aboard *adverb, preposition*
on or onto a ship, bus, train, or an aeroplane. *Climb* ***aboard!***

abolish *verb* abolishes, abolishing, abolished
to put an end to something.

aborigine (ab-o-ridge-a-nee) *noun* aborigines
one of the people who were the first to live in a country.
Aborigine one of the original people to live in Australia.
Word Building: Aboriginal

about *adverb, preposition*
This word has several uses. Here are some of the ways you can use it:
I got home at ***about*** *four o'clock.*
I read a book ***about*** *animals. She left all her toys lying* ***about.***

above *adverb, preposition*
This word has several uses. Here are some of the ways you can use it:
He looked up at the stars in the sky ***above.***
She hung the bilum ***above*** *the cupboard.*
He's in the grade ***above*** *me at school.*

absent *adjective*
away. *She was* ***absent*** *from school yesterday.*

abuse (a-buze) *verb* abuses, abusing, abused
1 to be cruel to someone or something.
2 to say rude things to someone.

accelerate (ak-sel-a-rate) *verb* accelerates, accelerating, accelerated
to move faster.
Word Building: accelerator, acceleration
The car passed the truck by gaining more ***acceleration.***

accent *noun* accents
the way people say their words. *a Scottish **accent**.*

accept *verb* accepts, accepting, accepted
to take what someone offers you. *He **accepted** the invitation to the party.*

access (ak-sess) *noun*
1 a means of getting to a particular place. *The **access** to the cave was down a steep mountainside.*
2 the right to visit or go near. *The children's parents were divorced but their father had **access** to them every weekend.*

accident (ak-si-dent) *noun* accidents
something bad which you did not plan to happen. *He broke his leg in a road **accident**.*
Word Building: accidentally

accompany *verb* accompanies, accompanying, accompanied
1 to go with someone. *Dad **accompanied** us to the station.*
2 to play a musical instrument while someone sings or dances. *She **accompanied** me on the piano.*

account *noun* accounts
1 a description or story about something that has happened. *He gave the police an **account** of the car accident.*
2 a list that tells you how much money you owe or have spent. *a bank **account***

accurate (ak-yu-ret) *adjective*
correct, exact. *He gave an **accurate** description of the thief.*
Word Building: accurately

accuse *verb* accuses, accusing, accused
to say that someone has done something wrong. *They **accused** me of breaking the window.*

ace *noun* aces
one of the four cards in a pack of cards marked to show it is number one. *the **ace** of clubs.*

ache (ake) *verb* aches, aching, ached
to have a pain that goes on hurting. *My stomach **aches** because I have eaten too much.*
Word building: ache *noun*
*He had an **ache** in his back.*

achieve *verb* achieves, achieving, achieved
to do or finish something after trying hard.

achievement *noun* achievements
something difficult or special that you have done. *Winning the competition was a great **achievement**.*

acid *noun* acids
a liquid that can burn your clothes and skin. *Lemon juice and vinegar contain weak **acids**.*

acrobat *noun* acrobats
someone who does exciting jumping and balancing tricks.

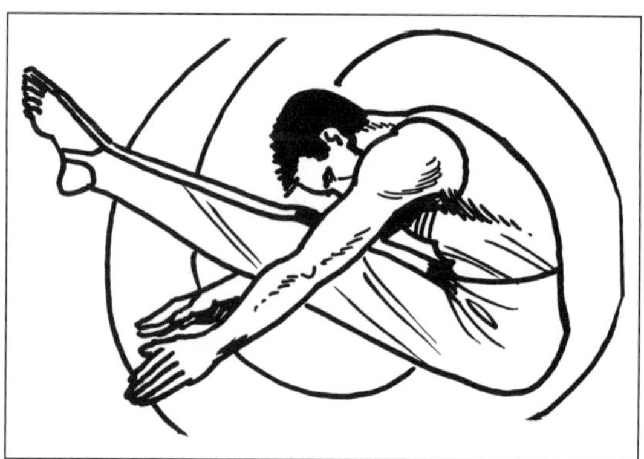

across *adverb, preposition*
1 from one side to the other. *He walked **across** the road.*
2 on the other side of something. *The garden is **across** the river.*
3 measuring from side to side. *The room is 3 metres **across**.*

act *verb* acts, acting, acted
1 to do something. *She **acted** quickly to put out the fire.*
2 to take part in a play.

action *noun* actions
1 something happening, especially something exciting. *I like movies with lots of **action**.*
2 something that a person has done. *The doctor's quick **action** saved her life.*

active *adjective*
busy, doing things, working.

activity *noun* activities
1 a lot of things happening and people doing things. *On sports day the school is full of **activity**.*
2 something that you do. *Swimming is one of her favourite **activities**.*

actor *noun* actors
a person who acts in a play.

actual *adjective*
real, true. *What is the **actual** date you started school?*
Word Building: actually

add *verb* adds, adding, added
1 to put something with something else. *You can **add** sugar to your tea.*
2 to put numbers together to make a bigger number. *If you **add** 2 and 2 you get 4.*

addict *noun* addicts
someone who finds something hard to give up and can't do without it. *The drug **addict** could not stop using drugs.*
Word Building: addicted, addiction

addition *noun*
putting numbers together. *We are doing **addition** and subtraction in maths.*

address *noun* addresses
the details of where a person lives that you put on a letter.

adjective *noun* adjectives
a word that tells you what someone or something is like. In *a tall man* and *a fast car*, the adjectives are *tall* and *fast*.

admire *verb* admires, admiring, admired
1 to think someone or something is very good.
2 to look at something and enjoy it. *We **admired** the lovely view.*

admit *verb* admits, admitting, admitted
1 to let someone come in. *No child under ten years of age can be **admitted**.*
2 to say you were the person who did something wrong. *He **admitted** that he broke the window.*

adopt *verb* adopts, adopting, adopted
to take someone into your family as your own child.

adore *verb* adores, adoring, adored
to love very much.

adult *noun* adults
someone who is fully grown.

advance *verb* advances, advancing, advanced
to move forward.

advantage *noun* advantages
something that helps you to do better than other people. *She has an unfair **advantage** because she is taller than us.*

adventure *noun* adventures
something exciting that happens to you.

adverb *noun* adverbs
a word that tells you how, when, or where something happens. In these sentences, *slowly*, *now*, and *somewhere* are adverbs: *He walks slowly. Do it now. I left my jumper somewhere.*

advertise *verb* advertises, advertising, advertised
to tell people about something to make them want to buy or use it.

advertisement *noun* advertisements
anything which advertises things.

advice (ad-vice) *noun*
something you say to someone to help them decide what to do. *My **advice** is to do your homework first.*

advise (ad-vize) *verb* advises, advising, advised
to tell someone what you think it would be best for them to do. *The doctor **advised** her to exercise more often.*

aerial (air-ee-ul) *noun* aerials
wires or metal rods for picking up or sending radio and television programs.

aeroplane, airplane *noun* aeroplanes, airplanes
a machine that can fly, with wings and an engine.

affect *verb* affects, affecting, affected
to make someone or something different in some way. *Her handwriting was **affected** by her sore finger.*

affection *noun*
the feeling you have for someone you like. *The class had a great **affection** for their teacher.*

afford *verb* affords, affording, afforded
to have enough money to pay for something. *I can't **afford** to buy you any more presents.*

afraid *adjective*
frightened. *I'm not **afraid** of dogs.*

after *preposition*
1 later than. *You finished **after** me.*
2 following. *I went swimming **after** school.*

afternoon *noun* afternoons
the time from the middle of the day until about 6 p.m.

afterwards *adverb*
later. *We had lunch and **afterwards** played in the garden.*

again *adverb*
once more. *Try **again**!*

against *preposition*
1 on the opposite side to. *We played **against** your team and won.*
2 on or next to. *He leaned **against** the wall.*

age *noun*
how old someone or something is. *She is tall for her **age**.*

agent *noun* agents
someone whose job it is to arrange things for people. *a travel **agent**.*

aggressive *adjective*
rough, violent, likely to attack people. *The dog looks very **aggressive**.*
Word Building: aggressively, aggression

ago *adverb*
in the past. *A long time **ago**.*

agony *noun*
extreme pain.

agree *verb* agrees, agreeing, agreed
to think the same as someone else. *My brother thinks he's really clever but I don't **agree**.*

agriculture *noun*
the work that farmers do, growing food.

aground *adverb*
touching the bottom in shallow water. *The ship ran **aground**.*

ahead *adverb*
in front. *I went on **ahead** to open the gate. She's **ahead** of me in maths.*

aibika *noun*
a traditional green vegetable with a five-fingered leaf and a green or red stem. ***Aibika** is a good soup vegetable.* [from Tok Pisin *aibika*]

aid *noun* aids
something that helps. *My bubu wears a hearing **aid**.*

aid *verb* aids, aiding, aided
to help. *We sent blankets to **aid** the victims of the earthquake.*

aid post *noun* aid posts
a small health centre in a village, town or settlement. *When we are sick we go to the **aid post** in our village.*

AIDS *noun*
a disease that can kill you, caused by a virus that affects the body's immune system. This word was made by using the first letters of the words Acquired Immune Deficiency Syndrome.

aim *verb* aims, aiming, aimed
1 to throw, kick, or shoot at something you are trying to hit. *He **aimed** the bow and arrow at the cuscus.*
2 to try to do something. *They **aimed** to reach the top of the mountain.*

air *noun*
what everyone breathes. *Let's go out for some fresh **air**.*

aircraft *noun* aircraft
any aeroplane or helicopter.

Air Nuigini *noun*
the national airline of PNG.

airport *noun* airports
a place where aeroplanes land and take off.

aisle (ile) *noun* aisles
a narrow path, usually between rows of seats. *Churches, cinemas, aeroplanes, and buses have **aisles**.*

alarm *noun* alarms
a warning sound or sign.

albatross *noun* albatrosses
a large sea bird with long wings.

album *noun* albums
1 a book to put things like photographs or stamps in.
2 a record with several pieces of music on it.

alcohol *noun*
a liquid which is part of drinks like beer and wine.

alcoholic *adjective*
containing alcohol.

alert *adjective*
lively and ready for anything.

alien *noun* aliens
1 a person from another country.
2 in stories, a person or creature from another planet.

alive *adjective*
living. *Is the pig still **alive**?*

all *adjective, pronoun*
1 everyone or everything. *Are you **all** listening? Put **all** your books on the table.*
2 the whole of something. *He's eaten **all** the rice.*

allergy (al-er-jee) *noun* allergies
a reaction that happens to some people when they eat certain foods or are near certain plants or other things.
Word Building: allergic
*The boy is **allergic** to the mangoes and his lips swell up when he eats them.*

alley *noun* alleys
a very narrow street.

alligator *noun* alligators
a kind of crocodile.

allow *verb* allows, allowing, allowed
to let something happen, to permit. *Mum **allowed** us to go out.*

all right *adjective, interjection*
1 safe and well, not hurt. *Are you **all right**?*
2 yes, I agree. ***All right**, I'll play.*

ally (al-lie) *noun* allies
a person or country fighting on the same side. *PNG and Australia were* ***allies*** *during the Second World War.*

almost *adverb*
very nearly. *We're* ***almost*** *home now.*

alone *adverb*
without others. *I feel frightened when I am* ***alone.***

along *adverb, preposition*
1 from one end to the other. *He ran* ***along*** *the top of the wall.*
2 forward. *She walked* ***along*** *slowly.*
Come along! hurry up.

aloud *adverb*
in a voice that can be heard. *Do not read to yourself—read* ***aloud.***

alphabet *noun* alphabets
all the letters people use in writing, arranged in a particular order.

alphabetical *adjective*
arranged in the order of the letters of the alphabet. The words in a dictionary are arranged in alphabetical order so that you can find them easily.

already *adverb*
1 by this time. *He was* ***already*** *there when we arrived.*
2 before now. *I've* ***already*** *done that.*

alright *adverb* see **all right**

also *adverb*
as well. *We had sago and* ***also*** *fish.*

altar *noun* altars
a special table used in religious ceremonies.

alter *verb* alters, altering, altered
to change. *The sign at the end of the road has been* ***altered.***

alteration *noun* alterations
a change in someone or something. *Mum made some* ***alterations*** *to my dress because it was too big.*

altitude (al-ti-tude) *noun*
How high something is above the level of the sea. *The aeroplane flew at a high* ***altitude.***

although *conjunction*
though. *We kept on running,* ***although*** *we were tired.*

altogether *adverb*
counting everything or everyone. *There are thirty-five in our class* ***altogether.***

aluminium (al-yu-**min**-ee-um) *noun*
a very light metal, coloured like silver.

always *adverb*
at all times, every time.

amateur (**am**-a-ter) *noun* amateurs
1 someone who does something as a hobby.
2 someone who takes part in a sport and is not paid.

amaze *verb* amazes, amazing, amazed
to surprise greatly. *She* ***amazed*** *everyone by winning the race.*

amazing *adjective*
surprising, wonderful. *He told us an* ***amazing*** *story.*

ambassador *noun* ambassadors
someone sent to a foreign country to represent his or her government.

ambition *noun* ambitions
something that you want to do very much. *Her* ***ambition*** *is to be a doctor.*

ambulance *noun* ambulances
a vehicle for taking injured or ill people to hospital.

ambush *verb* ambushes, ambushing, ambushed
to wait in a hiding-place and attack someone by surprise.

ammunition (am-yu-**nish**-en) *noun*
anything that is fired from a gun.

among *preposition*
1 in the middle of. *Your books must be somewhere* ***among*** *these.*
2 between three or more. *Share the peanuts* ***among*** *you.*

amount *noun* amounts
how much or how many there are. *He spent a large* ***amount*** *of money.*

amphibian (am-**fib**-ee-un) *noun* amphibians
an animal that can live on land as well as in water.
Word Building: amphibious

amuse *verb* amuses, amusing, amused
1 to make someone laugh or smile. *The old man* ***amused*** *the children with his funny stories.*
2 to keep someone happy or busy. *We played games to* ***amuse*** *ourselves.*
Word Building: amusing

anaesthetic (an-es-**thet**-ic) *noun* anaesthetics
a drug or gas or injection used so that you don't feel pain.

ancestor (**an**-ses-tor) *noun* ancestors
a member of the same family who lived long ago.

anchor (**ang**-kor) *noun* anchors
a heavy metal hook joined to a ship by a chain. It is dropped into the sea, where it lodges in the sea floor to keep the ship still.

ancient (**ain**-shent) *adjective*
very old. *The Great Wall of China is* ***ancient****—it was built hundreds of years ago.*

angel (**ain**-jel) *noun* angels
a messenger sent by God.

anger (**ang**-ger) *noun*
a strong feeling that you get when you are not pleased.

angle *noun* angles
the corner where two lines meet.

angry *adjective* angrier, angriest
feeling anger. *The teacher looked* ***angry*** *so I kept quiet.*
Word Building: angrily

animal *noun* animals
anything that lives and can move about. Birds, fish, snakes, ants and crocodiles are all animals.

ankle *noun* ankles
the thin part of the leg where it is joined to the foot.

anniversary *noun* anniversaries
a day when you remember something special that happened on the same day in another year. *16 September is the* ***anniversary*** *of PNG's independence.*

announce *verb* announces, announcing, announced
1 to tell a lot of people about something important. *They* ***announced*** *the winner of the competition.*
2 to introduce a program on radio or television.

announcement *noun* announcements
a public statement about something people need to know. *I have an important* ***announcement*** *to make.*

annoy *verb* annoys, annoying, annoyed
to make someone angry.

annual *adjective*
happening every year. *We have our* ***annual*** *school sports carnival in third term.*
Word Building: annually

another *adjective, pronoun*
1 a different one. *Choose* ***another*** *cap—that one is too big.*
2 one more. *You've had one mango—you can't have* ***another****.*

answer (**an**-ser) *noun* answers
something you say or write to someone who has said or written something to you. *the* ***answer*** *to a question, an* ***answer*** *to a letter.*

answer *verb* answers, answering, answered
to give or send an answer to someone. *Can anyone* ***answer*** *this question? Have you* ***answered*** *Uncle's letter?*

Antarctic *noun*
the very cold land and sea at the south of the earth.

antelope *noun* antelopes
a wild animal that looks like a deer, found in Africa and parts of Asia.

antenna *noun* antennas, antennae
1 a wire or rod used for receiving radio or television signals. *There are several radio* ***antennas*** *on our building.*
2 a feeler on the head of insects and some shellfish. *Insects usually have two* ***antennae.***

anthem *noun* anthems
a special song that is sung on important occasions. *A national* ***anthem*** *belongs to a country.*

antibiotic (an-ti-by-**ot**-ic) *noun* antibiotics
a type of medicine used to kill germs, e.g. penicillin.

anti-malarial *noun*
a drug used to fight malaria.

antiseptic *noun* antiseptics
a substance that kills germs.

anxious *adjective*
worried. *My mother was* ***anxious*** *when I was late home.*
Word Building: anxiously

any *adjective, pronoun*
1 some. *Have you got* ***any*** *money? I haven't* ***any.***
2 at all. *Are you* ***any*** *better?*
3 no special one. *Take* ***any*** *book you want.*

anybody, anyone *pronoun*
any person.

anything *pronoun*
any thing. *It's so dark, I can't see* ***anything.***

anywhere *adverb*
at, in, or to any place. *I can't find my book* ***anywhere.***

apart *adverb*
away from each other. *Those two dogs fight if you don't keep them* ***apart.***

ape *noun* apes
an animal like a large monkey with long arms and no tail.

apologise *verb* apologises, apologising, apologised
to say that you are sorry for doing something wrong.

apostrophe (a-**pos**-tro-fee) *noun* apostrophes
a mark like this **'** used to mark missing letters, or with *s* to show ownership. *It's going to rain. These are Vele's things.*

apparatus *noun*
special tools or equipment that you use for doing something. *This* ***apparatus*** *is used for scientific experiments.*

appeal *verb* appeals, appealing, appealed
to ask for something that you need. *He* ***appealed*** *for help.*

appear *verb* appears, appearing, appeared
1 to come and be seen. *He suddenly* ***appeared*** *from behind the tree.*
2 to seem. *It* ***appears*** *to be the wrong size.*

appearance *noun*
1 what someone looks like. *His* ***appearance*** *was very untidy.*
2 coming so that you can be seen. *The sudden* ***appearance*** *of the wild pig surprised everyone.*

appendix *noun* appendixes or appendices
1 the small tube inside the body that sometimes causes an illness called appendicitis.
2 a section added at the end of a book.

appetite *noun* appetites
the wish for food. *She lost her* ***appetite*** *while she was ill.*

applaud *verb* applauds, applauding, applauded
to clap to show that you are pleased. *The audience **applauded** very loudly.*

applause *noun*
clapping. *The **applause** lasted for ages.*

apple *noun* apples
a round, crisp, juicy fruit.

appoint *verb* appoints, appointing, appointed
to choose someone for a job. *The teacher will **appoint** a class helper.*
Word Building: appointment

appointment *noun* appointments
a time when you have arranged to meet someone. *I have an **appointment** at the doctor's tomorrow.*

approach *verb* approaches, approaching, approached
to come near to someone or something. *The aeroplane was **approaching** the airport.*
Word Building: approachable

appropriate *adjective*
suitable.
Word Building: appropriately

approve *verb* approves, approving, approved
to say that something is good or suitable.

approximate (a-**prok**-si-mut) *adjective*
not exact. *The **approximate** time of arrival is two o'clock.*
Word Building: approximately

approximate (a-**prok**-si-mate) *verb* approximates, approximating, approximated
to come close to. *Her calculation **approximates** the number of people who will be here.*

April *noun*
the fourth month of the year.

apron *noun* aprons
something worn over the front of the body to keep the clothes underneath clean.

aquarium *noun* aquariums
a large, glass container where fish are kept.

arc *noun* arcs
part of a curve

arch *noun* arches
a curved part of a bridge, building, or wall.

architect (**ar**-ki-tect) *noun* architects
a person who draws plans for buildings.

Arctic *noun*
the very cold land and sea at the north of the earth.

area *noun* areas
1 the size of a flat place. *We measured the **area** of the playground.*
2 a part of a place, town, country, or the world. *You must not play in this **area**. Desert **areas** have very little rain.*

arena *noun* arenas
a place that has been built to hold sporting events or shows.

argue *verb* argues, arguing, argued
to talk about something with people who do not agree with you. *Stop **arguing**, you two!*

argument *noun* arguments
talking in an angry or excited way to someone who does not agree with you.

arithmetic *noun*
the study and use of numbers.

arm *noun* arms
the part of the body between the shoulder and the hand.

armchair *noun* armchairs
a comfortable chair with parts at the side for you to rest your arms on.

arms *noun*
guns, knives, and other weapons used for fighting.

army *noun* armies
a large group of people trained to fight on land in a war.

around *adverb, preposition*
1 on all sides of something. ***Around** the village there was thick jungle.*
2 here and there. *Don't leave your books lying **around**.*

arrange *verb* arranges, arranging, arranged
to put in a certain order or place. ***Arrange** the chairs in a circle.*

arrangement *noun* arrangements
something that you have decided will happen. *We made an **arrangement** to meet after school.*

arrest *verb* arrests, arresting, arrested
to take someone prisoner. *The police **arrested** the gang of rascals.*

arrive *verb* arrives, arriving, arrived
to come to the end of a journey. *We **arrived** home at six o'clock.*

arrow *noun* arrows
1 a pointed stick that is shot from a bow.
2 a mark like this ⇒ that points to something.

art *noun* arts
drawing, painting, music, sculpture, and drama.

artery *noun* arteries
one of the tubes that carry your blood from your heart to other parts of your body.

article *noun* articles
1 a particular thing. *an **article** of clothing.*
2 a piece of writing. *an **article** in a magazine.*

artificial *adjective*
not natural, made by people or machines. ***artificial** flowers.*

ascend (a-send) *verb* ascends, ascending, ascended
to climb or go up.
Word Building: ascent
*The **ascent** of the mountain took several days.*

ash *noun* ashes
the grey powder left when something has been burned.

ashamed *adjective*
feeling very sorry, unhappy, and guilty about something.

ashore *adverb*
on land. *The sailors went **ashore**.*

ask *verb* asks, asking, asked
to speak in order to find out or get something. *'What's your name?' she **asked**.*

asleep *adjective*
sleeping.

aspirin *noun* aspirins
a small white pill. You swallow it when you have a pain to make you feel better.

assemble *verb* assembles, assembling, assembled
1 to put together. *You can **assemble** your model from the pieces provided.*
2 to gather together. *We will all **assemble** in the school grounds at two o'clock.*
Word Building: assembly

assess *verb* assesses, assessing, assessed
1 to say what you think the cost or value of something is.
2 to test students to find out what they have learned.

assist *verb* assists, assisting, assisted
to help.

assistant *noun* assistants
1 someone whose job is to help someone. *an **assistant** to the manager.*
2 someone who serves in a shop.

assorted *adjective*
different sorts put together.

asthma (ass-ma) *noun*
an illness that makes breathing difficult.

astonish *verb* astonishes, astonishing, astonished
to surprise someone very much.

astonishment *noun*
great surprise. *We stared in* ***astonishment*** *at the spaceship.*

astronaut *noun* astronauts
someone who travels in space.

astronomer (a-stron-o-mer) *noun* astronomers
someone who studies the sun, the stars, and the planets.

astronomy (a-stron-o-mee) *noun*
finding out about the sun, the stars, and the planets.

ate *verb* see eat

athlete *noun* athletes
someone who trains to be good at running, jumping, throwing, or other sports.

atlas *noun* atlases
a book of maps.

ATM *noun*
a bank machine from which you can get money when you use a special plastic card and number. ATM is short for Automated Teller Machine.

atmosphere *noun* atmospheres
the air around the Earth.

atom *noun* atoms
one of the very tiny things that everything is made up of.

attach *verb* attaches, attaching, attached
to join or fasten something to another thing. ***Attach*** *a label to your suitcase.*

attack *verb* attacks, attacking, attacked
to begin a fight.

attempt *verb* attempts, attempting, attempted
to try to do something. *The prisoner* ***attempted*** *to escape.*

attend *verb* attends, attending, attended
to be present somewhere. *Did he* ***attend*** *school yesterday?*

attendance *noun* attendances
being at a place in order to take part in something. ***attendance*** *at school.*

attention *noun*
careful listening, reading, or thinking.
pay attention take notice.

attic *noun* attics
a room or rooms inside the roof of a house.

attract *verb* attracts, attracting, attracted
1 to interest someone. *The toy* ***attracted*** *the baby's attention and he stopped crying.*
2 to make something come nearer. *The magnet* ***attracted*** *the small piece of metal.*

attractive *adjective*
pleasant to look at, beautiful.
Word Building: attractively

auction *noun* auctions
a sale when things are sold to the people who offer the most money for them.

audience *noun* audiences
people who have come to a place to see or hear something.

August *noun*
the eighth month of the year.

aunt, aunty *noun* aunts, aunties
the sister of your mother or father, or your uncle's wife.

aupa *noun*
a traditional green vegetable.

Aussie *noun* Aussies
(*informal*) an Australian.

Aussie Rules *noun*
the game of Australian Rules football.

author *noun* authors
someone who writes books or stories.

authority *noun* authorities
the power to make other people do as you say. *The police have the **authority** to stop speeding cars.*

autograph *noun* autographs
your name written by yourself. *I collect **autographs** of famous people.*

automatic *adjective*
able to work on its own without a person controlling it. *An **automatic** washing machine.*
Word Building: automatically

autumn (aw-tum) *noun*
the part of the year when leaves fall off the trees and it gets cooler.

available *adjective*
ready for you to buy or use. *More paper is **available** if you need it.*

avalanche (av-a-lanch) *noun* avalanches
a large amount of snow, rock, or ice sliding suddenly down a mountain. *The climbers were buried underneath an **avalanche**.*

avenue *noun* avenues
a road, often with trees along each side.

average *adjective*
ordinary or usual. *She's of **average** height for her age.*

avocado *noun* avocados
a pear-shaped tropical fruit with a rough green skin and a large seed in the middle.

avoid *verb* avoids, avoiding, avoided
to keep out of the way of someone or something.

awake *adjective*
not sleeping.

award *noun* awards
a prize. *an **award** for bravery.*

aware *adjective*
knowing about something. *I was **aware** of somebody watching me.*

away *adverb*
1 not here. *She is **away** today.*
2 to or in another place. *He ran **away**. Put your books **away** now.*

awe *noun*
a feeling of wonder, fear, or adoration. *The children were filled with **awe** as the chief demonstrated his hunting skills.*

awful *adjective*
(*informal*) very bad. *This tastes **awful**.*
Word Building: awfully

awkward *adjective*
1 difficult to do or use. *This big box is **awkward** to carry.*
2 clumsy. *He uses very **awkward** movements when he dances.*
3 not convenient. *They arrived at an **awkward** time.*

axe *noun* axes
a tool for chopping wood.

axle *noun* axles
a rod that goes through the centre of wheels.

baby *noun* babies
a very young child.

bachelor *noun* bachelors
a man who has not married.

back *noun* backs
1 the part behind or opposite the front. *The answers are in the* ***back*** *of the book. We sat in the* ***back*** *of the car.*
2 the part of a person or an animal between the neck and the bottom.

backward, backwards *adjective, adverb*
1 towards the back. *She fell* ***backwards*** *and hit her head.*
2 in the opposite way to usual. *You've got your singlet on* ***backwards.***

bacon *noun*
thin slices of dried or salty meat from a pig.

bacteria *plural noun*
tiny living things (germs), some of which cause diseases.

bad *adjective* worse, worst
1 of the kind that people do not want, or do not like. ***bad*** *manners, a* ***bad*** *smell.*
2 serious. *a* ***bad*** *accident.*
Word Building: badly
Are you ***badly*** *hurt?*

badge *noun* badges
something that you pin or sew on to your clothes, to show which school or club you belong to.

badminton *noun*
a game in which racquets are used to hit a shuttlecock back and forth over a net.

bag *noun* bags
a container made of plastic, paper, cloth, or leather that you carry things in.

bagarap *verb, adjective*
1 to break; to spoil.
2 broken, spoiled, damaged or wrecked. [from Tok Pisin *bagarap*].

bail, bails *noun*
one of the two pieces of wood that rest on top of cricket stumps.

bail *verb* bails, bailing, bailed
to scoop water out of a boat using a bucket.

bait *noun*
food put on a hook or in a trap to catch animals.

bake *verb* bakes, baking, baked
1 to cook or to be cooked in an oven. *I* ***baked*** *some scones.*
2 to make something very hot, or to be very hot. *The sun* ***baked*** *the ground hard.*
Word Building: baker, bakery

balance *noun* balances
a pair of scales for weighing things.

balance *verb* balances, balancing, balanced
to keep or make something steady, to be steady. *The boy* ***balanced*** *the soccer ball on his finger.*

balcony *noun* balconies
a platform with a rail around it outside an upstairs window.

bald *adjective*
without any hair on the head.

ball *noun* balls
1 a round object that you hit, kick, or throw in games. *a basket* ***ball.***
2 something round as in *a* ***ball*** *of string.*

balloon *noun* balloons
1 a small, coloured, rubber bag that you can blow up.
2 a very big bag filled with hot air or gas so that it floats in the sky.

bamboo *noun*
a tall plant with stiff, hollow stems.

ban *verb* bans, banning, banned
to say that no one can do a certain thing. *They have* ***banned*** *football in the playground.*

banana *noun* bananas
a long fruit with a thick yellow skin. An important food in many parts of PNG.

band *noun* bands
1 a group of people who play music together. *a string* ***band.***
2 a group of people. *a* ***band*** *of robbers.*
3 a thin strip of material. *a rubber* ***band.***

bandage *noun* bandages
a strip of material for wrapping around part of the body that has been hurt.

Band-Aid *noun* Band-Aids
a sticky patch you put over a cut or sore to cover it.

bandicoot *noun* bandicoots
a small marsupial with a long pointed head. It has sharp claws and feeds at night.

bang *noun* bangs
a sudden very loud noise.

bang *verb* bangs, banging, banged
to hit or shut with a loud noise. *Don't* ***bang*** *the door!*

banish *verb* banishes, banishing, banished
to send someone away from a place as a punishment.

bank *noun* banks
1 a place that looks after money and valuable things for people.
2 the ground near the edge of a river, canal or lake.
3 a sloping piece of ground.

banner *noun* banners
a flag with words on it. *The* ***banner*** *says 'Stop the war'.*

baptism *noun* baptisms
a Christian religious event where a person is sprinkled with water or put under water to show that they are new believers or members of a church.
Word Building: baptise

bar *noun* bars
1 a long piece of wood or metal.
2 a block of chocolate or soap.
3 a place that serves food and drinks at a counter. *a hotel* ***bar.***

barbecue *noun* barbecues
1 a metal frame for cooking meat over a fire.
2 an open-air party where food is cooked over a fire.

bare *adjective* barer, barest
1 without any clothes on.
2 without any covering or decoration. ***bare*** *walls.*

barely *adverb*
only just, hardly. *I was so tired that I could* ***barely*** *walk.*

baret *noun* barets
a man-made channel that is built as a shortcut across a loop in a river; a drain.

bargain *noun* bargains
1 a promise to give something in return for something else. *They made a **bargain** to swap the toys.*
2 something that costs much less than usual. *You can get **bargains** at sales in the big stores.*

bark *noun*
the hard covering on the trunk and branches of a tree.

bark *verb* barks, barking, barked
to make the sharp, loud sound a dog makes.

barn *noun* barns
a large building on a farm, where you keep animals or grain.

barramundi (bair-a-**mun**-dee) *noun*
a large freshwater fish, which is good to eat. This word probably comes from an Aboriginal language of central Queensland.

barrel *noun* barrels
1 a round, wooden container with flat ends. *a **barrel** of beer.*
2 the tube-shaped part at the front of a gun.

barren (**bair**-en) *adjective*
without trees or plants. ***barren** land.*

barrier (**bair**-ee-er) *noun* barriers
a fence or something that stands in the way.

base *noun* bases
the bottom part of something. *The **base** of the box was made of wood.*

baseball *noun*
1 a game played between two teams of nine players. After hitting the ball the batter runs around a diamond-shaped field with four bases to score a run.
2 the ball used in this game.

basement *noun* basements
the rooms in a building that are below the ground.

bashful *adjective*
shy.
Word Building: bashfully

basic (**bay**-sic) *adjective*
1 most important and necessary. *A person's **basic** needs are food, clothes, and somewhere to live.*
2 simple. ***basic** skills in first aid.*

basin (**bay**-sin) *noun* basins
a large bowl.

basket *noun* baskets
a container made of straw or thin strips of metal or plastic that you carry things in.

basketball *noun*
a game for two teams of five players who try to throw a ball into a high net.

bat *noun* bats
1 an animal like a mouse with wings that comes out at night.
2 a piece of wood for hitting a ball in a game.

bat *verb* bats, batting, batted
to have a turn at using the bat in games like cricket.

bath (rhymes with *path*) *noun* baths
a large container which you can fill with water to sit in and wash yourself all over.

bathe (**bayth**) *verb* bathes, bathing, bathed
1 to wash part of yourself carefully and gently. *He **bathed** his cut finger.*
2 to put a person or animal in water and wash him or her.

bathroom *noun* bathrooms
the room where you can have a bath or wash.

baton (**bat**-on or ba-**ton**) *noun* batons
1 a stick used by a conductor of an orchestra.
2 a stick that a runner in a relay-race passes to the next person in the team.

batsman *noun* batsmen
the person who uses the bat in cricket.

batter *noun* batters
1 a mixture of flour, eggs, and milk used to make pancakes or to cook fish in.
2 the person who uses the bat in softball or cricket.

batter *verb* batters, battering, battered
to damage something by hitting it again and again.

battery *noun* batteries
a closed container that gives electricity. You put batteries inside torches and radios to make them work.

battle *noun* battles
fighting between groups of people.

bawl *verb* bawls, bawling, bawled
to shout or cry loudly. *The hungry baby was **bawling**.*

bay *noun* bays
a place where the land bends inwards and sea fills the space.

be *verb* is, being, been
to exist. *I am **being** very good. I have **been** very good.*

beach *noun* beaches
land by the edge of the sea, covered with sand or small stones.

bead *noun* beads
a small ball of wood, glass, or plastic with a hole through the middle.

beak *noun* beaks
the hard pointed part of a bird's mouth.

beam *noun* beams
1 a long, strong piece of wood.
2 a line of light. *the **beam** of a torch.*

beam *verb* beams, beaming, beamed
to smile happily. *She **beamed** when she heard the good news.*

bean *noun* beans
a long, thin, green or yellow vegetable that contains seeds. It grows on a vine. *baked **beans**, runner **beans**.*

bear *noun* bears
a big wild animal with short, thick fur.

bear *verb* bears, bearing, bore, borne or born
1 to carry. *The bag was not strong enough to **bear** the weight of the vegetables.*
2 to put up with. *I couldn't **bear** the pain any longer.*
3 to give birth to. *I was **born** in Lae.*

beard *noun* beards
hair growing on a man's chin.

beast *noun* beasts
1 any big animal.
2 a horrible person.

beat *noun*
a regular rhythm. *Korom likes music with a strong **beat**.*

beat *verb* beats, beating, beat, beaten
1 to do better than someone else. *Kila always **beats** Gima in Maths.*
2 to hit often. *It's cruel to **beat** animals.*
3 to stir hard. *Seri **beat** the eggs to make some pancakes.*
4 to make a regular rhythm. *After running, my heart **beats** fast.*

beautiful *adjective*
1 very nice to look at, hear, or smell. *a **beautiful** picture.*
2 enjoyable, pleasant. ***beautiful** weather.*
Word Building: beautifully

beauty *noun*
if something has beauty you enjoy looking at it or listening to it. *the **beauty** of the sunset.*

became *verb* see **become**

because *conjunction*
for the reason that. *He was angry **because** I was late.*

become *verb* becomes, becoming, became, become
to come to be. *It suddenly **became** very cold yesterday.*

bed *noun* beds
1 a piece of furniture you sleep on, a place to sleep.
2 a piece of ground for growing flowers or vegetables. *a flower **bed**.*
3 the ground at the bottom of a sea or river. *the sea **bed**.*

bee *noun* bees
a flying insect that can make honey and lives with many others in a beehive.

beef *noun*
meat from a cow.

been see **be**

beer *noun* beers
a light brown alcoholic drink.

beetle *noun* beetles
an insect with hard wings and a shiny body.

beetroot *noun* beetroot
a round, dark red vegetable.

before *adverb, conjunction, preposition*
1 earlier than. *I was here **before** you.*
2 in front of. *It vanished **before** my eyes.*

beg *verb* begs, begging, begged
to ask for something in an anxious way.

began *verb* see **begin**

beggar *noun* beggars
someone who lives by asking other people for money, clothes, or food.

begin *verb* begins, beginning, began, begun
to start. *I'm **beginning** to understand. I have **begun** to learn the guitar. What time does the film **begin**?*

beginner *noun* beginners
someone who has just started learning something.

beginning *noun* beginnings
the start of something.

begun *verb* see **begin**

behave *verb* behaves, behaving, behaved
to show good or bad manners in front of other people. *He's **behaved** badly. She's **behaving** well.*
Behave yourself! Be good!

behaviour *noun*
how you behave.

behind *adverb, preposition*
at the back of. *He hid **behind** the wall.*

being *noun* beings
a creature. *They looked like **beings** from another planet.*

belief *noun* beliefs
what someone believes.

believe *verb* believes, believing, believed
to feel sure that something is true. *Do you **believe** in magic?*

bell *noun* bells
a piece of metal that rings when it is hit. *The **bell** rang at the end of the lesson.*

bellow *verb* bellows, bellowing, bellowed
to shout and make a lot of noise like an angry bull.

belly *noun* bellies
the stomach.

belong *verb* belo]ngs, belonging, belonged
1 to be someone's. *That pen **belongs** to me.*
2 to be part of something. *Lenus **belongs** to a football club.*
3 to be in the proper place. *Your coat **belongs** on the peg, not on the floor.*

belongings *noun*
things which belong to you. *Make sure you take your **belongings** when you get off the plane.*

below *adverb, preposition*
underneath; less than. *Write your address **below** your name. The temperature was **below** zero.*

belt *noun* belts
a stiff band of leather or other material that you wear around your waist.

bench *noun* benches
a wooden or stone seat for more than one person.

bend *noun* bends
a part of a road or river that is not straight. *She drove carefully around the **bend**.*

bend *verb* bends, bending, bent
1 to become or make something curved or not straight. *The branches were **bent** by the weight of the guavas.*
2 to lean over so that your head is nearer to the ground. *He **bent** down to tie his shoes.*

beneath *adverb, preposition*
underneath.

bent *verb* see **bend**

berry *noun* berries
a small round fruit with seeds in it. *blackberries, strawberries.*

berth *noun*
1 a sleeping place on a ship or train.
2 a place for a ship to tie up at a wharf.

berth *verb*
to tie up at a wharf.

beside *preposition*
at the side of. *a house **beside** the sea.*

besides *preposition*
as well as. *Ten people **besides** me also won prizes.*

best *adjective*
better than any other. *my **best** friend.*

bet *verb* bets, betting, bet
to say what you think will happen. If you are right you win money, but if you are wrong you lose money.

betel nut *noun* betelnuts
a nut with a bitter taste that is chewed (often with lime and daka) by people in the Pacific and South-East Asia.

betray *verb* betrays, betraying betrayed
1 to give away a secret.
2 to give information about your friends or country to the enemy.

better *adjective*
1 more useful, that you like more. *My new pen is **better** than my old one.*
2 more able at something. *She's **better** than me at swimming.*
3 well again after an illness. *I'm **better** now, thank you.*

between *adverb, preposition*
1 in the middle of two people or things. *I sat **between** Mum and Dad.*
2 among two. *Share the money **between** you.*

beware *verb*
be careful. ***Beware** of the dog.*

bewilder *verb,* bewilders, bewildering, bewildered
to puzzle or confuse someone.

bewitched *adjective*
under a spell.

beyond *adverb, preposition*
further than. *Don't go beyond the end of the road.*

biased (by-esd) *adjective*
unfairly liking one side more than another. *The referee was* ***biased.***

Bible *noun* Bibles
the holy book that is read in all Christian churches.

bicycle *noun* bicycles
a machine with two wheels and pedals, that you can ride.

big *adjective* bigger, biggest
large, of great size. *Port Moresby is a big city.*

bighead *verb*
to boast or disobey. [from Tok Pisin *bikhet*]

big man *noun*
a leader in a community in PNG. [from Tok Pisin *bikpela man*]

bike *noun* bikes
(*informal*) a bicycle.

bilas *noun*
1 traditional ornaments.
2 traditional body decorations.
3 smart clothes. [from Tok Pisin *bilas*]

bill *noun* bills
1 a piece of paper that tells you how much money you owe. *He paid all his* ***bills.***
2 a bird's beak.

billion *noun* billions
1,000,000,000; one thousand million.

billy-goat *noun* billy-goats
a male goat.

bin *noun* bins
a large container, often with a lid. *a rubbish* ***bin.***

binatang *noun*
an insect. [from Tok Pisin *binatang*]

bind *verb* binds, binding, bound
to tie together. *The prisoner's hands were* ***bound*** *behind his back.*

binoculars (bin-**ok**-yu-larz) *noun*
a special pair of glasses like two tubes joined together. When you look through them, things far away seem much nearer.

biodegradable (by-o-dee-**grade**-a-bl) *adjective*
able to rot, particularly in soil. *We bought* ***biodegradable*** *washing powder.*

biology *noun*
the study of living things.

bird *noun* birds
any animal with feathers, wings, and a beak.

bird of paradise *noun*
a native bird of PNG and Australia. The male bird has beautiful feathers often used as bilas in PNG.

birth *noun* births
the beginning of life, when a baby leaves its mother and starts to breathe.
date of birth the date when you were born.

birthday *noun* birthdays
the day each year when you remember the day you were born. *I had a party on my* ***birthday*** *this year.*

biscuit (**bis**-kit) *noun* biscuits
a kind of small, thin, dry cake.

bishop *noun* bishops
an important priest in the Christian church who is in charge of other priests.

bit *noun* bits
1 a very small amount of something. *a* ***bit*** *of bread,* ***bits*** *of paper.*
2 the part of a bridle that goes into a horse's mouth.

bit *verb* see **bite**

bitch *noun* bitches
a female dog.

A B C D E F G H I J K L M N O P Q R S T U V W X Y Z

bite *verb* bites, biting, bit, bitten
to use the teeth to cut into something. *Your dog's **bitten** me. Stop **biting** your nails! She **bit** into the mango.*

bitter *adjective*
1 having a sharp taste, not sweet.
2 unhappy because you are envious or disappointed.
Word Building: bitterly
*He cried **bitterly**.*

black *noun, adjective*
1 the colour of the sky on a very dark night.
2 with a dark skin.

blackberry *noun* blackberries
a small, soft, black berry that grows on bushes.

blade *noun* blades
1 the flat, sharp part of a knife or sword.
2 something shaped like a blade. *a **blade** of grass.*

blakbokis *noun*
a flying fox. [from Tok Pisin *blakbokis*]

blame *verb* blames, blaming, blamed
to say that some other person or thing is the cause of something bad that has happened. *Don't **blame** me if we're late!*

blank *adjective*
with nothing written or drawn on it. *a **blank** page.*

blanket *noun* blankets
a thick warm cover used on a bed.

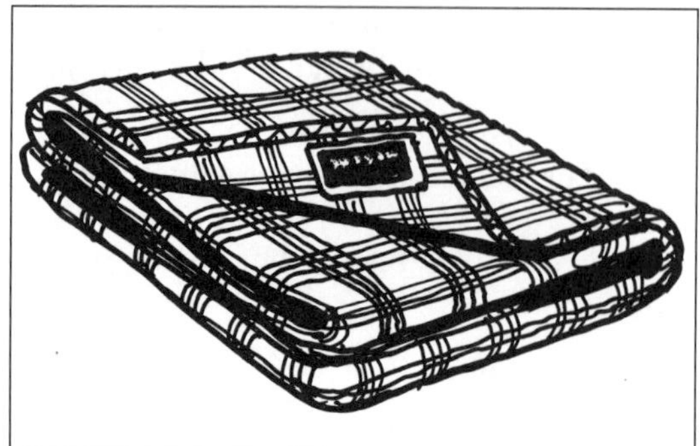

blast *noun* blasts
1 a sudden, rushing wind, a rush of air.
2 the loud sound that an explosion makes.

blast *verb* blasts, blasting, blasted
to blow up with explosives.

blaze *noun* blazes
a large, strong fire.

blaze *verb* blazes, blazing, blazed
to burn brightly. *The fire was **blazing**.*

bleach *noun*
a chemical that you use to kill germs or to make clothes whiter.

bleach *verb* bleaches, bleaching, bleached
to make something white.

bleat *verb* bleats, bleating, bleated
to make the sound sheep make.

bleed *verb* bleeds, bleeding, bled
to lose blood. *My nose is **bleeding**.*

blend *verb* blends, blending, blended
to mix together.

bless *verb* blesses, blessing, blessed
to ask God to look after someone and make them happy. *God **bless** you.*

blew *verb* see **blow**

blind *adjective*
not able to see.
Word Building: blindly

blind *noun* blinds
a cover over a window, which can be closed or opened.

blink *verb* blinks, blinking, blinked
to close your eyes and open them again very quickly.

blister *noun* blisters
a small swelling on the skin. It has liquid inside and hurts when you touch it.

blizzard *noun* blizzards
a storm with a lot of snow and wind.

blob *noun* blobs
a round drop of liquid, or a round lump of something. *a **blob** of ink.*

block *noun* blocks
1 a thick piece of something hard and solid. *a **block** of wood.*
2 a tall building with lots of flats or offices inside. *a **block** of flats, an office **block**.*

block *verb* blocks, blocking, blocked
to be in the way, or to put something in the way, so that nothing can get through. *A mob of sheep **blocked** the road.*

blond *adjective*
fair-haired.

blood *noun*
the red liquid that carries oxygen around inside your body.

bloom *verb* blooms, blooming, bloomed
to be in flower. *Bougainvillea **blooms** in the dry season.*

blossom *noun* blossoms
flowers on a tree. *apple **blossom**.*

blot *noun* blots
a spot of liquid spilt on something.

blow *verb* blows, blowing, blew, blown
1 to move in or with a current of air. *Iron was **blown** off the roof.*
2 to push air from your mouth or nose. *She **blew** up the balloon.*

blow *noun*
a hard knock or hit. *The cricket ball gave him a painful **blow** on his leg.*

blue *noun, adjective*
the colour of the sky on a fine day.

bluebottle *noun* bluebottles
a jellyfish with a poisonous sting.

blue-tongue *noun*
a large lizard with a broad blue tongue.

blunder *verb* blunders, blundering, blundered
1 to make a big mistake.
2 to move about very clumsily.

blunt *adjective* blunter, bluntest
not sharp. *a **blunt** knife.*

blur *verb* blurs, blurring, blurred
to make something look unclear. *My vision was **blurred** so I could not see clearly.*

blush *verb* blushes, blushing, blushed
to go red in the face because you feel shy or guilty.

boar *noun* boars
a male pig.

board *noun* boards
1 a long thin piece of wood.
2 a piece of wood used for a special purpose. *a notice-**board**.*

board *verb* boards, boarding, boarded
to get on an aeroplane, bus, ship, or train.

boast *verb* boasts, boasting, boasted
to talk in a way that shows you are much too proud of what you can do. *He **boasted** about how good he was at football.*

boat *noun* boats
something that floats and can take people or things over water.

body *noun* bodies
1 all of a person or animal that can be seen or touched.
2 all of a person but not the arms, legs, and head.
3 a dead person. *The police found a **body** in the river.*

bodyguard *noun* bodyguards
a person whose job is to protect someone.

bog *noun* bogs
a piece of ground so wet and soft that your feet sink into it.

boi haus (boy house) *noun*
a house, usually in the garden of the person's employer. [from Tok Pisin *haus boi*]

boil *noun* boils
a big painful spot on the skin.

boil *verb* boils, boiling, boiled
1 to bubble and give off steam. *Is the water* ***boiling****?*
2 to heat liquid until it boils. *I* ***boiled*** *the water to make tea.*
3 to be cooked or to cook something in boiling water. *We* ***boiled*** *the kaukau.*

bold *adjective* bolder, boldest
1 brave and not afraid.
2 large and easy to see. *bold handwriting.*
Word Building: boldly

bolt *noun* bolts
1 a piece of metal that you slide across to lock a door.
2 a thick metal pin like a screw. *nuts and* ***bolts****.*

bolt *verb* bolts, bolting, bolted
1 to lock something with a bolt. *Remember to* ***bolt*** *the back door.*
2 to rush off suddenly. *The cassowary* ***bolted****.*
3 to swallow food quickly without chewing it. *He* ***bolted*** *his dinner and went out to play.*

bomb *noun* bombs
a thing that explodes and hurts people or damages things.

bone *noun* bones
one of the hard white parts inside the body of a person or an animal that makes up the skeleton. *an ankle* ***bone****.*

bonfire *noun* bonfires
a large fire built in the open air.

bonnet *noun* bonnets
1 the part of a car that covers the engine.
2 a hat that is tied under the chin.

boo *verb* boos, booing, booed
to show that you don't like someone or something by shouting 'boo'.

book *noun* books
a number of pieces of paper joined together inside a cover, with words that you read.

book *verb* books, booking, booked
1 to arrange for something to be reserved for you. *Eli* ***booked*** *her plane ticket.*
2 to write someone's name in a book when they do something wrong. *The police* ***booked*** *her for speeding.*

bookcase *noun* bookcases
a piece of furniture made for holding books.

bookmark *noun* bookmarks
a piece of card for marking your place in a book.

boom *verb* booms, booming, boomed
to make a loud, deep sound. *The guns* ***boomed*** *away in the distance.*

boomerang *noun* boomerangs
a curved stick that comes back to the person who throws it.

boot *noun* boots
1 a kind of shoe that also covers the ankle or leg.
2 the part of a car for carrying luggage.

border *noun* borders
1 the narrow part along the edge of something. *a white tablecloth with a blue* ***border****.*
2 the line where two countries meet. *You need a passport to cross the* ***border****.*

bore *verb* bores, boring, bored
1 to make someone tired by being dull and uninteresting.
2 to make a hole with a tool.
3 see **bear** *verb*
Word Building: bored, boring

born, borne *verb* see **bear** *verb*

borrow *verb* borrows, borrowing, borrowed
to get the use of something for a short time and agree to give it back. *I've* ***borrowed*** *these library books.*

boss *noun* bosses
the person who is in charge.

both *adjective, pronoun*
the two of them. *Hold it in* ***both*** *hands. We* ***both*** *like swimming.*

bother *verb* bothers, bothering, bothered
1 to worry or annoy someone. *Is the loud music* ***bothering*** *you?*
2 to take trouble over doing something. *He never* ***bothers*** *to tidy his room.*

bottle *noun* bottles
a tall glass or plastic container with a narrow neck that you keep liquids in. *a* ***bottle*** *of cordial.*

bottom *noun* bottoms
1 the lowest part of anything.
2 the part of the body that you sit on.

bougainvillea *noun* bougainvilleas
a tropical climbing plant with brightly coloured, often purple, red or orange leaves around its small flowers.

bough (rhymes with *how*) *noun* boughs
a large branch of a tree.

bought (bawt) *verb* see **buy**

boulder (bowl-der) *noun* boulders
a large rock.

bounce *verb* bounces, bouncing, bounced
to spring back after hitting something hard.

bound *verb* bounds, bounding, bounded
1 to leap. *The dog* ***bounded*** *over the gate.*
2 bound to, certain to. *It's* ***bound*** *to rain if we go for a picnic.*

bound *verb* see **bind**

boundary *noun* boundaries
a line marking the edge of some land.

bow (rhymes with *go*) *noun* bows
1 a strip of bent wood with string joining each end. It is used for shooting arrows.
2 a wooden rod with strong hairs stretched along it and joining each end, for playing the violin and some other instruments with strings.
3 a knot with two loops and two ends. *The* ***bow*** *on your shoelace is undone.*

bow (rhymes with *cow*) *verb* bows, bowing, bowed
1 to bend your body or head forward to show respect. *He* ***bowed*** *to the Queen.*
2 the front part of a ship.

bowl *noun* bowls
a round, open container for liquid or food.

bowl *verb* bowls, bowling, bowled
to send a ball for the batsman to hit in cricket.

box *noun* boxes
a container, usually in the shape of a square or a rectangle. *a cardboard* ***box.***

box *verb* boxes, boxing, boxed
to fight with your fists.

boy *noun* boys
a male child or teenager.

bracelet *noun* bracelets
beads, a chain, or a ring worn around the arm.

bracket ***noun*** brackets
1 one of a pair of marks like these **( )** that you use in writing.
2 a piece of metal fixed to a wall to support something.

brag ***verb*** brags, bragging, bragged
to boast. *Bigheads **brag** a lot.*

braille (brale) ***noun***
a pattern of raised dots on paper so that blind people can read by touching them with their fingers.

brain ***noun*** brains
the part inside the head that controls the body of a person or an animal. It also lets you think and remember things.

brake ***noun*** brakes
the part of a car or bicycle that makes it slow down or stop.

branch ***noun*** branches
a part that sticks out from the trunk of a tree.

brand ***noun*** brands
the name of things you buy that show the maker. *a new **brand** of tea.*

brass ***noun***
a yellow metal made by mixing copper with zinc. ***brass** candlesticks.*

brave ***adjective*** braver, bravest
ready to do dangerous things without fear.
Word Building: bravely, bravery

bread (bred) ***noun***
a food made from flour and baked in the oven. *a loaf of **bread**.*

breadth (bredth) ***noun***
the measurement or distance from one side of something to the other; the width. *We measured the length and **breadth** of the garden.*

break (brake) ***noun*** breaks
1 a gap, a place where something is broken. *a **break** in the hedge.*
2 a short rest. *a **break** from work.*

break (brake) ***verb*** breaks, breaking, broke, broken
1 to make something go into smaller pieces. *I **broke** the window.*
2 to go into smaller pieces. *I dropped the cup and it **broke**.*
3 to fail to keep a law or promise. *He's **broken** the rules.*
break down If a car or machine breaks down, it stops working. *We were late because the car **broke down**.*

breakfast (brek-fast) ***noun*** breakfasts
the first meal of the day.

breast (brest) ***noun*** breasts
1 one of the two parts on the front of a woman's body that can produce milk to feed a baby.
2 a person's or animal's chest.

breath (breth) ***noun*** breaths
the air that a person breathes. *In Meudi they could see their **breath** in the frosty morning air.*

breathe (breeth) ***verb*** breathes, breathing, breathed
to take air into your lungs through your nose or mouth and send it out again.

bred ***verb*** see **breed** ***verb***

breed ***noun*** breeds
a particular kind of animal. *What **breed** of dog is that?*

breed ***verb*** breeds, breeding, bred
1 to produce young ones. *Birds **breed** in the mating season.*
2 to keep animals to get young ones from them. *Otto's friend **breeds** chickens.*

breeze ***noun*** breezes
a gentle wind.

bribe ***noun*** bribes
money or a present that you give to someone to tempt them to do something.

bribe *verb* bribes, bribing, bribed
to tempt someone to do something by offering them money.

brick *noun* bricks
a small block used in building.

bride *noun* brides
a woman on the day she gets married.

bridegroom *noun* bridegrooms
a man on the day he gets married.

bridge *noun* bridges
something built over a river, railway, or road so that people, cars, or trains can cross it.

brief *adjective* briefer, briefest
short. *a **brief** letter.*
Word Building: briefly

brigade (bri-**gade**) *noun* brigades
an organised group of people trained to do a special job. *The fire **brigade** saved the house from the fire.*

bright *adjective* brighter, brightest
1 with a lot of light. *a **bright** sunny day.*
2 with a strong colour. *a **bright** red dress.*
3 clever. *a **bright** boy.*
4 cheerful. *a **bright** smile.*
Word Building: brightly

brilliant *adjective*
very bright or very good.
Word Building: brilliantly

brim *noun* brims
1 the edge around the top of a container. *a cup filled to the **brim**.*
2 the part of a hat that sticks out around the edge. *a sun hat with a wide **brim**.*

bring *verb* brings, bringing, brought
1 to carry here. ***Bring** your book.*
2 to lead here. *Yesterday he **brought** his friend.*

brink *noun*
the edge of a dangerous place. *He trembled on the **brink** of the cliff.*

brisk *adjective* brisker, briskest
quick and lively. *a **brisk** walk.*
Word Building: briskly

bristle (bris-l) *noun* bristles
a short, stiff hair like the hairs on a brush.

brittle *adjective*
likely to break or snap. ***brittle** twigs.*

broad *adjective* broader, broadest
wide. *a **broad** river.*

broadcast *noun* broadcasts
a television or radio program.

bronchitis (bron-**ky**-tis) *noun*
an illness of part of the lungs that causes a very bad cough.

broke, broken *verb* see **break** *verb*

bronze *noun*
a brown metal made by mixing copper and tin. *The medal was made from **bronze**.*

brooch (broach) *noun* brooches
a piece of jewellery that you pin to your clothes.

broom *noun* brooms
a brush with a long handle that you sweep floors with.

brother (**bruth**-er) *noun* brothers
a man or boy who has the same parents as another person.
Word Building: brotherly, stepbrother

brother-in-law *noun* brothers-in-law
the brother of your husband or wife.

brought *verb* see **bring**

brow *noun* brows
1 the forehead. *He wiped the sweat from his **brow**.*
2 the top of a hill. *When they reached the **brow** of the hill they rested.*

brown *noun, adjective*
the colour of earth or clay.

bruise (brooz) *noun* bruises
a dark mark on your skin that comes after something hits it.

bruise (brooz) *verb* bruises, bruising, bruised
to give someone a bruise. *Gabriel fell and **bruised** his arm.*

brush *noun* brushes
a tool with short, stiff hairs. Brushes are used for making hair tidy, cleaning, sweeping, scrubbing, and painting. *a hair **brush**, a paint **brush**.*

brush *verb* brushes, brushing, brushed
to use a brush to do something. *I **brush** my teeth twice a day.*

bubble *noun* bubbles
a small ball of air or gas.

bubble *verb* bubbles, bubbling, bubbled
to form bubbles. *When water boils, it **bubbles**.*
Word Building: bubbly

bubu *noun*
the name shared between young and old relatives, usually between grandchildren and grandparents.

buck *verb* bucks, bucking, bucked
to jump with an arched back and stiff legs.

buck *noun* bucks
a male deer, or goat.

bucket *noun* buckets
a container with a handle but no lid, used for carrying liquid.

buckle *noun* buckles
a metal or plastic thing on the end of a belt that you use to join it to the other end.

bud *noun* buds
a flower or leaf before it has opened.

Buddhism (bood-izm) *noun*
a religion based on the teachings of Buddha, who lived in India a long time ago.
Word Building: Buddhist

budge *verb* budges, budging, budged
to move slightly.

budgerigar *noun* budgerigars
a kind of small, brightly coloured parrot.

bug *noun* bugs
1 an insect.
2 (*informal*) a germ, or an infectious illness. *a flu **bug**.*

build (bild) *verb* builds, building, built
to make something by putting parts together. *The bridge is **built** of stone.*

building *noun* buildings
something that has been built. *Houses, schools, theatres, shops, and churches are all **buildings**.*

built *verb* see **build**

bulb *noun* bulbs
1 the part of an electric lamp that gives light.
2 something that looks like an onion and is planted in earth. *Taro and some flowers grow from **bulbs**.*

bulge *verb* bulges, bulging, bulged
to swell out. *His pockets were **bulging** with peanuts.*

bulk *noun*
a large amount.

bull *noun* bulls
a male cow, elephant, or whale.

bulldozer *noun* bulldozers
a heavy machine that moves earth and makes land flat.

bullet *noun* bullets
a small piece of metal made to be fired from a gun.

bullock *noun* bullocks
a young, male ox.

bull's-eye *noun* bull's-eyes
the centre of a target.

bully *noun* bullies
someone who hurts or frightens a smaller or weaker person.

bully *verb* bullies, bullying, bullied
to hurt or frighten someone who is smaller or weaker than you.

bump *noun* bumps
a lump, a swelling.

bump *verb* bumps, bumping, bumped
to knock against something. *I **bumped** my head on the branch of the tree.*

bumper *noun* bumpers
a bar along the front or back of a car. It protects the car if it hits something.

bumpy *adjective* bumpier, bumpies
not flat but full of bumps. *a **bumpy** road.*

bun *noun* buns
a small, round cake or bread roll.

bunch *noun* bunches
a group of things joined or tied together. *a **bunch** of flowers.*

bundle *noun* bundles
a group of things tied together. *a **bundle** of sticks.*

bunk *noun* bunks
a bed that has another bed above or below it.

bunyip *noun* bunyips
an imaginary creature from Aboriginal stories, believed to live in swamps and waterholes. This word comes from Wemba-Wemba, an Aboriginal language of Victoria.

buoy (boy) *noun* buoys
a thing that floats in the sea to guide ships.

burden *noun* burdens
something that has to be carried.

burgle *verb* burgles, burgling, burgled
to break into a building to steal things.
Word Building: burglar, burglars, burglary, burglaries

burial *noun* burials
the burying of a dead person.

burn *verb* burns, burning, burned or burnt
1 to give out heat, light, and flames. *Paper **burns** easily.*
2 to damage something with heat. *Kora **burnt** the toast.*

burrow *noun* burrows
a hole in the ground that an animal lives in. *Bandicoots live in **burrows**.*

burst *verb* bursts, bursting, burst
1 to break open suddenly because there is too much inside. *The balloon **burst**.*
2 to make something break open. *Dorcas blew up the paper bag and **burst** it.*

bury (berry) *verb* buries, burying, buried
to put something or someone in a hole in the ground and cover it over.

bus *noun* buses
a large road vehicle for people to travel in.

bush *noun*
a forest of native trees. *a walk through the **bush**.*
Word Building: bushfire, bushwalking

business (biz-ness) ***noun*** businesses
1 buying and selling things. *the **business** of selling cars.*
2 a shop or firm or industry. *The tourist **business** is doing well.*

busy ***adjective*** busier, busiest
1 doing things all the time. *I'm very **busy** today.*
2 full of activity. *a **busy** street.*
Word Building: busily

butcher ***noun*** butchers
someone whose job is to cut up meat and sell it.

butter ***noun***
a yellow food made from milk.

butterfly ***noun*** butterflies
an insect with large white or coloured wings.

buttocks ***noun***
the part of the body you sit on, your bottom.

button ***noun*** buttons
a small round thing that you sew on clothes and push through a hole or loop to hold them together.

buy (by) ***verb*** buys, buying, bought
to get something by giving money for it. *I **bought** my car for K3000.*

buzz ***verb*** buzzes, buzzing, buzzed
to make the sound a bee makes.

by ***preposition***
1 at the side of. *I will stand **by** the gate and wait by my friend.*
2 because of someone's doing. *The toys were put away **by** John.*
3 not later than. *Please tidy the room **by** this afternoon.*

bye ***noun***
something said when leaving; short for goodbye.

bypass ***noun*** bypasses
a main road which goes round a town, not through it.

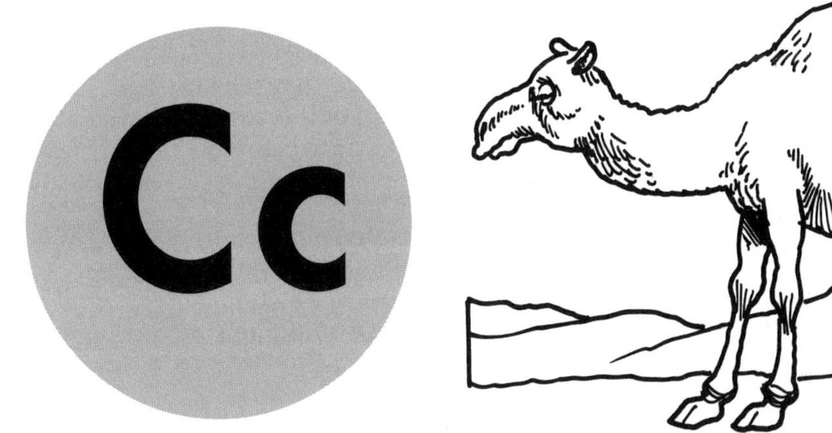

cab *noun* cabs
1 the part of a truck or train where the driver sits.
2 a taxi.

cabbage *noun* cabbages
a large round vegetable with a lot of green leaves.

cabin *noun* cabins
1 a room in a ship or aeroplane.
2 a small hut. *a log* ***cabin****.*

cabinet *noun* cabinets
a cupboard. *a kitchen* ***cabinet****.*

cable *noun* cables
strong, thick wire or rope.

cactus *noun* cacti
a plant with a thick green stem, covered in prickles. Cacti grow in hot, dry places and do not need much water.

café *noun* cafés
a place where you can buy a drink or food.

cage *noun* cages
a large box with bars across it for keeping animals or birds in.

cake *noun* cakes
a food that you make with flour, fat, eggs, and sugar, and bake in the oven.

calculate *verb* calculates, calculating, calculated
1 to find an answer by using mathematics: adding, subtracting, multiplying, and dividing.
2 to plan or intend to do something.
Word Building: calculator, calculation
A ***calculator*** *is a very useful machine for making* ***calculations****.*

calculator *noun* calculators
a machine that can do sums.

calendar *noun* calendars
a list showing all the days, weeks, and months in a year.

calf (kaf) *noun* calves
1 a young cow, elephant, or whale.
2 the part of your leg between the knee and the ankle.

call *verb* calls, calling, called
1 to speak loudly.
2 to give a name to someone or something. *They* ***called*** *the baby Tau.*
3 to tell someone to come to you. *Mother* ***called*** *us in for tea.*

calm *adjective* calmer, calmest
1 still. *a* ***calm*** *sea.*
2 not noisy or excited.

calorie *noun* calories
a unit used to measure the amount of energy produced by food.

came *verb* see come

camel (kam-el) ***noun*** camels
a big animal with one or two humps on its back.

camera ***noun*** cameras
a machine for taking photographs.

camouflage (kam-a-flahzh) ***verb*** camouflages, camouflaging, camouflaged
to hide something by making it look like its surroundings.

camp ***noun*** camps
a group of tents or huts where people live for a short time.

camp ***verb*** camps, camping, camped
to make a camp, or stay in a camp. *We went **camping** last summer.*

can ***noun*** cans
a tin. *a **can** of baked beans.*

can ***verb*** could
to be able to. *She **can** swim, but I **can't**. He **could** swim if he tried.*

cancel (kan-sl) ***verb*** cancels, cancelling, cancelled
to say that something which has been arranged will not happen. *The sports carnival was **cancelled**.*

cancer ***noun*** cancers
a serious disease in which lumps grow in the body.

candle ***noun*** candles
a stick of wax with string through the centre. It gives light as it burns.

cane ***noun*** canes
a long, thin stick, usually a stick of bamboo.

cannibal ***noun*** cannibals
a person who eats humans.

cannon ***noun*** cannons
a big gun that fires heavy metal balls.

canoe (ka-noo) ***noun*** canoes
a light, narrow boat that you move by using a paddle.

canteen ***noun*** canteens
1 a kind of café that sells food to people in a school, factory, or office.
2 a container in which you carry water to drink.

canvas (kan-vas) ***noun*** canvases
1 strong material for making things like tents.
2 material that you paint pictures on. *an artist's **canvas**.*

canvass (kan-vas) ***verb*** canvasses, canvassing, canvassed
to visit people to ask for votes, take orders for goods, or find out opinions.

canyon ***noun*** canyons
a long thin river valley with steep sides.

cap ***noun*** caps
1 a kind of hat, usually with a stiff brim at the front. *a peaked **cap**.*
2 a lid. *Put the **cap** back on the bottle.*

capable (kay-pa-bl) ***adjective***
able to do something. *You're **capable** of better work.*

capacity (ka-pass-a-tee) ***noun*** capacities
the largest amount a container can hold. *The **capacity** of this carton is one litre.*

capital ***noun*** capitals
1 the most important city in a country or state. *Port Moresby is the **capital** of Papua New Guinea.*
2 one of the big letters you put at the beginning of names and sentences. *A, B, C, D, and so on are **capital** letters.*

capsize ***verb*** capsizes, capsizing, capsized
to overturn. *The ship might **capsize** during the storm.*

capsule ***noun*** capsules
1 something that looks like a lolly, but has medicine inside.
2 a separate part at the front of a spaceship. It can move on its own away from the main part.

captain *noun* captains
1 a person in charge of a ship or aeroplane.
2 someone in charge of a team. *He's the **captain** of the school football team.*

captive *noun* captives
a person or an animal that is not free.

capture *verb* captures, capturing, captured
to catch someone. *The police **captured** the thieves.*

car *noun* cars
a machine with an engine that you drive along the road.

caravan *noun* caravans
a house on wheels that can be pulled by a car or truck from place to place.

card *noun* cards
1 thick, stiff paper.
2 a piece of card with a picture and a message on it. You send cards to people at special times like Christmas. *a birthday **card**.*
3 one of a set of small pieces of card with numbers or pictures on them, used in games. *a game of **cards**.*

cardboard *noun*
very thick, strong paper.

cardigan *noun* cardigans
a knitted jacket with buttons.

care *noun* cares
worry or trouble. *You should take more care with your schoolwork.*
to take care of to look after something. *Take **care** of the pigs for me.*

care *verb* cares, caring, cared
to be interested or concerned. *He doesn't care who wins.*
to care for someone to look after them.

careful *adjective*
making sure that you do things safely and well. *Be **careful** when you cross the road.*
Word Building: carefully

careless *adjective*
not careful, making mistakes.
Word Building: carelessly

caretaker *noun* caretakers
someone whose job is to look after a building. *the school **caretaker**.*

cargo *noun* cargoes
things taken by ship or aeroplane from one place to another.

cargo cult *noun* cargo cults
a belief held by a group of people that one day their ancestors will return with great wealth.

carnival *noun* carnivals
1 a sporting event. *Our school sports **carnival** is next week.*
2 a colourful procession with people wearing fancy dress.

carol *noun* carols
a song that people sing at Christmas.

carpenter *noun* carpenters
someone whose job is to make things out of wood.

carpet *noun* carpets
a thick cover for the floor.

carriage (ka-rij) *noun* carriages
1 one of the separate parts of a train where people sit.
2 a vehicle on wheels pulled by horses.

carried *verb* see **carry**

carrot *noun* carrots
a long, thin, orange vegetable.

carry *verb* carries, carrying, carried
to take people, animals, or things from one place to another. *I **carried** the books upstairs.*

carton *noun* cartons
a box made of cardboard or plastic. *a **carton** of milk.*

cartoon *noun* cartoons
1 a film that has drawings instead of actors.
2 a drawing that tells a joke.

cartridge *noun* cartridges
a case or tube that holds film, tape, or ink.

carve *verb* carves, carving, carved
1 to cut wood or stone to make a picture or a shape. *__carved__ out of wood.*
2 to cut off slices of meat.

case *noun* cases
1 a container. *a pencil __case__.*
2 a suitcase.

cash *noun*
coins or paper money.

casino (ka-see-no) *noun* casinos
a place where people gamble.

cassette *noun* cassettes
a small flat box with a tape inside it for recording or playing sounds or moving pictures. You put it inside a cassette player. *a video __cassette__.*

cast *noun* casts
all the actors in a play.

cast *verb* casts, casting, cast
to throw.

castle (kass-l) *noun* castles
a large, strong building with thick, stone walls. Castles were built so that people could defend themselves against their enemies.

casual (kazh-yoo-al) *adjective*
1 informal, not meant for important occasions. *I wore __casual__ clothes to the party.*
2 without thinking. *She upset me with her __casual__ remarks.*

casualty (kazh-ul-tee) *noun* casualties
a person killed or injured in an accident or in a war.

cat *noun* cats
a small, furry, meat-eating animal with a long tail often kept as a pet.

catalogue (kat-a-log) *noun* catalogues
a list of things you can buy or look at. *a __catalogue__ of library books.*

catamaran (kat-a-ma-ran) *noun* catamarans
a boat or raft with two hulls that are joined above the water.

catch *verb* catches, catching, caught
1 to capture. *The police __caught__ the bank robbers.*
2 to get hold of something. *I'll throw the ball and you try to __catch__ it.*
3 to get an illness. *I __caught__ a cold last week.*

caterpillar *noun* caterpillars
a grub that will turn into a butterfly or moth.

cathedral (ka-thee-dral) *noun* cathedrals
a big, important church.

cattle *noun*
cows and bulls kept by a farmer.

caught *verb* see **catch**

cauliflower *noun* cauliflowers
a vegetable with a thick white stalk covered in small, hard, white flowers.

cause *verb* causes, causing, caused
to make something happen. *The wind __caused__ the leaves to fall.*

caution (kaw-shun) *noun*
great care.

cautious (kaw-shus) *adjective*
taking care, doing what is safe.
Word Building: cautiously

cave *noun* caves
a big hole under the ground or inside a mountain.

cavern *noun* caverns
a big, deep cave.

CD *noun*
short for compact disc.

cease *verb* ceases, ceasing, ceased
to stop doing something.

ceiling (seel-ing) *noun* ceilings
the part of a room above your head.

celebrate *verb* celebrates, celebrating, celebrated
to do something special on an important day or when you are happy about something. *What shall we do to **celebrate** your birthday?*
Word Building: celebration

celery (sel-e-ree) *noun*
a vegetable with white long, green stalks that can be eaten raw.

cell (sell) *noun* cells
1 one of the small rooms where prisoners are kept in a prison.
2 the tiniest part of a living thing.

cellar *noun* cellars
a room underneath a building, used for storing things.

cello (chel-lo) *noun* cellos
a musical instrument like a big violin.

Celsius (sel-see-us) *adjective*
a way of measuring temperature, using a scale of 100 degrees where water freezes at 0 degrees and boils at 100 degrees.

cement (se-ment) *noun*
something used in building to stick bricks together.

cemetery (sem-a-tree) *noun* cemeteries
a place where dead people are buried.

centenary (sen-ten-a-ree) *noun* centenaries
a hundredth anniversary.
Word Building: centennial

centimetre *noun* centimetres
a measure for length. 100 centimetres make one metre.

centre (sen-ter) *noun* centres
1 the middle of something. *the **centre** of a circle.*
2 a place where you go to do certain things or to get certain things. *a sports **centre**.*

century *noun* centuries
a hundred years.

cereal (sear-ree-al) *noun* cereals
1 any plant grown by farmers for its seed.
2 a food made from the seed of plants such as corn and eaten at breakfast with milk.

cerebral palsy (ser-ra-bral pawl-see) *noun*
a brain injury which causes arms and legs to move jerkily.

ceremony (sair-uh-mo-nee) *noun* ceremonies
something important and serious that is done in front of other people.

certain (sert-n) *adjective*
1 sure. *Are you **certain**?*
2 one in particular. *a **certain** person.*

certificate *noun* certificates
a piece of paper that says you have done something special.

chain *noun* chains
a line made of metal rings fastened together. *an anchor **chain**.*

chair *noun* chairs
a seat for one person.

chalk *noun* chalks
1 a kind of soft white rock. ***chalk** cliffs.*
2 a white stick used for writing.

challenge *verb* challenges, challenging, challenged
to ask someone to try to do better than you at something. *He **challenged** me to a race.*

champion *noun* champions
someone who is the best in a sport or game, or who wins a competition. *a swimming **champion**.*

chance *noun* chances
1 a time when you can do something that you cannot do at other times. *This is our last **chance** to escape.*
2 the way things happen that have not been planned. *I saw him by **chance** on the PMV.*

change *noun*
the money you get back when you give more money than you need to pay for something.

change *verb* changes, changing, changed
1 to make or become different. *Tadpoles **change** into frogs.*
2 to give something and get something in return. *They **changed** places with each other.*

channel *noun* channels
1 a narrow sea.
2 a groove in the ground that water moves along.
3 a television station. *Which **channel** shall we watch?*

chant *verb* chants, chanting, chanted
to say words over and over again so that they sound like music.

chant *noun* chants
a tune, especially one that is often repeated.

chaos (kay-os) *noun*
a very confused state. *There was **chaos** in the village after the earthquake.*

chapel *noun* chapels
1 a kind of small church.
2 a small part of a church.

chapter *noun* chapters
a part of a book. *The book has ten **chapters**.*

character (kair-ek-ter) *noun* characters
1 someone in a story.
2 the sort of person you are. *The twins look the same, but they have very different **characters**.*

charge *noun* charges
1 the cost of something.
2 a sudden rush. *The army's **charge** was brave.*
to be in charge to have the job of organising or looking after something. *Mother left me **in charge** of the washing-up.*

charge *verb* charges, charging, charged
1 to ask a certain price. *They **charged** K5 for a watermelon.*
2 to rush at something and attack it. *The bull **charged**.*

charity (chair-i-tee) *noun* charities
a group of people who raise money to help others.

charm *noun* charms
1 a magic spell.
2 a small ornament which you wear to bring good luck.

charm *verb* charms, charming, charmed
1 to cast a spell over someone or something.
2 to make people like you.

charming *adjective*
attractive, pretty.

chart *noun* charts
1 a big map. *Sailors use **charts** of the sea.*
2 a large sheet of paper with information on it. *a temperature **chart**.*

chase *verb* chases, chasing, chased
to run after and try to catch a person or animal. *I saw the cat **chasing** a mouse.*

chat *verb* chats, chatting, chatted
to talk in a friendly way about things that are not important.

chatter *verb* chatters, chattering, chattered
1 to talk a lot or very quickly.
2 to make a rattling noise. *His teeth **chattered** with fear.*

cheap *adjective* cheaper, cheapest
costing less than usual.
Word Building: cheaply

cheat *verb* cheats, cheating, cheated
1 to trick someone in order to get something from them.
2 to try to do well in a test or game by breaking the rules.

check *verb* checks, checking, checked
to make sure something is correct or in proper condition. *Check your answers.*

check *noun*
a pattern of squares.

checkout *noun* checkouts
the place in a shop where you pay.

cheek *noun* cheeks
1 the side of your face below the eye.
2 rude behaviour or speech.

cheeky *adjective* cheekier, cheekiest
rude, not showing respect. *Don't be cheeky to the teacher.*
Word Building: cheekily

cheer *verb* cheers, cheering, cheered
to shout to show you are pleased or that you want your team to win.

cheerful *adjective*
looking or sounding happy.

cheese *noun* cheeses
food made by stirring milk until it becomes solid.

chemist (kem-ist) *noun* chemists
someone whose job is to make or sell medicines.

cheque (chek) *noun* cheques
a special piece of paper that a person can sign and use instead of money.

chest *noun* chests
1 a big, strong box.
2 the front part of your body between the neck and the waist.

chew *verb* chews, chewing, chewed
to keep biting food while you eat it.

chewing gum *noun*
a soft sticky substance that you chew but don't swallow.

chick *noun* chicks
a young bird.

chicken *noun* chickens
a bird kept for its meat and eggs.

chickenpox *noun*
an illness that gives you red spots that itch.

chief *adjective*
the most important.

chief *noun* chiefs
the person in charge.

child *noun* children
1 a young boy or girl.
2 a son or daughter.

chill *noun* chills
1 coldness
2 an illness that makes you shiver and feel hot at the same time.

chill *verb* chills, chilling, chilled
to make someone or something cold.
Word Building: chilly

chime *verb* chimes, chiming, chimed
to make a sound like a bell. *The clock chimed midnight.*

chimney *noun* chimneys
a tall pipe inside a house to take away the smoke from a fire.

chimpanzee *noun* chimpanzees
a small African ape.

chin *noun* chins
the part of the face that is under the mouth.

china *noun*
cups, saucers, and plates made of thin, hard material. *China breaks easily.*

chip *noun* chips
1 a small piece broken off something.
2 a piece of fried potato eaten hot.
3 a thin, crisp slice of fried potato eaten cold.

chip *verb* chips, chipping, chipped
to break or knock small pieces off something. *This cup is chipped.*

chirp *verb* chirps, chirping, chirped
to make short, sharp sounds like a bird.

chisel (chiz-zl) *noun* chisels
a tool with a short, sharp edge, for cutting stone or wood.

chocolate (chok-o-let) *noun* chocolates
sweet food made from cocoa and sugar.

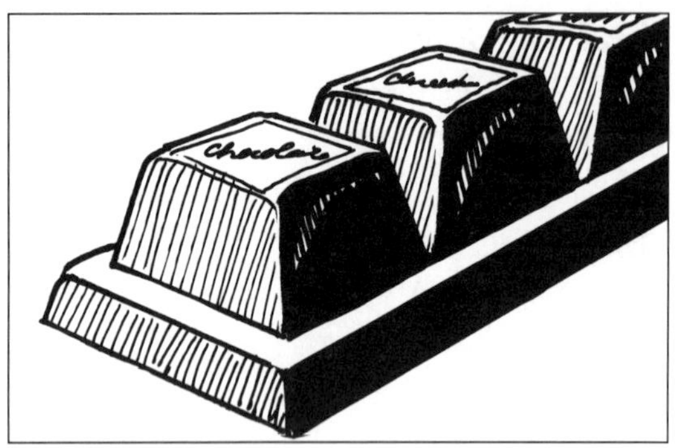

choice *noun* choices
1 choosing. *You can have first* ***choice****.*
2 a number of different things to choose from. *There's a* ***choice*** *of bananas, mangoes, or guavas.*

choir (kwire) *noun* choirs
a group of people who sing together.

choke *verb* chokes, choking, choked
1 to find it hard to get your breath because of something in your throat. *The smoke made him* ***choke****.*
2 to block up something. *The pond was* ***choked*** *with weeds.*

chook *noun* chooks
a slang word for a chicken or fowl.

choose *verb* chooses, choosing, chose, chosen
to take one thing instead of another, because you want to. *He* ***chose*** *a red shirt. Which book have you* ***chosen****?*

chop *noun* chops
a small, thick slice of pork or lamb.

chop *verb* chops, chopping, chopped
to cut something with a knife or axe.

choppy *adjective* choppier, choppiest
full of small waves, rough. *The sea was choppy.*

chopsticks *noun*
a pair of thin sticks held in one hand and used instead of a knife and fork, especially with Asian food.

chord (kord) *noun* chords
a combination of notes sung or played together.

chorus (kor-rus) *noun* choruses
the words repeated after every verse in a poem or song.

chose, chosen *verb* see choose

christen (kris-en) *verb* christens, christening, christened
to give a baby its name at a Christian ceremony in church.

Christianity (kris-tee-an-i-tee) *noun*
a religion followed by people who believe that Jesus Christ is the son of God.
Word Building: Christian, Christians

Christmas *noun* Christmases
the 25th December, when Jesus Christ's birthday is celebrated.

chrysalis (kris-a-lis) *noun* chrysalises
the cover a caterpillar makes around itself before it changes into a butterfly or moth.

chuckle *verb* chuckles, chuckling, chuckled
to laugh to yourself.

chunk *noun* chunks
a thick lump. *a* ***chunk*** *of bread.*

church *noun* churches
a building where Christians worship.

chute (shoot) *noun* chutes
a narrow, sloping passage, which objects can slide down or be dropped down. *The bag of money went down the* ***chute*** *into the bank vault.*

cicada (si-cay-da) *noun* cicadas
a flying insect. The males make a loud, high noise.

cigar (si-gar) *noun* cigars
tobacco leaves that are rolled and then smoked.

cigarette (sig-a-ret) *noun* cigarettes
a thin tube of paper with tobacco inside it for smoking.

cinema *noun* cinemas
a place where people go to see movies.

circle *noun* circles
1 a round shape like a ring or a wheel. *The edge of a **circle** is always the same distance from the centre.*
2 anything that makes this shape. *They danced in a **circle**.*

circle *verb* circles, circling, circled
to go in a circle.

circular *adjective*
like a circle. *A wheel is **circular**.*

circumference *noun* circumferences
the distance around the edge of a circle.

circumstances *noun*
the facts or details connected with something. *The police need to know the **circumstances** surrounding the accident.*

circus *noun* circuses
a show held in a big tent or building with animals, acrobats, and clowns.

citizen *noun* citizens
a person who belongs to a country, either by birth or by choice.
Word Building: citizenship

city *noun* cities
a large, important town.

claim *verb* claims, claiming, claimed
to ask for something that belongs to you. *She **claimed** her lost property.*

clamber *verb* clambers, clambering, clambered
to climb with difficulty, often using your hands to help. *They **clambered** over the rocks.*

clamp *verb* clamps, clamping, clamped
to grasp something tightly.

clamp *noun* clamps
a device for holding things tightly together.

clang *verb* clangs, clanging, clanged
to make a loud, deep ringing sound.

clap *verb* claps, clapping, clapped
to make a noise by hitting the palm of one hand with the palm of the other.

clash *verb* clashes, clashing, clashed
1 to make the sound cymbals make.
2 to disagree with someone. *Highland clans sometimes **clash** over land use.*

clasp *verb* clasps, clasping, clasped
to hold tightly.

class *noun* classes
1 a group of children who learn things together.
2 a group of people or things that are alike in some way. *There are many **classes** of animals.*

classroom *noun* classrooms
a room where children have lessons.

clatter *noun*
a noise made when hard objects hit each other.

clatter *verb* clatters, clattering, clattered
to make a rattling, annoying noise.

claw *noun* claws
one of the hard, sharp nails that some animals have on their feet. *The cuscus scratched me with her sharp **claws**.*

clay *noun*
a sticky kind of earth used for making things, because it keeps its shape and goes hard. ***clay** pots.*

clean *adjective* cleaner, cleanest
not dirty.
Word Building: cleanly

clean *verb* cleans, cleaning, cleaned
to make something clean.

clear *adjective* clearer, clearest
1 easy to see through, not cloudy or dirty. ***clear** water.*
2 easy to see, understand, or hear. *a **clear** photograph, a **clear** voice.*
3 free from things you don't want. *a **clear** road.*

clear *verb* clears, clearing, cleared
1 to become clearer. *The water will clear when the mud settles.*
2 to get rid of things that are in the way. *Please **clear** the table.*

clench *verb* clenches, clenching, clenched
to close your teeth, fingers, or fist tightly.

clerk (clark) *noun* clerks
1 someone who writes letters in an office. *an office **clerk**.*
2 someone who deals with money in a bank. *a bank **clerk**.*

clever *adjective* cleverer, cleverest
if you are clever, you can learn things quickly and easily.
Word Building: cleverly

click *verb* clicks, clicking, clicked
to make short, sharp sounds like the sound a light switch makes.

cliff *noun* cliffs
a steep hill made of rock close to the sea.

climate *noun* climates
the sort of weather that a place usually gets at different times of the year.

climax *noun* climaxes
the most exciting part of a story or an event, usually near the end.

climb *verb* climbs, climbing, climbed
to go up or down something high.

cling *verb* clings, clinging, clung
to hold tightly on to someone or something.

clinic *noun* clinics
a place where you can go to get help from doctors or nurses.

clip *noun* clips
1 a fastener for keeping things together or in place. *paper **clips**.*
2 a short piece from a film or TV program.

clip *verb* clips, clipping, clipped
to cut with scissors or shears.

clock *noun* clocks
a machine that shows you what time it is.

clockwise *adverb*
the direction a clock's hands move in. *Turn the handle **clockwise**.*

clockwork *adjective*
worked by a spring which you have to wind up.

clog *verb* clogs, clogging, clogged
to block up.

close (rhymes with *dose*) *adjective* closer, closest
1 very near. *They got **close** to the fire.*
2 careful. *Keep a **close** watch on the baby.*
Word Building: closely

close (rhymes with *doze*) *verb* closes, closing, closed
1 to shut. *Please **close** the door.*
2 to stop being open so that people cannot go there. *The shop was **closed**.*

cloth *noun*
material for making things like clothes and curtains.

clothe (kloath) *verb* clothes, clothing, clothed
to dress.

clothes, clothing *noun*
things you wear to cover your body.

cloud *noun* clouds
1 something white, grey, or black that floats in the sky. Clouds are made of drops of water that often fall as rain.
2 dust or smoke that looks like a cloud.

cloudy *adjective* cloudier, cloudiest
1 full of clouds. *a **cloudy** sky.*
2 hard to see through. ***cloudy** water.*

clown *noun* clowns
an amusing or foolish person.

club *noun* clubs
1 a group of people who meet together because they are interested in the same thing.
2 a thick stick used as a weapon.
3 a black clover leaf printed on some playing cards. *the ace of **clubs**.*

clue *noun* clues
something that helps you to find the answer to a puzzle.

clump *noun* clumps
a group of trees or plants growing close together.

clumsy *adjective* clumsier, clumsiest
likely to knock things over or drop things, because you move badly.

clung *verb* see **cling**

cluster *noun* clusters
1 a group of things growing together. *a **cluster** of berries.*
2 a group of people, animals, or things gathered around something.

clutch *noun* clutches
part of a car which is worked by the pedal for your left foot.

clutch *verb* clutches, clutching, clutched
1 to snatch at something. *The drowning man **clutched** the rope.*
2 to hold tightly. *She was **clutching** her doll and would not let go.*

clutter *noun*
a lot of things in an untidy mess.

coach *noun* coaches
someone who trains people in a sport. *a football **coach**.*

coal *noun* coals
hard, black rock that is burned to make heat. *a **coal** fire.*

coarse *adjective* coarser, coarsest
1 not delicate or smooth, rough. *coarse material.*
2 in large pieces. *coarse sand.*

coast *noun* coasts
the edge of land next to the sea. *the west **coast**. We went to the **coast** last Sunday.*

coat *noun* coats
1 a piece of clothing with sleeves that you wear on top of other clothes.
2 the hair or fur that covers an animal.
3 a covering. *a **coat** of paint.*

coax *verb* coaxes, coaxing, coaxed
to persuade gently. *We tried to **coax** the young boy into the water.*

cobweb *noun* cobwebs
a thin, sticky net spun by a spider to trap insects.

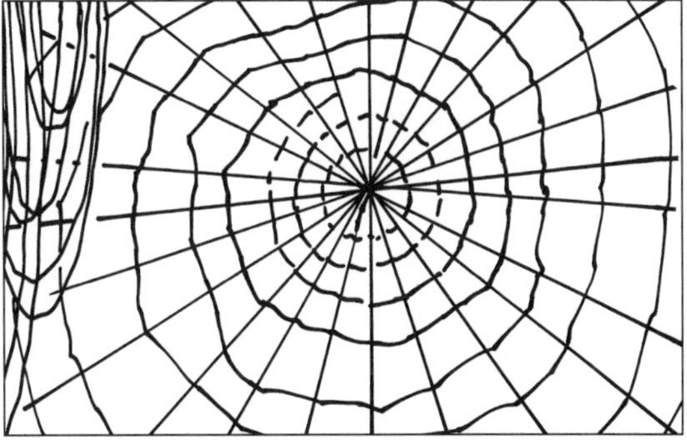

cockatoo *noun* cockatoos
a large Australian or New Guinean parrot with a crest on its head.

cocoa (ko-ko) *noun*
a brown powder used to make chocolate cakes.

cocoon (ko-**koon**) *noun* cocoons
the silky case a caterpillar spins to cover itself before it changes into a moth or butterfly.

coconut *noun* coconuts
a large, round nut that grows on a palm tree. It contains sweet, white flesh (meat) which is squeezed to make **coconut cream**, and is filled with a white liquid (**coconut milk**). A **coconut scraper** is used to remove the flesh from coconuts. **Coconut oil** is made by boiling the white flesh.

cod *noun* cod
a large sea fish that can be eaten.

code *noun* codes
1 a set of signs or letters for sending messages secretly or quickly. *Morse **code**.*
2 a set of rules.

coffee *noun* coffees
a hot drink made from roasted beans ground into a powder. *a cup of **coffee**, two **coffees** please.*

coffin *noun* coffins
the long box in which a dead person is put.

coil *verb* coils, coiling, coiled
to wind round and round in the shape of a circle or spiral. *The snake was **coiled** round a branch.*

coin *noun* coins
a piece of metal money.

cold *adjective* colder, coldest
not hot.

cold *noun* colds
an illness that makes you sneeze and blow your nose a lot.

collage (ko-**lazh**) *noun* collages
a picture made from small pieces of paper and material.

collapse *verb* collapses, collapsing, collapsed
to fall down. *The shed **collapsed** in the storm. People **collapsed** because it was so hot.*

collar *noun* collars
1 the part of your shirt or coat that goes around your neck.
2 something that goes around the neck of an animal. *a dog's **collar**.*

collect *verb* collects, collecting, collected
1 to bring things together from different places. *I **collect** foreign coins.*
2 to go and get someone or something. *She **collected** the children from school.*

collection *noun* collections
1 a set of things that have been collected. *a shell **collection**.*
2 money collected from many people for a special reason.

collector *noun* collectors
someone who collects things as a hobby or as a job.

college *noun* colleges
1 a place where you can go to study when you have left school.
2 a teachers' college, a technical college.

collide *verb* collides, colliding, collided
to hit someone or something by accident, while you are moving. *The car **collided** with a bus.*

collision *noun* collisions
a crash between two moving things.

colon *noun* colons
a mark like this **:** that you use in writing.

colony (**kol**-uh-nee) *noun* colonies
1 a group of settlers in a new country.
2 a place which is governed by another country.
Word Building: colonise or colonize, colonial

colour *noun* colours
any of the different effects you see from different kinds of light. Red, green, yellow, and blue are colours. *What is your favourite **colour**?*

colour *verb* colours, colouring, coloured
to use paint or crayon to put colour on something.

colourful *adjective*
1 full of bright colours.
2 lively, interesting. *Luke wrote a **colourful** description of the sing-sing.*

column (**kol**-um) *noun* columns
1 things on a list each below the other.
2 a thick stone post that supports something or decorates a building.

comb (rhymes with *home*) *noun* combs
a strip of plastic, wood, or metal with a row of thin parts like teeth, for making hair tidy.

combine *verb* combines, combining, combined
to join or mix together.

come *verb* comes, coming, came, come
1 to move here. *I **came** as soon as I could.*
2 to arrive. *Has the letter **come** yet?*

comedian (ko-**mee**-dee-an) *noun* comedians
someone who entertains people by making them laugh.

comedy (**kom**-e-dee) *noun* comedies
a funny play.

comet (**kom**-et) *noun* comets
a small, bright object with a long tail, moving across the sky.

comfort (**kum**-fert) *verb* comforts, comforting, comforted
to be kind and helpful to someone who is hurt or ill or unhappy.

comfortable (**kumf**-tra-bl) *adjective*
1 pleasant to use or to wear. *a **comfortable** chair, **comfortable** shoes.*
2 with no pain or worry. *Are you **comfortable**?*
Word Building: comfortably

comic *adjective*
funny.

comic *noun* comics
1 a paper with stories told in pictures.
2 a funny person.

comma *noun* commas
a mark like this **,** that you use in writing.

command *verb* commands, commanding, commanded
1 to tell someone to do something.
2 to be in charge of something.

comment *noun* comments
an opinion or a short explanation.

commentary (**kom**-en-tree) *noun* commentaries
a description of what is going on. *a football **commentary**.*

commercial (ka-**mer**-shal) *noun* commercials
an advertisement on TV or radio.

commit *verb* commits, committing, committed
to do something. *to **commit** a crime.*

common *adjective* commoner, commonest
ordinary, usual.

commonwealth *noun*
1 an independent nation or community.
2 The Commonwealth is an association of Britain and other countries such as PNG, Australia and New Zealand.

commotion (ka-**mo**-shn) *noun*
a lot of noise and moving about.

communicate (kom-**mew**-ni-kate) *verb* communicates, communicating, communicated
to tell something to someone else by talking or writing.
Word Building: communication
*Letters and phone calls are common forms of **communication**.*

community *noun* communities
the people living in one place.

community health worker *noun* community health workers
a health worker trained to treat simple health problems in villages, towns and settlements.

compact *adjective*
small and neat.
compact disc a kind of disc with music or information recorded or stored on it.

companion *noun* companions
a friend who is with you.

company *noun* companies
1 having an animal or another person with you so that you are not lonely. *The dog kept her **company**.*
2 a group of people who do things together. *a dance **company**.*

A B C D E F G H I J K L M N O P Q R S T U V W X Y Z

compare *verb* compares, comparing, compared
to try to see how like each other some things are.

compass *noun* compasses
1 an instrument with a needle that always points north. *The walkers used a **compass** to find their way home.*
2 an instrument for drawing circles.

compel *verb* compels, compelling, compelled
to force someone to do something.

compete *verb* competes, competing, competed
to take part in a race or competition.

competition (kom-pa-**tish**-shn) *noun* competitions
a test or game with a prize for the person who wins.

competitor (kum-**pet**-it-ter) *noun* competitors
a person who tries to win a competition.

complain *verb* complains, complaining, complained
to say that you are not pleased about something.
Word Building: complaint, complaints

complement *noun* complements
a thing that improves something or makes it complete. *That belt is a lovely **complement** to the outfit.*
Word Building: complementary, complement *verb*

complete *adjective*
whole, with nothing missing.
Word Building: completely

complete *verb* completes, completing, completed
1 to finish something. *You can play when you have **completed** your work.*
2 to make something whole. *I need one more piece to **complete** the jigsaw.*

complicate (**kom**-pli-kate) *verb* complicates, complicating, complicated
to make something difficult or complex.
Word Building: complication

complicated *adjective*
1 with a lot of different parts. *a **complicated** machine.*
2 difficult. *a **complicated** sum.*

compliment *noun* compliments
something nice you say about someone.

compose (kum-**pose**) *verb* composes, composing, composed
1 to make up or put something together. *The teacher asked us to **compose** a poem.*
2 to write music.

composer *noun* composers
someone who writes music.

composition *noun* compositions
1 a piece of music.
2 a story you have made up and written down.

compost *noun*
a mixture made up of leaves, scraps of food, and other materials, which is left to rot and then added to garden soil to help plants grow.
Word Building: compost *verb*

computer *noun* computers
a machine which stores information on tape or disk, organises it and then produces it when someone needs it.

conceal (kun-**seel**) *verb* conceals, concealing, concealed
to hide. *The money was **concealed** under the floor.*

conceit (kun-**seet**) *noun*
too much pride, vanity. *Hitolo was full of **conceit** when she won the prize.*
Word Building: conceited
*They were **conceited** about their ability to do the job.*

concentrate (kon-sen-trate) *verb* concentrates, concentrating, concentrated
to think hard about one thing. *I can't **concentrate** on my work!*
Word Building: concentration
Concentration is difficult when there is so much noise.

concern *verb* concerns, concerning, concerned
to be important or interesting to someone or something. *The information about the school trip **concerned** everyone.*

concerned *adjective*
worried. *When Edoa was late coming home, her mother became very **concerned**.*

concert *noun* concerts
music played for a lot of people.

conclude *verb* concludes, concluding, concluded
1 to finish. *The festival **concluded** with a firework display.*
2 to form an opinion. *When you didn't arrive, we **concluded** that you'd missed the transport.*

conclusion *noun* conclusions
what you believe or decide after thinking carefully. *We came to the **conclusion** that you were right.*

concrete *noun*
a mixture of cement and sand used for making buildings, paths, and bridges.

condemn (kun-**dem**) *verb* condemns, condemning, condemned
1 to say you don't like something. *We all **condemn** cruelty to animals.*
2 to say that someone is guilty. *The thief was **condemned** to spend three years in prison.*

condition *noun* conditions
1 the state something is in. *Is your car in a safe **condition**?*
2 something you must agree to before something can happen. *You can go out to play on the **condition** that you finish your homework first.*

conduct *verb* conducts, conducting, conducted
to stand in front of a band, choir, or orchestra and control the music the musicians play.
Word Building: conductor

cone *noun* cones
1 a shape with a flat, circular bottom and sides which come to a point at the top.
2 a case for seeds on some trees. *a pine **cone**.*

confess *verb* confesses, confessing, confessed
to say that you have done something wrong. *He **confessed** to breaking the window.*

confident (kon-fi-dent) *adjective*
1 brave and not afraid. *Sam is a **confident** swimmer.*
2 sure about something. *Rachael was **confident** that she knew the way.*
Word Building: confidence, confidently

conflict *noun* conflicts
a quarrel, a fight.

confuse *verb* confuses, confusing, confused
to mix people or things up. *He always **confuses** the names of the twins.*

congratulate *verb* congratulates, congratulating, congratulated
to tell someone how pleased you are about something special that has happened to them.
Word Building: congratulations
***Congratulations** on winning the race!*

conjunction *noun* conjunctions
a word that joins two parts of a phrase or sentence. *And*, *or*, *when*, and *because* are all conjunctions.

connect *verb* connects, connecting, connected
to join things together. *She **connected** the hose to the tap.*

conquer (kong-ker) *verb* conquers, conquering, conquered
to beat an enemy in a battle or war.

conscience (kon-shens) *noun*
a feeling inside you that tells you what is right and wrong. *Peter had a guilty **conscience** about breaking the window.*

conscious (kon-shus) *adjective*
awake and able to understand what is happening around you. *After the operation she slowly became **conscious**.*

consent *verb* consents, consenting, consented
to agree to let someone do something.

conserve *verb* conserves, conserving, conserved
to keep from harm, decay, or loss, for future use. *I will **conserve** my energy so that I don't get too tired.*
Word Building: conservation, conservationist
*A **conservationist** is concerned about the **conservation** of the natural environment.*

consider *verb* considers, considering, considered
to think carefully about something.

considerable *adjective*
large. *These books cost a **considerable** amount of money.*
Word Building: considerably

considerate *adjective*
kind and thoughtful in the way you behave.

consist *verb* consists, consisting, consisted
to be made up of. *Books **consist** of words and illustrations.*

consonant *noun* consonants
any letter of the alphabet except a, e, i, o, u and sometimes y.

constant *adjective*
going on all the time. ***Constant** chattering annoys the teacher.*
Word Building: constantly

construct *verb* constructs, constructing, constructed
to build. *a bridge **constructed** out of metal.*

consume *verb* consumes, consuming, consumed
to eat up, to use up.

contact *verb* contacts, contacting, contacted
to get in touch with someone. *I will **contact** the police.*

contact *noun* contacts
someone you get in touch with if you need information or help. *The didiman was a useful **contact** when I was doing my project.*

contain *verb* contains, containing, contained
to have something inside. *The box **contained** toys.*

container *noun* containers
anything that you can put other things into. Buckets, cups, bags, boxes, and jars are all containers.

container ship *noun* container ships
a ship on which cargo is carried in large containers.

content *adjective*
happy with what you have.
Word Building: contented, contentment, contentedly, discontent

contents (kon-tents) *noun*
what is inside a container or a book. *Be careful, the **contents** of this box are very fragile.*

contest (kon-test) *noun* contests
a competition.
Word Building: contestant

contest (kun-test) *verb* contests, contesting, contested
to enter a competition to try to win. *The two countries **contested** the control of the southern Pacific Ocean.*

continent *noun* continents
one of the seven very large areas of land in the world. *Australia is a **continent**.*

continual *adjective*
happening again and again. ***continual** interruptions.*
Word Building: continually
*She is **continually** late for school.*

continue *verb* continues, continuing, continued
to go on doing something. *They **continued** the game after lunch.*

continuous *adjective*
going on without stopping. *a **continuous** noise.*
Word Building: continuously
*It rained **continuously** for three hours.*

contract (kon-tract) *noun* contracts
an agreement. *The builder signed a **contract** to build the house.*
Word Building: contractor
*The **contractor** agreed to build the fence.*

contract (kun-tract) *verb* contracts, contracting, contracted
1 to make or become smaller or shorter.
2 to arrange an agreement with someone.
Word Building: contraction
*'Dr' is a **contraction** of 'doctor' and 'isn't' is a **contraction** of 'is not'.*

contract officer *noun* contract officers
a person working for the government for a fixed period of time.

contradict *verb* contradicts, contradicting, contradicted
to say the opposite of what someone else has said. *I said it was raining, but she **contradicted** me and said it was not raining.*

contrast (kun-trast) *verb* contrasts, contrasting, contrasted
to compare two things to show their difference.

contrast (kon-trast) *noun* contrasts
the amount of difference between two things.

contribute (kun-trib-yute) *verb* contributes, contributing, contributed
to give money or help to something.

control *verb* controls, controlling, controlled
to make someone or something do what you want. *I can't **control** my little sister.*

convenient *adjective*
easy to get at or use.
Word Building: conveniently

convent (kon-vent) *noun* convents
1 a place where nuns live and work together.
2 a school run by nuns.

conversation *noun* conversations
talking and listening to another person.

convict (kon-vict) *noun* convicts
a person who is put in prison for breaking the law.

convict (kun-vict) *verb* convicts, convicting, convicted
to find someone guilty of breaking the law.
Word Building: conviction

convince *verb* convinces, convincing, convinced
to make someone believe something. *He **convinced** her that ghosts were not real.*

cook *noun* cooks
someone whose job is to cook.

cook *verb* cooks, cooking, cooked
to get food ready to eat by heating it. *I'm learning to **cook**. I could smell something **cooking** in the kitchen.*

cool *adjective* cooler, coolest
not warm. *a **cool** wind.*

cooperate (ko-op-er-ate) *verb* cooperates, cooperating, cooperated
to work together for the same purpose. *The team members **cooperated** to win the final.*
Word Building: cooperation, coooperative, uncooperative

copper *noun*
a shiny brown or red metal. *Copper is used to make electrical wire and toea coins.*

copy *verb* copies, copying, copied
1 to write down or draw what is already written down or drawn. *She **copied** the poem in her best writing.*
2 to do exactly the same as someone else. *She always **copies** what I wear.*

copyright *noun*
a law that protects a person's writing, drawings, or music from being used by others without permission.

coral *noun*
a kind of rock made in the sea from the bodies of tiny creatures. Coral can be many colours.

cord *noun* cords
thin rope.

cordial *noun* cordials
a fruit-flavoured drink. *I like orange **cordial** best.*

core *noun* cores
the part in the middle of something. *an apple **core**.*

cork *noun* corks
a piece of the bark of a special kind of tree used as a stopper for a bottle.

corn *noun*
1 a cereal plant.
2 the seeds of these plants, used to make food.

corner *noun* corners
the point where two edges or streets meet.

coronation *noun* coronations
the time when someone is crowned as king or queen.

corps (kor) *noun*
an army unit.

corpse (korps) *noun* corpses
a dead body.

correct *adjective*
without any mistakes.
Word Building: correctly
*Have I spelt your name **correctly**?*

correct *verb* corrects, correcting, corrected
to show where the mistakes are in something and put it right. *The teacher **corrected** the homework.*

corridor *noun* corridors
a long narrow part of a building with rooms on each side of it.

cost *verb* costs, costing, cost
to have a certain price. *The dress **cost** K15.*

costly *adjective*
expensive, costing a lot. ***costly** repairs.*

costume *noun* costumes
1 clothes worn for acting in plays or stories.
2 special clothes worn in a particular country. *the national **costume** of Japan.*

cosy *adjective* cosier, cosiest
warm and comfortable. *a **cosy** room.*

cot *noun* cots
a small child's bed, with sides.

cotton *noun*
1 thread for sewing.
2 cloth made from a plant that grows in hot countries.
cotton wool soft, white, fluffy stuff used for cleaning cuts, removing make-up, and other things.

couch *noun* couches
a long seat that you can sit or lie on.

cough (kof) *verb* coughs, coughing, coughed
to make a sudden, loud noise to get rid of something in your throat. *Smoke and bad colds make people* ***cough****.*

could (rhymes with *good*) *verb* see **can**

council *noun* councils
a group of people chosen to plan and decide what should be done in a city or village.
Word Building: councillor
The Local Government Council is made up of ***councillors*** *from different villages.*

counsel *verb* counsels, counselling, counselled
to give advice to someone.
Word Building: counsellor

counsel *noun*
advice, suggestions. *The counsellor gave wise* ***counsel*** *to the student.*

count *verb* counts, counting, counted
1 to say the numbers in order. *My little brother can* ***count*** *from 1 to 10.*
2 to use numbers to find out how many people or things there are. *I* ***counted*** *ten fish in the pond.*

counter *noun* counters
1 the long table where you are served in a shop.
2 a small, round, flat piece of plastic used for playing some games.

counterfeit *adjective*
fake or false. *The money was* ***counterfeit****.*
Word Building: counterfeit *verb*

country *noun* countries
1 a land with its own people and laws. *Australia, Italy, and China are all* ***countries****.*
2 land that is not in the town. *Do you live in the town or in the* ***country****?*

couple *noun* couples
two people or things. *I've only got a* ***couple*** *of betel nuts left.*

courage *noun*
the ability to face danger or fear. *Koru showed a lot of* ***courage*** *when she had to go to hospital.*

course *noun* courses
1 the direction something goes in. *a ship's* ***course****.*
2 a piece of ground or water where some sport takes place. *a race* ***course****.*
3 a series of lessons. *a typing* ***course****.*

court *noun* courts
1 a piece of ground marked out for a game like netball or tennis.
2 the place where people decide whether someone is guilty of breaking the law. *a law* ***court****.*

courteous (ker-tee-us) *adjective*
polite.
Word Building: courtesy, courteously
He always behaves with great ***courtesy****.*

cousin (kuz-in) *noun* cousins
the child of your aunt or uncle.

cousin-brother *noun*
a male relative, a male clan member, or a close male friend.

cousin-sister *noun*
a female relative, a female clan member, or a close female friend.

cover *noun* covers
a piece of material which goes over or around something. *The book has a picture of a bird of paradise on the* ***cover****.*

cover *verb* covers, covering, covered
to put something over or around something else. *She **covered** him with a blanket.*

covering *noun* coverings
something which covers something else. *a **covering** of dust on the table.*

cow *noun* cows
a female animal kept by farmers for its milk.

coward *noun* cowards
someone who is afraid when they ought to be brave.

crab *noun* crabs
an animal with a shell, claws, and ten legs that lives in or near the sea.

crack *noun* cracks
1 a narrow gap or thin line where something is nearly broken. *There is a **crack** in this glass.*
2 a sudden loud noise. *a **crack** of thunder.*

crack *verb* cracks, cracking, cracked
1 to get or make a crack. *This mug is **cracked**. Be careful not to **crack** the glass.*
2 to make the sudden, sharp noise a dry twig makes when you break it.

crackle *verb* crackles, crackling, crackled
to make the cracking sounds burning wood makes.

craft *noun* crafts
a task which needs great skill; a skill. *Weaving is a **craft**.*

crafty *adjective* craftier, craftiest
clever in a sly sort of way.
Word Building: craftily

cramp *noun* cramps
a pain you get in your arm, leg, or stomach when a muscle tightens.

cramp *verb* cramps, cramping, cramped
to keep in a very small space.

crane *noun* cranes
1 a machine for lifting heavy things.
2 a large bird with very long legs.

crash *noun* crashes
1 an accident in which a car, truck, train, or plane hits something.
2 the noise of something crashing. *I heard a loud **crash** as the tree fell.*

crash *verb* crashes, crashing, crashed
to hit something with a loud noise.

crate *noun* crates
a box for carrying bottles or other things.

crater *noun* craters
1 a round opening at the top of a volcano.
2 a round hole in the ground made by something falling.

crawl *verb* crawls, crawling, crawled
1 to move on your hands and knees. *Babies **crawl** before they can walk.*
2 to move slowly. *The car **crawled** along in the dark.*

crayfish *noun* crayfish
a hard-shelled animal that looks like a lobster. Some types live in the sea and others in fresh water.

crayon *noun* crayons
1 a stick of coloured wax used for drawing.
2 a coloured pencil.

crazy *adjective* crazier, craziest
likely to do strange or silly things.
Word Building: crazily

cream *noun*
the thick yellowish liquid that comes to the top of milk.

crease *verb* creases, creasing, creased
to make a line in something by folding or pressing on it.

create *verb* creates, creating, created
to make something no one else has made or can make.
Word Building: creation, creator

creature (kree-cher) *noun* creatures
any animal.

creek *noun* creeks
a small river.

creep *verb* creeps, creeping, crept
1 to move along, keeping close to the ground. *We **crept** through the hole in the hedge.*
2 to move quietly or secretly. *We **crept** away and nobody saw us.*

crept *verb* see **creep**

crescent (kres-ent) *noun* crescents
something shaped in a curve like a new moon.

crest *noun* crests
1 the top of a hill or a wave.
2 a bunch of feathers on a bird's head.

crew *noun* crews
a group of people who work together on a boat or aeroplane.

cricket *noun*
1 a game played in a field by two teams with a ball, bats, and two wickets.
2 a brown insect like a grasshopper that makes a shrill sound by rubbing its wings together.

cried *verb* see **cry**

crime *noun* crimes
an activity such as stealing which is against the law.

criminal *noun* criminals
someone who has done something bad that is against the law.

crimson *noun, adjective*
a deep red colour.

cripple *verb* cripples, crippling, crippled
to hurt someone's legs so badly that they cannot walk. *She was **crippled** in an accident.*

crisp *adjective* crisper, crispest
1 very dry so that it breaks easily. *a **crisp** biscuit.*
2 firm and fresh. *a **crisp** apple.*

croak *verb* croaks, croaking, croaked
to make the hoarse sound a frog makes.

crocodile *noun* crocodiles
a large meat-eating reptile that lives in water and on land in some hot countries. It has short legs, a long body, and sharp teeth.

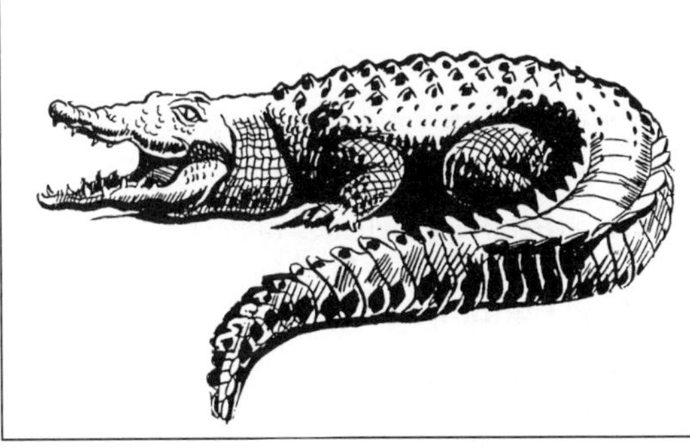

crook *noun* crooks
someone who cheats or robs people.

crooked *adjective*
not straight. ***crooked** teeth.*
Word Building: crookedly

crop *noun* crops
plants which are grown for food. *Taro and kaukau are **crops**.*

cross *adjective* crosser, crossest
angry, in a bad temper.
Word Building: crossly

cross *noun* crosses
a mark like **x** or **+**.

cross *verb* crosses, crossing, crossed
1 to move across something. *Take care when you **cross** the road.*
2 to make a shape like a cross. ***Cross** your arms.*
to cross something out to put a line through it.

crossing *noun* crossings
a place where you can cross a road.

crouch *verb* crouches, crouching, crouched
to lean forwards and bend your knees so that your bottom is almost touching the ground.

crow *noun* crows
a shiny-feathered big black bird.

crow *verb* crows, crowing, crowed
to make a sound similar to a rooster.

crowd *noun* crowds
a large number of people.

crown *noun* crowns
a big ring of silver or gold worn on the head by a king or queen.

crown *verb* crowns, crowning, crowned
to make someone a king or queen.

cruel *adjective* crueller, cruellest
very unkind.
Word Building: cruelly

cruise (krooz) *noun* cruises
a holiday on a big ship.

crumb (krum) *noun* crumbs
a tiny bit of bread or cake.

crumble *verb* crumbles, crumbling, crumbled
to break or fall into small pieces.

crumple *verb* crumples, crumpling, crumpled
to make something very creased. *crumpled clothes.*

crunch *verb* crunches, crunching, crunched
to eat with the noise you make when you eat hard biscuits.

crush *verb* crushes, crushing, crushed
to damage something by pressing it hard. *Carry the flowers carefully so you don't **crush** them.*

crust *noun* crusts
the hard part round the outside of bread.

crutch *noun* crutches
a stick that people who have hurt their legs can lean on when they are walking.

cry *verb* cries, crying, cried
1 to let tears fall from your eyes. *He was so upset that he **cried**.*
2 to shout.

crystal (kris-tl) *noun* crystals
1 a material which is hard and clear like glass.
2 a small, hard, shiny piece of something. ***crystals** of ice.*

cube (kyoob) *noun* cubes
the shape of dice. Cubes have six square sides that are all the same size.

cucumber (kyoo-kum-ber) *noun* cucumbers
a long, green vegetable eaten raw.

cuddle *verb* cuddles, cuddling, cuddled
to put your arms around a person or animal that you love.

culprit *noun* culprits
the person who is guilty.

culture *noun* cultures
the customs and way of life of a particular race or people.

cunning *adjective*
crafty.
Word Building: cunningly

cup *noun* cups
a small bowl-shaped container with a handle, for drinking from.

cupboard (kub-erd) *noun* cupboards
a piece of furniture or a space inside a wall. Cupboards have doors and usually some shelves.

curd *noun* curds
the thick, soft material formed when milk turns sour.
Word Building: curdle
*The milk had turned sour and **curdled**.*

cure (rhymes with *pure*) *verb* cures, curing, cured
to make someone well again.

curiosity *noun*
a wish to find out about things. *Out of **curiosity**, he opened the letter.*

curious *adjective*
1 wanting to know about something, inquisitive. *Eli is **curious** to know what she'll get for her birthday.*
2 unusual. *a **curious** smell.*
Word Building: curiously

curl *noun* curls
a piece of hair twisted into rings.

curl *verb* curls, curling, curled
to twist or bend into the shape of a ring. *The dog **curled** up by the fire.*

curly *adjective* curlier, curliest
with lots of curls. *curly hair.*

current *noun* currents
water, air, or electricity moving in one direction.

curriculum (ker-**rik**-yoo-lum) *noun* curricula
a statement of what schoolchildren are expected to learn.

curry *noun* curries
a cooked food with a spicy flavour. *vegetable **curry**.*

curse *noun* curses
an evil wish that something bad will happen to someone. *The sorcerer put a **curse** on the man.*

curse *verb* curses, cursing, cursed
to use bad language, to swear.

curtain (kert-n) *noun* curtains
a piece of cloth pulled in front of a window or stage to cover it.

curve *noun* curves
a line that is bent smoothly like the letter C.

cuscus *noun*
a furry animal with sharp claws which lives in trees and is active at night. In PNG it is hunted for food and its fur is used for bilas. [from Tok Pisin *cuscus*]

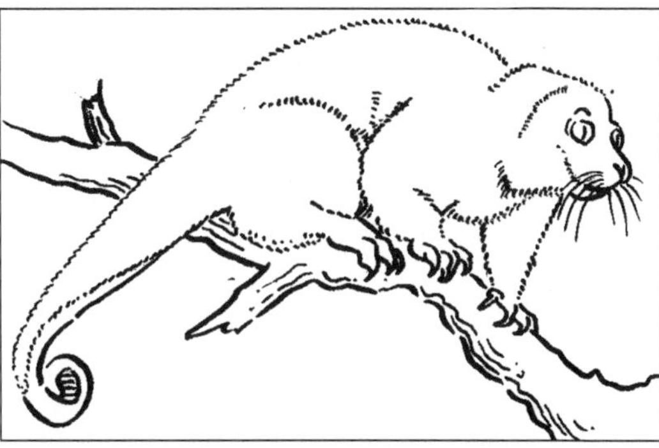

cushion (**kush**-un) *noun* cushions
a cloth bag filled with soft material so that it is comfortable to sit on or rest against.

custom *noun* customs
something that is usually done. *It is a **custom** to give presents at Christmas.*

customer *noun* customers
someone who uses a shop or a bank.

cut *noun* cuts
a small wound in the skin made by something sharp.

cut *verb* cuts, cutting, cut
1 to use a knife, axe, or scissors to divide, separate, or shape something.
2 to make something smaller or shorter. *They **cut** their hair.*

cutlery *noun*
knives, forks, and spoons.

cyclone (sy-klone) *noun* cyclones
a storm with very strong winds.

cylinder (sil-in-der) *noun* cylinders
the shape of a tin of baked beans or a toilet roll.

Dd

daffodil *noun* daffodils
a yellow flower that grows from a bulb in spring.

dagger *noun* daggers
a very short sword with two sharp edges.

daily *adjective, adverb*
every day, happening every day.

dainty *adjective* daintier, daintiest
delicate, pretty, and small.
Word Building: daintily, daintiness

dairy (dair-ree) *noun* dairies
a place where milk, cheese and butter are made or sold.

daisy *noun* daisies
a small flower with white or coloured petals.

daka *noun*
the fruit of the mustard plant, chewed with betel nut and lime. [from Tok Pisin *daka*]

dam *noun* dams
a wall built to hold water back.

damage *verb* damages, damaging, damaged
to harm something, to break or spoil it. *The house was badly **damaged** in the fire.*

damp *adjective* damper, dampest
a little wet, not quite dry. *Don't sit on the **damp** grass.*

damper *noun*
a simple kind of bread which is usually baked in the ashes of an outdoor fire.

dance *noun* dances
1 movements that you do to music.
2 a party where people dance.

dance *verb* dances, dancing, danced
to move about to music.
Word Building: dancer

dandelion *noun* dandelions
a wild plant which has yellow flowers, and balls of white feathery seeds which blow away.

danger (dain-jer) *noun* dangers
1 the chance that something harmful might happen. *That boy is in **danger** of falling off the wall.*
2 a person or thing that is dangerous. *Cats are a **danger** to baby birds.*

dangerous *adjective*
likely to kill or hurt you. *a **dangerous** road.*
Word Building: dangerously

dangle *verb* dangles, dangling, dangled
to hang loosely. *She sat on the fence with her legs **dangling**.*

dare *verb* dares, daring, dared
1 to be brave enough or rude enough to do something. *How **dare** you shout at me like that!*
2 to ask someone to do something to show how brave they are. *I **dare** you to climb that tree.*

daring *adjective*
very brave.

dark *adjective* darker, darkest
1 without any light. *a **dark** night.*
2 nearly black. ***dark** hair.*
3 not faint in colour. ***dark** red.*
Word Building: darkly, darkness

darn *verb* darns, darning, darned
to mend a hole in clothing with criss-cross stitches.

dart *noun* darts
a thing like a short arrow that you throw at a round board in the game of darts.

dart *verb* darts, darting, darted
to move suddenly and quickly. *The dog **darted** across the road.*

dash *noun* dashes
1 a hurried rush. *We made a **dash** for shelter from the rain.*
2 a long mark like this **–**.

dash *verb* dashes, dashing, dashed
to move very quickly. *She **dashed** into the house.*

data *noun*
facts or information, especially information for use in a computer.

date *noun* dates
1 the day, month, and year when something happens. *What **date** is your birthday?*
2 a sweet brown fruit that grows on a palm tree.

daughter (daw-ter) *noun* daughters
someone's female child.

dawn *noun*
the time of day when the sun rises.

day *noun* days
1 the twenty-four hours between midnight and the next midnight.
2 the part of the day when it is light.

daze *verb* dazes, dazing, dazed
to confuse or stun someone. *A blow on the head can **daze** you.*
Word Building: dazedly

daze *noun*
a confused state. *She was in a **daze** after the accident.*

dead *adjective*
not alive, not living.

deadly *adjective* deadlier, deadliest
likely to kill someone. ***deadly** poison.*

deaf (def) *adjective* deafer, deafest
not able to hear.

deal *noun*
a good deal, a great deal a lot.

deal *verb* deals, dealing, dealt
to give out. *I **dealt** the cards last time.*
to deal with to do what needs to be done.

dear *adjective* dearer, dearest
1 loved. *a **dear** friend.*
2 costing a lot of money. *Those shoes are too **dear**.*

death *noun* deaths
the end of life, dying.

debate (de-**bate**) *noun* debates
a public discussion or argument between two people or teams.

debate (de-**bate**) *verb* debates, debating, debated
to have a discussion or argument.

debt (det) *noun* debts
money that you owe someone.

decade (dek-aid) *noun* decades
ten years.

decay (de-kay) *verb* decays, decaying, decayed
to go bad or to rot.

deceit (de-seet) *noun*
making someone believe something you know is not true.

deceive (de-seev) *verb* deceives, deceiving, deceived
dishonesty, hiding the truth from someone.

December *noun*
the twelfth and last month of the year.

decide *verb* decides, deciding, decided
to make up your mind about something, to make a choice. *They* ***decided*** *to go to the lake.*

decimal (des-i-mal) *adjective*
using tens. *the* ***decimal*** *system.*
the decimal point the dot you put after whole numbers when you write fractions like this: 2.5.

decision (de-sizh-un) *noun* decisions
what you have decided.

deck *noun* decks
a floor in a ship.

declare *verb* declares, declaring, declared
to say something out loud for everyone to hear. *The tribe* ***declared*** *war on its enemy.*

decorate *verb* decorates, decorating, decorated
to make something look smart or pretty. *We* ***decorated*** *the classroom for the party.*

decrease *verb* decreases, decreasing, decreased
to make or become less. *The car* ***decreased*** *speed to go around the bend. Temperature* ***decreases*** *as night falls.*

deed *noun* deeds
something that you do. *a good* ***deed.***

deep *adjective* deeper, deepest
going a long way down from the top. ***deep*** *water, a* ***deep*** *hole.*
Word Building: deepen, deepening

deer *noun* deer
an animal that eats grass and can run fast. Male deer have horns called antlers.

defeat *verb* defeats, defeating, defeated
to beat someone in a game or battle.

defend *verb* defends, defending, defended
to keep someone or something safe from attack.
Word Building: defender

definite *adjective*
1 certain. *Is it* ***definite*** *that you can come?*
2 clear. *There is a* ***definite*** *improvement in your work.*
Word Building: definitely
I'm ***definitely*** *going swimming tomorrow.*

defy *verb* defies, defying, defied
to say or show that you will not obey someone. *She* ***defied*** *her parents and stayed out late.*

degree *noun* degrees
a unit of measurement for temperature or angles. You can write it using the sign °. *The temperature is 32° today. This angle measures 45°.*

delay *verb* delays, delaying, delayed
1 to make someone or something late. *The plane was* ***delayed*** *by heavy cloud.*
2 to put off doing something until later. *We'll have to* ***delay*** *giving out the prizes until everyone is here.*

deliberate *adjective*
done on purpose. *a* ***deliberate*** *mistake.*
Word Building: deliberately

delicate *adjective*
1 soft and fine. *a **delicate** flower.*
2 likely to get sick or broken.
*a **delicate** child, a **delicate** vase, **delicate** machinery.*
Word Building: delicately

delicious (de-**lish**-us) *adjective*
tasting or smelling very pleasant.
*a **delicious** cake.*

delight *verb* delights, delighting, delighted
to please very much. *The surprise gift **delighted** her.*

deliver *verb* delivers, delivering, delivered
to bring something to someone. *The mail is **delivered** once a week.*

delivery *noun* deliveries
delivering something. *The store was waiting for a **delivery** of tinned meat.*

demand *verb* demands, demanding, demanded
to ask for something that you think you ought to have.

demolish *verb* demolishes, demolishing, demolished
to knock something down and break it up. *The old house was **demolished**.*

demon (**dee**-man) *noun* demons
a wicked, evil spirit, a devil.

demonstrate (**dem**-on-strate) *verb* demonstrates, demonstrating, demonstrated
to show. *She's **demonstrating** how to make a bilum.*

demonstration (dem-on-**stray**-shun) *noun* demonstrations
1 showing people how to do something or how something works. *I'll give you a **demonstration**.*
2 a lot of people marching through the streets to show what they think about something.

den *noun* dens
1 a place where you can hide.
2 a place where a wild animal lives.

dengue fever *noun*
a tropical disease spread by mosquitoes which causes a fever and severe pains in our bones and joints.

dense *adjective* denser, densest
thick. ***dense** fog, a **dense** crowd.*

dent *verb* dents, denting, dented
to make a hollow in something hard, by hitting it. *Cars are often **dented** in accidents.*

dentist *noun* dentists
someone whose job is to look after teeth by cleaning them, filling them, or taking them out.

deny (de-**ny**) *verb* denies, denying, denied
to say that something is not true.
*She **denied** breaking the cup.*

deodorant *noun* deodorants
something that removes smell.

depart *verb* departs, departing, departed
to go away. *The plane **departs** at 3.20 this afternoon.*

department *noun* departments
a part of a business or government; a section of a large store. *Teachers are employed by the Education **Department**.*
Word Building: department store

depend *verb* depends, depending, depended
to trust someone or something to give you the help you need. *The blind man **depends** on his guide dog.*

deposit (de-**poz**-it) *noun* deposits
1 an amount of money paid into a bank.
2 a first payment for something.
*The boy paid a **deposit** on a new bike.*

deposit (de-**poz**-it) *verb* deposits, depositing, deposited
1 to put money into a bank account.
2 to put something into a special place.

depress *verb* depresses, depressing, depressed
to make someone feel sad.

depth *noun* depths
how deep something is. *Measure the depth of the hole.*

deputy (dep-yu-tee) *noun* deputies
the person who is second in charge and who takes over when the boss is away. *When the manager is away, her* ***deputy*** *takes over.*

descend (de-send) *verb* descends, descending, descended
to go down. *The plane started to* ***descend.*** *He* ***descended*** *the stairs slowly.*

describe *verb* describes, describing, described
to say what something or someone is like. *Can you* ***describe*** *her?*

description *noun* descriptions
words that tell you about someone or something. *Write a* ***description*** *of your house.*

desert (dez-ert) *noun* deserts
dry land where very few plants can grow.

desert (de-zert) *verb* deserts, deserting, deserted
to leave behind, to abandon. *The children* ***deserted*** *their friend who was in trouble.*

deserve (de-zerv) *verb* deserves, deserving, deserved
to have done something that makes people think you should get a reward or a punishment. *He was so brave he* ***deserves*** *a medal.*

design (de-zine) *verb* designs, designing, designed
to draw a plan or pattern for something.

desirable *adjective*
worth having or worth doing.

desire *verb* desires, desiring, desired
to want something very much.

desk *noun* desks
a kind of table where you can read, write, and keep books.

despair *verb* despairs, despairing, despaired
to give up hope.

desperate *adjective*
wanting something very much. *She was* ***desperate*** *for a drink of water.*
Word Building: desperately

despise *verb* despises, despising, despised
to dislike something or someone very much.

destination *noun* destinations
the place you are travelling to. *It took all day to reach our* ***destination.***

destroy *verb* destroys, destroying, destroyed
to break or spoil something so badly that it cannot be used again. *The house was* ***destroyed*** *by fire.*

destruction *noun*
the destroying of something. *the* ***destruction*** *of the native bush.*

detail *noun* details
a tiny piece of information about something. *She could remember every* ***detail*** *about the house.*

detect *verb* detects, detecting, detected
to find out, to uncover.

detective *noun* detectives
someone who tries to find out who did a crime.

detergent *noun* detergents
a kind of washing powder or liquid.

determined *adjective*
with your mind firmly made up. ***determined*** *to win.*

detest *verb* detests, detesting, detested
to hate.

detour (dee-toor) *noun* detours
a road or path used when you can't go the usual way.

develop *verb* develops, developing, developed
to grow or to become bigger or better. *Tadpoles **develop** into frogs.*

device *noun* devices
something that has been made for a special purpose. *A trolley is a useful **device**.*

devil *noun* devils
a wicked spirit.

devoted *adjective*
caring and loving. *The little boy was **devoted** to his pet cuscus.*

dew *noun*
tiny drops of water that form during the night on things outside.

diagonal (die-**ag**-on-l) *noun* diagonals
a slanting line drawn from one corner of something to the opposite corner.

diagram *noun* diagrams
a kind of picture that explains something. *The car book had a **diagram** of an engine.*

dial *noun* dials
a circle with numbers around it, on things like clocks or speedometers.

dial *verb* dials, dialling, dialled
to make a telephone call by turning a dial or pressing buttons. *He **dialled** 000 to call the police.*

diameter (die-**am**-a-ter) *noun* diameters
the distance across a circle, through the centre.

diamond *noun* diamonds
1 a very hard jewel like clear glass.
2 a shape with four sloping sides that are the same length. *Some playing cards have red **diamonds** printed on them.*

diarrhoea (die-a-**ree**-a) *noun*
an illness which makes you go to the toilet very often.

diary (**die**-a-ree) *noun* diaries
a book where you can write down what happens every day. *She kept a **diary** of her holiday.*

dice *noun* see **die** *noun*

dictator *noun* dictators
a ruler of a country who has unlimited power.
Word Building: dictatorship, dictatorial

dictionary *noun* dictionaries
a book where you can find out what a word means and how to spell it.

did *verb* see **do**

didiman *noun*
a government agricultural officer. [from Tok Pisin *didiman*]

die *verb* dies, dying, died
to stop living.

die *noun* dice
a small cube with each side marked with a different number of dots, from one to six. You use dice in various games.

diesel (**dee**-zl) *noun*
1 fuel for trucks or cars that work by burning oil, not petrol.
2 an engine that uses this fuel.

diet *noun* diets
1 special meals that some people must have to be healthy. *She went on a **diet** to lose weight.*
2 the food you normally eat. *We all need fruit and vegetables in our **diet**.*

differ *verb* differs, differing, differed
1 not to be the same. *The two flowers **differ** in colour.*
2 to disagree. *We **differ** about many things.*

difference *noun* differences
how different one thing is from another thing. *Can you spot the **difference** between these two pictures?*

A B C D E F G H I J K L M N O P Q R S T U V W X Y Z

different *adjective*
not like someone or something else. *She's very **different** from her sister.*

difficult *adjective*
not easy. *a **difficult** question.*

difficulty *noun* difficulties
something difficult.
with difficulty not easily.

dig *verb* digs, digging, dug
to move soil away to make a hole in the ground.

digest (die-jest) *verb* digests, digesting, digested
to change the food in your stomach so that your body can use it.
Word Building: digestion

digging stick *noun* digging sticks
a traditional gardening tool.

dignified *adjective*
looking serious and important. *a **dignified** old lady.*

dilute *verb* dilutes, diluting, diluted
to make a liquid weaker or thinner by adding water.

dim *adjective* dimmer, dimmest
not bright. *a **dim** light.*
Word Building: dimly

dimdim *noun*
a white person. [from a Milne Bay language *dimdim*]

dimple *noun* dimples
a small hollow on the skin.

din *noun*
a loud, annoying noise. *Stop making such a **din**!*

dine *verb* dines, dining, dined
to eat dinner.
Word Building: diner

dinghy (ding-gee) *noun* dinghies
a small rowing or sailing boat.

dinner *noun* dinners
the main meal of the day.

dinosaur *noun* dinosaurs
an animal like a huge lizard that lived millions of years ago.

dip *verb* dips, dipping, dipped
to put something into a liquid for a short time. *I **dipped** my toe into the water.*

direct *adjective*
as straight or as quick as it can be. *We walked the **direct** way home.*
Word Building: directly
*We went out **directly** after lunch.*

direct *verb* directs, directing, directed
1 to show someone the way. *Can you **direct** me to the airport?*
2 to be in charge of something. *to **direct** a play or film.*
Word Building: director

direction *noun* directions
the way you go to get somewhere. *Which **direction** is your house?*

dirt *noun*
dust or mud.

dirty *adjective* dirtier, dirtiest
marked with dirt or stains. *a **dirty** face.*

disabled *adjective*
not able to do some of the things other people can do, because you are ill, or because you have been injured.

disagree *verb* disagrees, disagreeing, disagreed
to think that someone else is wrong and that you are right.

disappear *verb* disappears, disappearing, disappeared
to go away and not be seen any more. *The bandicoot **disappeared** down the hole.*

disappoint *verb* disappoints, disappointing, disappointed
to make someone sad by not doing what they hoped.
Word Building: disappointing

disappointed *adjective*
sad because something was not as good as you had hoped. *She was **disappointed** because she did not win first prize.*

disapprove *verb* disapproves, disapproving, disapproved
to have a poor opinion of someone or something.

disaster *noun* disasters
something very bad that happens suddenly. Earthquakes and floods are natural disasters.

disc *noun* discs
1 any round, flat object.
2 a compact disc.

discharge *verb* discharges, discharging, discharged
1 to release somebody. *He was **discharged** from the army.*
2 to send out something. *Cars should not **discharge** too much exhaust.*

disciple (dis-sy-pl) *noun* disciples
a person who follows a religious leader.

discipline (dis-si-plin) *noun*
behaviour which shows that you have been trained to be obedient. *Our teacher likes to have **discipline** in the classroom.*

discourage *verb* discourages, discouraging, discouraged
to try to stop someone from doing something by telling them how difficult or bad it is. *She **discouraged** her children from smoking.*

discover *verb* discovers, discovering, discovered
to find out about something.
Word Building: discovery
*Scientists have made an important new **discovery**.*

discuss *verb* discusses, discussing, discussed
to talk about something with people who have different ideas about it.
Word Building: discussion, discussions

disease *noun* diseases
illness, sickness.

disgraceful *adjective*
so bad that it makes people ashamed of you. ***disgraceful** behaviour.*
Word Building: disgracefully

disguise *verb* disguises, disguising, disguised
to make yourself look different so that people will not recognise you. *The thief **disguised** himself as a policeman.*

disgust *verb* disgusts, disgusting, disgusted
to give someone a strong feeling of dislike. *The sight **disgusted** him.*
Word Building: disgusting
*Her behaviour was **disgusting**.*

dish *noun* dishes
1 a plate or bowl.
2 prepared food.

dishonest *adjective*
not honest.
Word Building: dishonestly

dislike *verb* dislikes, disliking, disliked
to feel that you do not like someone or something.

dismal (diz-mal) *adjective*
gloomy. ***dismal** weather.*
Word Building: dismally

A B C D E F G H I J K L M N O P Q R S T U V W X Y Z

dismiss *verb* dismisses, dismissing, dismissed
to send someone away. *The teacher **dismissed** the class at the end of the day.*

disobedient (dis-o-**beed**-ee-ent) *adjective*
not doing something that you are told to do. *The **disobedient** boy would not clean his room when his mother told him to.*
Word Building: disobedience

disobey (dis-o-**bay**) *verb* disobeys, disobeying, disobeyed
to fail to obey; to do what you have been told not to do.

display *noun* displays
a show or exhibition.

display *verb* displays, displaying, displayed
to show, to make a display.

disposable *adjective*
made to be thrown away after being used. ***disposable** nappies.*

disqualify *verb* disqualifies, disqualifying, disqualified
to take somebody out of a race or competition because he or she has broken the rules.
Word Building: disqualification

dissatisfied *adjective*
unhappy with a situation.
Word Building: dissatisfaction

dissolve (di-**zolv**) *verb* dissolves, dissolving, dissolved
to mix something in liquid so that it becomes part of the liquid. *You can **dissolve** sugar in hot tea.*

distance *noun* distances
the amount of space between two places.

distant *adjective*
far away.

distinct *adjective*
1 easy to see or hear. *The sound of the bellbird was quite **distinct**.*
2 different. *The two teams wear **distinct** colours.*
Word Building: distinctly

distinguish *verb* distinguishes, distinguishing, distinguished
to see or hear the difference between two things or people. *Most people can't **distinguish** between me and my twin sister.*

distress *noun*
a strong feeling of sadness or worry.

distribute *verb* distributes, distributing, distributed
to share out, to give out.

district *noun* districts
part of a province, town, city or country.

disturb *verb* disturbs, disturbing, disturbed
1 to stop someone from doing something. *Don't **disturb** the baby—she's asleep.*
2 to worry someone. *She was **disturbed** by the bad news.*

disturbance *noun* disturbances
something that upsets someone's peace or rest.

ditch *noun* ditches
a long, narrow hole dug to take away water from land.

dive *verb* dives, diving, dived
to jump head first into water.

divide *verb* divides, dividing, divided
1 to share something out. ***Divide** the money equally between you.*
2 to split something into smaller parts. *The cake was **divided** into eight pieces.*
3 to find out how many times one number goes into another. *Six **divided** by two is three, $6 \div 2 = 3$.*

division (di-**vizh**-un) ***noun*** divisions
dividing things or numbers into smaller amounts.

divorce ***noun*** divorces
the ending of a marriage.

dizzy *adjective* dizzier, dizziest
feeling as if everything is spinning around you.

do *verb* does, doing, did, done
1 to carry out an action. *Yaking* ***does*** *lots of jobs around the house, but her sister* ***doesn't****. What are you* ***doing*** *now?*
2 to finish. *I* ***did*** *my work before I went out to play. Have you* ***done*** *your homework?*

dock ***noun*** docks
a place where boats or ships are loaded and unloaded.

docket ***noun*** dockets
a piece of paper listing goods delivered, jobs done, or payments made.

doctor ***noun*** doctors
someone whose job is to help sick people to get better.

dodge *verb* dodges, dodging, dodged
to move quickly to get out of the way of something.

doe ***noun*** does
a female deer, rabbit, or hare.

does *verb* see do

dog ***noun*** dogs
a meat-eating animal which is easily trained and is often kept as a pet.

doll ***noun*** dolls
a toy in the shape of a person.

dolphin ***noun*** dolphins
a mammal that lives in the sea.

dome ***noun*** domes
a roof shaped like the top half of a ball.

done *verb* see do

donkey ***noun*** donkeys
an animal that looks like a small horse with long ears.

door ***noun*** doors
something that opens and closes at an entrance. *a car* ***door****, the bathroom* ***door****.*

dose ***noun*** doses
the amount of medicine someone has to take.

dot ***noun*** dots
a small spot, like a full stop.

double *adjective*
twice as much or as many.

doubt (rhymes with *out*) ***noun*** doubts
the feeling you have when you are not sure about something. *If you are in* ***doubt****, ask your teacher.*

doubt (rhymes with *out*) *verb* doubts, doubting, doubted
to feel not sure about something.
I ***doubt*** *that he will come to the party.*

doubtful *adjective*
not sure.
Word Building: doubtfully

dough (rhymes with *go*) ***noun***
a mixture of flour and water. Dough is used for making bread and cakes.

dove ***noun*** doves
a bird that looks like a small pigeon.

down *adverb, preposition*
to somewhere lower. *Run* ***down*** *the hill.*

down ***noun***
very soft feathers.

downward, downwards *adverb*
moving to somewhere lower. *The bird flew* ***downwards****.*

doze *verb* dozes, dozing, dozed
to be nearly asleep.

dozen (duz-n) *noun* dozens
a set of twelve. *one **dozen** eggs.*

drag *verb* drags, dragging, dragged
to pull something heavy along.

dragon *noun* dragons
a monster with wings, that you read about in stories.

drain *verb* drains, draining, drained
to get rid of water or other liquid from something. *The water **drained** down the sink. We washed the plates and left them to **drain**.*

drama *noun*
1 a play that is acted out.
2 exciting events. *The crowd watched the **drama** of the rescue at sea.*
Word Building: dramatic, dramatically, dramatise or dramatize

drank *verb* see **drink**

draught (draft) *noun* draughts
cold air that blows into a room.

draw *verb* draws, drawing, drew, drawn
1 to make a picture with a pen, pencil, or crayon.
2 to pull, to attract. *The man was **drawing** a trolley of coffee. The show **drew** a large crowd.*
3 to end a game with the same score on both sides. *We **drew** 1–1 on Saturday.*

drawer (dror) *noun* drawers
a box without a lid, that slides into a piece of furniture.

dread (dred) *noun*
great fear. *He has a **dread** of heights.*
Word Building: dread
*They **dread** the dry season.*

dreadful *adjective*
very bad. *a **dreadful** storm.*
Word Building: dreadfully

dreadlocks *noun*
hair in long, tightly-curled strands.

dream *noun* dreams
things you seem to see while you are asleep.

dream *verb* dreams, dreaming, dreamed or dreamt
to have dreams.

drench *verb* drenches, drenching, drenched
to make someone or something very wet all over.

dress *noun* dresses
a garment for women or girls which has a skirt and also covers the top half of the body.

dress *verb* dresses, dressing, dressed
to put clothes on.

drew *verb* see **draw**

dribble *verb* dribbles, dribbling, dribbled
to let liquid come out of your mouth without meaning to. *Babies often **dribble**.*

drift *verb* drifts, drifting, drifted
to be carried gently along by water or air. *The empty boat **drifted** along on the sea.*

drill *noun* drills
a tool for making holes.

drink *verb* drinks, drinking, drank, drunk
to swallow liquid. *Have you **drunk** your milk?*

drip *verb* drips, dripping, dripped
to let drops of liquid fall off.

drive *verb* drives, driving, drove, driven
1 to control a car, bus, train, or truck. *Fabian is learning to **drive**.*
2 to make someone or something move. *We **drove** the sheep into the shed.*

driver *noun* drivers
a person who drives a car, bus, PMV, or truck.

drizzle *noun*
very light rain.

droop *verb* droops, drooping, drooped
to hang down weakly. *a **drooping** flower.*

drop *noun* drops
a tiny amount of liquid. ***drops** of rain.*

drop *verb* drops, dropping, dropped
to fall or to let something fall.

drought (drowt) *noun* droughts
a long period of very dry weather.

drove *verb* see **drive**

drown *verb* drowns, drowning, drowned
to die because you are under water and cannot breathe.

drug *noun* drugs
1 a substance used to help you if you are ill or in pain.
2 a substance which affects your mind as if you were drunk.

drum *noun* drums
a hollow musical instrument that you strike with a stick or with your hands.

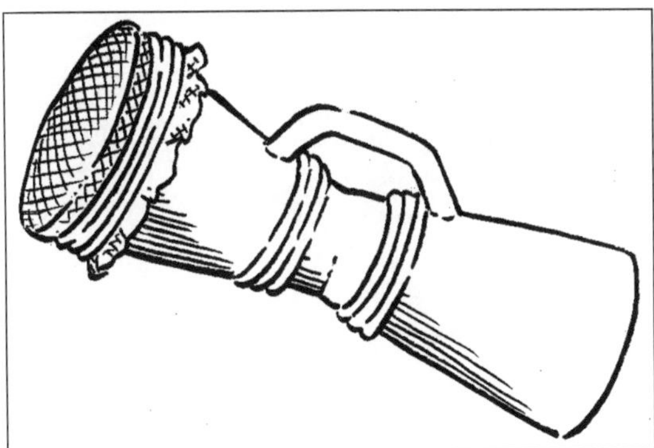

drunk *adjective*
not able to control what you say or do because you have drunk too much alcohol.

drunk *verb* see **drink**

dry *adjective* drier, driest
not damp or wet. ***dry** land.*

dual *adjective*
made up of two parts; double. *The plane had **dual** controls so that two people could fly it.*

duck *noun* ducks
a bird that lives near water. It has a wide, flat beak.

due *adjective*
expected. *The plane is **due** now.*
due to caused by. *The accident was **due to** the thick fog.*

duel *noun* duels
a fight between two people using the same kind of weapon. *a **duel** with spears.*

duet *noun* duets
a piece of music sung or played by two people.

dugong *noun* (**doo**-gong or **dyoo**-gong) dugongs
a marine mammal; a sea cow. *In PNG **dugongs** are eaten at special feasts.*

dukduk *noun*
1 a secret society in East New Britain.
2 a traditional costume shaped like a bird with a long neck. [from Tok Pisin *dukduk*]

dull *adjective* duller, dullest
1 not interesting. *a **dull** book.*
2 not bright. *a **dull** colour.*
3 not sharp. *a **dull** pain.*

dumb *adjective*
not able to speak.

dummy *noun* dummies
a piece of rubber made for a baby to suck.

dump *noun* dumps
a place where people leave rubbish.

dump *verb* dumps, dumping, dumped
1 to leave something you want to get rid of. *I hate to see people **dumping** rubbish in a ditch.*
2 to put something down quickly or carelessly. *I **dumped** my things on the floor.*

dungeon *noun* dungeons
a prison underneath a castle.

during *preposition*
while something else is going on. *I fell asleep **during** the movie.*

dusk *noun*
the dim light at the end of the day, before it gets dark.

dust *noun*
dry dirt that is like powder.

duty *noun* duties
what you ought to do. *It is your **duty** to look after your little brother on your way home from school.*

dwarf *noun* dwarfs
a very small person.

dye *verb* dyes, dyeing, dyed
to change the colour of something by putting it in a special liquid.

dying *verb* see die

dynamite *noun*
material that explodes when lit and is used for blowing things up.

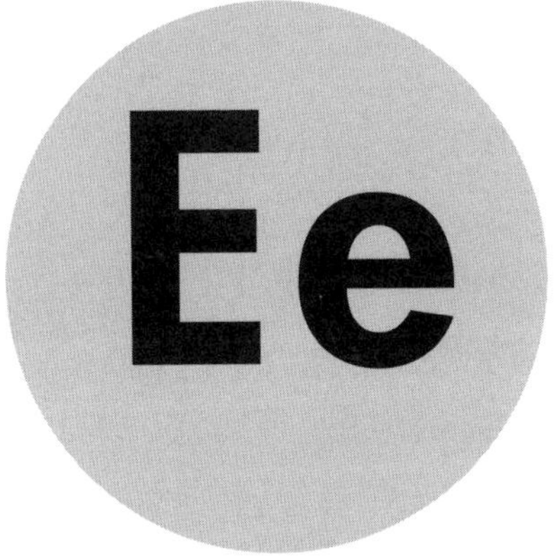

each *adjective, pronoun*
every. *She gave* ***each*** *child a present.*

eager *adjective*
wanting to do something very much. ***eager*** *to begin.*
Word Building: eagerly

eagle *noun* eagles
a large bird that hunts and eats small animals.

ear *noun* ears
the part of the body used for hearing.

early (er-lee) *adjective, adverb* earlier, earliest
1 near the beginning. ***early*** *in the day.*
2 sooner than we expected. *She came* ***early****.*

earn *verb* earns, earning, earned
to get money by working for it.

Earth *noun*
the planet that we all live on.

earth *noun*
the ground or soil in which plants grow.

earthquake *noun* earthquakes
a time when the ground suddenly shakes. Strong earthquakes can destroy buildings.

easel *noun* easels
a stand for holding a picture while you work on it.

east *noun, adjective*
the direction where the sun rises in the morning.

Easter *noun*
a time of year when Christians remember when Christ died and rose from the dead.

easy *adjective* easier, easiest
able to be done or understood without any trouble. *an* ***easy*** *sum.*
Word Building: easily

eat *verb* eats, eating, ate, eaten
to put food in your mouth and swallow it. *Have you* ***eaten*** *all the rice?*

eave (eev) *noun* eaves
the overhanging edge of the roof of a building.

eccentric (ek-sen-trik) *adjective*
behaving in a strange way; doing things in an odd or strange way. *The* ***eccentric*** *woman wore weird hats.*
Word Building: eccentricity

Echidna *noun* echidnas
a spiny mammal with a long snout and claws found in PNG and Australia; the spiny anteater.

echo (ek-o) *noun* echoes
a sound that you hear again as it bounces back off something solid. You often hear echoes in caves and tunnels.

eclipse (ee-klips) *noun*
the darkness that happens when either the Sun or the Moon is in shadow so that their light is blocked.

economy (ee-kon-o-mee) *noun* economies
1 the wealth that a country gets from business and industry. *The PNG **economy** relies heavily on the mining industry.*
2 The careful use or management of money or things.
Word Building: economic, economist, economically

edge *noun* edges
the part along the end or side of something. *the **edge** of the cliff.*

edit *verb* edits, editing, edited
1 to get a newspaper, magazine, or book ready for printing.
2 to put a story, film, or recording in the order you want.

editor *noun* editors
the person in charge of a book, newspaper, or magazine. Editors decide which stories and pictures will be printed.

educate *verb* educates, educating, educated
to teach people things they need to know like reading and writing.
Word Building: educator, education, educational

eel *noun* eels
a fish that looks like a snake.

effect *noun* effects
anything that happens because of something else. *The **effect** of acid rain is to make trees die.*

effort *noun* efforts
hard work at something you are trying to do.

egg *noun* eggs
1 an oval object with a thin shell, made by a hen and used as food.
2 one of the oval objects that baby birds, fish, insects, or snakes live inside until they are big enough to be born.

eight *noun* eights
the number 8.
Word Building: eighth

eighteen *noun*
the number 18.
Word Building: eighteenth

eighty *noun*
the number 80.
Word Building: eightieth

either (eye-ther or ee-ther) *pronoun*
one or the other of two people or things. *There are two dresses; you can have **either**.*

elastic *noun*
a strip of material that can stretch and then go back to its usual size.

elbow *noun* elbows
the bony part in the middle of the arm where it bends.

elder *adjective*
older. *Tau is Mary's **elder** brother.*
Word Building: elderly

elder *noun* elders
an old person whose advice is valued because of his or her experience. *Young people should respect the **elders** of their tribe.*

elderly *adjective*
old. *an **elderly** man.*

eldest *adjective*
oldest. *My brother is the **eldest** child in our family.*

elect *verb* elects, electing, elected
to choose somebody who will be in charge of something. *We **elected** a class captain.*

election *noun* elections
a time when people can vote to choose who will be in charge of their town, state or country.

electric, electrical *adjective*
worked by electricity. *an **electric** drill.*

electrician (ee-lek-**trish**-an) *noun* electricians
someone whose job is to work with, install and look after electrical equipment.

electricity *noun*
the power or energy used to give light and heat and to work machines. It comes along wires or from batteries.

electronic *adjective*
using electrical signals. TV sets, computers, and radios have electronic devices inside them.

elegant *adjective*
beautiful, smart, and pleasing to look at. *The woman wore **elegant** clothes.*
Word Building: elegance

elementary school *noun*
a school providing three years of education from prep to grade 2.

elephant *noun* elephants
a very big grey animal with tusks and a very long nose called a trunk.

elevator (el-a-vay-tor) *noun* elevators
a lift; a platform used for raising or lowering people or things to different floors in a building.

eleven *noun*
the number 11.
Word Building: eleventh

eliminate (ee-**lim**-i-nate) *verb* eliminates, eliminating, eliminated
to get rid of something. *I'll **eliminate** all the squares from this pattern.*

else *adverb*
different, other. *Ask someone **else**. Let's do something **else**.*

embark *verb* embarks, embarking, embarked
to get on a ship at the beginning of a journey.

embarrass *verb* embarrasses, embarrassing, embarrassed
to make someone feel shy and upset.
Word Building: embarrassed, embarrassing

embassy (**em**-ba-see) *noun* embassies
the building where an ambassador lives and works.

embrace *verb* embraces, embracing, embraced
to put your arms around someone to show you love them.

emerge *verb* emerges, emerging, emerged
to come out, to appear.

emergency *noun* emergencies
something very dangerous that suddenly happens. *Call the doctor—it's an **emergency**.*

emigrate *verb* emigrates, emigrating, emigrated
to go and live in another country.

em inap *interjection*
that's enough! [from Tok Pisin *em inap*]

em nau *interjection*
that's right; that's it. [from Tok Pisin *em nau*]

emotion *noun* emotions
a feeling you have, such as happiness, fear, sadness, or excitement.
Word Building: emotional

employ *verb* employs, employing, employed
to pay someone to work for you.
Word Building: employer, employers

empty *adjective*
with nothing in it or on it. *an **empty** box.*

empty *verb* empties, emptying, emptied
to take everything out of something. *He **emptied** his pocket.*

em tasol *interjection*
that's all; it's finished; it is over [from Tok Pisin *em tasol*]

encourage *verb* encourages, encouraging, encouraged
to give someone your support so that they will do something. *He **encouraged** me to dive from the diving board.*

encyclopedia *noun* encyclopedias
a book or set of books that tells you about all kinds of things.

end *noun* ends
the last part of something, the place where something stops.

end *verb* ends, ending, ended
to finish, to come to the end.

endanger *verb* endangers, endangering, endangered
to cause danger to someone or something. *Scientists try to protect **endangered** species of animals and plants.*

endeavour or **endeavor** (en-dev-or) *verb* endeavours, endeavouring, endeavoured
to try. *She **endeavoured** to finish cutting the grass before it became dark.*

endeavour or **endeavor** (en-dev-or) *noun* endeavours
an attempt. *He was proud of his **endeavours** at maths.*

enemy *noun* enemies
1 someone who wants to hurt you.
2 the people fighting against you.

energetic *adjective*
full of the strength you need to do a lot of things. *He is a very **energetic** football player.*

energy *noun*
1 the strength to do something.
2 the power that comes from coal, electricity, and gas. It makes machines work and gives us heat and light.

engaged *adjective*
1 having promised to marry someone. *They are **engaged** to be married.*
2 already occupied or being used. *Her telephone number is **engaged**.*
Word Building: engagement

engine *noun* engines
a machine that can make things move. *Most cars have petrol **engines**.*

engineer *noun* engineers
someone who makes machines, or plans the building of roads and bridges.

English *noun*
the language of England, now used in the United Kingdom, USA, PNG, Australia and most Commonwealth countries.

enjoy *verb* enjoys, enjoying, enjoyed
to like watching, listening to, or doing something. *Did you **enjoy** the movie?*

enormous *adjective*
very big.

enough (ee-nuff) *adjective, noun*
as much as is needed. ***enough** money. I have had **enough**.*

enter *verb* enters, entering, entered
1 to come or go in.
2 to take part in a race or a competition.

enterprising *adjective*
willing to take a risk and try something new.

entertain *verb* entertains, entertaining, entertained
to make time pass very pleasantly for people. *The clown **entertained** the children.*

entertainment *noun* entertainments
anything that entertains people.

enthusiasm *noun* enthusiasms
a very great interest in something.

enthusiastic *adjective*
so interested in something that you spend a lot of time doing it or talking about it.
Word Building: enthusiastically

entire *adjective*
whole. *The **entire** class was ill.*
Word Building: entirely

entrance *noun* entrances
the way into a place.

entry *noun* entries
1 a way into a place.
2 going or coming into a place. *The sign said 'No **entry**'.*
3 a person, animal, or thing in a competition. *There were many **entries** for the competition.*

envelope *noun* envelopes
a paper cover for a letter. *You write the address on the **envelope**.*

envious *adjective*
full of envy. If you feel envious, you want something that someone else has. *I'm **envious** because my brother has got a new bike.*
Word Building: enviously

environment *noun* environments
the world we live in, especially the plants, animals, and things around us which can make our lives nicer or nastier. *The didiman thinks that planting more trees will improve our **environment**.*

envy *noun*
a feeling you get when you would like to have something that someone else has.

episode *noun* episodes
one program in a radio or TV series. *We must wait until next week to see the next **episode**.*

equal *adjective*
the same as something else in amount, size, or value. *Everyone had an **equal** share of the food.*
Word Building: equally

equator *noun*
an imaginary line around the middle of the earth. Countries near the equator are very hot.

equip *verb* equips, equipping, equipped
to provide someone with everything necessary to do something. *Chefs must **equip** themselves for cooking.*

equipment *noun*
the things you need for doing something. *sports **equipment**.*

erase *verb* erases, erasing, erased
to rub out marks on something.

eraser *noun* erasers
a piece of rubber or plastic used to rub out pencil marks.

erosion (ee-ro-zhun) *noun*
the wearing away of soil, rock, or sand by water or wind.

errand *noun errands*
a short journey to take a message or fetch something for someone.

error *noun* errors
a mistake.

escalator *noun* escalators
a moving staircase.

escape *verb* escapes, escaping, escaped
1 to get free. *The prisoner* ***escaped****.*
2 to get away. *They* ***escaped*** *from the rain by going into a café.*

especially *adverb*
more than anything else. *I hate going to bed early,* ***especially*** *in the hot weather.*

essential *adjective*
necessary.

estimate *verb* estimates, estimating, estimated
to guess the amount, size, or price of something. ***Estimate*** *how long the table is.*

eucalypt (yoo-ka-lipt) *noun* eucalypts
a gum tree.

eucalyptus (yoo-ka-lip-tus) *noun*
1 a gum tree.
2 a strong-smelling oil from the leaves of a eucalyptus tree.

evaporate (ee-vap-o-rate) *verb* evaporates, evaporating, evaporated
1 to change from liquid into steam or vapour. *The puddle of water in the hot sun will soon* ***evaporate****.*
2 to disappear. *They seemed to* ***evaporate*** *into thin air.*
Word Building: evaporation

even *adjective*
1 level or equal. *At half-time the scores were* ***even****.*
2 able to be divided by two. *4, 6, and 8 are* ***even*** *numbers.*
Word Building: evenly
Spread the butter ***evenly****.*

evening *noun* evenings
the time at the end of the day before people go to bed.

event *noun* events
something important that happens. *The Gooroka show is a big* ***event****.*

eventually *adverb*
in the end.

ever *adverb*
at any time. *Have you* ***ever*** *climbed this tree?*

evergreen *noun* evergreens
any tree that has green leaves all through the year. *A pine tree is an* ***evergreen****.*

everlasting *adjective*
lasting forever.

every *adjective*
each. *I go swimming* ***every*** *week.*

everybody, everyone *pronoun*
every person.

everyday *adjective*
happening or used every day. *Going to the shops was an* ***everyday*** *event for him.*

everything *pronoun*
all things.

everywhere *pronoun*
in all places. *We've looked* ***everywhere*** *for the ball.*

evidence *noun*
anything that shows that something is true. *There was plenty of* ***evidence*** *that he was guilty.*

evil *adjective*
wicked.

exact *adjective*
just right. *Add the **exact** amount of water.*
Word Building: exactly

exaggerate (eg-zaj-er-ate) *verb* exaggerates, exaggerating, exaggerated
to say that something is bigger, better, larger, or more impressive than it really is.

exam, examination *noun* exams, examinations
an important test.

examine *verb* examines, examining, examined
to look at something very carefully.

example *noun* examples
1 anything that shows how something works or what it is like. *I copied the **example** from the book.*
2 a person or thing that should be copied. *He behaves so well he sets a good **example**.*

excellent *adjective*
very good.
Word Building: excellently

except *preposition*
not including, apart from. *Everyone got a prize **except** me.*

exchange *verb* exchanges, exchanging, exchanged
to give something and get something in return.

excite *verb* excites, exciting, excited
to give someone very strong feelings, to make someone excited.

excited *adjective*
very lively, interested, and eager. *We're getting very **excited** about the party.*

excitement *noun*
an excited feeling.

exclaim *verb* exclaims, exclaiming, exclaimed
to make a sudden sound because you are surprised or excited. *'I don't believe it!' she **exclaimed**.*

exclamation mark *noun* exclamation marks
a mark like this **!** put after words to show that they have been shouted or are surprising.

excursion (ex-sker-zhun) *noun* excursions
a short trip made by a group of people. *Our class went on an **excursion** to the river.*

excuse (rhymes with *goose*) *noun* excuses
words that try to explain why you have done wrong so that you will not get into trouble. *Her **excuse** for being late was that her transport was running late.*

excuse (rhymes with *choose*) *verb* excuses, excusing, excused
1 to forgive. *Please **excuse** our dog's bad behaviour.*
2 to allow someone not to do something. *I was **excused** from swimming because I had a cold.*

execute *verb* executes, executing, executed
to kill someone as a punishment.

exercise *noun* exercises
1 work that makes your body healthy and strong. *He gets his **exercise** by playing football.*
2 a piece of work that you do to make yourself better at something. *The maths book includes practice **exercises**.*

exhaust *noun*
1 the gases that come out from an engine.
2 the pipe that these gases come out of.

exhausted *adjective*
tired out.

exhausting *adjective*
making you very tired.

exhibit *verb* exhibits, exhibiting, exhibited
to display or show something. *The sculptor **exhibited** her work at the gallery.*
Word Building: exhibitor, exhibitionist

exhibition *noun* exhibitions
a group of things put on show so that people can come to see them. *an **exhibition** of paintings.*

exist *verb* exists, existing, existed
1 to be real, not imaginary. *Do ghosts **exist**?*
2 to live. *Camels **exist** in the desert.*

exit *noun* exits
the way out of a place.

expand *verb* expands, expanding, expanded
to get bigger. *A balloon **expands** when you blow air into it.*

expatriate (expat for short) *noun, adjective*
a person working in a foreign country, usually for a fixed time. *The missionary is an **expatriate**. An **expatriate** family lives in this house.*

expect *verb* expects, expecting, expected
to think something is very likely to happen. *The clouds are so dark I **expect** it will rain.*

expedition *noun* expeditions
a journey made for a special reason. *a shopping **expedition**.*

expel *verb* expels, expelling, expelled
to force something or someone out. *She was **expelled** from school.*

expensive *adjective*
costing a lot of money.

experience *noun* experiences
1 what you learn from things that you see and do. *The **experience** of riding in a car made him want to own one for himself.*
2 something that has happened to you. *a frightening **experience**.*

experiment *noun* experiments
a test to find out whether an idea works. *a scientific **experiment**.*

expert *noun* experts
someone who does something very well or knows a lot about something.

explain *verb* explains, explaining, explained
to make something clear to people so that they understand it.

explanation *noun* explanations
something said or written to help people to understand.

explode *verb* explodes, exploding, exploded
to make something burst or blow up with a loud bang.

explore *verb* explores, exploring, explored
to look carefully around a place for the first time. *Let's **explore** the cave.*

explosion *noun* explosions
a loud bang made by something bursting or blowing up.

explosive *noun* explosives
anything used for making things blow up.

export *verb* exports, exporting, exported
to send goods or services to other countries for sale.
Word Building: exporter

express *verb* expresses, expressing, expressed
to show your thoughts and feelings through words, actions, or looks.
Word Building: expressionless
*His face was **expressionless**.*

express *adjective*
going or sent very quickly. *express mail.*

expression *noun* expressions
the look on someone's face. *a happy expression.*

extend *verb* extends, extending, extended
1 to stretch out.
2 to make something longer.
3 to offer or give. *The boy will **extend** a welcome to his friends.*
extended family a family group that includes all your relatives and not just your parents and brothers and sisters.

extent *noun*
the length or area or amount of something.

exterior (ex-teer-ree-or) *noun*
the outside of something.

exterminate *verb* exterminates, exterminating, exterminated
to destroy completely.

external *adjective*
outside. *The **external** walls of the building were made of metal.*

extinct *adjective*
no longer existing. *Dinosaurs are extinct.*

extinguish *verb* extinguishes, extinguishing, extinguished
to put out a fire.

extra *adjective*
more than usual.

extract *verb* extracts, extracting, extracted
to pull out. *The dentist **extracted** one of my teeth.*

extraordinary *adjective*
very unusual. *The camel is an **extraordinary** animal. It can survive for weeks without water.*

extravagant (ex-trav-a-gant) *adjective*
spending more money or using more of something than people think you should.

extreme *adjective*
1 very great. ***extreme** cold.*
2 the furthest away. *the **extreme** corner of the playground.*
Word Building: extremely

eye *noun* eyes
1 the part of the body used for seeing.
2 the small hole in a needle.

eyebrow *noun* eyebrows
the curved line of hair above each eye.

eyelash *noun* eyelashes
one of the short hairs that grow in a fringe around each eye.

fable *noun* fables
a story about animals that teaches people something.

face *noun* faces
1 the front part of your head.
2 the front or side of something. *a clock **face**.*

face *verb* faces, facing, faced
1 to have your face towards something. *Can you all **face** the front of the class, please?*
2 to have the front towards something. *Kila's house **faces** the river.*

fact *noun* facts
something that we know is true. *It's a **fact** that the earth travels around the sun.*

factory *noun* factories
a building where people make things with machines. *a sugar **factory**.*

fade *verb* fades, fading, faded
to get paler or quieter so that it is harder to see or hear.

Fahrenheit (fair-en-hite) *adjective*
a way of measuring temperature, using a scale where water freezes at 32 degrees and boils at 212 degrees.

fail *verb* fails, failing, failed
1 not to do something you should do, or something you want to do. *Our team **failed** to win the match.*
2 not to pass a test or exam. *My brother **failed** his driving test.*

failure *noun* failures
someone or something that has failed.

faint *adjective* fainter, faintest
weak, hard to see or hear. ***faint** cries for help, a **faint** mark.*
Word Building: faintly

faint *verb* faints, fainting, fainted
to feel dizzy and become unconscious for a short time.

fair *adjective* fairer, fairest
1 light in colour. ***fair** skin.*
2 someone or something that is fair treats people equally or in the right way. *It's not **fair** if she gets more time than me.*
3 quite good but not very good. *She has a **fair** chance of winning.*

fair *noun* fairs
a place outside where you can go on rides and try to win things.

fairly *adverb*
to some extent but not a lot. *It's **fairly** warm today.*

faith *noun*
feeling that something is true.

faithful *adjective*
always ready to help your friends and do what you promised to do.
Word Building: faithfully

fake *noun* fakes
something not valuable that is made to look valuable. *The painting was a* ***fake****.*

fall *verb* falls, falling, fell, fallen
to go down quickly, to drop. *She* ***fell*** *downstairs and broke her arm.*

false *adjective*
1 not real. ***false*** *teeth.*
2 not true. *He gave a* ***false*** *name to the police.*
Word Building: falsely

fame *noun*
importance, glory. *The singer's* ***fame*** *had spread around the world.*

familiar *adjective*
well known to you. *a* ***familiar*** *face.*

family *noun* families
1 a parent or parents with a child or children.
2 a group of people or things that are closely related.

famine (fam-in) *noun* famines
a time when there is very little food. *There is* ***famine*** *in many parts of Africa.*

famous *adjective*
very well known.
Word Building: famously

fan *noun* fans
1 something that blows air.
2 a person who supports someone or something. *Raphael is a* ***fan*** *of our local football team.*

fancy *adjective*
decorated, pretty. ***fancy*** *cakes.*
fancy dress unusual clothes you dress up in for fun. *She went to the* ***fancy dress*** *party dressed as a witch.*

fang *noun* fangs
a long, sharp tooth. *the* ***fangs*** *of a dog.*

fantastic *adjective*
(*informal*) very good, wonderful.
Word Building: fantastically

fantasy *noun* fantasies
something you imagine; something that is more like a dream than real life.

far *adverb* farther, farthest
a long way. *Do you live* ***far*** *from the town? Esther lives* ***farther*** *from the town than I do.*

fare *noun* fares
the money people have to pay to travel on trains, buses, boats, or aeroplanes.

farewell *interjection*
goodbye.

farm *noun* farms
a piece of land where someone grows crops or keeps animals for food.

farmer *noun* farmers
someone who keeps a farm.

fashion *noun* fashions
the up-to-date way of dressing which most people like and try to copy.

fast *adjective, adverb* faster, fastest
1 moving quickly. *a* ***fast*** *car. He can run* ***fast****.*
2 showing a time that is later than the right time. *My watch is* ***fast****.*

fasten (fas-sn) *verb* fastens, fastening, fastened
1 to close something so that it will not come open. ***Fasten*** *the seat belt.*
2 to join something to something else. ***Fasten*** *a badge to your shirt.*

fastener (fas-a-ner) *noun* fasteners
something used for fastening things.

fat *adjective* fatter, fattest
1 with a large, round body. *a* ***fat*** *person.*
2 having too much fat. ***fat*** *meat.*

fat *noun*
1 the white, greasy part of meat.
2 one of the greasy things you use in cooking, such as butter or margarine.

fatal (fay-tl) *adjective*
causing death. *a* ***fatal*** *accident.*
Word Building: fatally
fatally *wounded.*

father *noun* fathers
a male parent.

fault *noun* faults
1 something wrong that spoils a person or thing.
2 if something bad is your fault, you made it happen. *It's your **fault** we missed the transport.*

favour (fay-vor) *noun* favours
something kind that you do for someone. *Please do me a **favour** and post those letters for me.*

favourite *adjective*
liked the most. *Pigs are my **favourite** animals.*

fawn *noun* fawns
a young deer.

fax *noun* faxes
a copy of a letter or a picture sent using telephone lines and a machine called a fax machine.

fear *noun* fears
the feeling you get when you think something bad is going to happen.

fear *verb* fears, fearing, feared
to be afraid of someone or something. *There is no need to **fear** the dark.*

feast *noun* feasts
a special meal for a lot of people.

feat *noun* feats
something you do that is brave or difficult. *Climbing Mount Everest was an amazing **feat**.*

feather *noun* feathers
one of the many light, soft things that cover a bird and help it to fly.

February *noun*
the second month of the year.

fed *verb* see feed

feeble *adjective* feebler, feeblest
weak.
Word Building: feebly

feed *verb* feeds, feeding, fed
1 to give food to a person or animal. *I **fed** the baby last night.*
2 to eat. *The pigs are **feeding** now.*

feel *verb* feels, feeling, felt
1 to touch something to find out what it is like. *The cuscus' fur **feels** soft.*
2 to experience something inside yourself. *I **feel** happy.*

feeling *noun* feelings
something that you feel inside yourself, like anger or love.

feet *noun* see foot

fell *verb* see fall

felt *noun*
a thick cloth made from wool that has been pressed flat.

felt *verb* see feel

female *noun* females
a person or animal of the sex that can become a mother.

feminine *adjective*
belonging to women, like women, suitable for women.

fence *noun* fences
a kind of wall made of wood, posts, stone, wire, or bricks.

fern *noun* ferns
a plant with leaves like feathers and no flowers.

ferocious (fe-ro-shus) *adjective*
fierce and dangerous. *a **ferocious** dog.*
Word Building: ferociously

ferry *noun* ferries
a boat that takes people from one side of a body of water to the other.

fertile *adjective*
able to grow a lot of healthy plants. ***fertile** land.*

fertiliser *noun* fertilisers
something you add to the soil to feed plants and make them grow better.

festival *noun* festivals
a time when people do special things to celebrate something. *a yam **festival**, a drama **festival**.*

fetch *verb* fetches, fetching, fetched
to go and get. *Please **fetch** my coat.*

fever *noun* fevers
an illness that makes your body get hotter than it should.

few *adjective, pronoun*
not many. *Few people were there.*
a few a small number.

fibre (fi-ber) *noun* fibres
1 a very thin thread. *cotton **fibres**.*
2 a substance in some foods which we need to digest things properly and make us healthy inside.

fiction (fik-shun) *noun*
stories about people and things that are not real.
Word Building: fictional, fictitious

fiddle *verb* fiddles, fiddling, fiddled
to play with something with your fingers. *Stop **fiddling** with your hair!*

fidget *verb* fidgets, fidgeting, fidgeted
to keep moving about in an annoying way. *Please don't **fidget**!*

field *noun* fields
a piece of ground with a fence around it and crops or grass growing on it. *a **field** of corn.*

fierce *adjective* fiercer, fiercest
angry or dangerous. *Wild pigs are **fierce** animals.*
Word Building: fiercely

fifteen *noun*
the number 15.
Word Building: fifteenth

fifty *noun*
the number 50.
Word Building: fiftieth

fig *noun* figs
a small, soft fruit, full of small seeds.

fight *verb* fights, fighting, fought
to take part in a struggle, battle, or war.

figure *noun* figures
1 one of the signs for numbers, such as *1*, *2*, and *3*.
2 the shape of a body. *a tall thin **figure**.*

file *noun* files
1 a line of people one behind the other. *Line up in single **file**.*
2 a flat tool that you rub against things to make them smooth. *a nail **file**.*
3 a box or cover that you keep papers in.
4 a collection of information on a computer.

fill *verb* fills, filling, filled
to make someone or something full. *Mary-Jane **filled** the jug with milk.*

film *noun* films
1 the thin roll of plastic you put in a camera for taking photographs.
2 moving pictures which tell a story, like those you see on television.

filthy *adjective* filthier, filthiest
very dirty.

fin *noun* fins
one of the thin, flat parts that stand out from a fish's body and help it swim.

final *adjective*
coming at the end. *The **final** entry in this dictionary is zucchini.*
Word Building: finally

final *noun* finals
a match played to decide the winner of a competition.

finalist (fine-a-list) *noun* finalists
a competitor in the final of a competition.

finch *noun* finches
a small bird with a short beak for eating seeds.

find *verb* finds, finding, found
to see or get or come across something, either by chance or because you have been looking for it. *I **found** 20 toea on the ground.*

fine *adjective* finer, finest
1 very thin, very small. ***fine** hair, **fine** sand.*
2 dry and sunny. ***fine** weather.*
3 very good. *a **fine** piece of work.*

fine *noun* fines
money someone has to pay as a punishment. *a speeding **fine**.*

finger *noun* fingers
one of the five separate parts at the end of the hand.

fingernail *noun* fingernails
the hard part at the end of each finger.

fingerprint *noun* fingerprints
the mark left on a surface by the tip of a finger.

finish *verb* finishes, finishing, finished
to end, to come to the end. *I've **finished** my work.*

fiord, fjord (fi-**jord**) *noun* fiords, fjords
a long, narrow strip of water between high cliffs, coming from the sea into the land.

fire *noun* fires
1 something which is burning.
2 something which gives us heat. *a gas **fire**.*

fire *verb* fires, firing, fired
to shoot. *to **fire** a gun.*

fire engine *noun* fire engines
a large vehicle that carries people to put out fires.

firefighter *noun* firefighters
a person whose job is to put out fires.

fireplace *noun* fireplaces
the part of the room where you can have a fire.

firewood *noun*
wood used for burning as fuel.

firework *noun* fireworks
a thing that burns or explodes with loud bangs and coloured lights.

firm *adjective* firmer, firmest
hard, solid.
Word Building: firmly

first *adjective, adverb*
before all others. *'A' is the **first** letter of the alphabet. I came **first** in the race.*

first aid *noun*
help that you give to a person who is hurt, before a doctor comes.

fish *noun* fishes or fish
an animal with scales and fins that lives and breathes in water.

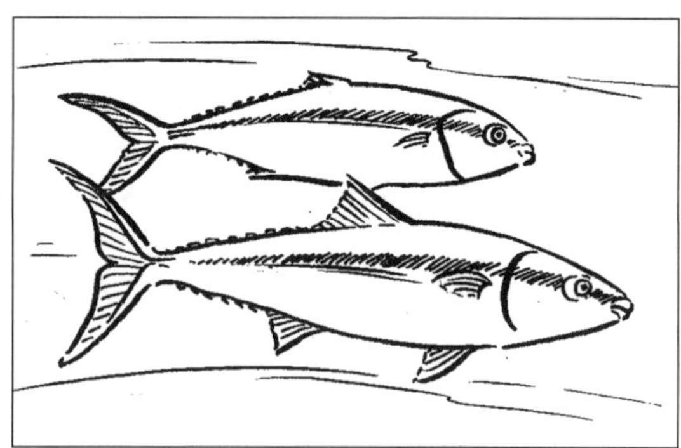

fish *verb* fishes, fishing, fished
to try to catch fish.

fist *noun* fists
a tightly-closed hand.

fit *adjective* fitter, fittest
1 healthy, strong. *Swimming helps to keep you **fit**.*
2 good enough. *Is this old bread **fit** to eat?*

fit *verb* fits, fitting, fitted
to be the right size and shape. *These jeans don't **fit** me.*

five *noun* fives
the number 5.
Word Building: fifth

five-corner *noun* five-corners
a type of fruit with five edges; a star fruit. [from Tok Pisin *faivkona*]

fix *verb* fixes, fixing, fixed
1 to join firmly to something. *Fix the shelf onto the wall.*
2 to mend. *She **fixed** the broken table.*

fizzy *adjective* fizzier, fizziest
with a lot of tiny bubbles that keep bursting. *fizzy drinks.*

flag *noun* flags
a piece of cloth, often with a coloured design on it, used as a sign or signal. *Every country has its own **flag**.*

flake *noun* flakes
a very light, thin piece of something. *A **flake** of pastry came off the pie.*
Word Building: flaky

flame *noun* flames
fire shaped like a pointed tongue. *a candle **flame**.*

flap *noun* flaps
a flat piece of something joined along one edge so that it covers an opening. *the **flap** of an envelope.*

flap *verb* flaps, flapping, flapped
to move up and down like a bird's wings, or from side to side. *The sails of the boat **flapped** in the wind.*

flash *verb* flashes, flashing, flashed
1 to shine suddenly and brightly. *The lights **flashed** on and off.*
2 to appear for a very short time. *The cars **flashed** past.*

flat *adjective* flatter, flattest
with no bumps or holes.

flat *noun* flats
a set of rooms to live in, which is part of a bigger building. *a block of **flats**.*

flatten *verb* flattens, flattening, flattened
to make something flat.

flatter *verb* flatters, flattering, flattered
to praise someone too much.

flavour *noun* flavours
the taste of something. *ten different flavours of drink.*

flavour *verb* flavours, flavouring, flavoured
to add something to food to make it taste different. *coconut **flavoured** sago.*

flea *noun* fleas
a small jumping insect that sucks blood.

flee *verb* flees, fleeing, fled
to run away.

fleece *noun* fleeces
the wool that covers a sheep.

flesh *noun*
the soft part of your body between the bones and skin.

flew *verb* see **fly**

flicker *verb* flickers, flickering, flickered
to burn or shine shakily. *The candle will **flicker** in the wind.*

flight *noun* flights
1 a journey through the air made by a bird or an aeroplane. *a **flight** from Wewak to Mount Hagen.*
2 an escape.
a flight of stairs a set of stairs.

flight attendant *noun* flight attendants
a person who works on the cabin of an aeroplane and cares for passengers.

flimsy *adjective* flimsier, flimsiest
thin, not very strong. *a curtain made of **flimsy** material.*

fling *verb* flings, flinging, flung
to throw something as hard as you can.

flipper *noun* flippers
a limb used by water animals for swimming. *Turtles have **flippers**.*

float *verb* floats, floating, floated
to stay on the surface of a liquid or in the air. *Wood **floats** on water.*

flock *noun* flocks
a large group of sheep or birds. *a **flock** of seagulls.*

flood *noun* floods
a lot of water that spreads over land that is usually dry.

flood *verb* floods, flooding, flooded
to flow over its banks. *The river burst its banks and **flooded**.*

floor *noun* floors
the part of a building or room that people walk on.

flop *verb* flops, flopping, flopped
1 to drop down suddenly. *She **flopped** into a chair, feeling exhausted.*
2 to hang loosely. *The expat's hair kept **flopping** into his eyes.*

flour *noun*
a powder made from wheat and used for making bread, scones and cakes.

flourish (**flur**-ish) *verb* flourishes, flourishing, flourished
to grow well. *The plants **flourished**.*

flow *verb* flows, flowing, flowed
to move along like a river.

flower *noun* flowers
the part of a plant that has petals and produces seeds.

flown *verb* see **fly**

flu *noun*
an illness that gives you a cold and makes you ache all over and feel very hot.

fluff *noun*
light, soft stuff that comes off wool, hair, or feathers.

fluffy *adjective*
light and soft like fluff.

fluid *noun* fluids
any substance that can flow, any liquid or gas.

flute *noun* flutes
a musical instrument which you play by blowing across a hole.

flutter *verb* flutters, fluttering, fluttered
to make quick flapping movements. *The baby bird **fluttered** its wings.*

fly *noun* flies
a small insect with wings.

fly *verb* flies, flying, flew, flown
to move along through the air. *Aeroplanes **fly** quickly across the sky.*

flying fox *noun* flying foxes
a large, fruit-eating bat.

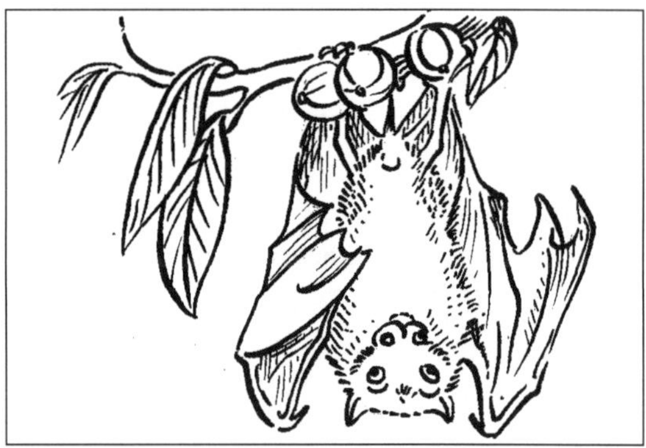

foam *noun*
1 a lot of small bubbles on top of a liquid.
2 a soft substance with a lot of small holes in it like a sponge. *Mattresses are often made of **foam**.*

focus *verb* focuses, focusing, focused
to set the lens of a camera, telescope, or projector so that you get a clear picture.

fog *noun* fogs
damp air that looks like thick smoke and is difficult to see through.

foil *noun* foils
a sheet of metal as thin as paper.

fold *verb* folds, folding, folded
to bend one part of something on top of another part. ***Fold** your clothes neatly please.*

folder *noun* folders
a large cover made of card for keeping your work in.

foliage (foe-lee-ij) *noun*
the leaves of a tree or other plant.

follow *verb* follows, following, followed
1 to go after. *A dog **followed** me.*
2 to go along. ***Follow** this road.*
3 to understand. *Did you **follow** what she said?*

fond *adjective* fonder, fondest
liking someone or something a lot. *She's very **fond** of her pet dog.*

food *noun* foods
anything that you eat to help you grow and be healthy.

fool *noun* fools
someone who is very silly.

foolish *adjective*
silly.
Word Building: foolishly

foot *noun* feet
the part of the body at the end of the leg that you stand on.

football *noun*
1 the game played by two teams with a round or oval ball that is kicked and sometimes handled. Australian Rules, Rugby and Soccer are football games.
2 the ball used in these games.

footpath *noun* footpaths
the path for people to walk on along the side of a street.

for *preposition*
this word has several uses. Here are some of the ways you can use it: *This present is **for** me. This knife is **for** cutting kaukau. I bought two pencils **for** a kina.*

forbid *verb* forbids, forbidding, forbade, forbidden
to say that someone must not do something. *Walking on the grass is **forbidden**.*

force *noun* forces
1 strength, power, violence. *They had to use **force** to open the door.*
2 an organised group of people, such as police or an army.

force *verb* forces, forcing, forced
to use power or violence to make a person or thing do what you want. *They **forced** him to give them the money.*

forecast *noun* forecasts
a statement about what someone thinks is going to happen. *a weather **forecast**.*

forehead *noun* foreheads
the part of the face above the eyebrows.

foreign (for-en) *adjective*
belonging to another country. *a **foreign** language.*

foreigner *noun* foreigners
a person who comes from another country.

forest *noun* forests
a lot of trees growing together in an area.

forge (forj) *verb* forges, forging, forged
to copy something because you want to trick people. *He was put in prison for **forging** his driving licence.*

forgery *noun* forgeries
a forged copy of something. *This certificate is a **forgery**.*

forget *verb* forgets, forgetting, forgot, forgotten
to fail to remember. *I **forgot** my money. I have **forgotten** her name.*

forgetful *adjective*
likely to forget; absent-minded. *They were so **forgetful** they left their homework at home.*
Word Building: forgetfulness

forgive *verb* forgives, forgiving, forgave, forgiven
to stop being angry with someone. *I **forgave** him when he said sorry.*

forgot, forgotten *verb* see forget

fork *noun* forks
a tool with three or four thin pointed parts called prongs.

form *noun* forms
1 the shape something has. *The carving was in the **form** of a bird.*
2 a printed paper with spaces where you have to write.

formal *adjective*
being very correct in what you say, do, or wear, because something important is happening.

fortnight *noun* fortnights
two weeks. *We get paid every **fortnight**.*

fortunate *adjective*
lucky.
Word Building: fortunately

fortune *noun* fortunes
1 a lot of money.
2 luck. *By good **fortune**, I met her in town.*

forty *noun*
the number 40.
Word Building: fortieth

forward, forwards *adverb*
in the direction that is in front of you.
to look forward to to wait for something with pleasure.

fossil *noun* fossils
part of a dead plant or animal that has been in the ground for millions of years and has become hard like rock.

foster *verb* fosters, fostering, fostered
to care for someone else's child as if he or she was one of your own family.

fought *verb* see fight

foul *adjective* fouler, foulest
1 dirty and nasty. *a **foul** smell.*
2 (*informal*) bad. ***foul** weather.*
3 against the rules. ***foul** play.*

found *verb* see find

foundations *noun*
the solid part under the ground that a building is built on.

four *noun* fours
the number 4.
Word Building: fourth

fourteen *noun*
the number 14.
Word Building: fourteenth

fowl *noun* fowls
a bird, like a chicken, that is kept for its eggs or meat.

fraction *noun* fractions
1 a number that is not a whole number. $\frac{1}{2}$, $\frac{5}{3}$, and $\frac{1}{4}$ are fractions.
2 a small part of something.

fracture *noun* fractures
a break or crack in something, especially a bone.

fragile (fraj-ile) *adjective*
easily broken. *Glass is **fragile**.*

fragment *noun* fragments
a small piece that has been broken off.

frail *adjective* frailer, frailest
not strong or healthy.

frame *noun* frames
1 a structure made of rods or bars, often to support something.
2 something that fits around a picture or around the lenses of a pair of glasses.

fraud *noun* frauds
a trick or a person who tries to cheat someone.

freak *noun* freaks
someone or something that is very strange or abnormal. *Everyone said that the very large pumpkin was a freak.*

free *adjective* freer, freest
1 able to do what you want or go where you want.
2 not costing anything.

free *verb* frees, freeing, freed
to let a person or animal go free after being shut in somewhere. *We will **free** the bird when it is well enough to fly.*

freeway *noun*
a large main road for fast traffic. *In Port Moresby there is a **freeway** which goes right across the city to the airport.*

freeze *verb* freezes, freezing, froze, frozen
1 to change into ice.
2 to be very cold. *My hands feel frozen.*

freezer *noun* freezers
a large refrigerator used for keeping food frozen.

frequent (free-kwent) *adjective*
happening often. ***frequent** showers.*
Word Building: frequently

fresh *adjective* fresher, freshest
1 new. ***fresh** bread.*
2 clean and cool. ***fresh** air.*
3 not tired. ***fresh** after a rest.*
Word Building: freshly

Friday *noun* Fridays
the day after Thursday.

friend *noun* friends
someone you like who likes you. ***Friends** like doing things together.*

friendly *adjective* friendlier, friendliest
behaving like a friend.

fright *noun* frights
sudden fear. *That loud noise gave me a **fright**.*

frighten *verb* frightens, frightening, frightened
to make someone afraid. *He's **frightened** of snakes.*
Word Building: frightened, frightening

fringe *noun* fringes
1 an edge.
2 a border of threads or strips of cloth on a blanket or garment.

frog *noun* frogs
a small animal with a smooth, wet skin. Frogs live near water and move by leaping and swimming.

from *preposition*
this word has several uses. Here are some of the ways you can use it: *people **from** Abtau; a present **from** Linda; 20 kilometres **from** the city; made **from** wood.*

front *noun* fronts
the side that people usually see first. *the **front** of the house.*

frost *noun* frosts
ice that looks like powder and covers things when the weather is very cold.

froth *noun*
a lot of small bubbles on the top of a liquid.

frown *verb* frowns, frowning, frowned
to have lines on your forehead because you are angry or worried.

froze, frozen *verb* see freeze

fruit *noun* fruits or fruit
the part of a plant which contains seeds and is often used as food.

fry *verb* fries, frying, fried
to cook in hot fat in a pan on top of a stove. ***fried** sago.*

fuel *noun* fuels
anything that is burned to make heat. *Wood is a **fuel**.*

full *adjective* fuller, fullest
holding as much as possible. *The PMV was **full**. A cup **full** of rice.*
full stop the dot which you put at the end of every sentence.

fumes (fewmz) *noun*
gases and smoke, which usually smell nasty. *car **fumes**.*

fun *noun*
amusement, enjoying yourself. *We had great **fun** at the river.*

fund *noun* funds
money that will be used for something special.

funeral (few-ne-ral) *noun* funerals
the ceremony when a dead person is buried or burned.

fungus *noun* fungi
a kind of plant that is not green and grows in damp places. Mushrooms are a kind of fungus.

funnel *noun* funnels
1 a chimney on a ship.
2 a tube with a wide top and a narrow bottom. It is used to pour things into containers with small openings.

funny *adjective* funnier, funniest
1 a person or thing that is funny makes you laugh, or makes you smile. *a **funny** joke.*
2 strange. *a **funny** smell.*

fur *noun* furs
the soft hair that covers some animals.

furious (few-ree-us) *adjective*
very angry.
Word Building: furiously

furniture *noun*
things such as beds and tables that you have inside a house or school.

furry *adjective* furrier, furriest
covered in fur.

further *adjective, adverb*
to a greater distance. *I swam **further** than you.*

fuse (fewz) *noun* fuses
1 a safety device fitted in electrical equipment.
2 a thing used to set off an explosion.

fuss *verb* fusses, fussing, fussed
to worry and bother too much about something that is not important.

fussy *adjective* fussier, fussiest
hard to please, always fussing.

future *noun*
the time that will come. *Nobody knows what will happen in the **future**.*

fuzzy *adjective* fuzzier, fuzziest
not clear. *The TV picture is **fuzzy**.*

A B C D E F G H I J K L M N O P Q R S T U V W X Y Z

gadget *noun* gadgets
a small, useful tool. *A penknife is a useful **gadget**.*

gag *noun* gags
something put over someone's mouth to stop them from talking or making a noise.

gag *noun* gags, gagging, gagged
1 to put something over someone's mouth to stop them from talking or making a noise.
2 to choke and almost vomit.

gain *verb* gains, gaining, gained
to get something that you need or that you did not have before. *We **gained** more points than the other team.*

galaxy *noun* galaxies
a large group of stars and planets. *The Milky Way is a **galaxy**.*

gale *noun* gales
a very strong wind.

galip *noun*
1 a tall tree with reddish timber.
2 the nut from this tree which is good to eat. [from Tok Pisin *galip*]

gallery *noun* galleries
a building or long room where paintings are shown. *an art **gallery**.*

gallop *verb* gallops, galloping, galloped
to go at the fastest speed a horse can go.

gamble *verb* gambles, gambling, gambled
to attempt to win money by playing a game that requires luck.

game *noun* games
something that you play at that has rules. *a **game** of softball, a card **game**.*

gang *noun* gangs
a group of people who do things together.

gap *noun* gaps
an empty space or time between two things. *We went through a **gap** in the fence.*

gape *verb* gapes, gaping, gaped
1 to open your mouth wide with surprise. *Nick just **gaped** at us when we told him he'd won.*
2 to be wide open. *He fell down a big **gaping** hole in the ground.*

garage (ga-**rahzh** or **ga**-rahzh) *noun* garages
1 the building where a car or bus is kept.
2 a place that sells petrol and mends cars.

garamut *noun*
1 a tree with a rough, twisted trunk.
2 a large hollow drum made from this tree. *The **garamut** is played in many parts of PNG, such as the Sepik and Ramu areas.* [from Tok Pisin *garamut*]

garbage (gar-bij) *noun*
rubbish or waste materials.

garden *noun* gardens
a piece of ground where vegetables, fruit, or flowers are grown.

garment *noun* garments
any piece of clothing. Shirts, dresses, and jeans are all garments.

gas *noun* gases
1 any substance that fills the space it's in, like air.
2 a gas that we burn to make heat. *a gas fire.*

gash *noun* gashes
a deep cut. *She fell over and got a nasty gash on her forehead.*

gasp *verb* gasps, gasping, gasped
to breathe in noisily and quickly because you are surprised or ill, or because you have been running. *'I can't run any further,' she* ***gasped.***

gate *noun* gates
a kind of door in a wall or fence round a piece of land.

gather *verb* gathers, gathering, gathered
1 to come together. *A crowd* ***gathered*** *to watch the fight.*
2 to bring together, to collect. *We* ***gathered*** *information for our project.*

gave *verb* see give

gay *adjective*
1 cheerful.
2 brightly coloured.
Word Building: gaily, gaiety

gaze *verb* gazes, gazing, gazed
to look at something for a long time.

gear *noun* gears
1 part of a bicycle or car. Gears help to control the speed of the wheels so that it is easier to go up and down hills.
2 the things needed for a job or sport. *netball* ***gear.***

gem *noun* gems
a valuable or beautiful stone.

general (jen-e-rul) *adjective*
1 concerning most people or things. *All adults can vote in a* ***general*** *election.*
2 not going into details. *He gave us a* ***general*** *idea of what he wanted.*
Word Building: generally

general (jen-e-rul) *noun* generals
an important officer in the army.

generous (jen-e-rus) *adjective*
always ready to give or share what you have.
Word Building: generously

genius (jee-nee-us) *noun* geniuses
a very clever person.

gentle *adjective* gentler, gentlest
quiet and kind, not rough.
Word Building: gently

gentleman *noun* gentlemen
a polite name for a man.

genuine (jen-yoo-en) *adjective*
real. ***genuine*** *gold.*

geography (jee-og-ra-fee) *noun*
the study of the earth, with its mountains, rivers, seas, and other parts.

geometry (jee-om-a-tree) *noun*
the study of lines, angles, surfaces, and solids.

germ *noun* germs
a tiny living thing, too small to see. Germs sometimes cause diseases.

get *verb* gets, getting, got
1 to receive, buy, or earn. *What did you **get** for your birthday? I'm going to the shop to **get** some food. Jo **got** K5 for washing the car.*
2 to become. *I **got** hot waiting outside.*

geyser (gy-zer) *noun* geysers
a spring in the ground that sends hot water high into the air.

ghost (rhymes with *most*) *noun* ghosts
the shape of a dead person that people think they have seen.

giant *noun* giants
a very big person.

giddy *adjective* giddier, giddiest
dizzy.

gift *noun* gifts
a present. *a birthday **gift**.*

gigantic *adjective*
very big.

giggle *verb* giggles, giggling, giggled
to laugh in a silly way.

gill *noun* gills
the part on each side of a fish that it breathes through.

ginger *noun*
a spice with a strong, hot taste.

giraffe *noun* giraffes
a very tall African animal with a very long neck.

girl *noun* girls
a female child or young person.

give *verb* gives, giving, gave, given
to let someone have something. *I **gave** Thomas a present for his birthday.*

glacier (glay-see-er) *noun* glaciers
a river of ice that moves very slowly down a mountain.

glad *adjective*
happy.
Word Building: gladly

glance *verb* glances, glancing, glanced
to look at something quickly.

glare *verb* glares, glaring, glared
1 to shine very brightly. *The sun **glared** down on us.*
2 to look angrily at someone. *They stood **glaring** at each other.*

glass *noun* glasses
1 a very hard substance that you can see through, used for making windows.
2 a kind of cup without a handle, made of glass.

glasses *noun*
a pair of lenses held in front of the eyes by a frame that fits over your nose and ears. Glasses help you see better.

gleam *verb* gleams, gleaming, gleamed
to shine with a soft light, especially one that comes and goes.

glide *verb* glides, gliding, glided
to move very smoothly. The seagull was ***gliding** over the water.*

glider *noun* gliders
a kind of aeroplane without an engine.

glimpse *verb* glimpses, glimpsing, glimpsed
to see something for only a few seconds. *She **glimpsed** the house from the window of the car.*

glisten (gliss-en) *verb* glistens, glistening, glistened
to shine like something with drops of water on it. *The grass **glistened** with dew.*

glitter *verb* glitters, glittering, glittered
to shine with a bright light that keeps coming and going. ***glittering** jewels.*

globe *noun* globes
1 a ball with the map of the whole world on it.
2 an electric light bulb.

gloom *noun*
1 darkness, dim light. *We could hardly see in the **gloom**.*
2 sadness, depression. *The girl had a look of **gloom** on her face.*
Word Building: gloomy, gloomier, gloomiest
*It was a **gloomy** day.*

glory *noun*
great fame. *the **glory** of winning a gold medal.*

glossy *adjective* glossier, glossiest
smooth and shiny.

glove *noun* gloves
a covering for the hand with separate parts for the thumb and each finger.

glow *verb* glows, glowing, glowed
to shine with a warm light.

glue *noun* glues
a substance used for sticking things together.

glutton *noun* gluttons
someone who eats too much.

gnarled (narld) *adjective*
twisted like the trunk of an old tree.

gnash (nash) *verb* gnashes, gnashing, gnashed
to grind your teeth together. *He **gnashed** his teeth in anger and frustration.*

gnaw (naw) *verb* gnaws, gnawing, gnawed
to keep biting or chewing on something hard like a bone.

go *verb* goes, going, went, gone
1 to move, to travel. *I **go** to school by bus.*
2 to work. *Is your clock **going**?*
3 to become. *She **went** very quiet when she heard the bad news.*

goal *noun* goals
1 the two posts the ball must go between to score a point in games like football.
2 a point scored in football, soccer, netball, and other games.

goat *noun* goats
a farm animal with horns, kept for its milk.

gobble *verb* gobbles, gobbling, gobbled
to eat quickly and greedily.

god *noun* gods
a person or thing that people worship.

goddess *noun* goddesses
a female god.

go finish *verb*
to leave somewhere for good. *The expats next door are **going-finish** next week.* [from Tok Pisin *go pinis*]

goggles *noun*
large glasses worn to protect the eyes from wind, water, dust, or bright lights.

gold *noun*
a valuable, shiny, yellow metal.

golden *adjective*
coloured like gold. *a **golden** cup.*

gone *verb* see go

gong *noun* gongs
a large metal disc which makes an echoing sound when you hit it.

good *adjective* better, best
1 what people like and praise. *a **good** story.*
2 kind and true. *a **good** friend.*
3 well behaved. *a **good** boy.*

goodbye *interjection*
the word you say when you are leaving someone.

goods *noun*
things that can be bought and sold.

goose *noun* geese
a large freshwater bird with a long neck.

gorgeous (gor-jus) *adjective*
beautiful, splendid. *a **gorgeous** day.*

gorilla *noun* gorillas
a large African ape.

gossip *verb* gossips, gossiping, gossiped
to talk a lot about other people, sometimes in an unkind way.

got *verb* see **get**

govern *verb* governs, governing, governed
to be in charge of a country or a group of people.

government *noun* governments
the group of people who govern a country or state.

governor (guv-er-nor) *noun* governors
1 a person who governs.
2 the chairman of a Provincial Assembly.

gown *noun* gowns
a loose, flowing garment usually worn to special events.

Governor-General *noun* Governors-General
the person who acts in place of the Queen in Papua New Guinea.

grab *verb* grabs, grabbing, grabbed
to take hold of something suddenly. *She **grabbed** her coat and ran.*

grace *noun*
1 beauty in the way someone moves.
2 a short prayer said before a meal.
Word Building: graceful, gracefully, gracious, graceless

grade *noun* grades
a class in some schools. *I will be in grade 3 next year.*

grade *verb* grades, grading, graded
to sort or divide into groups. *We had to grade the sticks into different sizes.*

gradual *adjective*
happening a little at a time. *The changes we made were **gradual**.*
Word Building: gradually

grain *noun*
the seed that grows in plants like wheat and is used for making food.

grains *noun*
tiny bits of something like sand or salt.

gram *noun* grams
a measure of weight. 1000 grams make 1 kilogram.

grammar *noun*
the rules for using words properly.

grand *adjective* grander, grandest
large, important.

grandchild *noun* grandchildren
a child of your son or daughter. Granddaughters and grandsons are grandchildren.

grandparent *noun* grandparents
a parent of your mother or father. Grandmothers and grandfathers are grandparents.

grant *verb* grants, granting, granted
to agree to give someone what they have asked for. *Her wish was **granted**.*

grape *noun* grapes
a small, soft green or purple fruit that grows in bunches.

grapefruit *noun* grapefruits
a sour-tasting fruit that looks like a big orange, but is yellow.

graph (graf) *noun* graphs
a diagram that helps you to compare different numbers or amounts of things. *We drew a **graph** showing how much rain fell in each month of the year.*

graphics *noun*
pictures, patterns, or designs. *computer **graphics**.*

grasp *verb* grasps, grasping, grasped
to get hold of something and hold it tightly. *She **grasped** my arm to stop herself from falling.*

grass *noun* grasses
a green plant with flat, narrow leaves that can be eaten by sheep and other animals.

grasshopper *noun* grasshoppers
an insect that makes a shrill sound and can jump a long way.

grass skirt *noun* grass skirts
a traditional skirt made from string and thin strips of leaf worn mostly by women in PNG and the Pacific.

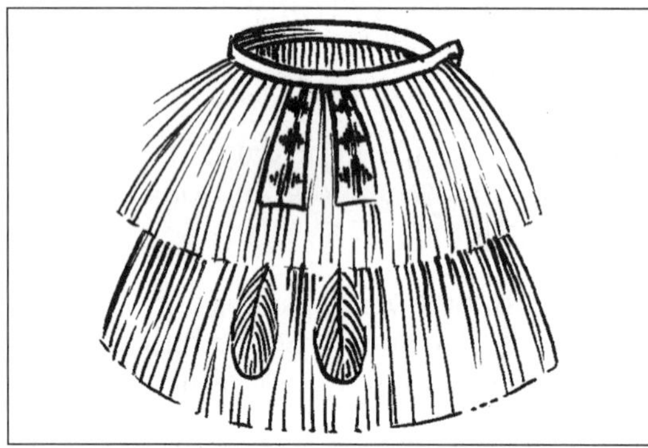

grate *verb* grates, grating, grated
1 to rub something against a rough surface so that it makes small pieces. *to **grate** cheese.*
2 to make a rasping noise.

grateful *adjective*
wanting to thank someone for what they have done. *I was **grateful** for her help.*
Word Building: gratefully

grave *noun* graves
a place where a dead person is buried in the ground.

gravel *noun*
a mixture of tiny stones and coarse sand. *a **gravel** path.*

gravity *noun*
the force that pulls everything towards the Earth.

gravy *noun*
a kind of hot brown sauce poured over meat.

graze *verb* grazes, grazing, grazed
1 to hurt the skin by rubbing hard against something.
2 to eat grass. *The sheep were **grazing** in the field.*

grease *noun*
thick, slippery stuff like oil.

greasy *adjective* greasier, greasiest
covered in grease, full of grease. *greasy hair.*

great *adjective* greater, greatest
1 big, impressive. *a **great** storm.*
2 admired by many people. *a **great** musician.*
3 (*informal*) very good. *We had a **great** time.*
Word Building: greatly

greed *noun*
a strong wish for much more than you need of something, such as money or food.
Word Building: greedy, greedier, greediest, greediness, greedily

green *noun, adjective*
the colour of grass.

greenhouse *noun* greenhouses
a glass building for growing plants in.

greet *verb* greets, greeting, greeted
to welcome someone or say hello.

greeting *noun* greetings
words or actions used when you meet someone.

grew *verb* see **grow**

grey *noun, adjective*
a colour or shade between black and white.

grief (greef) *noun*
a very sad feeling.

grill *verb* grills, grilling, grilled
to cook food on metal bars put under or over heat. ***grilled** steak.*

grille *noun*
a skin infection causing ring-shaped itching sores; ringworm. [from Tok Pisin *grile*]

grim *adjective* grimmer, grimmest
not kind, not pleased or cheerful. *She looked **grim**.*
Word Building: grimly

grin *verb* grins, grinning, grinned
to smile showing your teeth.

grind *verb* grinds, grinding, ground
to crush into tiny bits. *The wheat was **ground** into flour.*

grip *verb* grips, gripping, gripped
to hold tightly. *He **gripped** the handlebars as he went downhill.*

grit *noun*
tiny bits of stone or sand.

groan *verb* groans, groaning, groaned
to make a low sound because you are in pain or trouble.

groceries *noun*
food and household supplies.

groom *noun* grooms
1 a person who looks after horses.
2 another word for a bridegroom.

groove *noun* grooves
a long, narrow cut in something.

grope *verb* gropes, groping, groped
to try to find something by feeling for it when you cannot see. *In the dark she **groped** for the door.*

ground *noun* grounds
1 the earth. *The kite fell to the **ground**.*
2 a piece of land to play on. *a football **ground**.*

ground *verb* see **grind**

group *noun* groups
1 a number of people, animals, or things that belong together in some way. *a **group** of teenagers.*
2 people who play music together. *a pop **group**.*

grow *verb* grows, growing, grew, grown
1 to become bigger. *You've **grown** very quickly.*
2 to plant something in the ground and look after it. *We **grew** onions and tomatoes last year.*

growl *verb* growls, growling, growled
to make a deep, angry sound. *Angry dogs **growl**.*

grown-up *noun* grown-ups
a man or woman who is not a child any more.

growth *noun*
getting bigger, growing. *We measured the **growth** of the plants.*

grub *noun* grubs
a tiny creature that will become an insect.

grubby *adjective* grubbier, grubbiest
dirty. ***grubby** hands.*

grudge *noun* grudges
a bad feeling you have against someone, because you think they have harmed you.

gruesome *adjective*
horrible, disgusting.

gruff *adjective* gruffer, gruffest
with a deep, rough voice.
Word Building: gruffly

grumble *verb* grumbles, grumbling, grumbled
to complain; to be bad-tempered about something.

grunt *verb* grunts, grunting, grunted
to make the sound a pig makes.

guarantee (gair-un-tee) *noun* guarantees
a promise to mend or replace something if it goes wrong.

guard (gard) *verb* guards, guarding, guarded
to keep someone or something safe. *The dog was **guarding** the house.*

guardian (gar-dee-un) *noun* guardians
a person who is in charge of a child whose parents cannot look after him or her.

guava *noun*
1 a small tropical tree
2 the pale orange fruit with pink flesh which is good to eat from this tree.

guess (gess) *verb* guesses, guessing, guessed
to say what you think the answer is when you do not really know. *Did you **guess** the right answer?*

guest (gest) *noun* guests
a person who is invited to a party, or is making a visit to someone else's home.

guide (gide) *noun* guides
someone or something that shows you where to go or what to look at. *The **guide** took us round the museum.*
Guide a member of the Girl Guides Association.
guide dog a dog trained to help a blind person.

guilt (gilt) *noun*
the feeling that you have done something wrong.

guilty (gil-tee) *adjective* guiltier, guiltiest
1 responsible for doing something wrong. *He was **guilty** of stealing.*
2 feeling or looking as if you were guilty. *He had a **guilty** look.*

guinea pig (gin-ee pig) *noun* guinea pigs
a small, furry animal that has no tail.

guitar (gi-tar) *noun* guitars
a musical instrument with strings across it that you play with your fingers.

gull *noun* gulls
a kind of sea bird.

gully *noun* gullies
1 a small narrow valley made by running water.
2 a gutter or drain.

gulp *verb* gulps, gulping, gulped
to swallow very quickly. *Don't **gulp** your food!*

gum *noun* gums
1 the hard pink part of the mouth that holds the teeth.
2 a sweet substance that you chew. *chewing **gum**.*
3 a sticky substance from a gum tree.

gumboots *noun*
long rubber boots that you wear to keep your feet and legs dry.

gumi *noun*
1 rubber
2 a rubber tyre; a rubber tube [from Tok Pisin *gumi*]

gum tree *noun*
a tree from the eucalyptus family. Gum trees grow in parts of Papua New Guinea and Australia.

gun *noun* guns
a weapon that fires bullets or shells from a metal tube.

gurgle *verb* gurgles, gurgling, gurgled
to make the noise water makes as it goes down the plughole in a bath.

guria *noun*
1 an earthquake or earth tremor.
2 a crested pigeon found in parts of PNG.
3 a shaking attack on the body often associated with sorcery. [from Tok Pisin *guria*]

gush *verb* gushes, gushing, gushed
to move like water rushing out of a tap.

gust *noun* gusts
a sudden rush of wind or air.

gutter *noun* gutters
a long, narrow hollow at the side of a street or along the edge of a roof to take away rainwater.

gym (jim) *noun* gyms
short for gymnastics and gymnasium.

gymnastics (jim-nas-tics) *plural noun*
exercises for the body usually carried out in a gymnasium.

Hh

habit *noun* habits
anything that you do without thinking, because you have done it so often.

habitat *noun* habitats
the place where a plant or animal lives.

had *verb* see **have**

hail *noun*
small pieces of ice that fall from the sky like rain.

hair *noun* hairs
a soft covering that grows on the heads and bodies of people and other mammals.

hairdresser *noun* hairdressers
someone whose job is to wash, cut, and style people's hair.

hairy *adjective* hairier, hairiest
covered with hair.

half *noun* halves
one of the two equal parts something can be divided into. It can also be written as $\frac{1}{2}$. *Two **halves** make a whole.*

hall *noun* halls
1 the part inside a house near the front door.
2 a very big room. *a school **hall**.*
3 a large, important building or house. *Port Moresby has a City **Hall**.*

halo *noun* halos or haloes
a circle of light, especially shown around the head of a saint in pictures.

halt *verb* halts, halting, halted
to stop. *The bus **halted** at the red light.*

halter *noun* halters
a rope or strap put around an animal's head or neck so that it can be controlled.

ham *noun*
meat from a pig's leg.

hamamas *adjective*
happy, pleased [from Tok Pisin *hamamas*]

hamburger *noun* hamburgers
a bread bun containing a round portion of minced meat, with onion and lettuce.

hammer *noun* hammers
a heavy tool used for hitting nails.

hammock *noun* hammocks
a bed made of cloth or rope that you hang up at the two ends.

hand *noun* hands
the part of the body at the end of your arm.

handbag *noun* handbags
a small bag used for carrying money and other belongings.

handcuffs *noun*
a pair of metal rings used for locking someone's wrists together.

handicap *noun* handicaps
anything that makes it more difficult for you to do something. *help for children with physical **handicaps**.*

handicapped *adjective*
having some kind of handicap.

handle *noun* handles
the part of a thing made for you to hold it or work it by.

handle *verb* handles, handling, handled
to touch, feel, hold, or use something with your hands. *Please wash your hands before you **handle** the food.*

handlebars *noun*
the bar you hold to steer your bicycle.

handsome *adjective*
attractive.

hang *verb* hangs, hanging, hung
to attach the top part of something to a hook or nail. *I **hung** up my coat and went in. The towels were **hanging** on hooks.*

hangar *noun* hangars
a big shed for keeping an aeroplane in.

hanger *noun* hangers
something used for hanging up things. *coat **hangers**.*

happen *verb* happens, happening, happened
1 to take place. *How did the accident **happen**?*
2 to do something by chance. *I just **happened** to see it.*

happiness *noun*
the feeling you have when you are very pleased or enjoying yourself.

happy *adjective* happier, happiest
full of happiness.
Word Building: happily

harbour *noun* harbours
a place where boats can stay safely when they are not out at sea.

hard *adjective* harder, hardest
1 not soft. ***hard** ground.*
2 difficult. ***hard** sums.*
3 severe. *a **hard** punishment.*

hard *adverb*
a lot. *She works **hard**.*

hardly *adverb*
not easily. *After the accident I could **hardly** walk.*

hardware *noun*
tools, nails, wire, and other things made of metal.

harm *verb* harms, harming, harmed
to hurt or spoil someone or something.

harmful *adjective*
likely to do harm, bad for you. *Too much sugar can be **harmful** to your teeth.*

harp *noun* harps
a musical instrument. It has a large frame with strings stretched across it that are played with the fingers.

harsh *adjective* harsher, harshest
not kind or gentle. *a **harsh** voice.*
Word Building: harshly

harvest *noun* harvests
the time when farmers gather in the fruit or vegetables they have grown.

hassle *noun* hassles
(*informal*) something that annoys you or causes you a problem.

haste (hayst) *noun*
being too quick and not careful. *Hitolo forgot her books in her **haste**.*

hasty (hay-stee) *adjective* hastier, hastiest
quick and not careful, hurrying.
Word Building: hastily

hat *noun* hats
something that you wear to cover the top of your head.

hatch *verb* hatches, hatching, hatched
to break out of an egg.

hatch *noun* hatches
an opening in a wall or floor, usually with a covering. *The electrician climbed through the **hatch** to get under the house.*

hate *verb* hates, hating, hated
to have a very strong feeling against someone or something you do not like.

haul *verb* hauls, hauling, hauled
to pull something heavy. *They **hauled** the boat out of the river.*

haunt *verb* haunts, haunting, haunted
1 to visit a place as a ghost.
2 to stay in your mind. *The memory will **haunt** me forever.*

hausboi (house boy) *noun*
a man employed to work in a private house. [from Tok Pisin *hausboi*]

hausmeri (house meri) *noun*
a woman employed to work in a private house. [from Tok Pisin *hausmeri*]

haus tambaran *noun*
1 a spirit house.
2 a men's ceremonial house. [from Tok Pisin *haus tambaran*]

haus win *noun*
a garden house, usually without walls. [from Tok Pisin *haus win*]

have *verb* has, having, had
this word has several uses. Here are some of the ways you can use it:
1 to own. *Yaking **has** a new dog.*
2 to include, to contain. *Otto's class **has** thirty pupils.*
3 to enjoy, to suffer. *I was **having** a good time, but Bernadette **had** a cold.*
4 to receive, to get. *I **had** lots of presents on my birthday.*

hawk *noun* hawks
a bird that hunts and eats smaller animals.

hay *noun*
dry grass used to feed animals.

hazard *noun* hazards
something that may be a risk or a danger.
Word Building: hazardous

hazy *adjective* hazier, haziest
misty, not clear. ***hazy** sunshine.*

he *pronoun*
a male person or animal being talked about.
Word Building: he's (he + is); he'd (he + had or would); he'll (he + will)

head *noun* heads
1 the part of a person or animal that contains the brain, eyes, and mouth.
2 the person in charge.

headache *noun* headaches
a pain in the head that goes on hurting.

headdress *noun* headdresses
a decorative covering for the head. In PNG many clans wear highly decorated wigs as headdresses.

heading *noun* headings
words you write as a title at the top of a piece of writing.

headline *noun* headlines
words in large print at the top of a piece of writing in a newspaper.

headquarters *noun*
the place from which the people organising something send out orders. *The **headquarters** for the Department of Education is in Waigani.*

heal *verb* heals, healing, healed
1 to become well again. *The cut on my foot **healed** slowly.*
2 to make someone well again. *The doctor **healed** the sick man.*

health (helth) *noun*
how well your body is, how you are feeling.

healthy (hel-thee) *adjective* healthier, healthiest
1 not ill or injured in any way. ***healthy** children.*
2 good for your health. ***healthy** food.*

heap *noun* heaps
an untidy pile. *Don't throw your clothes in a **heap** on the floor!*

hear *verb* hears, hearing, heard
to take in sounds through the ears. *I **heard** you shout so I came.*

heart *noun* hearts
1 the part of the body that pumps the blood around inside.
2 your feelings. *She has a kind **heart**.*

heat *noun*
the feeling you get from a fire or from the rays of the sun.

heat *verb* heats, heating, heated
to make something hot. ***Heat** up some milk.*

heave (heev) *verb* heaves, heaving, heaved
to lift or pull something heavy. *We **heaved** the box of books onto the table.*

heaven (hev-en) *noun*
1 God's home.
2 a very happy place.

heavy (hev-ee) *adjective* heavier, heaviest
weighing a lot, hard to lift.

hedge *noun* hedges
a kind of wall made by bushes growing close together.

heel *noun* heels
the back part of your foot.

height (hite) *noun* heights
how high something is. *We measured the **height** of the door.*

heir (sounds like *air*) *noun* heirs
the person who will be given money, property, or a title when their owner dies. *Prince Charles is **heir** to the throne of England.*

held *verb* see **hold**

helicopter *noun* helicopters
a kind of aircraft without wings. It can go straight up because it has a large propeller on the top.

hell *noun*
a place where some people believe wicked people are punished after they die.

hello *interjection*
the word you say when you meet someone.

helmet *noun* helmets
a strong covering that protects the head. *Motorcyclists must wear a crash **helmet**.*

help *verb* helps, helping, helped
to do something useful for someone else.
Word Building: helper, helpers

helpful *adjective*
giving help; useful.
Word Building: helpfulness

helping *noun* helpings
an amount of food put on your plate at one time. *Bubu gave us big **helpings** of food.*

helpless *adjective*
not able to look after yourself.
Word Building: helplessly

hem *noun* hems
the edge of a piece of cloth, that is folded under and sewn down. *The **hem** of her skirt is coming undone.*

hemisphere (hem-is-fear) *noun* hemispheres
1 one half of the earth.
2 a shape like half a ball.

hen *noun* hens
1 a female bird.
2 one of the birds which lay the eggs we eat.

heptagon *noun*
a shape with seven sides.

her *adjective, pronoun*
1 belonging to the woman or girl you are talking about. *Is that **her** dress?*
2 a word used to refer to a girl, woman, or female animal. *I went with **her**.*

herb *noun* herbs
a plant used in cooking to make the food taste good. *Parsley and mint are **herbs**.*

herd *noun* herds
a group of animals that live and feed together. *a **herd** of cattle or deer.*

here *adverb*
in, at, or to this place. *Come **here**! **Here's** my book.*

hermit *noun* hermits
someone who lives alone and keeps away from people.

hero *noun* heroes
someone who has done something very brave.

heron (hair-un) *noun* herons
a wading bird with a long neck.

herself *pronoun*
she and no one else. *She told me **herself**.*
by herself on her own. *She liked to work **by herself**.*

hesitate *verb* hesitates, hesitating, hesitated
to wait a bit before you do or say something, because you are not sure about it.

hexagon *noun* hexagons
a shape with six sides.

hibernate *verb* hibernates, hibernating, hibernated
to sleep for a long time during the cold weather. *Bats, tortoises, and bears all **hibernate**.*

hibiscus *noun*
a tropical plant with large brightly coloured flowers.

hiccup *verb* hiccups, hiccuping, hiccuped
to make a sudden, sharp gulping sound. You sometimes hiccup when you eat or drink too quickly.

hide *verb* hides, hiding, hid, hidden
1 to go to a place where people cannot see you. *I was **hiding** behind a tree.*
2 to put something in a secret place. *He **hid** his money under his mattress.*

high *adjective, adverb* higher, highest
1 going a long way up. *a **high** mountain.*
2 a long way above the ground. ***high** clouds.*
3 measuring from top to bottom. *The door is two metres **high**.*
4 above what you expect. ***high** prices.*
5 of a sound that is not deep or low. *a **high** voice.*

Highlands *noun*
the mountainous country in central mainland PNG.
Word building: highlander. *The people from Goroka are **highlanders**.*

highlighter *noun* highlighters
a pen with bright coloured ink used to make words on paper stand out.

highway *noun* highways
an important road.

hijack *verb* hijacks, hijacking, hijacked
to seize control of an aeroplane or other vehicle and force the person in charge to make it go somewhere else.

hill *noun* hills
ground that is higher than the ground around it.

him *pronoun*
a word used to refer to a boy, man, or male animal. *I went with **him**.*

himself *pronoun*
he and no one else. *He told me **himself**.*
by himself on his own. *He walked home by **himself**.*

hind *adjective*
at the back. *The dog stood on its **hind** legs.*

hinder *verb* hinders, hindering, hindered
to delay or prevent something from happening. *His work was **hindered** by the children.*

hinge *noun* hinges
a metal fastener that joins a door to a wall and lets the door swing open and closed.

hint *noun* hints
1 a slight clue or suggestion. *Lenus gave me a **hint** that she wanted a book for her birthday.*
2 a useful idea. *He gave us some **hints** on how to draw people.*

hint *verb* hints, hinting, hinted
to give a slight clue or suggestion.

hip *noun* hips
1 the bony part of the body that sticks out where your leg joins the side of your body.
2 a red berry on a rose bush.

hippopotamus *noun* hippopotamuses
a very large, heavy, African animal that lives near water. It is sometimes called a hippo for short.

hire *verb* hires, hiring, hired
to pay to get the use of something. *You can **hire** cars at the airport.*

hiri *noun, adjective*
a trading expedition, from the Port Moresby area to the Gulf of Papua, to exchange pottery for sago.

Hiri Motu *noun*
a language developed from the Motu language to allow communication and trade between the Motu people and other Papuans in PNG.

his *adjective*
belonging to the man or boy you are talking about. *Is that **his** car?*

hiss *verb* hisses, hissing, hissed
to make the long 'sss' sound that snakes make.

history *noun*
things that happened in the past.

hit *verb* hits, hitting, hit
to knock; to touch something roughly or violently.

hive *noun* hives
a kind of box for keeping bees in.

hoard (hord) *noun* hoards
a secret store of money or other things.

hoarse (hors) *adjective* hoarser, hoarsest
sounding rough and deep. *a **hoarse** voice.*
Word Building: hoarsely

hoax (hokes) *noun* hoaxes
a trick played on someone.

hobble *verb* hobbles, hobbling, hobbled
to walk with difficulty because there is something wrong with your leg or foot.

hobby *noun* hobbies
something interesting that people like doing in their spare time. *My **hobbies** are reading and swimming.*

hoe *noun* hoes
a tool for getting rid of weeds.

hold *verb* holds, holding, held
1 to have something in your hands. *Maha **held** the ladder while Jaydee climbed up.*
2 to have room inside for something. *The box **held** six books.*
Word Building: holder, holders

hole *noun* holes
a gap or opening made in something.

holiday *noun* holidays
time off from school or work.

hollow *adjective*
with an empty space inside. *a **hollow** tree.*
Word Building: hollow, hollows

holly *noun* hollies
a tree that has shiny, prickly leaves and red berries.

holy *adjective* holier, holiest
special because it belongs to God.

home *noun* homes
the place where you live.

homesick *adjective*
sad because you are away from home.

homework *noun*
school work that a student has to do at home.

honest (on-est) *adjective*
not stealing, cheating, or telling lies.
Word Building: honestly

honey *noun*
sweet, sticky food made by bees.

honour (on-er) *noun*
great respect.

hood *noun* hoods
the part of a coat that you put over your head in bad weather

hoof *noun* hoofs or hooves
the hard part that covers a horse's foot

hook *noun* hooks
a bent or curved piece of metal or other material, for hanging things on or for catching hold of things.

hookworm *noun* hookworms
a worm that lives in the intestines of people and other animals.

hoop *noun* hoops
a big wooden or metal ring used in games.

hoot *verb* hoots, hooting, hooted
to make a sound like an owl or the horn of a car.
Word Building: hooter, hooters

hop *verb* hops, hopping, hopped
1 to jump on one foot.
2 to move by jumping. *The blackbird **hopped** across the lawn.*

hope *verb* hopes, hoping, hoped
to want something to happen. *I'm* ***hoping*** *to go to Goroka in the holidays.*
Word Building: hopeful, hopefully

hopeless *adjective*
1 very bad at doing something. *He was* ***hopeless*** *at swimming.*
2 impossible, without hope. *It was* ***hopeless*** *trying to drive through the mud.*

hopscotch *noun*
a game where you throw or kick a stone into squares drawn on the ground, then hop on the other squares in the pattern.

horde *noun* hordes
a large crowd or gang.

horizon (ho-**rize**-on) *noun*
the line where the sky and the land or sea seem to meet. *I can see a ship on the* ***horizon****.*

horizontal (hor-i-**zon**-tal) *adjective*
flat and level like the horizon; the opposite of vertical.

horn *noun* horns
a kind of pointed bone that grows on the heads of some animals, like cows.

horrible *adjective*
1 nasty. *a* ***horrible*** *taste.*
2 frightening. *a* ***horrible*** *shock.*
Word Building: horribly

horrid *adjective*
horrible, unkind.

horror *noun*
very great fear.

horse *noun* horses
a big animal with hooves that can carry people and pull things.

horseshoe *noun* horseshoes
a piece of metal shaped like the letter U, fixed on the bottom of a horse's hoof.

hose *noun* hoses
a long plastic or rubber tube that water can go through.

hospital *noun* hospitals
a place where people who are ill or hurt are looked after.

hostage *noun* hostages
a person who is kept as a prisoner or threatened with harm until a demand is met.

hostile *adjective*
unfriendly, acting like an enemy.

hot *adjective* hotter, hottest
very warm, giving off a lot of heat.
hot *weather, a* ***hot*** *fire.*

hotel *noun* hotels
a building where you can pay to stay the night and to have meals.

hour (our) *noun* hours
a measure of time. There are 60 minutes in 1 hour.

house *noun* houses
a building where people live.

hover (**hov**-er) *verb* hovers, hovering, hovered
1 to stay in one place in the air.
The helicopter ***hovered*** *overhead.*
2 to wait near someone or something and have nothing to do. *She* ***hovered*** *about by the house waiting for the car.*

how *adverb*
1 a word that you use to ask questions.
How *old are you?* ***How*** *are you? Very well, thank you.*
2 in what way. *Show me* ***how*** *to do it.*

however *adverb*
and yet; but. *Jane fell down.* ***However****, she did not hurt herself.*

howl *verb* howls, howling, howled
to give a long, loud cry like an animal in pain.

A B C D E F G H I J K L M N O P Q R S T U V W X Y Z

hub *noun* hubs
the part at the centre of a wheel, where the spokes meet.

huddle *verb* huddles, huddling, huddled
to keep close to others in a group because you are cold or frightened.

hug *verb* hugs, hugging, hugged
to hold someone in your arms to comfort them or show you love them.

huge *adjective*
very big.

hum *verb* hums, humming, hummed
to sing a tune with your lips closed.

human, human being *noun* humans, human beings
any man or woman or child.

humble *adjective* humbler, humblest
modest, not too proud.
Word Building: humbly

humorous *adjective*
funny, amusing. *a **humorous** story.*

hump *noun* humps
a bump, a round lump. *The car slowed down as it approached the **hump** in the road.*

hundred *noun* hundreds
the number 100.
Word Building: hundredth

hung *verb* see hang

hunger *noun*
the need for food.

hungry *adjective* hungrier, hungriest
feeling the need for food.
Word Building: hungrily

hunt *verb* hunts, hunting, hunted
1 to go after an animal because you want to kill it. *Young crocodiles have to learn to **hunt**.*
2 to look carefully for something. *I've **hunted** everywhere for my keys but I can't find them.*
Word Building: hunter, hunters

hurl *verb* hurls, hurling, hurled
to throw something as far as you can.

hurricane *noun* hurricanes
a storm with a very strong wind.

hurry *verb* hurries, hurrying, hurried
1 to move quickly. *She **hurried** away to catch her transport.*
2 to try to do something quickly. *He **hurried** to finish before the bell.*
3 to try to make someone be quick or do something faster. *Don't **hurry** me along.*

hurt *verb* hurts, hurting, hurt
1 to make a person or animal feel pain. *Stop **hurting** me!*
2 to feel pain. *My leg **hurts**.*

hurtle *verb* hurtles, hurtling, hurtled
to move very quickly. *The rocket **hurtled** through space.*

husband *noun* husbands
a man married to someone.

hush *verb* hushes, hushing, hushed
to tell someone to be quiet. ***Hush!** Don't wake the baby!*

hustle (**hus**-sl) *verb* hustles, hustling, hustled
1 to hurry.
2 to push someone along roughly.

hut *noun* huts
a small building made of wood.

hymn (him) *noun* hymns
a song that praises God.

hyphen *noun* hyphens
a mark like this - that you use in writing to join parts of words together, such as grown-up.

hypnotise (**hip**-no-tize) *verb* hypnotises, hypnotising, hypnotised
to send someone into a state like a deep sleep, so that you can control what they do.
Word Building: hypnotist, hypnotists

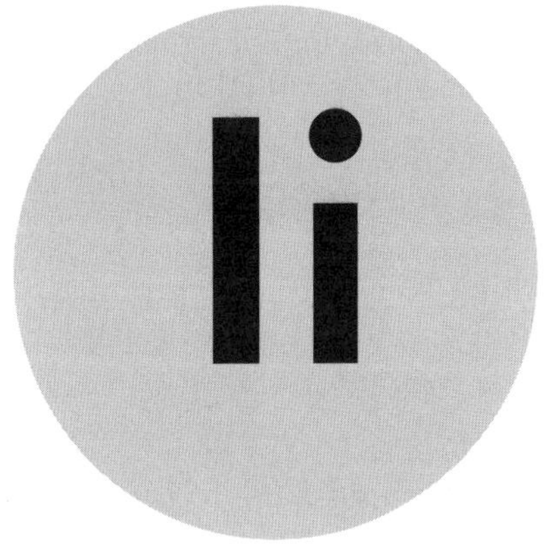

I *pronoun*
a word used by somebody to refer to himself or herself.
Word Building: I'd (I + had or should or would); I'll (I + shall or will); I've (I + have); I'm (I + am)

ice *noun*
water that has frozen hard.

iceberg *noun* icebergs
a very big piece of ice floating in the sea.

ice block *noun*
water flavoured with cordial then frozen in plastic tubes.

ice cream *noun* ice creams
a sweet frozen food that is made from milk.

icing *noun*
a mixture of sugar and other things spread over cakes to decorate them.

icy *adjective* icier, iciest
1 very cold. *an **icy** wind.*
2 slippery, covered with ice. ***icy** roads.*

idea *noun* ideas
1 something you have thought of. *I've got an **idea**. Let's go to the beach.*
2 a picture in your mind. *The film gives you an **idea** of what China is like.*

ideal *adjective*
just what you want. ***ideal** weather for a picnic.*

identical *adjective*
exactly the same. ***identical** twins.*

idiot *noun* idiots
a very stupid person.

idle *adjective* idler, idlest
doing nothing. ***idle** hands.*

idol *noun* idols
1 someone or something that people worship as a god.
2 a famous person that people love. *a pop **idol**.*

ignorant *adjective*
lacking knowledge. *He's very **ignorant** about computers.*

ignore *verb* ignores, ignoring, ignored
to take no notice of someone. *I said hello to her, but she **ignored** me.*

ill *adjective*
not well, in bad health. *I feel too **ill** to go to school.*

illegal (il-lee-gal) *adjective*
against the law. *It is **illegal** to drive a car if you do not have a driving licence.*

illness *noun* illnesses
a disease; something that makes people ill. *Malaria, tuberculosis, and colds are **illnesses**.*

illustrate *verb* illustrates, illustrating, illustrated
to add pictures to show something more clearly. *a book **illustrated** with colour photographs.*

illustration *noun* illustrations
a picture in a book.

imaginary (i-**maj**-i-nair-ee) *adjective*
not real, existing only in your mind. *Dragons are **imaginary** animals.*

imagination (im-aj-i-**nay**-shun) *noun*
the power to imagine things. *You have to use your **imagination** to write stories.*

imagine (i-**maj**-in) *verb* imagines, imagining, imagined
to make a picture in your mind of something you cannot see. *I closed my eyes and tried to **imagine** I was on the beach.*

imitate *verb* imitates, imitating, imitated
to copy a person or animal. *He **imitated** the teacher's voice.*

imitation *noun* imitations
a copy that is not as valuable as the real thing. *It's not a real diamond, it's only a glass **imitation**.*

immediate *adjective*
happening or done straight away.
Word Building: immediately
*Come here **immediately**!*

immense *adjective*
very big.

impatient *adjective*
not patient, not wanting to wait. *Don't be so **impatient**! It's your turn next.*
Word Building: impatiently

imperfect *adjective*
not perfect.

impertinent (im-**per**-ti-nent) *adjective*
rude, cheeky.

implore *verb* implores, imploring, implored
to beg someone to do something.

important *adjective*
1 well known and special. *an **important** person.*
2 If something is important, you must think about it carefully and seriously. *an **important** message.*

impossible *adjective*
not possible. *It's **impossible** to undo this knot.*

impress *verb* impresses, impressing, impressed
to make people think you are very good at something. *She **impressed** her friends with her trumpet playing.*

impression *noun* impressions
a vague idea or feeling. *I get the **impression** he doesn't like us.*

impressive *adjective*
so wonderful that you will always remember it. *an **impressive** firework display.*

imprison *verb* imprisons, imprisoning, imprisoned
to put someone in prison.

improve *verb* improves, improving, improved
1 to become better. *Her cold is **improving**.*
2 to make something better. *He **improved** his handwriting.*

improvement *noun* improvements
a change that makes something better. *There has been a lot of **improvement** in Korom's work this term.*

in *preposition*
This word is used to show position or location: at, inside; during. *She's **in** town today. The milk is **in** the cup. It's cold **in** the night.*
Word Building: indoors (in + doors); inland (in + land); inside (in + side)

inaccurate *adjective*
not accurate, not exact.

include *verb* includes, including, included
to make something part of a group of other things. *The children **included** the new girl in all their games.*

income *noun* incomes
the money which a person gets to live on.

inconvenient *adjective*
happening at a time when you want to do something else. *My friend came over at an **inconvenient** time. We were having lunch.*

incorrect *adjective*
not correct, wrong. *an **incorrect** answer.*

increase *verb* increases, increasing, increased
to become bigger or greater, or to make something bigger or greater. *The number of children in my class has **increased** from 30 to 32.*

incredible *adjective*
not to be believed. *His story about dinosaurs was **incredible**.*

incubate (in-kew-bate) *verb* incubates, incubating, incubated
to hatch eggs by keeping them warm.
Word Building: incubator, incubation

indeed *adverb*
really. *He's very rich **indeed**.*

independent *adjective*
free; not controlled or strongly affected by others; not dependent.
Word Building: independence, independently

index *noun* indexes
a list at the back of a book, arranged in alphabetical order. It tells you what things are in the book and where to find them.

indicate *verb* indicates, indicating, indicated
to point or show something.
Word Building: indication, indicator

indignant *adjective*
angry because someone has said or done something unfair. *I was very **indignant** when she said I was lazy.*
Word Building: indignantly

individual *adjective*
for one person or thing. *He had **individual** lessons to help him learn to read.*

individual *noun* individuals
one single person.

indoors *adverb*
inside a building.

industry *noun* industries
1 work done in factories.
2 all the companies that make the same thing. *Japan has a big car **industry**.*
Word Building: industrial
*The building is in an **industrial** part of town.*

infant *noun* infants
a baby or very young child.

infect *verb* infects, infecting, infected
to give your germs or sickness to someone else.
Word Building: infection, infectious

infectious (in-fek-shus) *adjective*
likely to spread to others. *an **infectious** illness.*

inferior (in-fear-ree-or) *adjective*
not as good or important as something else.
Word Building: inferiority

inferno *noun* infernos
a fierce fire.

inflammable (in-flam-a-bl) *adjective*
easily set on fire.
Word Building: flammable (Note: flammable means the same as inflammable.)

inflate *verb* inflates, inflating, inflated
to fill something with air or gas.
Word Building: inflatable

inflation *noun*
a general rise in prices.

influence *verb* influences, influencing, influenced
to have the power to change what someone thinks or does.

inform *verb* informs, informing, informed
to tell someone something. *You should **inform** the police of the accident.*

informal *adjective*
not formal, not strict. ***informal** clothes, an **informal** party.* Words in this dictionary marked '*informal*' are used when you talk to friends and at other times when you don't need to be very proper.

information *noun*
facts, news, or words that tell you about something. *We are gathering **information** about rainforests.*

infuriate (in-few-ree-ate) *verb* infuriates, infuriating, infuriated
to make very angry.

ingenious (in-jee-nee-us) *adjective*
clever at thinking of new ways to do things.

ingredient *noun* ingredients
one of the things you mix together when you cook something. *Flour is one of the **ingredients** in most cakes.*

inhabit *verb* inhabits, inhabiting, inhabited
to live in a place.

inherit (in-hair-it) *verb* inherits, inheriting, inherited
to receive money or property from someone who has died.
Word Building: inheritance, inheritor

initial *noun* initials
the first letter of a name. *William Mollomb's **initials** are W. M.*

initiate (in-ish-ee-ate) *verb* initiates, initiating, initiated
1 to start something.
2 to make someone a member of a society or group, often during a special ceremony.

inject *verb* injects, injecting, injected
to use a hollow needle to put medicine through someone's skin into his or her body.
Word Building: injection

injure *verb* injures, injuring, injured
to harm, to damage. *A cat **injured** a baby bird.*

injury *noun* injuries
damage done to part of your body, such as a cut or a broken bone.

ink *noun* inks
a coloured liquid used for writing with a pen.

inland *adjective, adverb*
in a part of the country that is not near the sea.

in-law *noun* in-laws
a member of a person's, husband's or wife's family; tambu.

innocent *adjective*
not guilty, not doing wrong.
Word Building: innocently

inquire (in-kwire) *verb* inquires, inquiring, inquired
to ask a question, to seek information. *I will **inquire** about the weather.*
Word Building: inquiry, inquiries
*There was an official **inquiry** into the cause of the accident.*

inquisitive *adjective*
always wanting to find out about things, fond of asking questions.
Word Building: inquisitively

insect *noun* insects
a small animal with six legs and no backbone. *Flies, ants, butterflies, mosquitoes, and bees are all **insects**.*
Word Building: insecticide
***Insecticide** kills insects.*

insert *verb* inserts, inserting, inserted
to put something into a hole or a slot. *He **inserted** a cassette into the cassette player.*

inside *adjective, adverb, preposition*
in something. *Come **inside**; it's raining.*

insist *verb* insists, insisting, insisted
to be very firm in asking, saying, or doing something. *He **insists** on coming with us.*

inspect *verb* inspects, inspecting, inspected
to look carefully at people or things. *The detectives **inspected** the room for fingerprints.*

instant *adjective*
made or done very quickly.

instantly *adverb*
immediately, without waiting.

instead *adverb, preposition*
in place of something else. *They made tea **instead** of coffee.*

instinct *noun* instincts
something that makes people and animals do things they have not learned to do—they can just do them. *Spiders spin webs by **instinct**.*
Word Building: instinctive
*Animals have an **instinctive** fear of fire.*

instruct *verb* instructs, instructing, instructed
1 to tell someone how to do something.
2 to give orders to someone.
Word Building: instructor

instructions *noun*
words that tell you how to do something. *Read the **instructions** before using this glue.*

instrument *noun* instruments
1 a tool or machine used for doing a job. *A microscope is an **instrument** for looking at very tiny things.*
2 something used for making musical sounds. *Violins and flutes are musical **instruments**.*

insult *verb* insults, insulting, insulted
to hurt someone's feelings by being rude. *She **insulted** me by saying I was stupid.*

intelligent *adjective*
clever; able to learn and understand things easily.
Word Building: intelligently

intend *verb* intends, intending, intended
to mean to do something. *Did you **intend** to push me?*

intense *adjective*
very great. ***intense** heat.*

intentional *adjective*
done on purpose.

interest *verb* interests, interesting, interested
to make someone want to find out more, look, or listen.
Word Building: interested

interesting *adjective*
making you want to find out more, making you want to look or listen.

interfere *verb* interferes, interfering, interfered
to take part in something that has nothing to do with you.

interior (in-teer-ree-or) *noun* interiors
the inside of something. *The **interior** of the house was beautifully decorated.*

interjection *noun* interjections
a word you say when you greet someone or you are surprised or angry. *Hello, Hurray*, and *Oh* are all interjections. In writing, interjections often have an exclamation mark like this **!** after them.

internal *adjective*
on the inside of something. *The X-rays allowed the doctor to look at the man's **internal** organs.*
Word Building: internally

international *adjective*
of or between different countries. ***international** travel.*

Internet *noun*
the huge system linking computers around the world for communication and the sharing of information.

interpret (in-ter-pret) *verb* interprets, interpreting, interpreted
1 to explain what something means.
2 to translate from one language to another.
Word Building: interpreter, interpretation
*The **interpreter** translated the book from French to English.*

interrupt *verb* interrupts, interrupting, interrupted
to stop someone from carrying on with what they are saying or doing. *Don't **interrupt** me while I'm doing my homework.*

intersect *verb* intersects, intersecting, intersected
to cross each other. *The lines **intersect** at the corner.*
Word Building: intersection
*There are traffic lights at the **intersection**.*

interview *verb* interviews, interviewing, interviewed
to ask someone questions to find out what they are like, or what they think, or what they know.
Word Building: interviewer
*a television **interviewer**.*

introduce *verb* introduces, introducing, introduced
to make someone or something known to other people. *Toropo **introduced** me to her friend.*

introduction *noun* introductions
1 being introduced to someone.
2 a short part at the beginning of a book or piece of music.

invade *verb* invades, invading, invaded
1 to go into another country to try to capture it.
2 to go where you are not supposed to go and make trouble. *The crowd **invaded** the football pitch.*
Word Building: invasion

invalid (in-va-lid) *noun* invalids
someone who is weak because they are ill or injured.

invent *verb* invents, inventing, invented
1 to be the first person to make or think of a new thing. *The telephone was **invented** by Alexander Graham Bell.*
2 to make something up. *He **invented** the whole story.*
Word Building: inventor

invertebrate (in-ver-te-bret) *noun* invertebrates
an animal that does not have a backbone.

investigate *verb* investigates, investigating, investigated
to try to find out as much as you can about something.

invisible *adjective*
not able to be seen. *The ghost was* ***invisible****.*

invitation *noun* invitations
words that ask you politely to come. *a party* ***invitation****.*

invite *verb* invites, inviting, invited
to ask someone politely to come or do something.

iron *noun* irons
1 a strong, heavy metal.
2 a flat piece of metal with a handle. It is heated and used for making clothes smooth and flat.

irrigate (ear-i-gate) *verb* irrigates, irrigating, irrigated
to supply land with water using channels or pipes.
Word Building: irrigation

irritable *adjective*
easily annoyed.

irritate *verb* irritates, irritating, irritated
to keep annoying someone. *Don't ask so many questions. It* ***irritates*** *me.*

is *verb* see be

Islam *noun*
the religion of Muslim people, started by a teacher called Muhammed. People who follow Islam call God Allah.
Word Building: Islamic

island (eye-land) *noun* islands
a piece of land with water all round it.

isle (ile) *noun* isles
an island.

isolate (eye-so-late) *verb* isolates, isolating, isolated
to keep something or someone apart from others. *We must* ***isolate*** *the plants which are diseased.*
Word Building: isolation

italics *noun*
sloping letters printed *like this.*

itch *verb* itches, itching, itched
to have a feeling in your skin that makes you want to scratch.

item *noun* items
any one thing in a list or group of things. *The first* ***item*** *on the shopping list is cheese.*

its *adjective*
belonging to it. *The dog chased* ***its*** *tail.*

it's
1 it is. *It's raining.*
2 it has. *I think* ***it's*** *stopped raining.*

itself *pronoun*
it and nothing else. *The bird was washing* ***itself****.*
by itself on its own. *The security light comes on* ***by itself*** *when it gets dark.*

ivy *noun* ivies
a climbing plant with shiny leaves.

A B C D E F G H I J K L M N O P Q R S T U V W X Y Z

Jj

jab *verb* jabs, jabbing, jabbed
to poke at someone or something roughly, often with something sharp. *She* ***jabbed*** *me in the ribs with her elbow.*

jack *noun* jacks
1 a tool for lifting up a car when you want to change a wheel.
2 the card between the ten and the queen in a pack of cards. *the* ***jack*** *of hearts.*

jacket *noun* jackets
a short coat.

jackpot *noun* jackpots
an amount of prize money that gets bigger until someone wins it.

jagged (jag-ed) *adjective*
with a sharp, uneven edge. ***jagged*** *rocks.*

jail *noun* jails
a prison.

jam *noun* jams
1 fruit boiled with sugar until it is thick. *raspberry* ***jam****.*
2 a lot of people or cars crowded together so that it is difficult to move. *a traffic* ***jam****.*

jam *verb* jams, jamming, jammed
to become stuck tight so that it is hard to move. *Our back door keeps getting* ***jammed****.*

January
the first month of the year.

jar *noun* jars
a container like the glass ones used for jam.

jaw *noun* jaws
1 the lower part of the face.
2 one of the bones that hold the teeth.

jazz *noun*
a kind of music first played and sung by African Americans.

jealous (jel-us) *adjective*
unhappy because someone else has more or does better than you. *I was very* ***jealous*** *of Ben's new bicycle.*
Word Building: jealousy, jealously

jeans *noun*
trousers usually made of strong blue cotton cloth.

jeep *noun* jeeps
a very strong, small car.

jeer *verb* jeers, jeering, jeered
to laugh at someone in a rude, scornful way.

jelly *noun* jellies
a sweet, slippery food that shakes when you move it.

jellyfish *noun* jellyfish
a sea animal that looks rather like jelly.

jerk *verb* jerks, jerking, jerked
to move suddenly or clumsily.

jet *noun* jets
1 a liquid or gas coming quickly out of a small opening. *A **jet** of water spurted out of the broken pipe.*
2 a fast aeroplane.

jetty *noun* jetties
a long stone or wooden wall that sticks out into a sea, bay, or river. You can tie boats to it.

Jew *noun* Jews
someone whose religion is Judaism.

jewel *noun* jewels
a valuable and beautiful stone. *Diamonds and rubies are **jewels**.*

jewellery (joo-el-ree) *noun*
necklaces, bracelets, rings, and brooches.

jigsaw *noun* jigsaws
1 a puzzle made up of many different pieces that fit together to make a picture.
2 a saw that can cut curved shapes.
Word Building: jigsaw puzzle

jingle *verb* jingles, jingling, jingled
to make the sound tiny bells make.

jingle *noun* jingles
a short song or poem with a simple rhyme.

job *noun* jobs
1 the work that a person does to earn money. *Sam has a **job** in the tradestore on weekends.*
2 a particular piece of work you have to do. *It's my **job** to wash up.*

jockey *noun* jockeys
someone who rides horses in races.

joey *noun* joeys
a young kangaroo or wallaby.

jog *verb* jogs, jogging, jogged
1 to run slowly.
2 to push against something. *He **jogged** my elbow and I spilled my drink.*

join *verb* joins, joining, joined
1 to put or fix two things together.
2 to become a member of a group. *I've **joined** a swimming club.*

joint *noun* joints
1 the place where two parts fit together. *The ankle is the **joint** between the foot and the leg.*
2 a large piece of meat. *a **joint** of pork.*

joke *noun* jokes
something you say or do to make people laugh.

joke *verb* jokes, joking, joked
to make jokes.
Word Building: joker, jokers

jolly *adjective* jollier, jolliest
happy and cheerful.

jolt *noun* jolts
a sudden movement. *The PMV started with a **jolt**.*

jolt *verb* jolts, jolting, jolted
to move or move something quickly and suddenly.

journey (jer-nee) *noun* journeys
the travelling people do to get from one place to another place. *We went on a **journey** around the coast of Manus.*

joy *noun*
happiness.

joyful *adjective*
happy, cheerful.
Word Building: joyfully

Judaism (Jew-day-izm) *noun*
the religion of the Jewish people, which teaches that there is only one God.

judge *noun* judges
a person who judges.

judge *verb* judges, judging, judged
1 to say whether someone is guilty or not guilty.
2 to say whether something is good or bad, right or wrong.

judo (jew-doe) *noun*
a Japanese method of wrestling and self-defence in which weapons are not used.

jug *noun* jugs
a container with a handle, used for holding and pouring water or other liquids. *a water **jug**.*

juggle *verb* juggles, juggling, juggled
to keep two or more things in the air by throwing and catching them quickly. *The clown **juggled** three balls.*

juice (joos) *noun* juices
the liquid in fruit and vegetables. *orange **juice**.*

July *noun*
the seventh month of the year.

jumble *noun*
a lot of different things all mixed up.

jumbo *adjective*
very large.
Word Building: jumbo jet

jump *verb* jumps, jumping, jumped
to move up suddenly from the ground into the air.

junction *noun* junctions
a place where roads or railway lines meet.

June *noun*
the sixth month of the year.

jungle *noun* jungles
a forest in a very hot, damp country.

junior (joon-yer) *adjective*
younger. *The boys in the **junior** team are all under 14.*

junk *noun*
1 useless things that people do not want any more.
2 a Chinese sailing boat.

junk food *noun*
unhealthy food usually containing a lot of sugar or salt and fat. *My favourite **junk** food is potato chips.*

jury (joo-ree) *noun* juries
a group of people in a law court who decide whether someone is guilty or innocent.
Word Building: juror
*Each person on a jury is called a **juror**.*

just *adjective*
right and fair, what the law says ought to happen. *a **just** punishment.*

just *adverb*
1 exactly. *It's **just** what I want.*
2 hardly. *I **just** caught the bus.*
3 recently. *She has **just** gone.*
4 only. *I'll **just** be a minute.*

kai or **kaikai** *noun*
1 food.
2 a meal. [from Tok Pisin *kaikai*]

kalabus *noun*
a prison. [from Tok Pisin *kalabus*]

kalamansi *noun*
a small tropical fruit with a sharp taste like a lemon or a lime.

kalang *noun*
1 an earring.
2 a gold-lipped shell.

kalapua *noun*
a cooked banana. [from Tok Pisin *kalapua*]

kambang *noun*
the lime used for chewing with betel nut. [from Tok Pisin *kambang*]

kanaka *noun* kanakas
an ignorant person. [from Tok Pisin *kanaka*]

kangaroo *noun* kangaroos
an animal with strong back legs for jumping. Female kangaroos have pouches in which they carry their babies.

kapkap *noun*
a circular ornament made from turtle shell, which is carved into an openwork pattern and fixed on to a white shell disc.

kapul *noun*
a possum, tree-kangaroo or cuscus. [from Tok Pisin *kapul*]

karate (ka-rot-ee) *noun*
a style of fighting originally from Japan. People do karate as a sport.

kaukau *noun*
the sweet potato. [from Tok Pisin *kaukau*]

kava *noun*
an alcoholic drink used in ritual ceremonies in Polynesia, Fiji, Vanuatu and parts of PNG.

kayak (ky-ak) *noun* kayaks
a small canoe with a cover to keep out water.

kebab *noun* kebabs
pieces of meat and other food cooked on a long spike called a skewer.

keel *noun* keels
the long piece of wood or metal along the bottom of a boat that holds it together.

keen *adjective* keener, keenest
1 sharp or strong. *Dogs have a* ***keen*** *sense of smell.*
2 very interested in something. *Sam is* ***keen*** *on pop music.*

keep *verb* keeps, keeping, kept
1 to have something as your own and not get rid of it. *He **kept** the money he found.*
2 to make something stay as it is. *Try to **keep** your clothes clean.*
3 to look after something. *She **keeps** chickens.*

kennel *noun* kennels
a little hut for keeping a dog in.

kerb *noun* kerbs
the line of concrete or stone along the edge of the pavement.

kernel *noun* kernels
1 the part inside the shell of a nut that you can eat.
2 a grain or seed without its covering.

kerosene *noun*
a liquid made from oil, that is burnt to make heat.

kettle *noun* kettles
a container made to boil water in.

key *noun* keys
1 a piece of metal shaped so that it fits into a lock.
2 a small lever pressed with the finger. Pianos, typewriters, and computers have keys.

keyboard *noun* keyboards
1 a set of keys arranged in rows, like those on a piano or computer.
2 an electronic musical instrument with a keyboard like the one on a piano.

kiap *noun*
a patrol officer, government officer or district officer. [from Tok Pisin *kiap*]

kick *verb* kicks, kicking, kicked
to hit with your foot.

kid *noun* kids
1 a young goat.
2 (*informal*) a child.

kid *verb* kids, kidding, kidded
to tease someone, especially by telling funny, false stories.

kidnap *verb* kidnaps, kidnapping, kidnapped
to take someone away and keep them prisoner until you get what you want.

kill *verb* kills, killing, killed
to cause the death of someone or something.
Word Building: killer, killers

kilogram (kil-o-gram) *noun* kilograms
a measure of weight.
One kilogram = 1000 grams.

kilometre (kil-o-mee-ter or ki-**lom**-e-ter) *noun* kilometres
a measure of length.
One kilometre = 1000 metres.

kina *noun*
1 the currency of PNG.
2 a gold-lipped pearl shell used as money before colonial times. [from Tok Pisin *kina*]

kind *adjective* kinder, kindest
friendly, ready to help other people.

kind *noun* kinds
a sort, a type. *A terrier is a **kind** of dog.*

kindam *noun*
a prawn or a lobster. [from Tok Pisin *kindam*]

king *noun* kings
a man who has been crowned as ruler of a country.

kingdom *noun* kingdoms
a land that is ruled by a king or queen.

kingfisher *noun* kingfishers
a bright blue bird that lives near water and catches fish.

kiss *verb* kisses, kissing, kissed
to touch someone with your lips because you are fond of them.

kitchen *noun* kitchens
the room where food is cooked.

kite *noun* kites
a light frame covered in cloth or paper and flown in the wind at the end of a long piece of string.

kitten *noun* kittens
a very young cat.

kiwi *noun* kiwi
a brown New Zealand bird that cannot fly. It has a long bill and no tail, and feeds at night.

kiwifruit *noun* kiwifruit
a hairy brown fruit with green flesh that is grown in New Zealand.

klinki pine *noun*
a type of tree grown widely in PNG for its timber.

knead (need) *verb* kneads, kneading, kneaded
to press and stretch something soft, like bread dough, with your hands.

knee *noun* knees
the bony part in the middle of the leg where it bends.

kneel *verb* kneels, kneeling, kneeled
to get down on your knees.

knew *verb* see know

knickers (nik-ers) *noun*
underpants worn by women and girls.

knife (nife) *noun* knives
a tool with a long, sharp edge for cutting things.

knight (nite) *noun* knights
1 a man who has been given the title Sir. *Sir Michael Somare is a* ***knight****.*
2 a man in armour who rode into battle on a horse.

knit (nit) *verb* knits, knitting, knitted
to use wool and a pair of long needles to make clothes.

knob (nob) *noun* knobs
the round handle on a door or drawer.

knock *verb* knocks, knocking, knocked
to hit something hard.
to knock someone out to make them unconscious by hitting them.

knot (not) *noun* knots
the twisted part where pieces of string, rope, cotton, or ribbon have been tied together.

know (no) *verb* knows, knowing, knew, known
1 to have something in your mind. *Maru* ***knows*** *the names of all the football teams.*
2 to be able to remember or recognise someone or something. *I don't* ***know*** *that girl. Who is she?*

knowledge (naw-lej) *noun*
things that you know and understand. *He has a lot of* ***knowledge*** *about animals.*

knuckle (nuk-kl) *noun* knuckles
one of the places where the fingers bend.

kuka *noun*
a crab. [from Tok Pisin *kuka*]

kula *noun*
an annual ceremonial exchange of gifts between islands in the Milne Bay province.

kulau *noun*
1 a green coconut that has liquid which is good for drinking.
2 the liquid itself. [from Tok Pisin *kulau*]

kumu *noun*
any green leaves which are good to eat. [from Tok Pisin *kumu*]

kumul *noun*
a bird of paradise. [from Tok Pisin *kumul*]

kunai *noun*
a tall, long-bladed grass. [from Tok Pisin *kunai*]

kundu *noun*
a drum which is narrower in the middle than at each end and has skin stretched over one end only. [from Tok Pisin *kundu*]

kuru *noun*
laughing sickness; a disease found only in PNG.

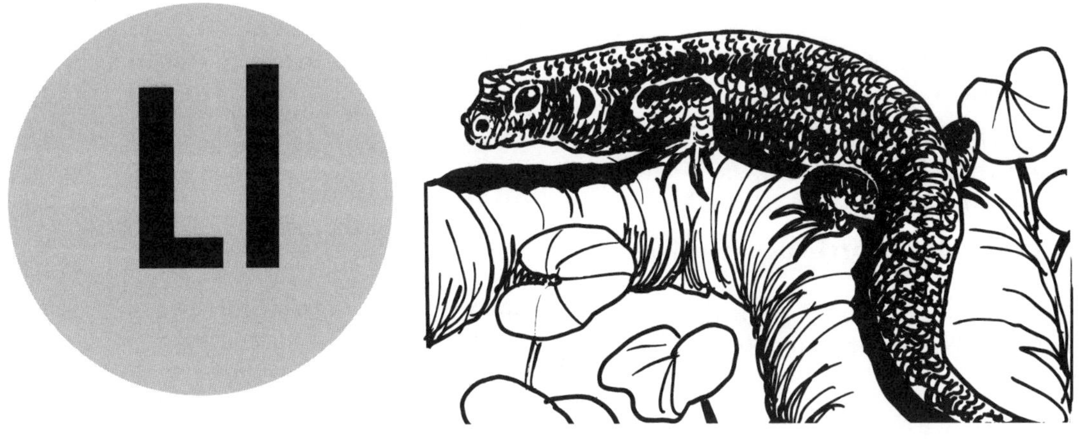

label *noun* labels
a piece of material, card, or sticky paper put on something to show what it is, whose it is, or where it is going.

laboratory (la-**bor**-ra-tree) *noun* laboratories
a room or building where scientific work is done.

labour *noun*
1 hard work.
2 the time when a woman is giving birth to a baby.

lace *noun* laces
1 thin, pretty material with a pattern of holes in it. *a lace collar.*
2 a piece of thin cord used to tie up a shoe.

lack *verb* lacks, lacking, lacked
to be without something. *The team lacked a good goalkicker.*

ladder *noun* ladders
two long bars with short bars between them (called rungs) that you can climb up or down.

ladle *noun* ladles
a big, deep spoon used for serving soup.

lady *noun* ladies
a polite name for a woman.

lagatoi or **lakatoi** *noun*
a large sailing boat, made from several dugout canoes tied together, used during hiri voyages. [from Motu *lakatoi*]

Lahara *noun*
1 the season when winds blow from the north-west.
2 winds which blow from the north-west.

laid *verb* see **lay**

lain *verb* see **lie** *verb*

lair (rhymes with *hair*) *noun* lairs
a wild animal's home.

lake *noun* lakes
a large area of water with land all around it.

lamb *noun* lambs
a young sheep.

lame *adjective*
not able to walk properly. *The horse is lame.*

lamington (**lam**-ing-tun) *noun* lamingtons
a square of sponge cake covered with chocolate icing and coconut.

lamp *noun* lamps
something that gives light where you want it. *a desk lamp.*

land *noun* lands
1 the dry part of the earth's surface.
2 a country. *foreign **lands**.*

land *verb* lands, landing, landed
to arrive by boat or aeroplane. *The plane **landed** at Mendi airport.*

landlady, landlord *noun* landladies, landlords
the owner of a house or flat that someone pays rent to live in.

lane *noun* lanes
1 a narrow road.
2 a strip of road for one line of traffic. *Some motorways have six **lanes**.*

language (lang-gwij) *noun* languages
words spoken or written by people. *foreign **languages**.*

lantern *noun* lanterns
a container for a light, which the light can shine through without being blown out by the wind.

lap *noun* laps
1 the level place you make with the top of your legs when you sit down. *The baby sat on my **lap**.*
2 one time around a race course or swimming pool.

lap *verb* laps, lapping, lapped
to drink with the tongue, as a cat does. *The cat **lapped** up all the milk.*

laplap *noun*
a piece of cloth worn by men and women tied loosely around the waist like a skirt. [from Tok Pisin *laplap*]

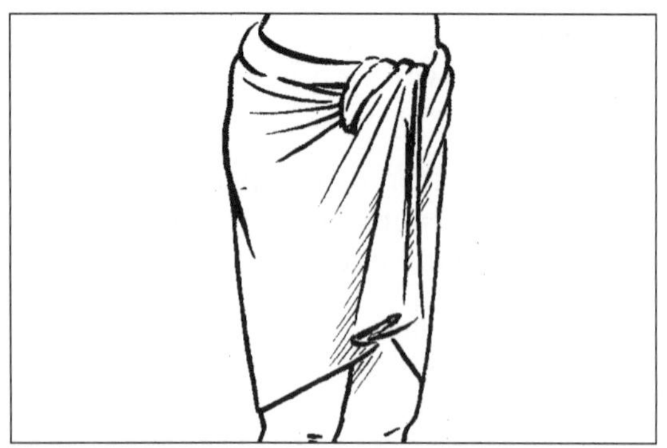

lapun *noun*
an old person. [from Tok Pisin *lapun*]

large *adjective* larger, largest
big; more than average in size.

larva *noun* larvae
an insect in the first stage of its life after it comes out of the egg.

lash *verb* lashes, lashing, lashed
1 to tie tightly to something.
2 to hit hard, as if with a whip. *The rain **lashed** against the window.*

lasso *noun* lassoes
a long rope with a loop at the end, tied so that the loop can get bigger or smaller. *Cowboys use **lassoes** for catching cattle.*

last *adjective*
coming after all the others. *Will the **last** person close the door?*

last *verb* lasts, lasting, lasted
to go on, to continue. *The movie **lasted** two hours.*

latch *noun* latches
a fastener on a gate or door.

late *adjective* later, latest
1 after the expected time. *The plane was **late**.*
2 near the end of a day, month, or year. *We arrived **late** afternoon.*

lately *adverb*
not long ago, recently. *Have you seen Kila **lately**?*

laugh (laf) *verb* laughs, laughing, laughed
to make sounds that show that you are happy or think something is funny.

laughter (laf-ter) *noun*
the sound of laughing.

laulau *noun*
a small red fruit which is good to eat, a Malay apple. [from Tok Pisin *laulau*]

launch *noun* launches
a large boat with an engine.

launch *verb* launches, launching, launched
1 to put a boat into the water.
2 to send off a rocket or spaceship.

laundry *noun* laundries
1 clothes that need to be washed.
2 a room or place where dirty clothes and sheets are washed.

Laurabada *noun*
winds which blow from the south-east.

lava *noun*
very hot, melted rock that flows out of a volcano.

law *noun* laws
a rule or set of rules that everyone in a country must keep.

lawn *noun* lawns
the part of a garden that is covered with short grass.

lawyer *noun* lawyers
a person who helps people with the law or argues for them in court.

lay *verb* lays, laying, laid
1 to put something down. *I **laid** the papers out on the desk.*
2 to produce an egg. *Hens **lay** eggs.*

layer *noun* layers
something flat that lies over or under another surface. *a **layer** of dust on the floor.*

lazy *adjective* lazier, laziest
a person who is lazy does not want to work.
Word Building: lazily

lead (rhymes with *bed*) *noun*
a very heavy, grey metal.

lead (rhymes with *seed*) *noun* leads
a strap you fasten to a dog's collar so that you can control it.

lead (rhymes with *seed*) *verb* leads, leading, led
1 to go in front. *You **lead** and we'll follow you.*
2 to be in charge of other people. *The captain **led** her team with great skill.*
Word Building: leader, leaders

leaf *noun* leaves
one of the flat green parts that grow on trees and other plants.

league (leeg) *noun* leagues
a group of teams that play matches against each other.

leak *verb* leaks, leaking, leaked
to have a hole or crack that liquid or gas can get through. *The bottle is **leaking**.*

lean *adjective* leaner, leanest
not fat. ***lean** meat.*

lean *verb* leans, leaning, leaned or leant
1 to bend your body towards something. *I **leaned** forward.*
2 to rest against something. ***Lean** against me if you are tired.*
3 to make something slope. ***Lean** your ladder against the wall.*

leap *verb* leaps, leaping, leaped or leapt
to jump. *They **leaped** into the swimming pool.*

leap year *noun* leap years
a year when February has 29 days. A leap year comes every four years.

learn *verb* learns, learning, learned or learnt
1 to find out about something. *We're **learning** about our culture.*
2 to find out how to do something. *I **learned** to swim last year.*

least *adjective, adverb, pronoun*
less than all the others, the smallest in amount. *It was the **least** expensive coat in the shop. Mandy has lots of money, Sam has less and Julie has the **least**.*

leather (le*th*-er) *noun*
a strong material made from the skins of animals.

A B C D E F G H I J K L M N O P Q R S T U V W X Y Z

leave *verb* leaves, leaving, left
1 to go from a person or place. *What time do you **leave** for school?*
2 to let something stay where it is. ***Leave** your books on the table near the door.*

lecture *noun* lectures
a talk to an audience by a teacher or an expert.

led *verb* see lead *verb*

ledge *noun* ledges
a narrow shelf like the one that sticks out under a window.

left *verb* see leave

left *adjective, adverb*
on the side opposite the right.

left-handed *adjective*
If you are left-handed you use the left hand to write and do other important things.

leg *noun* legs
1 one of the parts of the body an animal uses to stand, walk, and run.
2 one of the upright pieces that support a table or chair.

legal (lee-gl) *adjective*
allowed by the law. *It is not **legal** to steal.*
Word Building: legally

legend *noun* legends
an old story handed down from the past.

leisure (lezh-yer) *noun*
time when you can do what you want because you do not have to work.

lemon *noun* lemons
a yellow fruit with a sour taste.

lemonade *noun*
a clear fizzy drink with lemon flavour.

lend *verb* lends, lending, lent
to let someone have something of yours for a short time. *Torot **lent** me his bike yesterday.*

length *noun* lengths
how long something is.

lens *noun* lenses
a curved piece of glass or plastic that makes light go where it is needed. *Glasses, cameras, and telescopes have **lenses**.*

leopard (lep-ard) *noun* leopards
a big, wild cat found in Africa and Asia. It has yellow fur with black spots on it.

less *adjective*
smaller in amount. *Please make **less** noise.*

lessen *verb* lessens, lessening, lessened
to become less or to make something less. *The medicine will help to **lessen** the pain.*

lesson *noun* lessons
1 the time when someone is teaching you. *a maths **lesson**.*
2 something that you have to learn. *Road safety is an important **lesson** for everyone.*

let *verb* lets, letting, let
1 to allow someone to do something. *Sam **let** me ride his bike.*
2 to allow someone to use a house or building if they pay money. *She **lets** her house at the beach to people on holiday.*

letter *noun* letters
1 one of the signs used for writing words, such as a, b, or c.
2 a written message sent to another person.

lettuce *noun* lettuces
a vegetable with large green leaves that you usually eat uncooked.

level (lev-l) *adjective*
1 flat and smooth. ***level** ground.*
2 equal. *The two teams are **level** with 10 points each.*

lever (lee-ver) *noun* levers
a bar that is pulled down to lift something heavy or make a machine work.

liar *noun* liars
someone who tells lies.

library (lie-bre-ree) *noun* libraries
a building or room where a lot of books are kept for people to use.

lice *noun* see **louse**

licence *noun* licences
a printed paper that says that you can do, own, or use something.

lick *verb* licks, licking, licked
to move your tongue over something.

lid *noun* lids
a cover for a box or jar.

lie *noun* lies
something you say that you know is not true. *Don't tell **lies**.*

lie *verb* lies, lying, lied
to say something that you know is not true.

lie *verb* lies, lying, lay, lain
1 to rest with your body flat, as it is in bed. *We **lay** on the bed and went to sleep.*
2 to be or stay on something. *Leaves **lay** on the ground.*

life *noun* lives
being alive, the time between birth and death. *The doctor saved her **life**.*

lifelike *adjective*
looking like a real person. *The wax models were very **lifelike**.*

lifetime *noun*
all the time that you are alive. *There have been a lot of changes in my bubu's **lifetime**.*

lift *noun* lifts
1 a machine for taking people or things up and down inside a building.
2 a free ride in someone's car.

lift *verb* lifts, lifting, lifted
1 to move something up to a higher level. ***Lift** the box onto the shelf.*
2 to pick up. *Dobi **lifted** the baby up onto her lap.*

light (lite) *adjective* lighter, lightest
1 not heavy, not weighing a lot. *a **light** suitcase.*
2 not dark, with plenty of light. *a **light** room.*
3 pale. ***light** colours.*

light (lite) *noun* lights
1 what you need to be able to see things. Light comes from the sun, the stars, fires, and lamps.
2 any device which provides light. *electric **lights**.*

light (lite) *verb* lights, lighting, lit
1 to provide light so that you can see something. *At Christmas they **lit** the church with candles.*
2 to start something burning. *We tried to **light** the fire.*

light-hearted *adjective*
cheerful, not worried.

lightning *noun*
the bright light that flashes in the sky in a thunderstorm.

like *preposition, conjunction*
nearly the same as another person or thing. *Teresa looks **like** her mother.*

like *verb* likes, liking, liked
to think someone or something is nice. *Do you **like** ice cream?*

likely *adjective* likelier, likeliest
probable, expected to happen or to be true. *It is **likely** to rain.*

limb (lim) ***noun*** limbs
a leg, arm, or wing.

lime pot ***noun*** lime pots
a container for storing lime to be chewed with betel nut.

limit ***noun*** limits
a line or point that people cannot or should not pass. *a speed **limit**.*

limp ***adjective*** limper, limpest
not stiff; drooping. *The cardboard went **limp** when it got wet.*

limp ***verb*** limps, limping, limped
to walk with difficulty because you have hurt your leg or foot.

line ***noun*** lines
1 a long mark like this ____ .
2 a row of people or things.
3 all the words that are beside each other on a page. *I don't know the next **line** of the poem.*

linen (lin-en) ***noun***
strong cloth used for making sheets and tablecloths.

linger ***verb*** lingers, lingering, lingered
to be slow to leave. *Don't **linger** in the playground after school.*

lining ***noun*** linings
a layer you put inside something to make it thicker or to protect it.

link ***noun*** links
one of the rings in a chain.

link ***verb*** links, linking, linked
to join things together.

lion ***noun*** lions
a large, light brown wild cat found in Africa and India.

lioness ***noun*** lionesses
a female lion.

lip ***noun*** lips
one of the parts of your face which make the top and bottom edges of your mouth.

lipstick ***noun*** lipsticks
colour that can be put on your lips.

liquid (lik-wid) ***noun*** liquids
anything that is like water or oil.

list ***noun*** lists
a group of things or names written down one after the other.

listen (lis-sn) ***verb*** listens, listening, listened
to pay attention in order to hear something.

lit ***verb*** see **light** ***verb***

literature (lit-ra-cher) ***noun***
books, plays, and poetry.

litre (lee-ter) ***noun*** litres
a measure for liquid. *a **litre** of paint.*

litter ***noun*** litters
1 paper, empty packets, bottles, and other rubbish, dropped or left lying about.
2 all the young animals born to the same mother at the same time.

little ***adjective*** littler, littlest
1 not big. *a **little** village.*
2 not much. *I've got very **little** money.*

live (rhymes with *dive*) ***adjective***
alive, living. ***live** animals in a cage.*

live (liv) ***verb*** lives, living, lived
1 to be alive, so that you can feed and develop as animals and plants should do.
2 to have your home somewhere.

lively ***adjective*** livelier, liveliest
full of life and energy. *a **lively** kitten.*

livestock ***noun***
farm animals.

living ***adjective***
being alive. *The children looked in the pond for **living** creatures.*

lizard (liz-erd) ***noun*** lizards
a reptile with skin like a snake and four legs.

load *noun* loads
things that you carry or deal with at one time. *The truck brought another* ***load*** *of sand. He was carrying* ***loads*** *of books.*

load *verb* loads, loading, loaded
1 to put things on to something that will carry them. ***Load*** *the suitcases into the car boot.*
2 to put bullets into a gun. ***Load*** *the gun.*
3 to put film into a camera.

loaf *noun* loaves
bread in the shape it was baked in.

loan *noun* loans
anything that is lent to someone.

local *adjective*
of a place near you. *We go to the* ***local*** *school.*

lock *noun* locks
1 a fastening for a door, gate, or box which is opened with a key.
2 a piece of hair.

lock *verb* locks, locking, locked
to fasten with a key.

locust (lo-kust) *noun* locusts
a kind of grasshopper that flies in a large group and eats all the plants in an area.

logic (loj-ik) *noun*
the study of correct reasoning patterns.

logical (loj-i-kl) *adjective*
sensible, reasonable.

loiter *verb* loiters, loitering, loitered
to stand about with nothing to do.

lonely *adjective* lonelier, loneliest
1 sad because you are on your own.
2 far from others. *a* ***lonely*** *house.*

long *adjective* longer, longest
1 measuring a lot from one end to the other. *a* ***long*** *road.*
2 taking a lot of time. *a* ***long*** *holiday.*

long *verb* longs, longing, longed
to want something which you have to wait for. *I* ***longed*** *for a drink.*

long house *noun*
a large communal house built in some villages.

longlong *adjective*
crazy, insane. [from Tok Pisin *longlong*]

look *verb* looks, looking, looked
1 to use your eyes, to turn your eyes towards something.
2 to seem. *The dog* ***looks*** *friendly.*
to look after to take care of someone or something. *My sister will* ***look after*** *our dog when we go on holidays.*
to look for to try to find something.

loom *noun* looms
a machine for weaving cloth.

loom *verb* looms, looming, loomed
to appear large and frightening.

loop *noun* loops
a ring made in rope, wire, thread, or ribbon.

loose *adjective* looser, loosest
1 not tight. *My tooth is* ***loose.***
2 free, not fixed or tied up. *The animals were all* ***loose.***

loosen *verb* loosens, loosening, loosened
1 to make looser. *He* ***loosened*** *his collar.*
2 to get looser.

lord *noun* lords
a nobleman.

lorikeet *noun* lorikeets
a small, brightly coloured parrot.

lose (looz) *verb* loses, losing, lost
1 to be without something because you cannot find it. *I've **lost** my coat.*
2 to be without something you once had. *He's **lost** one of his front teeth.*
3 to be beaten in a game. *Our team **lost** the match.*

lost *adjective*
not able to find the right way. *Don't get **lost**!*

lot *noun* lots
a large number, a large amount. *We ate a **lot** of mangoes.*
the lot everything. *We were so hungry that we ate **the lot**.*

lotion (lo-shun) *noun* lotions
a liquid that is put on the skin.

loud *adjective* louder, loudest
easy to hear, making a lot of noise.

lounge (lownj) *noun* lounges
a room where you can relax.

lounge (lownj) *verb* lounges, lounging, lounged
to stand, sit or move lazily.

louse *noun* lice
a small insect that lives on animals. It sucks the blood of animals or the juices of plants, and it lays eggs called nits.

love (luv) *noun*
the strong feeling you have when you like someone very much.

love (luv) *verb* loves, loving, loved
1 to feel love for someone.
2 to like something. *I **love** watching films.*

lovely (luv-lee) *adjective* lovelier, loveliest
1 beautiful.
2 pleasing. *a **lovely** idea.*

low *adjective* lower, lowest
not high.

lower (lo-er) *verb* lowers, lowering, lowered
to bring something down. *He **lowered** the flag.*

loyal *adjective*
always doing your duty; faithful to someone.

luck *noun*
things that happen that you have not planned.

lucky *adjective* luckier, luckiest
having good luck. *The dog ran across the road and was **lucky** not to be hit by a car.*
Word Building: luckily

luggage (lug-ij) *noun*
bags, boxes, and suitcases taken by someone on a journey.

lukewarm *adjective*
only slightly warm. ***lukewarm** water.*

lullaby (lul-a-by) *noun* lullabies
a song that is sung to send a baby to sleep.

luluai *noun*
a village or tribal chief appointed by the government in colonial times. [from Tok Pisin *luluai*]

lump *noun* lumps
1 a solid thing with no clear shape. *a **lump** of clay.*
2 a swelling. *I've got a **lump** on my head where I hit it when I fell.*

lunar (loo-nar) *adjective*
to do with the moon. *A **lunar** eclipse happened last week.*

lunch *noun* lunches
a meal eaten in the middle of the day.

lung *noun* lungs
one of the two parts inside the body used for breathing.

lurch *verb* lurches, lurching, lurched
to lean suddenly to one side. *The PMV **lurched** and the passengers were thrown about.*

lure *verb* lures, luring, lured
to tempt someone into a trap.

luxury (luck-sha-ree) ***noun*** luxuries
something expensive that you like very much but do not really need.

lying *verb* see lie

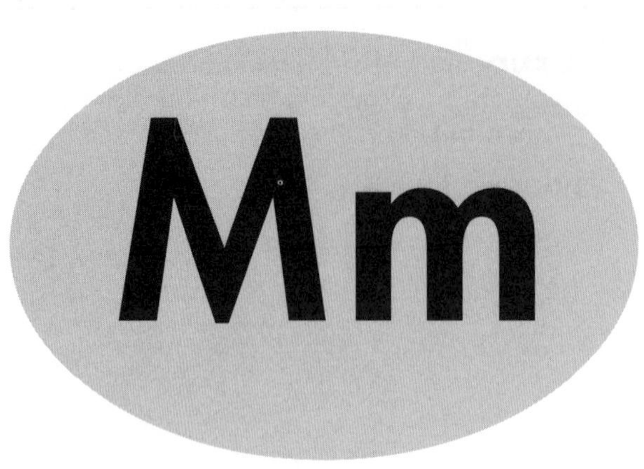

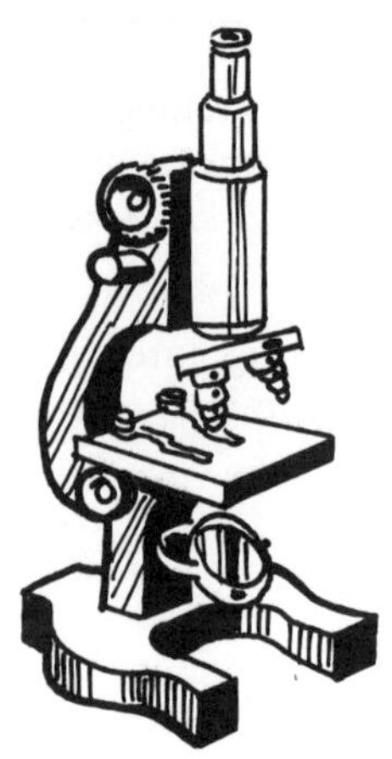

machine (ma-**sheen**) *noun* machines
a thing with several parts that work together to do a job or to make something. *a washing **machine**.*

machine-gun *noun* machine-guns
a gun that can keep firing very quickly for a long time.

machinery (ma-**sheen**-a-ree) *noun*
1 the parts of a machine. *the **machinery** inside a clock.*
2 a group of machines. *The factory has bought some new **machinery**.*

mad *adjective* madder, maddest
1 ill in the mind.
2 very silly.
3 very angry.

made *verb* see **make**

magani *noun*
a small kangaroo; a wallaby. [from Motu *magani*]

magazine *noun* magazines
a thin book that comes out every week or month with different stories and pictures in it.

maggot *noun* maggots
a tiny worm that comes from an egg laid by a fly.

magic (**maj**-ik) *noun*
the power to do wonderful things or clever tricks that people cannot usually do.
Word Building: magical, magically

magician (ma-**jish**-in) *noun* magicians
1 a person in stories who knows a lot about magic and uses it.
2 a person who does magic tricks to amuse people.

magnet *noun* magnets
a piece of metal that can make pieces of iron or steel come and stick to it.

magnificent *adjective*
very good or beautiful. *a **magnificent** palace.*

magnify (**mag**-ni-fy) *verb* magnifies, magnifying, magnified
to make something look bigger. *We **magnified** the insect under the microscope.*

mail *noun*
letters, cards, and parcels sent through the post.

main *adjective*
the most important. *a **main** road.*

mainly *adverb*
almost completely, most of all.

maize *noun*
a tall kind of corn with large seeds.

major (may-jer) *adjective*
great; larger; more important. *Doing our work neatly was of **major** importance to the teacher.*

major (may-jer) *noun* majors
an important army officer.

majority (ma-jor-i-tee) *noun* majorities
most of a group; the largest number. *The **majority** of my friends play netball.*

makau *noun* makaus
a small freshwater fish found in the Sepik River which is good to eat fresh or smoked. [from Tok Pisin *makau*]

make *verb* makes, making, made
1 to get something new by putting other things together. *Edoa **made** a dress.*
2 to cause something to happen. *The balloon **made** a loud bang when it burst.*
3 to force someone to do something. *Mother **made** me tidy up my room.*

make-up *noun*
cream, lipstick, and powder that can be put on your face to make it look beautiful. *Actors wear **make-up** to make them look different.*

male *noun* males
a person or animal of the sex that can become a father.

mall *noun* malls
1 an area without traffic where people can walk and shop.
2 a shopping centre.

mammal *noun* mammals
any animal that has hair and can feed its babies with its own milk. Whales, lions, and people are all mammals.

man *noun* men
a grown-up male human being.

manage *verb* manages, managing, managed
1 to be in charge of a shop or factory.
2 to be able to do something although it is difficult. *The box was heavy but she **managed** to carry it.*

mane *noun* manes
the long hair along a horse's back or on a lion's head and neck.

mangle *verb* mangles, mangling, mangled
to crush or cut up badly.

mango *noun* mangoes or mangos
a sweet, yellowish, tropical fruit.

manioc *noun*
tapioca; cassava. [from Tok Pisin *manioc*]

manner *noun*
the way something happens or is done.

manners *noun*
the way you behave when you are with other people. *It's bad **manners** to talk with your mouth full.*

manoeuvre (ma-noo-ver) *noun* manoeuvres
a planned and controlled move. *That was a very clever **manoeuvre** on the part of the general.*

manoeuvre (ma-noo-ver) *verb* manoeuvres, manoeuvring, manoeuvred
to make a planned and controlled move. *She **manoeuvred** the car into a tight parking space.*

mantelpiece *noun* mantelpieces
the shelf above a fireplace.

manual (man-yoo-al) *adjective*
done with the hands. *The car had **manual** controls.*

manual (man-yoo-al) *noun* manuals
a handbook. *Read the **manual** carefully before you start to put the model together.*

manufacture *verb* manufactures, manufacturing, manufactured
to make things in a factory with machines.

manure *noun*
waste matter from animals' bodies used to fertilise the ground.

many *adjective, pronoun*
a large number of people or things.

Māori *noun* Māori
a person whose ancestors were the first race to live in New Zealand.

map *noun* maps
a drawing of a town, a country, or the world. Maps show you where roads, mountains, and rivers are.

marathon *noun* marathons
a running race which goes on for about 42 kilometres.

marble *noun* marbles
1 a small, glass ball used in some games.
2 a kind of smooth stone used for building or making statues.

March *noun*
the third month of the year.

march *verb* marches, marching, marched
to walk like soldiers on parade.

mare *noun* mares
a female horse.

margarine (mar-jo-reen) *noun*
a food that looks and tastes like butter, but is not made from milk.

margin (mar-jin) *noun* margins
the empty space between the edge of a page and the writing or pictures.

marita *noun*
a type of pandanus which bears a fruit that is good to eat. [from Tok Pisin *marita*]

mark *noun* marks
1 a stain, spot, or line that spoils something. *dirty **marks** on the wall.*
2 a sign or number put on a piece of work to show how good it is.

mark *verb* marks, marking, marked
to put marks on something.

market *noun* markets
a group of stalls selling food and other things.

marmalade *noun*
jam made from oranges, grapefruit, or lemons.

maroon *verb* maroons, marooning, marooned
to leave someone in a wild and lonely place without any way of escaping from it. *He was **marooned** on the island after the storm.*

marriage (mair-ij) *noun* marriages
1 a wedding.
2 the state of being married. *They had a long and happy **marriage**.*

marry *verb* marries, marrying, married
to become someone's husband or wife. *Boroma and Mairi got **married** last Saturday.*

marsh *noun* marshes
a piece of very wet ground.

marsupial (mar-soo-pee-al) *noun* marsupials
an animal such as a tree kangaroo or magani that carries its young in a pouch for a time after birth.

marvellous *adjective*
wonderful.
Word Building: marvellously

masculine (mas-kew-lin) *adjective*
belonging to men, like men, suitable for men.

mash *verb* mashes, mashing, mashed
to crush something to make it soft and get rid of the lumps. ***mashed** potato.*

mask *noun* masks
a covering worn on the face to protect or hide it.

maski *interjection*
it doesn't matter; forget it; leave it alone; never mind. [from Tok Pisin *maski*]

mass *noun* masses
1 a large number or amount. ***masses** of flowers.*
2 a Roman Catholic church service.

massive *adjective*
very big. *a **massive** rock.*

mast *noun* masts
a tall pole that holds up a ship's sails, a flag, or an aerial.

masta *noun*
a white man. Commonly used in colonial times in PNG. [from Tok Pisin *masta*]

master *noun* masters
a person who is in control of people or animals. *The dog ran to its **master**.*

mat *noun* mats
a small piece of carpet or other material put on the floor.

match *noun* matches
1 a small, thin stick that gives a flame when rubbed on something rough.
2 a game played between two sides. *a football **match**.*

match *verb* matches, matching, matched
to look the same as something else. *In some card games you have to find the pictures which **match**.*

mate *noun* mates
1 one of a pair of birds or animals that have come together to produce young ones.
2 (*informal*) a friend.

mate *verb* mates, mating, mated
to come together as a pair so that the female can produce young ones.

material (ma-teer-ree-al) *noun* materials
1 something that you use to make other things. *Wood and bricks are building **materials**.*
2 cloth, anything that is woven and used to make things like clothes or curtains.

maternity (ma-ter-na-tee) *noun*
the state of being a mother.
maternity ward part of a hospital where a woman may go when it is time for her baby to be born.

mathematics, maths *noun*
the study of numbers, measurement, and shapes.

matter *noun* matters
1 a substance or material. *waste **matter**.*
2 something you need to do or to think about. *There is an important **matter** we have to talk about.*
What's the matter? What is wrong?

matter *verb* matters, mattering, mattered
to be important. *It doesn't **matter** if you are a bit late.*

mattress *noun* mattresses
the thick, soft part of a bed.

maul *verb* mauls, mauling, mauled
to treat roughly or injure something or someone by rough handling.

mauswara *verb*
to talk nonsense.
Word building: mauswara man or mauswara meri, a joker. [from Tok Pisin *mauswara*]

May *noun*
the fifth month of the year.

may *verb* might
1 can. ***May** I go out to play?*
2 will perhaps. *It **might** rain later.*

mayor *noun* mayors
the person in charge of the council in a town or city.

maze *noun* mazes
a set of lines or paths that twist and turn so much that it is very easy to lose the way. *a **maze** of winding streets.*

meal *noun* meals
the food you eat at breakfast, lunch, or dinner.

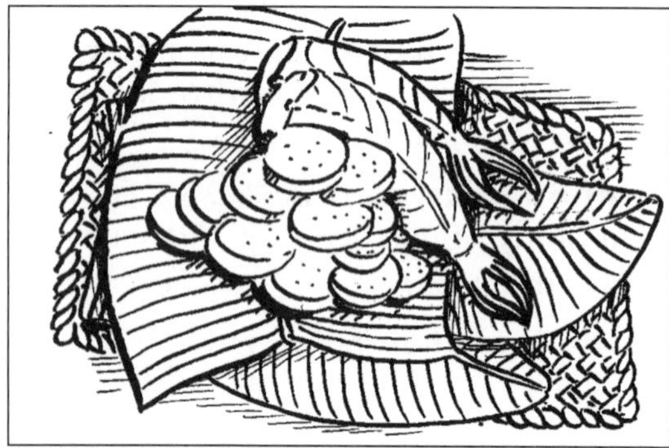

mean *adjective* meaner, meanest
not ready to give or share things.

mean *verb* means, meaning, meant
1 to plan in your mind. *I **meant** to tell him, but I forgot.*
2 to have a meaning. *This dictionary tells you what words **mean**.*

meaning *noun* meanings
the meaning of the words you use is what you want other people to know when they hear or read those words. *If you don't know the **meaning** of a word, look it up in the dictionary.*

meanwhile *adverb*
during the time something else is happening. *You clean the table. **Meanwhile** I'll prepare the lunch.*

measles (mee-zuls) *noun*
an illness that makes red spots appear on the skin.

measure (mezh-er) *noun* measures
a unit used for measuring. *Kilograms and grams are **measures** for weight.*

measure (mezh-er) *verb* measures, measuring, measured
1 to find out the size or amount of something. *I **measured** the box with a ruler.*
2 to be a certain size or amount. *This room **measures** 4 metres across.*

measurement (mezh-er-ment) *noun* measurements
how much something measures. *What are the **measurements** of this table?*

meat *noun* meats
the flesh of animals used as food.

mechanic (ma-kan-ik) *noun* mechanics
a person who works with or repairs machines. *a car **mechanic**.*

mechanical (ma-kan-i-kl) *adjective*
done or made by machinery. *They used a **mechanical** digger to make a ditch.*

medal (med-l) *noun* medals
a piece of metal in the shape of a coin, star, or cross given to someone very brave or very good at something. *She won a gold **medal** at the South Pacific Games.*

medallist (med-a-list) *noun* medallists
someone who has won a medal. *an Olympic gold **medallist**.*

meddle *verb* meddles, meddling, meddled
to take part in something or touch something that has nothing to do with you. *Don't **meddle** with the papers on my desk.*

media (mee-dee-ya) *plural noun*
the ways in which news and entertainment are passed on to everyone, such as TV, radio, and newspapers.

medicine (med-i-sin) ***noun*** medicines
liquid or tablets that a sick person has to swallow in order to get better again.
Word Building: medical
*Tau is a **medical** orderly in our village aidpost.*

medium (mee-dee-um) ***adjective***
of middle size.

meek ***adjective*** meeker, meekest
gentle and not proud.
Word Building: meekly

meet ***verb*** meets, meeting, met
1 to come together with someone.
*Let's **meet** at the river at two o'clock.*
2 to see someone for the first time.
*Have you **met** Nora?*
3 to join together with something.
*Our house is on the corner where the two roads **meet**.*

meeting ***noun*** meetings
a group of people who have come together to talk about something or to listen to someone.

Melanesia ***noun***
The south-western Pacific including PNG.
Word building: Melanesian, a native of Melanesia.

melody (mel-o-dee) ***noun*** melodies
music that makes a pattern or tune.

melon (mel-un) ***noun*** melons
a large, juicy fruit with a yellow or green skin.

melt ***verb*** melts, melting, melted
to change to a liquid when made warmer. *Ice **melts** if you take it out of the fridge.*

member ***noun*** members
someone who belongs to a club or group. ***member** of parliament.*

memorial ***noun*** memorials
something made in memory of an important person or event. *The people built a **memorial** to remember the soldiers who fought in the war.*

memory (mem-o-ree) ***noun*** memories
1 the power to remember things.
*Have you got a good **memory**?*
2 anything that is remembered.
*The old man had happy **memories** of when he was a boy.*

mend ***verb*** mends, mending, mended
to make a damaged thing as useful as it was before.

mental ***adjective***
in the mind, of the mind. ***mental** illness.*

mention (men-shun) ***verb*** mentions, mentioning, mentioned
to speak or write a little about something. *She **mentioned** that she was going on holiday.*

menu (men-yoo) ***noun*** menus
a list of the different kinds of food you can choose for your meal.

mercy ***noun***
being kind to someone instead of punishing them. *Show **mercy** to the prisoners.*

meri ***noun***
a woman, girl or wife. [from Tok Pisin *meri*]

meri blaus ***noun***
a loose blouse with short sleeves, usually worn with a laplap. [from Tok Pisin *meri blaus*]

mermaid ***noun*** mermaids
a creature in stories that looks like a woman but has a fish's tail instead of legs.

merry ***adjective*** merrier, merriest
happy and lively.
Word Building: merrily

mess *noun*
something that is untidy, dirty, or mixed up. *Don't leave your clothes in a* ***mess.***

message *noun* messages
words that you send to a person when you cannot speak to him or her yourself.

messenger *noun* messengers
someone who takes a message to someone else.

met *verb* see **meet**

metal (met-l) *noun* metals
something hard that melts when it is very hot. Gold, silver, iron, and tin are kinds of metal.

meteor (mee-tee-or) *noun* meteors
a piece of rock or metal that moves through space and burns up when it gets near the earth.

meter *noun* meters
a machine that measures how much of something has been used. *an electricity* ***meter.***

method *noun* methods
the way you choose to do something.

metre (mee-ter) *noun* metres
a measure for length.
1000 metres = 1 kilometre.

metric system *noun*
a decimal system for counting, measuring, and weighing things.

mice *noun* see **mouse**

microphone *noun* microphones
a machine that is used to broadcast or record sound, or to make it louder.

microscope *noun* microscopes
an instrument that makes it possible to see very tiny things by making them look much bigger.

microscopic *adjective*
so small that you can only see it under a microscope.

midday *noun*
twelve o'clock in the day.

middle *noun* middles
1 the part of something that is the same distance from all its sides or edges or from both its ends. *An avocado has a stone in the* ***middle.***
2 after the beginning and before the end. *The phone rang in the* ***middle*** *of the night.*

midnight *noun*
twelve o'clock at night.

might *verb* see **may** ***verb***

mighty (my-tee) *adjective* mightier, mightiest
very strong or powerful.

migrant (my-grant) *noun* migrants
a person who goes to live in another country.

migrate (my-grate) *verb* migrates, migrating, migrated
to move to another place or country.
Some birds ***migrate*** *to a warmer place when the weather gets cold.*
Word Building: migration
The bird watchers were waiting for the ***migration*** *of the swallows.*

mild *adjective* milder, mildest
1 gentle. *a* ***mild*** *curry is not very hot.*
2 not too bad. *a* ***mild*** *illness.*
Word Building: mildly

mile *noun* miles
a measure of distance.
One mile = roughly 1.6 kilometres.

military *adjective*
of, for, or by soldiers.

milk *noun*
a white liquid that mothers and some female animals feed their babies with.

mill *noun* mills
1 a place with machinery for making corn into flour.
2 a kind of factory. *a paper* ***mill.***

millennium *noun* millenniums or millennia
a period of one thousand years.

millimetre (mil-i-mee-ter) *noun* millimetres
a measure of length. *There are 10 **millimetres** in 1 centimetre.*

million (mil-yun) *noun* millions
the number 1,000,000.
Word Building: millionth

millionaire (mil-yun-air) *noun* millionaires
a rich person who has more than a million dollars.

mime *verb* mimes, miming, mimed
to tell someone something by using actions not words.

mimic *verb* mimics, mimicking, mimicked
to copy what someone says or does in order to make fun of them.

mince *noun*
meat cut into very small pieces.

mind *noun* minds
the power to think, feel, and understand.

mind *verb* minds, minding, minded
to be worried or upset by something. *Do you **mind** missing the party?*

mine *noun* mines
1 a place where people work to dig coal, metal, jewels, or salt out of the ground.
2 a bomb hidden in the ground or the sea to blow up things that come close to it.

miner *noun* miners
someone who works down a mine.

mineral (min-a-rul) *noun* minerals
any useful or valuable rock that people get out of the ground.

miniature (min-a-cher) *adjective*
tiny, but just like something much bigger. *a **miniature** painting.*

mingle *verb* mingles, mingling, mingled
to mix. *I will **mingle** with the other people at the party.*

minimum *noun*
the smallest possible amount or number. *The teacher wants a **minimum** of noise.*
Word Building: minimal

minor (my-nor) *adjective*
small, less important. *The teacher made a **minor** alteration to my work*

minority (my-nor-i-tee) *noun* minorities
the smaller number of things or people in a group. *Only a **minority** of the children wanted to go home.*

minister *noun* ministers
1 someone who serves God by being in charge of a church.
2 an important member of a government.

mint *noun* mints
1 a green plant used in cooking to flavour food.
2 a sweet that tastes of mint.
3 a place where coins are made.

minus *preposition*
with the subtraction of. *Six **minus** two is four,* $6 - 2 = 4$.

minute (my-newt) *adjective* minuter, minutest
very small.

minute (min-it) *noun* minutes
a measure of time. *There are 60 **minutes** in one hour.*

miracle (meer-a-kl) *noun* miracles
something wonderful that has happened, although it did not seem possible. *It's a **miracle** no one was hurt in the car crash.*

mirage (mi-rahzh) *noun* mirages
a trick of the light that makes people see things that are not really there, such as pools of water in deserts.

mirror *noun* mirrors
a piece of glass, in which you can see yourself.

misbehave *verb* misbehaves, misbehaving, misbehaved
to be naughty.

miscarriage *noun* miscarriages
the birth of a baby before it has developed enough to stay alive.

mischief *noun*
silly or bad behaviour that gets you into trouble.

mischievous (mis-che-vus) *adjective*
often getting into mischief, naughty. *The* ***mischievous*** *puppy chewed my shoes.*

miser (my-zer) *noun* misers
someone who likes to save money, but hates spending it.

miserable (miz-ra-bl) *adjective*
very unhappy.
Word Building: miserably

misery (miz-a-ree) *noun*
suffering, being miserable.

misfortune *noun* misfortunes
bad luck.

mislead *verb* misleads, misleading, misled
to give someone an idea that is not true.

miss *verb* misses, missing, missed
1 to fail to hit, catch, see, hear, or find something. *I tried to hit the ball but I* ***missed*** *it. I* ***missed*** *the bus again.*
2 to be sad because someone is no longer with you. *I'll* ***miss*** *all my old friends when we move house.*

missile *noun* missiles
a weapon or object which is thrown or fired through the air.

missing *adjective*
lost. *We're looking for a* ***missing*** *person.*

mission (mish-un) *noun* missions
an important job that someone is sent away to do.

missis *noun*
1 a word used by Papua New Guineans to refer to the woman they work for.
2 a word used by some Papua New Guineans to refer to any white woman, or someone's wife. [from Tok Pisin *misis*]

mist *noun* mists
damp air that it is difficult to see through.

mistake *noun* mistakes
something that you have done or thought that is wrong.

mistake *verb* mistakes, mistaking, mistook, mistaken
to get the wrong idea about someone or something. *I* ***mistook*** *her for a friend of mine.*

misty *adjective* mistier, mistiest
full of mist, covered with mist.

misunderstand *verb* misunderstands, misunderstanding, misunderstood
to get the wrong idea about something.

mix *verb* mixes, mixing, mixed
to put different things together to make something new. ***Mix*** *yellow and blue paint together to make green.*

mixture *noun* mixtures
something made of different things mixed together. *a cake* ***mixture****.*

moan *verb* moans, moaning, moaned
1 to make a soft sound that shows you are in pain or trouble.
2 to grumble. *The class* ***moaned*** *about missing the swimming lesson.*

moat *noun* moats
a ditch dug around a castle and usually filled with water.

mob *noun* mobs
a noisy or angry crowd of people.

mobile *adjective*
that can move or be moved easily. *a* ***mobile*** *phone.*

mobile *noun* mobiles
a decoration which you hang up so that it can move about in the air.

mock *adjective*
not real. *a* ***mock*** *battle.*

mock *verb* mocks, mocking, mocked
to make fun of someone.

model *noun* models
1 a small copy of something. *a* ***model*** *aeroplane.*
2 someone whose job is to wear new clothes to show people what they look like.

moderate (mod-er-et) *adjective*
not too little and not too much. *Uncle drives at a* ***moderate*** *speed.*
Word Building: moderately

modern *adjective*
of the kind that is usual now. *a* ***modern*** *house.*

modest (mod-est) *adjective*
1 not boasting. *You didn't tell me you could sing so well—you're very* ***modest!***
2 shy. *He was too* ***modest*** *to undress on the beach.*
Word Building: modestly

moist *adjective* moister, moistest
damp, just a little bit wet.

Moka *noun*
a ceremonial exchange of pigs and shells in the Western Highlands.

molten *adjective*
melted. ***molten*** *metal.*

moment *noun* moments
a very small amount of time.

monarch *noun* monarchs
a ruler who is a king, queen, emperor, or empress.

monastery (mon-as-tair-ee) *noun* monasteries
a house where monks live and work.

Monday *noun* Mondays
the day after Sunday.

money (mun-ee) *noun*
the coins and pieces of paper used when people buy and sell things.

monitor (mon-i-tor) *verb* monitors, monitoring, monitored
to check on the progress of something. *We had to* ***monitor*** *the growth of the plants for our science project.*

monitor (mon-i-tor) *noun* monitors
someone who is given a special job to do at school.

monk *noun* monks
a religious man who lives with other monks, away from the rest of the world.

A B C D E F G H I J K L **M** N O P Q R S T U V W X Y Z

monkey (mung-kee) *noun* monkeys
an animal with hands, feet it can use like hands, long arms, and a tail.

monster *noun* monsters
a large, frightening animal in stories.

month *noun* months
a measure for time. There are twelve months in a year.

monument (mon-yoo-ment) *noun* monuments
a statue or building made so that people will remember someone or something. *a* ***monument*** *to soldiers who died in the war.*

mood *noun* moods
the way you feel. *in a good* ***mood.***

Moon *noun* moons
the object that goes around the Earth and shines in the sky at night. *There is a full* ***Moon*** *tonight.*

mop *noun* mops
a bundle of strings or other material on the end of a stick, used to wipe things clean.

moral *noun* morals
a lesson about what is right or wrong. *a story with a* ***moral.***

more *adjective, pronoun, adverb*
a bigger number or amount. *You've got* ***more*** *lollies than I have. I like guavas* ***more*** *than pineapple.*

morning *noun* mornings
the time from the beginning of the day until the middle of the day.

mortar *noun*
a mixture of sand, cement, and water, used in building to stick bricks together.

mosaic (mo-zay-ik) *noun* mosaics
a picture made from coloured pieces of paper, glass, stone, or wood.

mosque (mosk) *noun* mosques
a building where Muslims worship.

mosquito (mo-skee-toe) *noun* mosquitoes
an insect that sucks blood.

moss *noun* mosses
a plant that grows in damp places and has no flowers.

most *adjective, pronoun, adverb*
more than any other. *Which story did you like the* ***most?***

motel *noun* motels
a kind of hotel for people who are travelling by car.

moth *noun* moths
an insect like a butterfly, that flies usually at night.

mother *noun* mothers
a female parent.

motive (mo-tiv) *noun* motives
a reason for doing something.

motor *noun* motors
an engine, the part of a machine that makes it go.

motorbike, motorcycle *noun* motorbikes, motorcycles
a kind of bicycle with an engine.

motorist *noun* motorists
a person who drives a car.

Motu *noun*
1 the people who live on the Papuan coast near Port Moresby.
2 the language these people speak, which is also one of the official languages of PNG.

mould (rhymes with *old*) *noun* moulds
1 a kind of fungus that sometimes grows on food that has gone bad.
2 a container for making things set in the shape that is wanted. *a jelly* ***mould.***

mound *noun* mounds
a pile of earth.

mount *verb* mounts, mounting, mounted
to get onto a horse or bicycle so that you can ride it.

mountain *noun* mountains
a very high hill.

mourn (morn) *verb* mourns, mourning, mourned
to feel very sorry because someone or something has died or left.
Word Building: mourner

mouse *noun* mice
a small, furry animal with a long tail.

moustache (mus-stash) *noun* moustaches
hair that grows above a man's top lip.

mouth *noun* mouths
the part of the face that you use for eating and speaking.

move *verb* moves, moving, moved
1 to put something in another place. *Let's **move** the table over there.*
2 to go from one place to another. *We're **moving** house soon.*

movement *noun* movements
moving. *a sudden **movement**.*

movie *noun* movies
moving pictures that tell a story, seen in a cinema or on video.

mow (mo) *verb* mows, mowing, mowed, mown
to cut grass.

mower (mo-er) *noun* mowers
a machine that cuts grass.

much *adjective*
a lot. *I haven't got **much** money. I don't like carrots **much**.*

mud *noun*
wet soil.
Word Building: muddy
*a **muddy** field.*

Mud man *noun* Mud men
a person in the traditional costume of white mud, which is worn by the men of Asaro in the Eastern Highlands.

muffled *adjective*
hard to hear, not clear. ***muffled** cries for help.*

mug *noun* mugs
a big cup.

muli *noun*
limes and lemons.
Word building: switmuli, orange [from Tok Pisin *muli*]

muli water *noun*
a drink made from lemons, limes or oranges; lemonade.

multiply *verb* multiplies, multiplying, multiplied
to make something a number of times bigger. *Two **multiplied** by four is eight,* $2 \times 4 = 8$.

mum, mummy *noun* mums, mummies
(*informal*) mother.

mumu *noun*
a method of cooking food wrapped in leaves in a pit using hot stones. [from Tok Pisin *mumu*]

mumble *verb* mumbles, mumbling, mumbled
to speak quietly in a way that is not clear so that it is difficult to hear you.

mumps *noun*
an illness that makes the sides of the face swell.

munch *verb* munches, munching, munched
to chew noisily. ***munching** an apple.*

murder *verb* murders, murdering, murdered
to kill someone on purpose.

murmur *verb* murmurs, murmuring, murmured
to speak in a very soft, low voice.

muruk *noun*
a cassowary. [from Tok Pisin *muruk*]

muscle (mus-sl) *noun* muscles
one of the parts inside you which you use to make your body move.

museum (mew-**zee**-um) *noun* museums
a place where a lot of interesting things are kept for people to go and see.

mushroom *noun* mushrooms
a kind of fungus with a stem and a cap, like an umbrella.

music (**mew**-zik) *noun*
the sounds made by someone singing or playing a musical instrument.

musical (**mew**-zi-kl) *adjective*
1 having to do with music. ***musical** instruments.*
2 good at music.

musician (mew-**zish**-un) *noun* musicians
a person who sings or plays or composes music.

Muslim *noun* Muslims
someone who follows the religion of Islam.

mussel *noun* mussels
a small sea creature that lives inside a black shell.

must *verb*
have to, be forced to, have a duty to. *You **must** go to school.*

mustard *noun*
a yellow substance which gives a strong, hot taste to food.

muster *verb* musters, mustering, mustered
to gather people or animals together in one place.

mute *adjective*
1 unable to speak.
2 silent. *They stood and listened in **mute** amazement.*
Word Building: muted, mutely

mutiny (**mew**-ti-nee) *noun* mutinies
an attack made by soldiers or sailors against the officers in charge of them.

mutter *verb* mutters, muttering, muttered
to speak in a low, quiet voice. *People often **mutter** if they are angry.*

muzzle *noun* muzzles
1 an animal's nose and mouth.
2 a cover put over an animal's mouth so that it cannot bite.

my *adjective*
belonging to me. ***my** book.*

myself *pronoun*
I and no one else. *I can do it **myself**.*
by myself on my own. *I walked home **by myself**.*

mysterious (mis-**teer**-ee-us) *adjective*
strange and puzzling.
Word Building: mysteriously

mystery (**mis**-tree) *noun* mysteries
something strange and puzzling that has happened.

myth (mith) *noun* myths
1 an old story, a legend.
2 a story that is not true.

nag *verb* nags, nagging, nagged
to keep telling someone that you are not pleased and that they ought to behave differently. *She **nagged** him to tidy his room.*

nail *noun* nails
1 the hard part at the end of each finger and toe. *finger**nails**, toe**nails**.*
2 a small thin piece of metal with a sharp point at the end. It is used for fastening pieces of wood together.

nail *verb* nails, nailing, nailed
to join things or fix something with nails. *I **nailed** the two pieces of wood together.*

naked *adjective*
without any clothes on.

nambawan *noun*
1 the best. *Chocolate ice-cream is **nambawan**.*
2 the most important. *He's the **nambawan** teacher in the school.* [from Tok Pisin *nambawan*]

name *noun* names
the word you use to call or talk about someone or something.

name *verb* names, naming, named
to give a name to someone or something. *They **named** their baby Lenus.*

nappy *noun* nappies
a piece of cloth or paper used to cover a baby's bottom.

narrate (**nair**-rate) *verb* narrates, narrating, narrated
to tell a story.

narrative (**nair**-ra-tiv) *noun* narratives
a story.
Word Building: narrator, narration

narrow *adjective* narrower, narrowest
not wide. *a **narrow** road.*

narrowly *adverb*
only just. *We were **narrowly** beaten by the other team.*

nasty *adjective* nastier, nastiest
bad, not nice. *a **nasty** person.*

nation (**nay**-shun) *noun* nations
a country and the people who live in it.

national (**nash**-a-nl) *adjective*
belonging to one country. *He's wearing the **national** costume of Greece.*

national *noun* nationals
a person born in PNG. *There were **nationals** and expats at the party.*

national high school *noun*
a school providing two years of education from grade 11 to grade 12.

native *noun* natives
someone born in a place. *a **native** of Scotland.*

native *adjective*
coming from or belonging to a place. *native birds. The bird of paradise is **native** to PNG.*

natnat *noun*
a mosquito. [from Tok Pisin *natnat*]

natural (nach-e-rl) *adjective*
1 made by nature, not by people or machines. *the **natural** beauty of the Snowy Mountains.*
2 normal. *It is **natural** for birds to fly.*
Word Building: naturally

nature (nay-cher) *noun*
1 plants, animals, the sea, and everything else in the world that was not made by people.
2 what a person or animal is really like. *My dog has a gentle **nature**.*

naughty (naw-tee) *adjective* naughtier, naughtiest
badly behaved. *the **naughtiest** boy in the class.*

navigate *verb* navigates, navigating, navigated
to make sure that a ship, aeroplane, or car is going in the right direction.

navy *noun* navies
a group of ships and the people trained to use them for fighting.

navy *adjective*
dark blue. ***navy** blue trousers.*

near *adjective, adverb* nearer, nearest
not far away. *We live **near** the school. Where is the **nearest** store?*

nearly *adverb*
almost, not quite. *It's **nearly** 3 o'clock. We're **nearly** home.*

neat *adjective* neater, neatest
clean and tidy.
Word Building: neatly
*Please fold your clothes up **neatly**.*

necessary (nes-a-sair-ee) *adjective*
having to be done. *It is **necessary** to water plants in dry weather.*
Word Building: necessarily

neck *noun* necks
the part of the body that joins the head to the shoulders.

necklace (nek-les) *noun* necklaces
beads, jewels, or a chain worn round the neck.

nectar *noun*
a sweet liquid inside flowers. *Bees collect **nectar** to make honey.*

need *verb* needs, needing, needed
1 to be without something that you ought to have or that is necessary. *Plants and animals **need** water.*
2 to have to do something. *I **need** to go to the hospital.*

needle *noun* needles
1 a very thin, pointed piece of metal with a hole at one end. *You use **needles** for sewing. I can't thread this **needle**.*
2 one of a pair of long sticks used for knitting. *knitting **needles**.*
3 a very thin, pointed leaf. *Pine trees have **needles**.*

negative *adjective*
meaning 'no' or 'not'. *When we asked for a biscuit we received a **negative** answer.*

neglect *verb* neglects, neglecting, neglected
to leave something alone and not look after it.

neighbour (nay-bor) *noun* neighbours
someone who lives next door or near to you.

neighbourhood (nay-bor-hood) *noun* neighbourhoods
the area near where you are or where you live. *Is there a shop in the **neighbourhood**?*

neither (nie-ther or nee-ther) *pronoun*
not either. *'I don't like betel nut.' 'Neither do I.'*

nephew (nef-you) *noun* nephews
the son of a brother or sister.

nerve *noun* nerves
one of the small parts inside the body that carry messages to and from the brain, so that the body can feel and move.

nervous *adjective*
1 afraid and excited because of something you have to do. *Are you **nervous** about going to the new school?*
2 easily frightened. *a **nervous** animal.*

nest *noun* nests
a cosy place made by birds, mice, and some other animals for their babies.

net *noun* nets
material made of threads or wires joined together with holes between.

netball *noun*
a game where two teams of seven players try to throw a ball through a big round net.

nettle *noun* nettles
a plant with its stem and leaves covered in hairs that sting.

network *noun* networks
a system of things such as radio stations or computers that are linked together. *A television **network**.*

neutral *adjective*
not taking sides. *The referee has to be **neutral**.*

never *adverb*
not ever.

new *adjective* newer, newest
1 just bought or made. *a **new** bike.*
2 different. *my **new** school.*

New Guinea *noun*
1 the island on which Irian Jaya and PNG are located.
2 the northern part of PNG formerly administered by Germany.

news *noun*
words that tell you about something that has just happened.

newspaper *noun* newspapers
large sheets of paper folded together, with the news printed on them. Most newspapers come out every day.

next *adjective*
1 nearest, closest. *My friend lives in the **next** village.*
2 that comes after this one. *We're going on holiday **next** week.*

nibble *verb* nibbles, nibbling, nibbled
to eat something by biting off a little at a time.

nice *adjective* nicer, nicest
pleasant, of the kind you like.
Word Building: nicely

nickname *noun* nicknames
a name that your family or friends call you instead of your real name.

niece (nees) *noun* nieces
the daughter of your brother or sister.

night (nite) *noun* nights
the time when it is dark.

nightmare (nite-mair) *noun* nightmares
a frightening dream.

nil *noun*
nothing. *We won the match by four goals to **nil**.*

nimble *adjective* nimbler, nimblest
able to move quickly and easily.

nine *noun* nines
the number 9.
Word Building: ninth

nineteen
the number 19.
Word Building: nineteenth

ninety
the number 90.
Word Building: ninetieth

nits *noun*
the eggs of a small insect called a louse.

noble *adjective* nobler, noblest
1 good, honest, and not selfish. ***noble** thoughts.*
2 of a rich important family. *a **noble** prince.*

nobody *pronoun*
no person. *There was **nobody** at home.*

nocturnal (nok-ter-nal) *adjective*
active at night. *Bats are **nocturnal** animals.*

nod *verb* nods, nodding, nodded
to move your head up and down, as you do to show you agree with someone.

nogat *interjection*
a word used to deny or refuse something. [from Tok Pisin *nogat*]

noise *noun* noises
1 a sound. *Did you hear a **noise**?*
2 a loud and unpleasant sound. *Stop that **noise**!*

noisy *adjective* noisier, noisiest
making an unpleasant noise.
Word Building: noisily

none *pronoun*
not any or not one. *I wanted some more rice but there is **none** left.*

non-fiction *noun*
books and stories about real things and true events.

nonsense *noun*
something that does not mean anything.

noodles *noun*
food rather like spaghetti.

noon *noun*
twelve o'clock in the day.

noose *noun* nooses
a loop you make in a rope. A knot in the rope slips along and makes the loop smaller or larger.

nor *conjunction*
and not. *You can't do it; **nor** can I. Neither Yaking **nor** Toropo are at school today.*

normal *adjective*
usual, ordinary.
Word Building: normally
*I **normally** get up at 6.30.*

north *noun*
the direction to your left when you face east.

nose *noun* noses
the part of the face that is used for breathing and smelling.

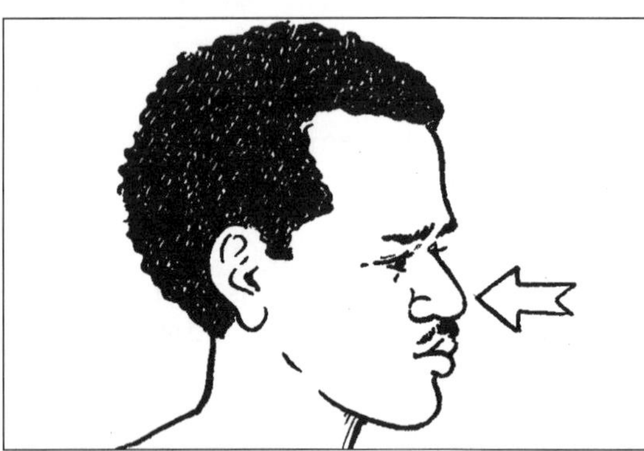

nostril *noun* nostrils
one of the two holes at the end of the nose for taking in air.

not *adverb*
a word used to change the meaning of another word to its opposite. *I do **not** want to do my homework.*

note *noun* notes
1 a few words written down to remind you of something. *Make a **note** of the address.*
2 a short letter. *a thank you **note**.*
3 one sound in music. *I'll play the first few **notes**, then you join me.*
4 a piece of paper money. *a K20 **note**.*

nothing *noun*
not anything.

notice *noun* notices
a special piece of information, written on a poster or read out at assembly.

notice *verb* notices, noticing, noticed
to see something and think about it. *Daure **noticed** that his mother looked tired.*

nought (nawt) *noun* noughts
the sign for nothing, 0.

noun *noun* nouns
a word that is the name of a person, place, thing, or idea. *Tau, Morobe, chair, and happiness are all **nouns**.*

nourishing *adjective*
good for you. ***nourishing** food.*

novel (nov-l) *noun* novels
a long story which fills a book.

novelty (nov-el-tee) *noun* novelties
something new or unusual.

November *noun*
the eleventh month of the year.

now *adverb*
at this time. *Do you want to go **now**?*

nowhere *adverb*
not anywhere.

nozzle *noun* nozzles
the part at the end of a piece of pipe where a spray of liquid or powder comes out.

nuclear (new-klee-ar) *adjective*
using energy that results from splitting an atom.

nude *adjective*
without any clothes.

nudge *verb* nudges, nudging, nudged
to push someone with your elbow to make them notice something.

nugget *noun* nuggets
a small piece of something. *gold **nuggets**.*

Nuigini *noun*
New Guinea. [from Tok Pisin *Nu Gini* or *Nui Gini*]

nuisance (new-sense) *noun* nuisances
someone or something that causes trouble. *It's a **nuisance** that we missed the bus.*

numb (num) *adjective*
not able to feel anything. *My legs get **numb**.*

number *noun* numbers
the word or sign that tells you how many. 1, 2, and 3 are numbers.

numerous (new-mer-us) *adjective*
many.

nun *noun* nuns
a religious woman who lives with other nuns, away from the world in a nunnery.

nurse *noun* nurses
someone whose job is to look after people who are ill, hurt, or old.

nurse *verb* nurses, nursing, nursed
1 to look after or feed a baby.
2 to look after someone who is ill, hurt, or old.

nursery *noun* nurseries
1 a room in a house for very young children to sleep and play in.
2 a place where plants are grown from seed.

nut *noun* nuts
1 a fruit with a hard shell and a kernel inside that you can eat. *a galip **nut**.*
2 a piece of metal with a hole in it which you screw on the end of a long piece of metal called a bolt. *You use **nuts** and bolts to join things together.*

nuzzle *verb* nuzzles, nuzzling, nuzzled
to rub something with the nose.

nylon *noun*
a strong thin material for making clothes and other things.

oak *noun* oaks
a large tree with seeds called acorns.

oar *noun* oars
a long pole with a flat part at one end, used for rowing a boat.

oasis (oh-**ay**-sis) *noun* oases
a place with water and trees in a desert.

oath *noun* oaths
a serious promise.

oats *noun*
a plant grown by farmers. Its seed is used to make food for humans and animals.

obedient (oh-**bee**-dee-ent) *adjective*
willing to do what you are told.
Word Building: obediently

obey (oh-**bay**) *verb* obeys, obeying, obeyed
to do what you are told.

object (**ob**-jekt) *noun* objects
1 anything that you can see or touch. *There were some interesting **objects** in the museum.*
2 the object of a sentence is the person or thing that has an action done to it. In the sentence *Vaitania threw the ball*, the ***object*** of the verb is *'the ball'*.

object *verb* objects, objecting, objected
to say that you do not like or agree with something. *We **objected** to their bad language.*
Word Building: objection, objections

oblong *noun* oblongs
a rectangle, the shape of a page of a book.

observe *verb* observes, observing, observed
to watch carefully. *We **observed** the bird building its nest.*

obstacle (**ob**-sta-kl) *noun* obstacles
something that is in the way and stops you from doing what you want to do.

obstinate *adjective*
hard to persuade; sticking to your own ideas even if they might be wrong.
Word Building: obstinately

obstruct *verb* obstructs, obstructing, obstructed
to stop something getting past. *Please don't **obstruct** the path to the kitchen.*
Word Building: obstruction

obtain *verb* obtains, obtaining, obtained
to get, to buy, to be given. *Where can I **obtain** tickets for the game?*

obvious *adjective*
easy to see or understand.
Word Building: obviously

occasion (o-**kay**-shun) *noun* occasions
the time when something happens. *Your birthday is a special **occasion**.*

occasional (o-**kay**-zhun-l) *adjective*
happening sometimes, not regular.
Word Building: occasionally

occupation (ok-yew-**pay**-shun) *noun* occupations
any job or hobby.

occupy *verb* occupies, occupying, occupied
1 to live in or use something. *Is this seat **occupied**?*
2 to keep someone busy and interested. *Keeping young children **occupied** is a hard job.*

occur (oh-**ker**) *verb* occurs, occurring, occurred
1 to happen. *When did the accident **occur**?*
2 to come into your mind. *An idea **occurred** to me.*

ocean (**oh**-shun) *noun* oceans
a big sea. *the Pacific **Ocean**.*

o'clock *adverb*
by the clock. *one **o'clock**.*

octagon *noun* octagons
a shape with eight sides.

October *noun*
the tenth month of the year.

octopus *noun* octopuses
a sea creature with eight arms.

odd *adjective* odder, oddest
1 strange. *an **odd** person.*
2 not even. *Five is an **odd** number.*
3 not alike. ***odd** shoes.*

odds and ends *noun*
various things that you do not really want.

odour or **odor** *noun* odours, odor
a smell.
Word Building: odourless, deodorant
*Some people use deodorant under their arms to keep **odours** away.*

of *preposition*
this word has several uses. Here are some of the ways you can use it: *a glass **of** milk, the 1st **of** June, the front **of** the book, a box made **of** wood.*

off *adverb, preposition*
this word has several uses. Here are some of the ways you can use it:
1 down from. *He fell **off** the fence.*
2 not working. *The electricity is **off**.*
3 away. *The rascals ran **off**.*

offend (o-**fend**) *verb* offends, offending, offended
to hurt someone's feelings.

offensive *adjective*
nasty and very annoying. *an **offensive** smell.*

offer *verb* offers, offering, offered
1 to hold out something so that another person can take it if they want it. *She **offered** me a piece of cake.*
2 to say that you are willing to do something. *He **offered** to lay the table.*

office *noun* offices
a room with desks and telephones, where people work.

officer *noun* officers
1 a person in charge of others in the army, navy, or air force.
2 a member of the police force.

official (o-**fish**-al) *adjective*
done or made or said by someone in charge. *Is it **official** that we've got a holiday next week?*
Word Building: officially

offsider *noun* offsiders
a partner, assistant or friend. *The **offsider** in the PMV collected the money from the passengers.*

often (**off**-en or **oft**-en) *adverb*
many times. *We **often** go swimming on Saturday.*

okari nut *noun* okari nuts
a purple-red nut with a white centre that is good to eat. [from Tok Pisin *okari*]

oil *noun* oils
a thick, slippery liquid. You can use various kinds of oil as fuel, to make machinery work better, and in cooking.

old *adjective* older, oldest
1 born or made a long time ago. *an* ***old*** *man, an* ***old*** *car.*
2 known for a long time. *an* ***old*** *friend.*

old-fashioned *adjective*
of the kind that was usual a long time ago. ***old-fashioned*** *clothes.*

olive (ol-iv) *noun* olives
1 an evergreen tree with a small, bitter fruit.
2 the fruit of this tree.

Olympic Games (oh-**lim**-pik) *noun*
a series of sporting contests held every four years, in which competitors from many countries take part.
Word Building: Olympics, Olympian

omit *verb* omits, omitting, omitted
to leave out. ***Omit*** *verse 2 and sing verses 3 and 4.*

on *adverb, preposition*
this word has several uses. Here are some of the ways you use it:
1 in a certain position. ***on*** *the wall.*
2 at a certain time. ***on*** *my birthday.*
3 about. *A book* ***on*** *dinosaurs.*
4 working. *The radio is* ***on****.*

once (wuns) *adverb*
1 one time. *She only missed school* ***once*** *this term.*
2 at one time. ***Once*** *dinosaurs roamed the Earth.*
at once immediately, now. *Come here* ***at once****!*

one (wun) *noun* ones
the number 1.

onion (**un**-yun) *noun* onions
a round, white vegetable with a very strong flavour.

only *adjective, adverb*
this word has several uses. Here are some of the ways you can use it: *There is* ***only*** *one pawpaw left. It's* ***only*** *4 o'clock. I* ***only*** *touched it. I didn't break it.*
an only child a child with no brothers or sisters.

ooze *verb* oozes, oozing, oozed
to come slowly through a hole or small opening. *Blood* ***oozed*** *from the cut.*

open *adjective*
not closed, allowing people or things to go through or in. *an* ***open*** *door.*

open *verb* opens, opening, opened
to make something open.

opening *noun* openings
a space, a way through. *We crawled through a small* ***opening*** *in the hedge.*

operate (**op**-er-ate) *verb* operates, operating, operated
1 to work a machine or tool. *Can you* ***operate*** *a drill?*
2 to fix up a part of your body that is sick or hurt. This is done by a doctor who usually puts you to sleep for a short time and uses special tools to work on the body part.
Word Building: operation, operator
The boy had an ***operation*** *to fix his broken leg.*

A B C D E F G H I J K L M N **O** P Q R S T U V W X Y Z

opinion (oh-pin-yun) ***noun*** opinions
what you think of something. *In your* ***opinion****, which colour looks best?*

opponent (o-pone-ent) ***noun*** opponents
a person with whom you argue or fight or play a game against. *We beat our* ***opponents*** *easily.*

opportunity (op-or-tyoo-ni-tee) ***noun*** opportunities
a good chance to do something.

oppose (o-poze) ***verb*** opposes, opposing, opposed
to fight or argue or play against someone or something.

opposite (op-o-sit) ***adjective, adverb,*** preposition
1 facing. *the* ***opposite*** *side of the road.*
2 completely different. *North is the* ***opposite*** *direction to South.*

opposite (op-o-sit) ***noun*** opposites
something that is as different as possible from another thing. *Hot and cold are* ***opposites.***

or ***conjunction***
a word used to show a difference or give a choice. *You can have an apple* ***or*** *a banana.*

orange (or-inj) ***noun*** oranges
1 a round, juicy fruit with a thick peel.
2 the colour of this fruit.

orbit ***noun*** orbits
the path of something moving round the sun or a planet in space.

orchard (or-cherd) ***noun*** orchards
a place where a lot of fruit trees grow. *an apple* ***orchard.***

orchestra (or-kes-tra) ***noun*** orchestras
a large group of people playing musical instruments together.

ordeal ***noun*** ordeals
a time when you have to put up with great pain or trouble.

order ***noun*** orders
1 a statement that you must do something. *Soldiers must always obey* ***orders.***
2 the way that you place people or things together. *alphabetical* ***order.***

order ***verb*** orders, ordering, ordered
1 to tell someone to do something. *The officer* ***ordered*** *the soldiers to march.*
2 to ask for something to be brought to you. *He* ***ordered*** *fish and chips.*

orderly ***adjective***
properly arranged, well behaved.

ordinary ***adjective***
usual, normal, not special.

ore ***noun*** ores
rock with metal in it. *iron* ***ore.***

organ ***noun*** organs
1 a musical instrument with one or more keyboards like a piano. Organs usually have pedals and pipes.
2 a part of the body such as the heart or the lungs, that has a special job to do.

organise ***verb*** organises, organising, organised
1 to get people working together to do something.
2 to plan and arrange things like parties, concerts, or holidays.

origin (or-i-jin) ***noun*** origins
The beginning point of something

original (o-rij-i-nal) ***adjective***
1 first, existing from the beginning. *Our car still has the* ***original*** *tyres.*
2 new, not copied. *an* ***original*** *idea.*
Word Building: originally

ornament ***noun*** ornaments
something put in a place to make it look pretty.

orphan ***noun*** orphans
a child whose mother and father are dead.

other (rhymes with *brother*) *adjective, pronoun*
not the same as this. *I like the* ***other*** *biscuits better. I can't find my* ***other*** *shoe.*

otherwise *adverb, conjunction*
or else. *Hurry up* ***otherwise*** *we'll be late.*

ought (awt) *verb*
should. *I* ***ought*** *to go now.*

our *adjective*
belonging to us. *Come to* ***our*** *house.*

ourselves *pronoun*
we and no one else. *We made* ***ourselves*** *some sandwiches.*
by ourselves on our own, without help. *We painted the shed* ***by ourselves.***

out *adjective, adverb*
this word has several uses. Here are some of the ways you can use it: *Mirou went* ***out*** *today. Put the light* ***out*** *please. The sun has come* ***out*** *again. Fish can't live* ***out*** *of water.*

outback *noun*
the regions of Australia that are far inland and a long way from the cities.

outdoor *adjective*
outside a building in the open air. *They like* ***outdoor*** *activities.*
Word Building: outdoors
We played cricket ***outdoors.***

outfit *noun* outfits
a set of clothes you wear together. *Dorcas bought a new* ***outfit*** *to wear at her sister's wedding.*

outlaw *noun* outlaws
a lawless person, a robber.

outline *noun* outlines
a line around the edge of something, that shows its shape. *It was dark but we could still see the* ***outline*** *of the houses.*

outside *adjective, adverb, preposition*
not inside. *We went* ***outside*** *to play in the garden.*

outside *noun*
the surface or edge of something, the part farthest from the middle. *The* ***outside*** *of a coconut is brown and hairy and the inside is white.*

outstanding *adjective*
unusually good.

outwards *adverb*
away from the middle. *We stood in a circle facing* ***outwards.***

oval (oh-val) *noun, adjective*
the shape of an egg.

oven (uv-en) *noun* ovens
the part of a stove where food can be baked or roasted.

over *adverb, preposition*
this word has several uses. Here are some of the ways you can use it: *We climbed* ***over*** *the fence. I won't buy it if it costs* ***over*** *K20. Come straight home when school is* ***over.*** *She put a jumper* ***over*** *her shirt.*

overboard *adverb*
over the side of a boat into the water. *I nearly fell* ***overboard!***

overcome *verb* overcomes, overcoming, overcame
to control or defeat. *She tried to* ***overcome*** *her fear of the dark.*

overflow *verb* overflows, overflowing, overflowed
to come over the sides of a container, because there is too much in it. *Turn off the taps. The bath is* ***overflowing!***

overgrown *adjective*
covered with plants you do not want. *an* ***overgrown*** *garden.*

overhead *adjective, adverb*
above the head. *overhead wires, a plane flying overhead.*

overseas *adverb*
in or to another country. *She is living overseas.*

overtake *verb* overtakes, overtaking, overtook, overtaken
to catch up and pass someone.

overturn *verb* overturns, overturning, overturned
to push or knock something over.

owe (rhymes with *go*) *verb* owes, owing, owed
to have to pay money to someone.

owl *noun* owls
a bird with large eyes that hunts smaller animals at night.

own *adjective, pronoun*
my own mine and no one else's. *my own room.*
on my own by myself. *I played on my own today.*

own *verb* owns, owning, owned
to be able to keep something because it belongs to you.

ox *noun* oxen
a large animal kept for its meat or for pulling carts.

oxygen (ox-ee-jen) *noun*
a gas in the air that everyone needs to breathe in order to stay alive.

oyster *noun* oysters
a sea creature that lives inside a pair of shells.

pace *noun* paces
1 a single step in walking or running. *Take one **pace** backwards.*
2 the speed at which someone or something is moving. *The boat was moving at a very fast **pace**.*

pace *verb* paces, pacing, paced
to walk slowly and evenly. *The man **paced** around the room.*

pack *noun* packs
1 a group of dogs or wolves.
2 a set of cards used in games.

pack *verb* packs, packing, packed
to put things into a box, bag, or suitcase.

package (pak-ij) *noun* packages
something wrapped in paper; a parcel.

packet *noun* packets
a small box or bag that you buy things in. *a **packet** of biscuits.*

pad *noun* pads
1 sheets of writing paper joined together along one edge so that you can tear a sheet off when you need it.
2 material used as a kind of cushion to protect something.

pad *verb* pads, padding, padded
1 to protect something or make it more comfortable with a pad of soft material.
2 to walk softly.

paddle *noun* paddles
a length of wood with a flat part at one end, used to make a canoe move through water.

paddle *verb* paddles, paddling, paddled
1 to walk about in shallow water. *We went **paddling** in the sea.*
2 to move a canoe through water. *We **paddled** down the river.*

paddock *noun* paddocks
1 an area of land with a fence around it and crops or grass growing on it.
2 an area of land with a fence around it in which farm animals may be kept.

padlock *noun* padlocks
a lock that you use on gates and suitcases.

page *noun* pages
a piece of paper that is part of a book.

paid *verb* see **pay**

pain *noun* pains
the unpleasant feeling you have when part of your body is injured or you are ill.
Word Building: painful, painfully

paint *noun* paints
a substance you can use to make coloured pictures or to give things a new colour.

paint *verb* paints, painting, painted
to use paint to make a picture or to colour something.
Word Building: painter, painters

painting *noun* paintings
a picture that has been painted.

pair *noun* pairs
two people, animals, or things that belong together. *a **pair** of shoes.*

palace (pal-ess) *noun* palaces
a very large house where a king, queen, or some other very important person lives.

pale *adjective* paler, palest
1 almost white. *a **pale** face.*
2 light in colour. *a **pale** blue sky.*

palm *noun* palms
1 the inside of the hand between the fingers and wrist.
2 a tropical tree with large leaves and no branches.

pan *noun* pans
a metal pot that you use for cooking. *a frying **pan**, a sauce**pan**.*

pancake *noun* pancakes
flour, milk, and egg mixed together and fried.

panda *noun* pandas
an animal found in China. Giant pandas look like large black and white bears.

pane *noun* panes
a piece of glass in a window.

panel (pan-l) *noun* panels
a long, flat piece of wood or metal that is part of a door, wall, or piece of furniture.

panic (pan-ik) *noun*
sudden fear that cannot be controlled. *He felt **panic** when he saw the fire.*

pant *verb* pants, panting, panted
to take short, quick breaths, usually after running.

panther *noun* panthers
a wild animal like a very big black cat.

pants *noun*
1 underpants.
2 trousers.

paper *noun* papers
1 thin material used to write on, to make books with, and to wrap things in. *a sheet of **paper**, a **paper** bag.*
2 a newspaper.

Papua *noun*
the southern part of mainland PNG.

Papuan *noun* Papuans
a person who was born in Papua.

Papuan black *noun* Papuan blacks
a snake that lives in parts of Papua and has a deadly bite.

parachute (pair-a-shoot) *noun* parachutes
a large piece of cloth that opens up like an umbrella when a cord is pulled. It is tied to someone's back so that they can jump out of an aeroplane and float safely down to the ground.

parade (pa-rade) *noun* parades
people moving in a procession, while other people watch them.

paradise (pair-a-dise) *noun*
a wonderful place where people are happy; heaven.

paragraph (pair-a-graf) *noun* paragraphs
a group of lines of writing. You begin each new paragraph on a new line.

parallel (pair-a-lel) *adjective*
the same distance from each other all the way along. ***Parallel** lines never meet.*

paralysed *adjective*
someone who is paralysed cannot move or feel anything.

parcel (par-sl) *noun* parcels
something wrapped up ready to be carried or posted.

pardon *verb* pardons, pardoning, pardoned
to forgive.

parent (pair-ent) *noun* parents
1 a person who has a child.
2 an animal that has young ones.

park *noun* parks
a large space with grass and trees where anyone can walk or play.

park *verb* parks, parking, parked
to leave a car somewhere until you need it again.

parliament (par-la-ment) *noun* parliaments
the people who are elected to make the laws of a country.

parrot *noun* parrots
a brightly coloured bird with a curved beak.

parsley *noun*
a green plant used in cooking to flavour food.

part *noun* parts
anything that belongs to something bigger. *I've only read* ***part*** *of the story so far.*
part of speech any of the groups into which words are divided in grammar, such as *adjective, adverb, noun,* or *verb*.

particular (pa-tik-yoo-ler) *adjective*
1 only this one and no other. *I wanted this* ***particular*** *colour.*
2 choosing carefully, fussy. *She's* ***particular*** *about what she eats.*
Word Building: particularly

partly *adverb*
not completely.

partner *noun* partners
one of two people who do things together.

party *noun* parties
a group of people enjoying themselves together. *a birthday* ***party***.

pass *verb* passes, passing, passed
1 to go by. *On my way to school I* ***pass*** *the swamp.*
2 to give someone something they want, but cannot reach themselves. *Please* ***pass*** *the salt.*
3 to be successful in a test. *She's* ***passed*** *her driving test.*

passage (pas-sij) *noun* passages
a corridor.

passbook *noun* passbooks
a customer's record of money put into or taken out of a savings account at a bank.

passenger (pas-sen-jer) *noun* passengers
a person who is travelling in a bus, car, ship or aeroplane, but is not driving it.

passionfruit (pash-un-froot) *noun*
a small, purple-skinned fruit with pulp and seeds which are good to eat.

passport *noun* passports
a small book with your name and photograph in it. You must take it with you when you go to another country.

password *noun* passwords
a group of secret numbers, letters, or words.

past *adjective, adverb, preposition*
this word has several uses. Here are some of the ways you can use it:
We watched the cars go ***past***. *The bus goes* ***past*** *the school. It's half-****past*** *six.*

past *noun*
the time that has gone. *In the* ***past***, *there were no towns, roads, cars, or aeroplanes.*

pasta (pah-sta or pas-ta) *noun*
a food made from flour and water. *Spaghetti is a kind of* ***pasta***.

paste (payst) *noun*
1 a sticky substance used for sticking things together.
2 a soft wet mixture which is easy to spread.

pasture *noun*
land covered in grass that cattle, sheep, or horses can eat.

pat *verb* pats, patting, patted
to touch someone or something gently with an open hand. *Tanai* ***patted*** *the dog on the head.*

patch *noun* patches
1 a small piece of material put over something to mend it or protect it.
2 a small piece of something. *There is a **patch** of blue in the sky.*

patent (pay-tent) *noun* patents
government permission given to someone to be the only person to make or sell an invention.

path *noun* paths
a narrow way that you can walk along to get somewhere. *a **path** beside the river.*

patient *adjective*
able to wait for a long time without getting angry.
Word Building: patiently, patience
*Learning to sew takes a lot of **patience**.*

patient *noun* patients
someone who is ill and being looked after by a doctor.

patrol (pa-**trole**) *noun* patrols
a group of soldiers or policemen who move around a place to guard it.

patrol box *noun* patrol boxes
a large metal box carried on patrol (by patrol officers) containing official papers etc.

patrol officer *noun* patrol officers
a government official in colonial times; a kiap.

patter *verb* patters, pattering, pattered
to make the light, tapping sound rain makes against a window.

pattern *noun* patterns
1 lines, shapes, or colours on something to make it look interesting or attractive. *a dress with a flowery **pattern**.*
2 anything that people copy in order to make something. *I bought some material and a **pattern** to make a new dress.*

pause *verb* pauses, pausing, paused
to stop for a very short time.

pave *verb* paves, paving, paved
to cover a street, driveway, or path with tar, stones, or cement.
Word Building: pavement

paw *noun* paws
an animal's foot.

pawpaw *noun* pawpaws
1 an oval-shaped tropical fruit with soft orange flesh which is good to eat.
2 the tree which bears this fruit.

pay *verb* pays, paying, paid
to give money in return for something.

pay-back *noun*
revenge.

Pay Friday *noun*
government payday, the second Friday of each month.

payment *noun* payments
money that you pay for something.

pea *noun* peas
a tiny, round, green vegetable that grows with others inside a pod.

peace *noun*
1 a time free from war.
2 a time of quiet and rest. *We enjoy the **peace** and quiet when the baby is asleep.*

peaceful *adjective*
quiet, calm.
Word Building: peacefully

peach *noun* peaches
a round, soft, juicy fruit with a large stone and a fuzzy skin.

peak *noun* peaks
the top of a mountain.

peanut *noun* peanuts
a tiny, round nut that grows in a pod in the ground.

pear *noun* pears
a juicy fruit that is round at the bottom and more narrow where the stalk is.

pearl (perl) *noun* pearls
a small, shiny, white ball found inside the shells of some oysters and is used in jewellery.

pebble *noun* pebbles
a small, round stone.

peck *verb* pecks, pecking, pecked
to use the beak to pick up food or push at something.

peculiar (pe-**kew**-lee-ar) *adjective*
strange. *This pawpaw has a* ***peculiar*** *taste.*
Word Building: peculiarly

pedal *noun* pedals
a part of a bicycle or other machine that you press with your foot to make it work.

peddle *verb* peddles, peddling, peddled
to go from house to house trying to sell things.

pedestrian (pe-**des**-tree-an) *noun* pedestrians
someone who is walking.

peel *noun*
the skin on some fruit and vegetables. *lemon* ***peel.***

peel *verb* peels, peeling, peeled
to take the skin off something. *Nick* ***peeled*** *the potatoes.*

peer *verb* peers, peering, peered
to get very close to something to look at it.

peg *noun* pegs
1 a clip for fixing washing on a line. *a clothes* ***peg.***
2 a short wooden or metal rod to hang things on. *Hang your coats on the* ***pegs.***

pekpek *noun*
faeces (human waste).
Word Building: pekpek wara, diarrhoea. [from Tok Pisin *pekpek*]

pelican *noun* pelicans
a bird with a very large beak.

pelt *verb* pelts, pelting, pelted
to throw a lot of things at someone. *They* ***pelted*** *the wild dog with rocks.*

pen *noun* pens
a thing that you use for writing with ink.

penalty (**pen**-al-tee) *noun* penalties
a punishment. *The* ***penalty*** *for speeding is to pay a fine.*

pencil *noun* pencils
a thin stick of wood with black or coloured stuff in the middle, for writing or drawing with.

pendulum (**pen**-dew-lum) *noun* pendulums
a stick with a weight hanging from its end so that it swings backwards and forwards. Some large old-fashioned clocks have pendulums to make them work.

penetrate (**pen**-a-trate) *verb* penetrates, penetrating, penetrated
to make or find a way through something. *The hot sun* ***penetrated*** *his thin shirt.*

penguin (**pen**-gwin) *noun* penguins
a black and white bird that swims in the sea but cannot fly.

penknife *noun* penknives
a small knife that folds up so that you can carry it with you safely.

pentagon *noun* pentagons
a shape with five sides.

people (pee-pl) *noun*
men, women, and children.

pepper *noun*
a spice used to flavour food.

peppermint *noun* peppermints
a lolly with a strong mint flavour.

perch *noun* perches
anything that a bird rests on when it is not flying.

percussion instrument *noun* percussion instruments
any musical instrument that is banged, hit, or shaken. Kundus, garamuts and rattles are percussion instruments.

perfect *adjective*
so good that it cannot be better.
Word Building: perfectly

perform *verb* performs, performing, performed
to do something in front of a lot of people. *We **performed** the school play in front of our parents.*
Word Building: performer, performers

performance *noun* performances
something done in front of a lot of people.

perfume *noun* perfumes
1 a nice smell.
2 a liquid with a nice smell that you put on your body. *a bottle of **perfume**.*

perhaps *adverb*
possibly. ***Perhaps** it will rain tomorrow.*

peril (pair-il) *noun* perils
danger.

perimeter (pa-rim-e-ter) *noun*
the distance around the edge of something. *We measured the **perimeter** of the playground.*

period (peer-ee-ud) *noun* periods
a length of time. *What **period** of history are you studying?*

perish (pair-ish) *verb* perishes, perishing, perished
to die. *The fishermen **perished** in the storm.*

permanent (per-ma-nent) *adjective*
lasting forever or for a very long time.
Word Building: permanently

permission (per-mish-un) *noun*
words that say something is allowed.

permit *noun* permits
written permission to do something. *a **permit** to export carvings.*

permit *verb* permits, permitting, permitted
to allow.

persist *verb* persists, persisting, persisted
to carry on doing something no matter what happens.

person *noun* persons
a man, woman, or child.

personal *adjective*
1 by, or for, or belonging to a particular person. *my **personal** belongings.*
2 about a particular person. *Don't make rude **personal** remarks.*
Word Building: personally

persuade (per-swayd) *verb* persuades, persuading, persuaded
to get someone to agree to something. *Dorcas **persuaded** her mother to let her go to the school dance.*

pest *noun* pests
any person, animal, or plant that causes a lot of trouble.

pester *verb* pesters, pestering, pestered
to keep worrying someone by asking questions. *Wilson **pestered** his father about getting a new pair of football boots.*

pet *noun* pets
any animal which you keep so that you can enjoy its company.

petal (pet-l) *noun* petals
one of the separate, coloured parts of a flower.

petrol *noun*
a liquid that you put in cars to make them work.

pew *noun* pews
one of the long wooden seats in a church.

pharmacy (far-ma-see) *noun* pharmacies
a place where medicines are made and sold.
Word Building: pharmacist
*A **pharmacist** knows about different drugs and their effects.*

phone (fone) *noun* phones
a telephone.

phone (fone) *verb* phones, phoning, phoned
to use a telephone to speak to someone.

photo (fo-toe) *noun* photos
a photograph.

photocopier (fo-toe-kop-ee-er) *noun* photocopiers
a machine which makes copies of things written or printed on paper.

photograph (fo-ta-graf) *noun* photographs
a picture taken on film with a camera.

photograph (fo-ta-graf) *verb* photographs, photographing, photographed
to take a photograph of something.

phrase (fraze) *noun* phrases
a group of words that you use together as part of a sentence.

physical (fiz-i-kl) *adjective*
having to do with the body.
physical education physical exercise that you do at school.

piano *noun* pianos
a large musical instrument with white and black keys that you press with your fingers.

pick *verb* picks, picking, picked
1 to choose. *We **picked** Michael as captain of the football team.*
2 to take something up from where it is. *I **picked** up some shells on the beach.*
3 to take flowers or fruit from plants and trees. *I've **picked** some flowers for you.*

pickup *noun*
a ute, a small truck or PMV.

picnic *noun* picnics
a meal eaten in the open air away from home. *a **picnic** lunch.*

picture *noun* pictures
a painting, drawing, or photograph.

pidgin *noun* pidgins
a trade language. Tok Pisin and Hiri Motu are pidgin languages.

pie *noun* pies
meat, vegetables, or fruit covered with pastry and baked. *an apple **pie**.*

piece (pees) *noun* pieces
a part of something. *a **piece** of cake, **pieces** of broken glass.*

pier (peer) *noun* piers
a long structure built out into the sea.

pierce *verb* pierces, piercing, pierced
to make a hole through something.

pig *noun* pigs
an animal with short legs and a curly tail kept by farmers. Bacon, ham, and pork come from pigs.

A B C D E F G H I J K L M N O P Q R S T U V W X Y Z

pigbel *noun*
a disease of the stomach commonly found in the Highlands.

pigeon (pij-en) *noun* pigeons
a grey bird that often lives in towns.

piglet *noun* piglets
a young pig.

pigtail *noun* pigtails
a plait of hair.

pikelet *noun* pikelets
a small pancake that you eat cold with butter on it.

pikinnini *noun*
a baby or a child. [from Tok Pisin *pikinini*]

pile *noun* piles
a number of things put on top of one another. *a **pile** of books.*

pilgrim *noun* pilgrims
someone who makes a journey to a holy place.

pill *noun* pills
a small, round tablet that you take if you are ill.

pillar *noun* pillars
a wooden or stone post that helps to hold up a building.

pillow *noun* pillows
the cushion that you rest your head on in bed.

pilot *noun* pilots
1 someone who flies an aeroplane.
2 someone who steers a ship in narrow, difficult places.

pimple *noun* pimples
a small, round swelling on the skin.

pin *noun* pins
a thin piece of metal, with a sharp point. You use it to hold pieces of material or paper together.

PIN *noun*
a special group of numbers or letters given to a person to use when they want to do something like get money from an automatic teller machine. The word comes from the first letter of the words **p**ersonal **i**dentification **n**umber.

pinch *verb* pinches, pinching, pinched
1 to squeeze skin between your thumb and finger so that it hurts.
2 (*informal*) to steal. *Who **pinched** my pencil?*

pine *noun* pines
a tree with leaves like needles that do not fall in winter. ***pine** cones.*

pineapple *noun* pineapples
a large fruit with a yellow inside. It has stiff, pointed leaves and a thick skin covered in lumps

pink *noun, adjective*
a pale red colour.

pioneer *noun* pioneers
1 someone who is the first to do something.
2 one of the first people to go to live in a new country.

pip *noun* pips
a seed of a fruit such as an apple or orange.

pipe *noun* pipes
1 a tube for gas or liquid to go along.
2 a tube with a small bowl at one end, used for smoking tobacco.

pirate *noun* pirates
someone on a ship, who attacks and robs other ships.

pistol *noun* pistols
a small gun.

pit *noun* pits
a deep hole.

pitch *noun* pitches
1 ground marked out for cricket, soccer, or another game.
2 how high or low a sound is.

pitch ***verb*** pitches, pitching, pitched
1 to throw or toss something.
2 to put up a tent.

pitpit ***noun***
a type of wild sugar cane, the bottom part of which is good to eat. [from Tok Pisin *pitpit*]

pity ***noun***
the feeling you have when you are sorry that someone is in pain or trouble.

pity ***verb*** pities, pitying, pitied
to feel pity for someone.

pizza (peet-za) ***noun*** pizzas
a flat piece of dough covered with tomato sauce, cheese, and other things, and baked.

place ***noun*** places
1 a particular building, area, or spot. *We went to our favourite* ***place*** *for a picnic. Please put the book back in the right* ***place****.*
2 where you are in a race or test. *Seri finished in second* ***place****.*

place ***verb*** places, placing, placed
to put something somewhere. ***Place*** *your rubbish in the bin. Where have you* ***placed*** *the arrow?*

plague (playg) ***noun*** plagues
1 a dangerous illness that spreads very quickly.
2 a large number of pests. *There was a* ***plague*** *of mice in the village.*

plain ***adjective*** plainer, plainest
1 ordinary, not especially attractive. *a* ***plain*** *dress.*
2 easy to understand. *He gave me* ***plain*** *instructions.*

plain ***noun*** plains
a large area of flat ground. *You can see a long way over the* ***plain****.*

plait (plat) ***noun*** plaits
a long piece of plaited hair.

plait (plat) ***verb*** plaits, plaiting, plaited
to twist together three pieces of hair, rope, or wool by crossing them over and under each other.

plan ***noun*** plans
1 a set of ideas about how to do something. *The builder had a* ***plan*** *for the house he was building.*
2 a map of a building or a town.

plan ***verb*** plans, planning, planned
to decide what you are going to do and how to do it. *We* ***planned*** *to have a picnic in the holidays.*

plane ***noun*** planes
1 an aeroplane.
2 a tool for making wood smooth.

planet ***noun*** planets
any of the objects in space that move around the sun. The Earth is a planet.

plank ***noun*** planks
a long, flat piece of wood.

plant ***noun*** plants
a living thing that is not an animal. *Trees, flowers, and mushrooms are all* ***plants****.*

plant ***verb*** plants, planting, planted
to put something in the ground to grow.

plaster ***noun*** plasters
a soft mixture that goes hard when it dries. Plaster is used for covering walls.

plastic *noun, adjective*
a light, strong material that is made in factories and used for making all kinds of things. ***plastic** spoons, **plastic** bags.*

plate *noun* plates
a flat dish for eating from.

platform *noun* platforms
a raised place where people stand so that other people can see them.

play *noun* plays
a story acted in a theatre or on television.

play *verb* plays, playing, played
1 to have fun. *Maria **plays** with her friends on Saturdays.*
2 to take part in a game. *Tau likes **playing** football.*
3 to make music with a musical instrument. *Can you **play** the piano?*

playful *adjective*
wanting to play, full of fun. *a **playful** kitten.*

playground *noun* playgrounds
a place out of doors where children can play.

plead (pleed) *verb* pleads, pleading, pleaded
to beg for something that you want very much. *She **pleaded** with her parents to buy a dog.*

pleasant (plez-ant) *adjective*
pleasing, nice.
Word Building: pleasantly

please *verb* pleases, pleasing, pleased
1 to make someone happy.
2 the polite word you use when you are asking for something. ***Please** may I have another mango?*

pleasure (plezh-er) *noun*
the feeling people have when they are pleased.

pleat *noun* pleats
a fold in the material of a dress or skirt.

pleated *adjective*
with pleats.

plenty *noun*
a lot of something, as much as you need.

pliers *noun*
a tool for holding something tightly or for bending or breaking wire.

plod *verb* plods, plodding, plodded
to walk slowly and heavily.

plot *noun* plots
a secret plan.

plot *verb* plots, plotting, plotted
to plan something secretly.

plough (rhymes with *how*) *noun* ploughs
a machine used on farms for digging and turning over the soil.

plough *verb* ploughs, ploughing, ploughed
to dig and turn over the soil with a plough.

pluck *verb* plucks, plucking, plucked
1 to pull a feather, flower, or fruit from the place where it is growing.
2 to pull at something and let it go quickly. *People play guitars by **plucking** the strings.*

plug *noun* plugs
1 a thing on the end of a wire which fits in an electric socket.
2 a round piece of rubber or plastic which stops water from running out of a bath or sink.
3 anything you use to fill a hole.

plum *noun* plums
a juicy fruit with a smooth skin and a stone.

plumber (plum-er) *noun* plumbers
a person whose job is to put in taps, water pipes, and water tanks, or to mend them.

plump *adjective* plumper, plumpest
rather fat.

plunder *verb* plunders, plundering, plundered
to rob.
Word Building: plunderer

plunge (plunj) *verb* plunges, plunging, plunged
to jump suddenly into water, or to put something suddenly in water.

plural *adjective*
the form of a word you use when you are talking about more than one person or thing. *The **plural** of 'book' is 'books'. The **plural** of 'child' is 'children'.*

plus *preposition*
added to. *Three **plus** three is six, 3 + 3 = 6.*

pneumonia (new-**moan**-ya) *noun*
a serious illness that makes it painful to breathe.

pocket *noun* pockets
a small bag in your clothes that you put things in.

pod *noun* pods
a long thin part of some plants that has seeds inside. *Peas grow in **pods**.*

poem *noun* poems
a piece of writing with a special rhythm and lines that may rhyme.

poet *noun* poets
a person who writes poetry.

poetry *noun*
poems.

point *noun* points
1 the sharp end of something. *the **point** of a needle.*
2 a particular place or time. *We should soon reach the **point** where we can see the sea.*
3 a mark scored in a game. *Our team scored the most **points**.*
4 the reason for doing something. *The **point** of going to school is to learn.*

point *verb* points, pointing, pointed
1 to show where something is by holding your finger out towards it.
2 to aim a weapon. *He **pointed** the gun at the target.*

pointed *adjective*
with a point at the end.

poisin *noun*
a form of sorcery. [from Tok Pisin *poisin*]

poison (**poy**-zun) *noun* poisons
any liquid, powder, or plant that will kill or harm you if you swallow it.
Word Building: poisonous
*Don't eat that mushroom; it might be **poisonous**.*

poke *verb* pokes, poking, poked
to push hard with the end of your finger or a stick.

pokies *noun*
a place where poker machines can be played.

polar bear *noun* polar bears
a very large, white bear that lives in the Arctic.

pole *noun* poles
1 a long, round stick, a tall post.
2 one of the two ends of the earth.
South Pole the cold place that is the farthest south in the world.
North Pole the cold place that is the farthest north in the world.

police *noun*
the people whose job is to catch criminals and prevent crimes from happening.

Police Motu *noun*
an old name for Hiri Motu.

polish *noun* polishes
a substance which helps to make something shine. *furniture **polish**.*

polish *verb* polishes, polishing, polished
to rub the surface of something to make it shine.

polite (po-**lite**) *adjective* politer, politest
having good manners. *a **polite** boy.*
Word Building: politely

politician (pol-i-**tish**-en) *noun* politicians
a person who works in the government.

politics (**pol**-i-tiks) *noun*
the work of government.

pollen *noun*
yellow powder in a flower which wind or insects take to other flowers so that they can produce seeds.

pollute (po-**loot**) *verb* pollutes, polluting, polluted
to make air, water, and other things dirty and dangerous. *Many rivers are **polluted** with chemicals from factories.*

pollution (po-**loo**-shun) *noun*
dirty and unhealthy air or water. *Smoke and waste from factories cause **pollution**.*

Polynesia *noun*
the region of the Pacific between Hawaii, New Zealand and Easter Island.
Word building: Polynesian, a native of Polynesia. *Samoans are **Polynesians**.*

pond *noun* ponds
a very small lake.

pool *noun* pools
a small area of water.

poor *adjective* poorer, poorest
1 having very little money.
2 bad. ***poor** work, **poor** light.*

pop *noun*
a kind of popular music.

pop *verb* pops, popping, popped
to make a sound like a small explosion.

popcorn *noun*
kernels of a special kind of maize that are heated until they burst, making light, fluffy balls for eating.

poppy *noun* poppies
a bright red flower.

popular *adjective*
liked by a lot of people. *Kila is the most **popular** girl in the class.*

population (pop-yoo-**lay**-shun) *noun*
the number of people who live in a place.

porch *noun* porches
a small place with a roof, in front of the door of a building.

pore *noun* pores
one of the tiny openings in your skin.

pore *verb* pores, poring, pored
to think deeply about something. *He **pored** over the problem for a long time.*

pork *noun*
meat from a pig.

porridge *noun*
a hot food made from oats boiled in water or milk, sometimes eaten for breakfast.

port *noun* ports
a large place where ships can stay safely in the water when they are not at sea.

portable *adjective*
able to be carried about easily.
*a **portable** radio.*

portion (**por**-shun) *noun* portions
the part or amount given to you.
*Get a small **portion** of chips.*

portrait *noun* portraits
a picture of a person.

position (po-**zish**-un) *noun* positions
1 the place where something is or should be. *This is a good **position** to pitch the tent.*
2 how the body and its parts are arranged. *a sitting **position**.*

positive *adjective*
completely sure. *I am **positive** I gave you the book.*

possess (po-zess) ***verb*** possesses, possessing, possessed
to own. *They lost everything they **possessed** in the fire.*

possession (po-zesh-un) ***noun*** possessions
something that you own. *Be careful with other people's **possessions**.*

possibility ***noun*** possibilities
something that might happen. *There is a **possibility** that it will rain tomorrow.*

possible *adjective*
if something is possible, it can happen or it can be done. *Is it **possible** to mend my shoe?*
Word Building: possibly

possum ***noun*** possums
a small, long-tailed animal that lives in trees and feeds at night. The female carries her babies in a pouch.

post (rhymes with *most*) ***noun*** posts
1 an upright pole fixed in the ground. *fence **posts**.*
2 the service that delivers letters, cards, parcels, and other mail to people.
Word Building: postal, post office
*Gima is a **postal** worker.*

post (rhymes with *most*) ***verb*** posts, posting, posted
to send a letter, parcel, or postcard.

postcard ***noun*** postcards
a piece of card that you can write a message on and post.

poster ***noun*** posters
a large notice for everyone to read.

postpone ***verb*** postpones, postponing, postponed
to put off until later. *They **postponed** the race until the rain had stopped.*

pot ***noun*** pots
a deep round container, such as a teapot or a cooking pot.

potato (po-tay-toe) ***noun*** potatoes
a round white vegetable with a brown skin that you dig out of the ground.

pottery ***noun***
cups, plates, and other things made out of baked clay.

pouch ***noun*** pouches
1 a small bag.
2 a pocket of skin that some animals, such as kangaroos, have for carrying their babies in.

poultry (pole-tree) ***noun***
birds kept for their meat and eggs or meat. *Chickens and turkeys are **poultry**.*

pounce ***verb*** pounces, pouncing, pounced
to attack something by jumping on it suddenly. *The cat **pounced** on the mouse.*

pour ***verb*** pours, pouring, poured
to make liquid go out of a container. *Godfrey **poured** me a glass of milk.*

pout ***verb*** pouts, pouting, pouted
to stick out your lips when you are sulky or not pleased.

powder ***noun***
anything that is very dry and made up of many separate tiny bits, like flour or dust.

power *noun* powers
1 the ability to do what you want, or make other people do what you want. *the **power** of the government.*
2 strength. *the **power** of the storm.*

powerful *adjective*
strong, having a lot of power.
*a **powerful** engine, a **powerful** leader.*
Word Building: powerfully

practical *adjective*
1 useful or easy to do. *a **practical** idea.*
2 a person who is able to do useful things. *She's very **practical**.*

practically *adverb*
nearly, almost. *I've **practically** finished.*

practice *noun*
something you keep doing in order to get better at it. *softball **practice**.*

practise *verb* practises, practising, practised
to do something over and over again in order to get better at doing it. *If you keep **practising** you will soon improve.*

praise (prayz) *verb* praises, praising, praised
to say that someone or something is very good.

pram *noun* prams
a kind of cot on wheels for a baby.

prawn *noun* prawns
a small sea creature with a shell, which you can eat.

pray *verb* prays, praying, prayed
to talk to God.

prayer (rhymes with *care*) *noun* prayers
talking to God.

preach *verb* preaches, preaching, preached
to give a religious talk, as a minister does in church.
Word Building: preacher, preachers

precede *verb* precedes, preceding, preceded
to come before or go in front of something or someone. *The man **preceded** his wife.*

precious (presh-us) *adjective*
very valuable. ***precious** jewels.*

precipice (pres-i-pis) *noun* precipices
a cliff, a very steep rock, or a very steep part of a mountain.

precise (pre-sise) *adjective*
exact, correct.
Word Building: precisely

predator (pred-a-tor) *noun* predators
any animal that hunts and eats other animals.
Word Building: predatory

predict (pree-dict) *verb* predicts, predicting, predicted
to say what will happen in the future. *They are **predicting** that it will rain this weekend.*
Word Building: prediction

prefer (pre-fer) *verb* prefers, preferring, preferred
to like one person or thing more than another person or thing. *She **preferred** singing to dancing.*

pregnant *adjective*
expecting a baby.

prehistoric *adjective*
belonging to a time very long ago. ***prehistoric** animals.*

premature (pre-ma-tyoor) *adjective*
happening too soon; being born early. *a **premature** baby.*
Word Building: prematurely

premier (prem-ee-er) *noun* premiers
the head of a provincial government.

premiere (prem-ee-air) *noun*
the first time something is shown or done for an audience.

prepare *verb* prepares, preparing, prepared
to get something ready. *We **prepared** lunch.*
Word Building: preparation

preposition (prep-o-**zish**-un) *noun* prepositions
a word that goes at the front of some phrases. In these phrases *to*, *from*, *at*, and *with* are ***prepositions***: *to the school, from bubu, at the beach, with a stick.*

preschool *noun* preschools
a place for children to go to learn and play before they start school.

prescribe *verb* prescribes, prescribing, prescribed
to order something to be done.

prescription (pre-**scrip**-shun) *noun* prescriptions
a note from a doctor to a chemist saying what medicine you need.

present (**prez**-ent) *adjective*
1 happening now, or existing now. *the **present** queen.*
2 here. *All the children are **present**.*
at present now.

present (**prez**-ent) *noun* presents
something you give to or get from someone. *a wedding **present**.*

present (prez-**ent**) *verb* presents, presenting, presented
1 to give something to someone on a special occasion. *The principal **presented** the prizes.*
2 to introduce someone or something. *to **present** a television programme or a concert.*
Word Building: presenter, presenters *a television **presenter**.*

presently (**prez**-ent-lee) *adverb*
soon.

preserve (pree-**zerv**) *verb* preserves, preserving, preserved
1 to keep safe, not destroy. *Some old buildings in Port Moresby have been **preserved**.*
2 to do things to food so that it will not go bad. *You can **preserve** vegetables by freezing them.*

president *noun* presidents
1 the person in charge of a society, club or business.
2 the person elected to lead some countries, such as the United States of America.

press *verb* presses, pressing, pressed
1 to push hard on something. ***Press** the doorbell.*
2 to make clothes smooth and flat with an iron.

pressure (**presh**-er) *noun*
a force which presses or pushes. *the air **pressure** in a car tyre.*

pretend *verb* pretends, pretending, pretended
to try to make someone believe something that is not true. *Samuel **pretended** he was ill.*

pretty *adjective* prettier, prettiest
pleasant to look at, attractive.
Word Building: prettily

prevent *verb* prevents, preventing, prevented
to stop something from happening. *Close the door to **prevent** the room getting cold.*

preview *noun* previews
a special look at something before most people see it. *We went to a **preview** of the new film.*

previous (**pree**-vee-us) *adjective*
coming just before. *We got things ready on the **previous** day.*
Word Building: previously

prey (pray) *noun*
any animal hunted and eaten by other animals.
birds of prey birds that hunt and eat other animals.

price *noun* prices
the amount of money you have to pay for something.

priceless *adjective*
very valuable.

prick *verb* pricks, pricking, pricked
to make a tiny hole with something sharp.

pride *noun*
the feeling people have when they are proud.

priest (preest) *noun* priests
a person who leads people in religious ceremonies.

primary *adjective*
the first of something or the most important. *Young children go to* ***primary*** *school. The* ***primary*** *character in the story is named Oliver.*

primary school *noun*
a school providing six years of education from grade 3 to grade 8.

prime minister *noun* prime ministers
the leader of a government.

prince *noun* princes
the son of a king or queen.

princess *noun* princesses
1 the daughter of a king or queen.
2 the wife of a prince.

principal (prin-si-pl) *adjective*
most important, chief. *This map only shows the* ***principal*** *towns.*
Word Building: principally

principal (prin-si-pl) *noun* principals
the person in charge of a school.

principle (prin-si-pl) *noun* principles
an important rule.

print *verb* prints, printing, printed
1 to write with letters that are not joined together.
2 to use a machine that puts words or pictures onto paper.
Word Building: printer, printers

prism (priz-em) *noun* prisms
1 a piece of glass that breaks up light into the colours of the rainbow.
2 in mathematics, a three-dimensional object with parallel ends that are equal triangles.

prison (priz-en) *noun* prisons
a place where criminals are kept as a punishment.
Word Building: prisoner, prisoners

private (pry-vit) *adjective*
1 not open to everyone. *a* ***private*** *road.*
2 not known by other people. ***private*** *thoughts.*

prize *noun* prizes
something that you give to a person who wins a game or competition.

probable (prob-a-bl) *adjective*
likely to be true or to happen.
Word Building: probably
I'll ***probably*** *go swimming tomorrow.*

problem *noun* problems
something that is difficult to understand or answer.

procedure (pro-see-joor) *noun* procedures
an orderly way of doing things. *We followed the normal* ***procedure*** *for organising teams.*
Word Building: procedural

proceed *verb* proceeds, proceeding, proceeded
to go on. *The parade* ***proceeded*** *slowly along the street.*

process (pro-ses) *noun* processes
a series of actions for doing or making something. *the* ***process*** *of making cheese from milk.*

procession (pro-**sesh**-un) *noun* processions
a group of people moving along in a long line.

prod *verb* prods, prodding, prodded
to push something with the end of a finger or stick.

produce (pro-**doos**) *verb* produces, producing, produced
1 to make. *Cows* ***produce*** *milk.*
2 to bring something out so that it can be seen. *The teacher* ***produced*** *a chart from his desk.*
3 to organise a play, film, or television program.

profit (**prof**-it) *noun* profits
the extra money got by selling something for more than it cost to buy or make. *If you buy a pig for K200 and sell it for K210, you have made K10* ***profit.***

program *noun* programs
1 a talk, play, or show on the radio or television.
2 a list for people at a play or concert telling them about what they will see or hear.

progress (**prog**-res) *noun*
moving forward, or getting better.
to make progress to move forward, or to get better.

prohibit *verb* prohibits, prohibiting, prohibited
to say that people must not do something. *Smoking is* ***prohibited.***

project *noun* projects
1 a piece of work where you find out as much as you can about something interesting and write about it. *I'm doing a* ***project*** *on traditional science.*
2 a plan. *a* ***project*** *to build a new classroom.*

projector *noun* projectors
a machine for showing slides or movies on a screen.

promise (**prom**-iss) *verb* promises, promising, promised
to say that you will certainly do or not do something. *Don't forget—you* ***promised*** *to help me wash the car.*

prompt *adjective* prompter, promptest
without delay. *a* ***prompt*** *reply.*
Word Building: promptly

prong *noun* prongs
one of the thin, pointed parts on the end of a fork.

pronoun *noun* pronouns
a word that you use in place of a noun. *He*, *she*, *it*, *you*, and *they* are all ***pronouns.***

pronounce *verb* pronounces, pronouncing, pronounced
to say a sound or word in a certain way. *How do you* ***pronounce*** *your name?*

pronunciation (pro-nun-see-**ay**-shun) *noun*
the way you pronounce something.

proof *noun*
something that proves that an idea is true.

prop *verb* props, propping, propped
to support something so that it does not fall or sag.

propel *verb* propels, propelling, propelled
to drive forward.

propeller *noun* propellers
a set of blades that spin round. Propellers are fixed to aeroplanes, helicopters, and ships to make them move.

proper (prop-er) *adjective*
correct, suitable. *Put the books back in their **proper** places.*
Word Building: properly

proper name, proper noun *noun* proper names, proper nouns
the name of a person or place. You write a proper name with a capital letter: Aisi, Kerema.

property *noun* properties
1 a house or other building with land around it.
2 things that belong to you.

prophet (prof-et) *noun* prophets
1 a great religious teacher.
2 someone who tells you what he or she thinks is going to happen.

prosecute (pros-e-cute) *verb* prosecutes, prosecuting, prosecuted
to make someone go to court so that they can be punished if they have done wrong. *Trespassers will be **prosecuted.***

prosper *verb* prospers, prospering, prospered
to become successful or rich.
Word Building: prosperous
*She is a **prosperous** businesswoman.*

protect *verb* protects, protecting, protected
to keep safe from danger. *I wore a hat to **protect** me from the hot sun.*
Word Building: protection

protest *verb* protests, protesting, protested
to say or show that you think what someone else is saying or doing is wrong.

proud *adjective* prouder, proudest
very pleased with yourself or with someone else who has done well. *Hitolo was **proud** when her brother won a prize.*

prove (proov) *verb* proves, proving, proved
to show that an idea is true.

proverb (prov-erb) *noun* proverbs
a short, well-known saying which gives advice, such as 'Many hands make light work'.

provide *verb* provides, providing, provided
to give something that someone needs. *Cows **provide us with** milk.*

province (prov-ins) *noun* provinces
one of the large areas that PNG and some other countries are divided into. *the East Sopik **province**.*

provincial high school *noun*
a school providing four years of education from grade 7 to grade 10.

provoke *verb* provokes, provoking, provoked
to make someone angry. *If you **provoke** the dog, he may bite you.*

prowl *verb* prowls, prowling, prowled
to move about like an animal looking for something to kill and eat.

prune *noun* prunes
a dried plum.

pry *verb* pries, prying, pried
to try to find out about something that has nothing to do with you. *He liked to **pry** into other people's business.*

psalm (salm) *noun* psalms
one of the hymns in the Bible.

public *adjective*
open to everyone.
in public where anyone can see or hear; not in private.

publish *verb* publishes, publishing, published
to have something printed so that a lot of people can get a copy. *This dictionary was **published** by Oxford University Press.*
Word Building: publisher, publishers

puddle *noun* puddles
a small pool of water.

puff *verb* puffs, puffing, puffed
to blow out a small amount of smoke or air at a time.
puffed out out of breath.

pukpuk *noun*
a crocodile. [from Tok Pisin *pukpuk*]

pull *verb* pulls, pulling, pulled
to get hold of something and make it come towards you.

pulley *noun* pulleys
a wheel with a rope around it, used for lifting heavy things.

pulp *noun*
1 the soft inside part of a fruit.
2 a soft, wet mixture of something, especially for making paper.

pulpit *noun* pulpits
the high wooden desk in a church, where the priest or minister stands to talk to the people.

pulse *noun*
the throbbing you can feel in a vein as the blood is pumped around your body.

pump *noun* pumps
a machine for pumping air or liquid in or out of something, or along pipes. *a water* ***pump****.*

pump *verb* pumps, pumping, pumped
to force air or liquid in or out of something, or along pipes. *I've got to* ***pump*** *up the tyres on my car.*

pumpkin *noun* pumpkins
a very large, round fruit with a hard orange or green skin.

pumpkin tips *noun*
the tips of the green leaves of the pumpkin plant eaten as a vegetable.

punch *noun* punches
a tool for making holes in paper or other materials.

punch *verb* punches, punching, punched
1 to hit someone with your fist.
2 to make a hole with a punch.

punctual *adjective*
exactly on time.
Word Building: punctually

punctuation (punk-choo-**ay**-shun) *noun*
marks such as commas and full stops put into a piece of writing to make it easier to read.

puncture *noun* punctures
a hole in something. *The tyre is flat because of a* ***puncture****.*

punish *verb* punishes, punishing, punished
to make somebody suffer because they have done wrong.

punishment *noun* punishments
something you have to suffer if you have done wrong.

pupil (**pew**-pil) *noun* pupils
1 someone who has a teacher.
2 the black spot at the centre of the eye.

puppet *noun* puppets
a kind of doll, with a head and limbs that you can move by pulling strings or wires, or by fitting it over your hand like a glove.

puppy *noun* puppies
a very young dog.

purchase *verb* purchases, purchasing, purchased
to buy. *They* ***purchase*** *their supplies from the same store each fortnight.*

pure *adjective* purer, purest
with nothing else mixed with it. ***pure*** *water.*

puripuri *noun*
sorcery, magic, poisin. [from Tok Pisin *puripuri*]

purple *noun, adjective*
a colour, between red and blue.

purpose (**pur**-pus) *noun* purposes
what someone means to do.
on purpose deliberately, not by accident. *I didn't push you* ***on purpose****.*

purposely *adverb*
on purpose.

purr *verb* purrs, purring, purred
to make the sound a cat makes when it is very pleased.

purse *noun* purses
a small bag for holding money.

pursue *verb* pursues, pursuing, pursued
to go after someone and try to catch them.

push *verb* pushes, pushing, pushed
to use your hands to move something away from you.

put (rhymes with *foot*) *verb* puts, putting, put
to move something to a place, to leave something in a place. *Please* ***put*** *the book back on the shelf.*
to put something off to decide to do it later instead of now. *I decided to* ***put off*** *doing my homework till later.*
to put up with something to let it happen without complaining even if you don't like it. *We had to* ***put up with*** *the noise until the police came.*

puzzle *noun* puzzles
a problem or question that is hard to solve. *a jigsaw* ***puzzle.***

puzzle *verb* puzzles, puzzling, puzzled
to make you think hard to find the answer. *The riddle* ***puzzled*** *me.*

pyjamas (pa-**jom**-us) *noun*
trousers and a jacket worn in bed.

pygmy (**pig**-mee) *noun* pygmies
a person, animal, or plant that is very small.

pyramid (**peer**-a-mid) *noun* pyramids
1 a large, stone building made by the ancient Egyptians to hold the body of a dead king or queen.
2 the shape of a pyramid.

python (**pie**-thon) *noun* pythons
a large, tropical, non-poisonous snake that kills its prey by winding around it and crushing it.

quack *verb* quacks, quacking, quacked
to make the sound a duck makes.

quadrilateral (kwod-ri-**lat**-er-al) *noun* quadrilaterals
any four-sided shape.

quaint *adjective* quainter, quaintest
unusual but pleasant. *a **quaint** building.*

quake *verb* quakes, quaking, quaked
to shake because you are very frightened. *She was **quaking** with fear.*

qualify *verb* qualifies, qualifying, qualified
1 to pass a test or exam so that you are allowed to do something. *Korom has **qualified** as a doctor.*
2 to get enough points to go on to the next part of a competition.

quality *noun* qualities
how good or bad something is. *Torot's mangoes are always top **quality**.*

quantity *noun* quantities
an amount. *Add a small **quantity** of salt.*

quarrel *verb* quarrels, quarrelling, quarrelled
to talk angrily with someone because you do not agree.

quarry *noun* quarries
a place where people cut stone out of the ground so that it can be used for building. *a chalk **quarry**.*

quarter *noun* quarters
one of the four equal parts something can be divided into. It can also be written as $\frac{1}{4}$.

quay (kee) *noun* quays
a place where ships can be loaded and unloaded.

queen *noun* queens
1 a woman who has been crowned as ruler of a country.
2 a king's wife.

quench *verb* quenches, quenching, quenched
1 to put an end to someone's thirst. *Water **quenches** your thirst.*
2 to use water to put out a fire. *The firefighters soon **quenched** the flames.*

query (**kweer**-ee) *noun* queries
a question.

query (**kweer**-ee) *verb* queries, querying, queried
to ask a question.

quest *noun* quests
a long search.

question *noun* questions
something that you ask when you want to find out or get something.
question mark the mark **?** that you write at the end of a question.

queue (kew) *noun* queues
a line of people waiting for something.

quick *adjective* quicker, quickest
1 done in less time than usual. *a **quick** snack.*
2 fast. *Our canoe was **quicker** than theirs.*
Word Building: quickly
*Come as **quickly** as you can!*

quicksand *noun* quicksands
loose, wet sand that can swallow up people, animals, and other things.

quiet *adjective* quieter, quietest
1 without any noise. *The night was still and **quiet**.*
2 not loud, not making a lot of noise. ***quiet** music.*
Word Building: quietly
*Please close the door **quietly**.*

quit *verb* quits, quitting, quitted or quit
to give up or leave something. *He **quit** his job last year.*
Word Building: quitter

quite *adverb*
1 completely. *I'm not **quite** sure.*
2 not very but fairly. *I'm **quite** cold.*

quiver *verb* quivers, quivering, quivered
to shake because you are very cold or frightened.

quiz *noun* quizzes
a game in which people try to answer a lot of questions.

quotation (kwo-**tay**-shun) *noun* quotations
words written or spoken that were written or spoken by someone else first. *a **quotation** from a poem.*
Word Building: quotation marks
Quotation marks *" " are a punctuation mark used to show what someone said.*

quote *verb* quotes, quoting, quoted
to repeat words which were first said or written by someone else. *The teacher **quoted** some lines from a play.*

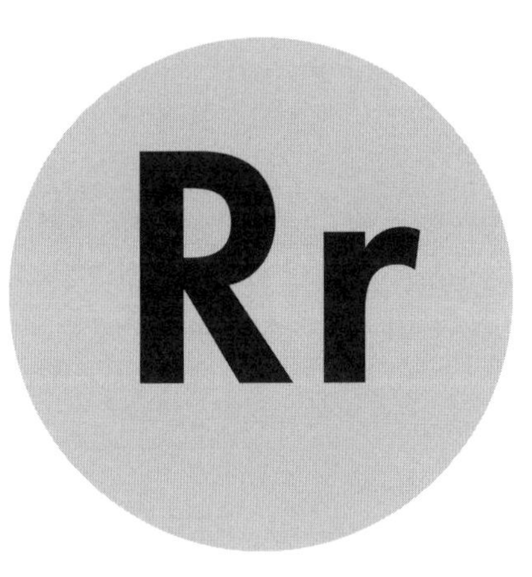

rabbi (rab-eye) *noun* rabbis
a teacher or leader of the Jewish religion.

rabbit *noun* rabbits
a furry animal with long ears. Rabbits live in holes they have dug in the ground.

race *noun* races
1 a competition to find who is fastest.
2 a group of people who come from the same part of the world and have the same colour skin, the same type of hair, and so on.
Word Building: racial

race *verb* races, racing, raced
to have a race against someone.

racist *noun* racists
a person who treats other people unfairly because they belong to a different race.

rack *noun* racks
a kind of shelf made of bars that you can put things on or in. *a luggage rack.*

racket *noun* rackets
(*informal*) a lot of loud noise.

racquet or **racket** (rak-et) *noun* racquets
a bat with a long handle and a frame with strings stretched across it, used in games like tennis.

radar (ray-dar) *noun*
a way of finding where a ship or aeroplane is and how fast it is travelling using radio waves.

radiator *noun* radiators
a part of a car that has water in it to keep the engine cool.

radio *noun* radios
a machine that picks up signals sent through the air and changes them into words or music that you can listen to.

radius *noun* radii
the distance from the centre of a circle to the edge.

raffle *noun* raffles
a way of getting money by selling tickets with numbers on them. People who buy tickets with lucky numbers on them win prizes.

raft *noun* rafts
a flat boat made of pieces of wood joined together and used instead of a boat.

rafter *noun* rafters
one of the long, sloping pieces of wood that hold up a roof.

rag *noun* rags
a small piece of cloth that you use for cleaning.
rags clothes that are very old and torn. *She was dressed in rags.*

rage *noun* rages
great anger.

raid *noun* raids
a sudden attack on a place. *a bank **raid**.*

rail *noun* rails
1 a bar or rod.
2 a long metal bar that is part of a railway line.

railway *noun* railways
1 the set of metal bars that trains travel on.
2 a train service that carries people and things.

rain *noun*
drops of water that fall from the sky.
Word Building: rainy
*a **rainy** day.*

rainbow *noun* rainbows
the curved band of different colours you see in the sky when the sun shines through rain.

rainforest *noun* rainforests
a large forest in a tropical part of the world.

raise (rayz) *verb* raises, raising, raised
1 to lift up or make something higher.
2 to gather together the money needed for something. *We need to **raise** money for the school trip.*

raisin *noun* raisins
a dried grape used in cooking.

rake *noun* rakes
a tool used in the garden. It has a long handle and a row of short spikes.

rake *verb* rakes, raking, raked
to move or smooth something with a rake. *He **raked** up the dead leaves.*

rally *noun* rallies
1 a lot of people who have come together for a big meeting.
2 a race for cars or motorcycles.

rambutan *noun* rambutans
a tropical fruit with a red hairy skin which is good to eat.

ran *verb* see **run**

ranch *noun* ranches
a large American farm with a lot of cattle or horses.

rang *verb* see **ring**

ranger *noun* rangers
a person whose job is to look after a national park.

rank *noun* ranks
1 a title or job that shows how important someone is. *The **rank** of general is higher than the **rank** of captain.*
2 a row of people. *The soldiers stood in neat **ranks**.*

rap *noun* raps
the sound you make when you knock on a door quickly.

rapid *adjective*
very quick.
Word Building: rapidly

rapt *adjective*
very happy about or entertained by something. *I was **rapt** in the film.*

rare *adjective* rarer, rarest
not often found. *Dugongs are **rare** animals.*
Word Building: rarely

rash *noun* rashes
red spots or patches that suddenly come on the skin.

rat *noun* rats
an animal like a large mouse.

rate *noun* rates
1 speed. *The snail moved at a slow **rate**.*
2 cost. *What is the **rate** for posting a letter to Australia?*

rather *adverb*
1 fairly, quite. *It's **rather** cold.*
2 more willingly. *I'd **rather** have a guava than a mango.*

ration (rash-un) *noun* rations
the amount you are allowed to have when food or other things are shared out among people. *You can't have any more, because you've had your **ration**.*

rational *adjective*
reasonable; able to think clearly. *My maths teacher is a very **rational** woman.*

rattle *verb* rattles, rattling, rattled
to make quick, hard noises by shaking something. *Many people wear **rattles** on their arms and legs when they dance in a sing-sing.*

rave *verb* raves, raving, raved
to talk in a very excited or enthusiastic way.

ravenous (rav-en-us) *adjective*
very hungry.

ravine (ra-veen) *noun* ravines
a deep, narrow valley between mountains.

raw *adjective*
not cooked. *a **raw** tomato.*

ray *noun* rays
a thin line of light. *the sun's **rays**.*

razor *noun* razors
a thin, sharp blade used for shaving.

reach *verb* reaches, reaching, reached
1 to stretch out the hand in order to touch something. *He **reached** for a coconut.*
2 to arrive at a place. *We **reached** home by 6 o'clock.*

react *verb* reacts, reacting, reacted
to act in response to something that has happened to you. *He **reacted** in surprise when she smiled at him.*
Word Building: reaction
*What was the teacher's **reaction** when you broke the window?*

read (reed) *verb* reads, reading, read
to look at and understand words that are written down.
Word Building: reader, readers

ready (red-ee) *adjective*
1 prepared and willing to do something. *Are you **ready** to go?*
2 fit to be used or eaten at once. *Is dinner **ready**?*

real *adjective*
1 true. *John is not his **real** name.*
2 not a copy. ***real** gold.*
Word Building: really
*I'm **really** hungry.*

realistic *adjective*
like the real thing. *The acting in the film was very **realistic**.*

realise *verb* realises, realising, realised
to know or understand something. *I suddenly **realised** that everyone was waiting for me.*

rear *noun* rears
the back part of something. *Sit at the **rear** of the bus.*

rear *verb* rears, rearing, reared
1 to look after children or young animals until they are big. *She **reared** the puppies.*
2 to stand on the back legs and lift the front legs into the air. *The horse **reared** in fright and the rider fell off.*

reason *noun* reasons
anything that explains why something has happened. *Is there any* ***reason*** *why you are late?*

reasonable (reez-un-a-bl) *adjective*
1 fair or right. *a* ***reasonable*** *price.*
2 willing to listen to reasons. *Be* ***reasonable****! I can't do all the work.*
Word Building: reasonably

rebel (ree-**bell**) *verb* rebels, rebelling, rebelled
to decide not to obey the people in charge.

recall (ree-**call**) *verb* recalls, recalling, recalled
to remember.

receipt (ree-**seet**) *noun* receipts
a piece of paper which proves that you have paid for something.

receive (ree-**seev**) *verb* receives, receiving, received
to get something that has been given or sent to you. *Did you* ***receive*** *my letter?*

recent (**ree**-sent) *adjective*
done or made a short time ago. *Is this a* ***recent*** *photo of your brother?*
Word Building: recently

recess (ree-**ses** or **ree**-ses) *noun* recesses
a short time when work stops.

recipe (**res**-a-pee) *noun* recipes
instructions that tell you how to cook something.

recite *verb* recites, reciting, recited
to say a poem or something else that you have learnt by heart.

reckless *adjective*
likely to do silly or dangerous things. *a* ***reckless*** *driver.*
Word Building: recklessly

reckon *verb* reckons, reckoning, reckoned
1 to count or add up. *Yaking* ***reckoned*** *up how much money she had left.*
2 to feel sure. *I* ***reckon*** *our side will win on Saturday.*

recognise (**rek**-og-nize) *verb* recognises, recognising, recognised
to know who someone is because you have seen them before.

recommend (rek-o-**mend**) *verb* recommends, recommending, recommended
1 to tell someone that another person or thing is useful. *Can you* ***recommend*** *a good hotel?*
2 to tell someone in a helpful way what you think they should do. *I* ***recommend*** *that you see a doctor.*

record (**rek**-ord) *noun* records
1 a written list of things you have done, seen, or found out. *We keep a* ***record*** *of the birds we see.*
2 the best that has been done so far. *Mirou's time for the race was a* ***record****.*

record (ree-**kord**) *verb* records, recording, recorded
1 to put music or other sounds onto a tape or disc.
2 to write down things you have done, seen, or found out.

recorder *noun* recorders
a wooden or plastic musical instrument that you play by blowing into one end.

recover *verb* recovers, recovering, recovered
1 to get better after being ill.
2 to get something back that you have lost. *The police* ***recovered*** *the stolen car.*

recreation (rek-ree-**ay**-shun) *noun*
hobbies or games people like playing in their spare time.

rectangle *noun* rectangles
a flat, four-sided shape with four right angles.
Word Building: rectangular

recycle *verb* recycles, recycling, recycled
to use paper, glass, or other things again instead of throwing them away.

red *noun, adjective*
the colour of blood.

red emperor *noun*
a red reef fish that is very good to eat.

reduce (ree-**doos**) *verb* reduces, reducing, reduced
to make smaller or less. ***Reduce** speed when you approach a bend in the road.*

reed *noun* reeds
a plant like tall grass with a strong stem that grows near water.

reef *noun* reefs
a line of rocks just below or just above the surface of the sea. *a coral **reef**.*

reel *noun* reels
a round piece of wood, metal, or plastic on which you wind things like cotton or film.

reel *verb* reels, reeling, reeled
to lose your balance because you feel dizzy.

refer *verb* refers, referring, referred
1 to talk about someone or something. *When I said some people are stupid, I wasn't **referring** to you!*
2 to look in a book for information. *If you don't know how to spell a word, you can **refer** to the dictionary.*

referee (ref-e-**ree**) *noun* referees
someone who makes sure that the players in a game keep to the rules.

reference (**ref**-rens) *noun* references
1 a mention of something.
2 a place in a book or file where information can be found.
3 a letter listing the work someone has done, and how well he or she did it.

reflect *verb* reflects, reflecting, reflected
1 to send back light from a shiny surface.
2 to show an image of something, as a mirror does. *The trees were **reflected** in the still water.*
3 to think seriously about something.
Word Building: reflection, reflections

refresh *verb* refreshes, refreshing, refreshed
to make a tired person feel fresh and strong again. *a **refreshing** drink.*

refreshments *plural noun*
drinks and snacks.

refrigerator (ree-**frij**-e-ray-tor) *noun* refrigerators
a kind of cupboard that keeps food and drink cold and fresh, often called a fridge.

refugee (ref-yoo-**jee**) *noun* refugees
a person who had to leave his or her country because of a war.

refund *noun* refunds
money that is paid back. *You can get a **refund** on the unused ticket.*

refuse (**ref**-yoos) *noun*
rubbish.

refuse (ree-**fyooz**) *verb* refuses, refusing, refused
to say you will not do something you have been asked to do. *She **refused** to tidy her room.*

regard *verb* regards, regarding, regarded
to think of someone or something in a certain way. *He **regarded** me as a friend.*

region (**ree**-jun) *noun* regions
a part of a country or the world. *the Highlands **regions** of PNG.*

A B C D E F G H I J K L M N O P Q R S T U V W X Y Z

regret *verb* regrets, regretting, regretted
to be sad or sorry about something you have done or something that has happened.

regular (reg-yoo-luh) *adjective*
1 always happening at certain times. ***regular** meals.*
2 usual, normal. *Who is your **regular** teacher?*
Word Building: regularly

rehearsal (ree-her-sl) *noun* rehearsals
a practice for a concert or play.

rehearse *verb* rehearses, rehearsing, rehearsed
to practise something before you do it in front of an audience.

reindeer (rain-deer) *noun* reindeer
a deer that lives in very cold countries.

reins (rains) *noun*
the two long straps used for guiding a horse.

reject *verb* rejects, rejecting, rejected
to refuse to accept someone or something. *The piglet was **rejected** by its mother.*

rejoice *verb* rejoices, rejoicing, rejoiced
to be very happy about something.

relate *verb* relates, relating, related
1 to tell or describe something.
2 to connect or compare one thing with another.
Word Building: relation, relationship, unrelated

related *adjective*
belonging to the same family.

relative *noun* relatives
someone who is related to you.

relax *verb* relaxes, relaxing, relaxed
to rest and let your body become less stiff. *She **relaxed** on the bed.*

relay *verb* relays, relaying, relayed
to pass on a message.

release *verb* releases, releasing, released
to set someone free.

relent *verb* relents, relenting, relented
to become less angry or less strict than you were at first. *Mother **relented** and let us go for a swim.*

reliable *adjective*
trustworthy, able to be counted on. *a **reliable** friend.*

relic (rel-ik) *noun* relics
something very old that was left by people who lived long ago.

relief (ree-leef) *noun*
the feeling you have when you are no longer in trouble, pain, or danger.

relieve (ree-leev) *verb* relieves, relieving, relieved
1 to end some worry or pain. *The tablet will **relieve** your headache.*
2 to take over from someone. *The night nurse will **relieve** the day nurse.*

relieved (ree-leevd) *adjective*
happy because you are no longer in trouble, pain, or danger.

religion *noun* religions
what people believe about God or gods, and how they worship.
Word Building: religious

reluctant *adjective*
not wanting to do something. *She was **reluctant** to leave her baby at home.*
Word Building: reluctantly

rely *verb* relies, relying, relied
to trust someone or something to help you. *The blind man **relied** on his dog.*

remain *verb* remains, remaining, remained
to stay after other people or things have gone. ***Remain** where you are!*

remainder *noun* remainders
what is left over.

remains *plural noun*
1 ruins. *the **remains** of an old church.*
2 a dead body. *His **remains** are buried in the cemetery.*

remark *verb* remarks, remarking, remarked
to say something that you have thought or noticed. *'It's very hot today,' she **remarked**.*

remarkable *adjective*
so unusual that you remember it.
Word Building: remarkably

remedy (rem-e-dee) *noun* remedies
a way of making something better. *Vitamin C is a good **remedy** for colds.*

remember *verb* remembers, remembering, remembered
to bring something into your mind when you want to. *I can't **remember** his name.*

remind *verb* reminds, reminding, reminded
to make or help someone remember something.

remote *adjective* remoter, remotest
far away.

remove *verb* removes, removing, removed
to take something off or away. *He **removed** the dishes when we had finished eating.*

rent *noun* rents
the money that you pay every week or month to live in a place or use something that belongs to another person.

rent *verb* rents, renting, rented
to pay to live in a place or use something that belongs to another person. *to **rent** a flat.*

repair *verb* repairs, repairing, repaired
to mend something that is broken or doesn't work anymore. *Can you **repair** my radio?*

repay *verb* repays, repaying, repaid
to pay back what you owe.

repeat *verb* repeats, repeating, repeated
to say or do the same thing again.
Word Building: repeatedly, repetition

repent *verb* repents, repenting, repented
to be very sorry about something you have said or done. *She **repented** after she had been so unkind.*

replace *verb* replaces, replacing, replaced
1 to put something back. *He **replaced** the book on the shelf.*
2 to take the place of another person or thing. *We have a new car to **replace** the old one.*

reply *noun* replies
an answer.

reply *verb* replies, replying, replied
to answer.

report *noun* reports
1 something that someone says or writes about something that has happened. *a news **report**.*
2 something that teachers write about your work. *a school **report**.*

report *verb* reports, reporting, reported
to tell or write about something that has happened. *We **reported** the accident to the police.*
Word Building: reporter, reporters

represent (rep-ree-**zent**) *verb* represents, representing, represented
1 to be a picture or model of something. *These red lines on the map **represent** roads.*
2 to be chosen from a larger group to do something you are good at. *She **represented** the school in the speaking competition.*

reproduce *verb* reproduces, reproducing, reproduced
1 to make a copy of something.
2 to produce babies.
Word Building: reproduction, reproductions

reptile *noun* reptiles
an animal with cold blood that lays eggs. *Snakes, crocodiles, and lizards are **reptiles**.*

reputation (rep-yoo-tay-shun) *noun* reputations
the things everyone says or thinks about a person. *She has a **reputation** for being noisy.*

request *verb* requests, requesting, requested
to ask politely for something.

require *verb* requires, requiring, required
to need.

rescue (res-kew) *verb* rescues, rescuing, rescued
to save from danger.

research *noun* researches
careful study to find out more about something.

resemble (ree-zem-bl) *verb* resemble, resembling, resembled
to look or sound like another person or thing. *Raka **resembles** his father.*

reserve (ree-zerv) *verb* reserves, reserving, reserved
1 to ask someone to keep a place or a seat for you. ***Reserve** a seat for the show.*
2 to keep something for later. ***Reserve** some taro for tomorrow.*

reservoir (rez-ev-wah) *noun* reservoirs
a lake with a dam at one end where water is stored.

resign (ree-zine) *verb* resigns, resigning, resigned
to give up your job.

resist (ree-zist) *verb* resists, resisting, resisted
to fight against something and not give way.

resources *noun*
things which are useful for making things or for making our lives better. *Oil is one of our most important natural **resources**.*

respect *noun*
the feeling you have for someone you like and admire.

respond *verb* responds, responding, responded
to answer.

responsible *adjective*
in charge and likely to take the blame if anything goes wrong.

rest *noun* rests
a time which you spend sleeping or being still and quiet. *We climbed the hill and had a **rest** at the top.*
the rest the people or things that are left. *If you don't want **the rest**, I'll eat it.*

rest *verb* rests, resting, rested
to stop doing things for a time so that you can get your strength back. *Halfway up the hill we sat down to **rest**.*

restaurant (rest-a-ront or rest-ront) *noun* restaurants
a place where you can buy a meal and eat it.

restore (ree-stor) *verb* restores, restoring, restored
to make something as good as it was before.

result (ree-**zult**) *noun* results
1 anything that happens because of other things. *I got up late and as a **result** I missed the bus.*
2 the score or marks at the end of a game, competition, or test.

retire *verb* retires, retiring, retired
to stop working because you are too old or ill.

retreat *verb* retreats, retreating, retreated
to go back because it is too dangerous to carry on. *The soldiers **retreated**.*

return *verb* returns, returning, returned
1 to go back to a place. *We **returned** home at tea time.*
2 to give something back. *Koru **returned** the book to the library.*

reveal *verb* reveals, revealing, revealed
to let something be seen or known.

revenge (ree-**venj**) *noun*
a wish to hurt someone because they have hurt you or one of your friends.

reverse *verb* reverses, reversing, reversed
to go backwards.

revise *verb* revises, revising, revised
1 to go back over something and change it. *I'll **revise** my story by changing the ending.*
2 to go back over something so that you learn it.

revolt *verb* revolts, revolting, revolted
to say that you will not obey the people in charge.

revolting *adjective*
horrible, disgusting.

revolution (rev-o-**loo**-shun) *noun* revolutions
a fight to get rid of the government and put a new kind of government in its place.

revolve *verb* revolves, revolving, revolved
to turn round and round like a wheel.

reward *noun* rewards
a present given to someone because of something good they have done.

rhinoceros (ry-**noss**-e-rus) *noun* rhinoceroses
a big, wild animal with a horn on its nose, found in Africa and Asia. It is often called a rhino for short.

rhyme *verb* rhymes, rhyming, rhymed
to have the same sound at the end as another word. *Bat **rhymes** with mat.*

rhythm (**rith**-m) *noun* rhythms
the pattern made in music or poetry by the strong and weak sounds.

rib *noun* ribs
one of the curved bones above the waist.

ribbon *noun* ribbons
a strip of nylon, silk, or some other material.

rice *noun*
white or brown grains that you cook and eat.

rich *adjective* richer, richest
having a lot of money.

rid *verb*
to get rid of to make someone or something go away.

riddle *noun* riddles
a question or puzzle that is a joke.

ride *noun* rides
a journey in a PMV or car, or on a bus, train, horse or bicycle.

ride *verb* rides, riding, rode, ridden
1 to sit on something and be carried along on it. *to **ride** a horse.*
2 to travel in a car, bus, or train.
Word Building: rider, riders

ridge *noun* ridges
a long, narrow part higher than the rest, like the line along the top of a roof.

ridiculous *adjective*
so silly that people laugh.
Word Building: ridiculously

rifle *noun* rifles
a long gun that is held against the shoulder when it is fired.

right *adjective*
1 on the side opposite the left. *Most people write with their **right** hand.*
2 correct. *the **right** answer.*
3 fair. *It is not **right** to cheat.*

right *adverb*
correctly. *Have I spelt your name **right**?*

right-handed *adjective*
if you are right-handed you use the right hand to write and do other important things.

rim *noun* rims
the edge round the top of a round container or round the outside of a wheel. *the **rim** of a cup.*

rind *noun* rinds
the skin on bacon, cheese, or fruit.

ring *noun* rings
1 a circle.
2 a circle of metal worn on a finger. *a wedding **ring**.*

ring *verb* rings, ringing, rang, rung
1 to make a sound like a bell.
2 to make a telephone call to someone. *We **ring** Bubu every Sunday.*

rinse *verb* rinses, rinsing, rinsed
to wash something in clean water after using soap.

riot *noun* riots
violent, noisy behaviour by a crowd of people.

rip *verb* rips, ripping, ripped
to tear.

ripe *adjective* riper, ripest
fruit that is ripe is ready to eat.

ripple *noun* ripples
a tiny wave on the surface of water.

rise *verb* rises, rising, rose, risen
1 to go upwards. *The sun **rises** in the east.*
2 to get up. *They all **rose** as she came in.*

risk *noun* risks
the chance that something bad or dangerous might happen.

risky *adjective* riskier, riskiest
dangerous.

rival *noun* rivals
someone trying to win the same prize as you are.

river *noun* rivers
a large amount of water that flows into the sea.

road *noun* roads
a wide, sealed path that cars, buses, and other vehicles go along.

roam *verb* roams, roaming, roamed
to move around without trying to get anywhere. *They **roamed** all over the hills.*

roar *verb* roars, roaring, roared
to make the loud, deep sound a lion makes.

roast *verb* roasts, roasting, roasted
to cook meat or vegetables in the oven or over a fire.

rob *verb* robs, robbing, robbed
to steal something from someone.
Word Building: robber, robbers, robbery

robot (roe-bot) *noun* robots
a machine in a factory controlled by a computer. ***Robots** can work like a person.*

rock *noun* rocks
something hard and heavy that is part of mountains, hills, and the ground.

rock 'n' roll *noun*
a type of popular music.

rock *verb* rocks, rocking, rocked
to move gently backwards and forwards or from side to side.

rocket *noun* rockets
1 a jet engine that is used to make a spacecraft fly.
2 a firework joined to a stick. Rockets shoot high into the air when they are lit.

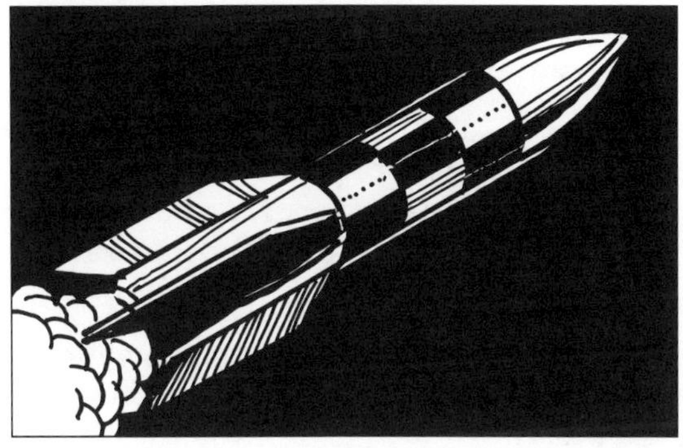

rod *noun* rods
a long, thin, round piece of wood or metal.

rode *verb* see **ride**

rodent *noun* rodents
an animal that gnaws things. Rats and mice are rodents.

rodeo (ro-day-o) *noun* rodeos
a contest where people show their skill in riding horses and catching cattle.

roll *noun* rolls
1 a long round shape made by rolling something up. *a* ***roll*** *of carpet.*
2 a very small loaf of bread.

roll *verb* rolls, rolling, rolled
to turn over and over like a ball moving along the ground.

roof *noun* roofs
the part that covers the top of a building.

room *noun* rooms
1 one of the spaces with walls around it inside a building.
2 enough space for something.

roost *noun* roosts
the place where a bird rests at night.

rooster *noun* roosters
a male chicken.

root *noun* roots
the part of a plant that grows under the ground.

rope *noun* ropes
a lot of strong threads twisted together.

rose *noun* roses
a flower with a sweet smell and thorns on its stem.

rose *verb* see **rise**

rosella (ro-**zel**-la) *noun* rosellas
a brightly coloured, long-tailed parrot.

rosy *adjective* rosier, rosiest
coloured like a pink or red rose.

rot *verb* rots, rotting, rotted
to go soft or bad so that it cannot be used. *We should eat the fruit before it* ***rots****.*

rotten *adjective*
1 so soft or bad that it cannot be used. ***rotten*** *wood, a* ***rotten*** *apple.*
2 (*informal*) very bad. *a* ***rotten*** *joke.*

rough (ruff) *adjective* rougher, roughest
1 not smooth or flat. ***rough*** *wood.*
2 not gentle. ***rough*** *seas.*
3 not exact. *a* ***rough*** *guess.*

round *adjective*
shaped like a circle or ball. *a* ***round*** *mirror.*

roundabout *noun* roundabouts
a place where roads meet, where cars must drive around in a circle.

route (root) *noun* routes
the way you go to get to a place.

row (rhymes with *how*) *noun* rows
1 a quarrel.
2 a lot of noise.

row (rhymes with *toe*) *noun* rows
people or things arranged in a straight line.

A B C D E F G H I J K L M N O P Q R S T U V W X Y Z

row (rhymes with *toe*) ***verb*** rows, rowing, rowed
to use oars to make a boat move.

royal ***adjective***
belonging to a king or queen.

royalty ***noun***
kings, queens, and their families.

rub ***verb*** rubs, rubbing, rubbed
to move something backwards and forwards against another thing.
*I **rubbed** my hands together to keep warm.*

rubber ***noun*** rubbers
1 a strong material that stretches, bends, and bounces. ***Rubber** is used for making car tyres.*
2 a piece of rubber for removing pencil marks.

rubbish ***noun***
1 things that are not wanted or needed.
2 nonsense. *You're talking **rubbish**!*

rudder ***noun*** rudders
a flat part at the end of a boat or aeroplane. It moves to make the boat or aeroplane go left or right.

rude ***adjective*** ruder, rudest
not polite.

rug ***noun*** rugs
a thick blanket or a mat.

rugby ***noun***
a football game with an oval ball that can be carried or kicked.

rugged (rug-ged) ***adjective***
1 rough and not even.
2 rocky.

ruin ***noun*** ruins
a building that has fallen down.

ruin ***verb*** ruins, ruining, ruined
to spoil something completely. *The rain **ruined** our picnic.*

rule ***noun*** rules
something that everyone ought to obey.
*When you play a game, you must obey the **rules**.*

rule ***verb*** rules, ruling, ruled
1 to be in charge of a country and the people who live there.
2 to draw a straight line with a ruler.

ruler ***noun*** rulers
1 someone who rules a country.
2 a strip of wood, metal, or plastic with straight edges, used for measuring and drawing lines.

rumble ***verb*** rumbles, rumbling, rumbled
to make the deep, heavy sound thunder makes.

rumour ***noun*** rumours
something that a lot of people are saying, although it might not be true.

run ***verb*** runs, running, ran
1 to use your legs to move quickly.
2 to flow. *The river **runs** into the sea.*
3 to control something. *Who **runs** this company?*
Word Building: runner, runners

run ***noun*** runs
1 a time spent running. *We took the dog for a **run**.*
2 a point scored in cricket, softball, or baseball.

rung ***noun*** rungs
one of the short bars on a ladder.

rung ***verb*** see **ring**

runner-up ***noun*** runners-up
a person or team that finishes in second place.

runway ***noun*** runways
a surface that aeroplanes take off from and land on.

rural ***adjective***
to do with the areas outside towns and cities. *Most villages in PNG are in the **rural** areas.*

rush *verb* rushes, rushing, rushed
to move very quickly.

rust *noun*
a rough, red surface that covers iron that has got wet.
Word Building: rusty

rustle (rus-sl) *verb* rustles, rustling, rustled
to make the light sounds dry leaves make when they are blown by the wind.

sack *noun* sacks
a large bag made of strong material. *a sack of coffee.*
to get the sack (*informal*) to lose your job.

sacred (say-kred) *adjective*
with a special religious meaning. *A church is a **sacred** building.*

sacrifice (sak-ri-fise) *noun* sacrifices
1 something you like which you give up in order to help someone.
2 a gift offered to God.

sad *adjective* sadder, saddest
not happy.
Word Building: sadly

safe *adjective* safer, safest
if you are safe, you are not in any danger.
Word Building: safely

safe *noun* safes
a strong metal box with a lock where you can keep money or things like jewellery.

safety *noun*
a time or place without danger. *The firefighter carried her to **safety**.*

sag *verb* sags, sagging, sagged
to go down in the middle. *The bed **sagged** under his weight.*

sago *noun*
a starchy food made from the stems of the sago palm; saksak. ***Sago** is the main food eaten by people from the Sepik province.*
Word building: sago grub, sago palm

said *verb* see say

sail *noun* sails
a large piece of strong cloth which makes a boat move along when the wind blows into it.

sail *verb* sails, sailing, sailed
to travel in a boat.

sailor *noun* sailors
a person who works on a ship.

saint *noun* saints
a very good and holy person.

sake *noun*
purpose, reason. *Will you do it for the **sake** of your health?*

saksak *noun*
sago [from Tok Pisin *saksak*]

salad (sal-ad) *noun* salads
a mixture of vegetables eaten raw or cold.

salary (sal-a-ree) *noun* salaries
money paid to someone regularly, usually each fortnight for the work they do.

sale *noun* sales
1 the selling of things. *These carvings are not for **sale**.*
2 a time when things in a shop are sold at lower prices than usual.

saliva (sa-lie-va) *noun*
a liquid in your mouth that helps you to eat your food.

salmon (sam-on) *noun* salmon
a large fish with pink flesh that you can eat.

salt *noun*
a white powder put on food to give it flavour.
Word Building: salty, saltier, saltiest

salute (sa-**loot**) *verb* salutes, saluting, saluted
to touch your forehead with your hand, as soldiers do to show respect.

same *adjective*
not different in any way. *Yamog goes to the **same** school as me.*

sample *noun* samples
a small amount that shows what something is like. *free **samples** of soap.*

sand *noun* sands
powder made of tiny bits of rock that you find in deserts and next to the sea.

sandal *noun* sandals
a light shoe with straps that you wear in warm weather.

sandwich *noun* sandwiches
two slices of bread and butter with a different food between them. *a meat **sandwich**.*

sandy *adjective*
covered with sand, full of sand. ***sandy** beaches.*

sane *adjective* saner, sanest
normal and healthy in your mind; not mad.
Word Building: sanity, insane

sang *verb* see sing

sanguma *noun*
a form of sorcery. [from Tok Pisin *sanguma*]

sank *verb* see sink

sap *noun*
the sticky liquid that carries food through plants and trees.

sapling *noun* saplings
a young tree.

sarcastic *adjective*
if you are sarcastic, you say something funny in an unkind way. *Vagi hates it when her brother makes **sarcastic** remarks.*

sarep or **saref** *noun*
a long knife with a curved end used for cutting grass. [from Tok Pisin *sarip, sarep*]

sari *noun* saris
a long piece of cloth worn as a dress by Indian women and girls.

sash *noun* sashes
a wide ribbon worn around the waist.

sat *verb* see sit

satellite *noun* satellites
a planet or spacecraft that moves in space around another planet. *The moon is a **satellite** of the earth.*
satellite dish a kind of antenna in the shape of a dish for receiving television signals from a satellite.

satin *noun*
smooth cloth that is very shiny on one side.

satisfactory *adjective*
good enough but not very good. *Her work is **satisfactory**.*

satisfy *verb* satisfies, satisfying, satisfied
to be good enough to please someone; to give someone what they want or need.

Saturday *noun* Saturdays
the first day of the weekend.

sauce *noun* sauces
a thick liquid put on food. *tomato sauce.*

saucepan *noun* saucepans
a metal pan with a long handle used for cooking.

saucer *noun* saucers
a small plate for putting a cup on.

sausage *noun* sausages
a skin tube stuffed with tiny pieces of meat and bread.

savage *adjective*
wild and fierce. *a **savage** attack by a large dog.*
Word Building: savagely

save *verb* saves, saving, saved
1 to take someone or something away from danger. *The doctor **saved** her life.*
2 to keep something, especially money, to use later.

savings *noun*
money that you put in a bank so that you can use it later.

saw *noun* saws
a tool with a wide, thin blade with sharp teeth. You move a saw backwards and forwards across a piece of wood to cut it.

saw *verb* saws, sawing, sawed, sawn
to use a saw to cut wood.

saw *verb* see see

sawdust *noun*
a powder that comes from wood when it is cut with a saw.

say *verb* says, saying, said
to use the voice to make words. *'Hello,' he **said**.*

saying *noun* sayings
a sentence or phrase which people often use. *'The early bird catches the worm' is an old **saying**.*

scab *noun* scabs
a piece of hard skin that covers a cut or graze while it is getting better.

scabies *noun*
a skin disease which causes itching.

scaffolding *noun*
planks fixed to poles and put around a building so that builders and painters can stand on them.

scald *verb* scalds, scalding, scalded
to burn yourself with very hot liquid.

scale *noun* scales
1 one of the thin, hard flakes that cover the skins of animals such as fish and snakes.
2 a set of musical notes.
Word Building: scaly

scale *verb* scales, scaling, scaled
to climb something. *We **scaled** the mountain at dawn.*

scales *plural noun*
a machine for weighing things.

scalp *noun* scalps
the skin covering the top of the head where the hair grows.

scamper *verb* scampers, scampering, scampered
to run about quickly.

scandal *noun*
unkind talk about someone who is supposed to have done something wrong.

scar *noun* scars
a mark left on your skin by a cut or burn after it has healed.

scarce (skairs) *adjective* scarcer, scarcest
not enough, not often found, rare. *Water is **scarce** in the desert.*

scarcely (skairs-lee) *adverb*
only just, hardly. *He was so frightened he could **scarcely** speak.*

scare *verb* scares, scaring, scared
to frighten. *Are you **scared** of the dark?*

scarecrow *noun* scarecrows
something that looks like a person and is put in a field to frighten away birds.

scarf *noun* scarves
a piece of material that is worn around the neck or head.

scarlet *noun, adjective*
bright red.

scary *adjective* scarier, scariest
frightening. *The **scary** story frightened the children.*

scatter *verb* scatters, scattering, scattered
to throw small things so that they fall in many different places. *She **scattered** some crumbs for the birds.*

scene (seen) *noun* scenes
1 the place where something happens. *the **scene** of the crime.*
2 part of a play.

scenery (seen-a-ree) *noun*
1 things that you can see around you when you are out in the country. *beautiful mountain **scenery**.*
2 things on a stage of a theatre to make it look like a real place.

scent (sent) *noun* scents
1 a liquid with a sweet smell.
2 a pleasant smell. *the **scent** of ginger.*
3 an animal's smell. *a deer's **scent**.*

scheme (skeem) *noun* schemes
a plan.

scholarship (skol-er-ship) *noun* scholarships
money given to someone in order to help them to go on studying.

school (skool) *noun* schools
the place where children go to learn.

science (sy-ens) *noun* sciences
knowledge about the world that people get by studying things and testing ideas about the way they work.

scientific (sy-en-**tif**-ik) *adjective*
having to do with science.

scientist (sy-en-tist) *noun* scientists
someone who studies science.

scissors (siź-ers) *plural noun*
a tool for cutting that has two sharp blades joined together.

scold *verb* scolds, scolding, scolded
to tell someone you are angry with them because of what they have done. *Avia **scolded** the dog for eating her food.*

scone (skon) *noun* scones
a small cake or bun.

scoop *noun* scoops
a deep spoon for lifting up and measuring out things.

scoop *verb* scoops, scooping, scooped
to use a tool or your arms or hands to gather things together and lift them up.

scooter *noun* scooters
1 a motorbike with a small engine.
2 a small vehicle with two wheels that you ride by standing on it with one foot and pushing with the other.

scorch *verb* scorches, scorching, scorched
to make something so hot that it goes brown.

score *noun* scores
1 the number of points or goals scored by each side in a game.
2 twenty.

score *verb* scores, scoring, scored
to get a point or points in a game.

scorn *noun*
the feeling that you have when you think someone or something is not good enough. *She looked at him with **scorn** and hatred.*

scout *noun* scouts
someone sent ahead to find out things, usually about an enemy.

scramble *verb* scrambles, scrambling, scrambled
to use your hands and feet to climb up or down something. *We **scrambled** over the rocks.*
scrambled eggs eggs mixed up with milk and cooked.

scrap *noun* scraps
1 a small piece. *a **scrap** of material.*
2 something that you do not want any more but that is made of material that can be used again. ***scrap** paper.*

scrape *verb* scrapes, scraping, scraped
to move a rough or sharp thing across something. ***Scrape** the mud off your shoes.*

scratch *verb* scratches, scratching, scratched
1 to cut or make a mark on something with a sharp thing.
2 to rub your skin to stop it itching.

scream *verb* screams, screaming, screamed
to make a loud cry that shows you are hurt or afraid.

screech *verb* screeches, screeching, screeched
to make a loud, high sound. *An owl **screeched** in the night.*

screen *noun* screens
1 the flat glass part of a television or computer where words or pictures appear.
2 the flat surface where films are shown at the cinema.
3 a kind of thin wall that can be used to hide something.
4 a sheet of thin wire put over a window to keep out insects.

screw *noun* screws
a kind of nail with a slot on the top and ridges round the sharp end. You put it in a hole and twist it to fix things together.

screw *verb* screws, screwing, screwed
1 to fix something with a screw.
2 to turn or twist something to make it tighter.

screwdriver *noun* screwdrivers
a tool for turning a screw until it fits tightly into something.

scribble *verb* scribbles, scribbling, scribbled
to write or draw quickly and untidily.

scroll *verb* scrolls, scrolling, scrolled
to move the words or pictures on your computer screen up or down, to see what comes after or before them.

scrub *verb* scrubs, scrubbing, scrubbed
to rub something hard with a brush to clean it.

scrub *noun*
land that is thickly covered with low trees and shrubs.

scuba (skoo-ba) *noun*
equipment to help you to breathe under water.
Word Building: scuba diver

sculptor *noun* sculptors
an artist who makes things in stone, wood, clay, or metal.

sculpture *noun* sculptures
a statue or something else made by a sculptor.

scurry *verb* scurries, scurrying, scurried
to run with short, fast steps.

sea *noun* seas
the large area of salty water that covers large parts of the earth.

seafood *noun*
fish, prawns, scallops, oysters, and other animals found in the sea that you can eat.

seagull *noun* seagulls
a white or grey sea bird with a loud cry.

seal *noun* seals
a furry animal that lives in the sea and on land.

seal *verb* seals, sealing, sealed
to close something by sticking two parts together. *Did you* ***seal*** *the envelope?*

seam *noun* seams
the line where two pieces of material are sewn together.

search *verb* searches, searching, searched
to look carefully for something.

season *noun* seasons
1 one of the four parts of the year. Spring, summer, autumn, and winter are the seasons.
2 a period of time when something happens, as in the wet season.

seat *noun* seats
a chair or stool or anything else that people sit on.

seaweed *noun* seaweeds
a plant that grows in the sea.

second *adjective, adverb*
coming after the first. *February is the* ***second*** *month of the year.*

second *noun* seconds
a measure of time. There are 60 seconds in one minute.

secondary school *noun*
A school providing four years of education from grade 9 to grade 12.

second-hand *adjective*
not new, already owned by someone else.

secret (see-kret) *adjective*
not known by everybody; not to be told or shown to other people.
Word Building: secretly

secret (see-kret) *noun* secrets
something which is not to be told or shown to other people.

secretary (sek-re-tair-ee) *noun* secretaries
someone whose job is to write letters, answer the telephone, and organise things in an office.

section (sek-shun) *noun* sections
1 a part of something.
2 the piece of land that a person's house is built on.

secure *adjective* securer, securest
safe or firm. *Make sure the ladder is* ***secure*** *before you climb it.*
Word Building: securely, security

see *verb* sees, seeing, saw, seen
1 to use your eyes to look at something.
2 to understand. *Do you* ***see*** *what I mean?*

seed *noun* seeds
a tiny thing that a plant can grow from.

seedling *noun* seedlings
a young plant.

seek *verb* seeks, seeking, sought
to try to find.

seem *verb* seems, seeming, seemed
to make you think something is true. *Nou* ***seems*** *sad today.*

seen *verb* see see

see-saw *noun* see-saws
a piece of wood or metal that is balanced in the middle and can go up and down when people sit on the ends.

A B C D E F G H I J K L M N O P Q R S T U V W X Y Z

seize (seez) *verb* seizes, seizing, seized
to take hold of something suddenly. *The thief **seized** the bag and ran.*

seldom *adverb*
not often.

select *verb* selects, selecting, selected
to choose.

self *noun* selves
everything in a person that makes them different from anyone else.

selfish *adjective*
If you are selfish you only think about yourself and don't care what other people want.
Word Building: selfishly

sell *verb* sells, selling, sold
to give in return for money. *I **sold** my pig yesterday.*

semicircle *noun* semicircles
half of a circle.

semicolon *noun* semicolons
a mark like this **;** that you use in writing.

semifinal *noun* semifinals
a match played to decide who plays in the final.

send *verb* sends, sending, sent
to make a person or thing go somewhere. ***Send** for an ambulance!*

senior *adjective*
older or more important.

sensation *noun* sensations
1 anything that you can feel happening to yourself. *The cold water gave me a tingling **sensation**.*
2 something exciting that happens.

sense *noun* senses
1 the power to see, hear, smell, feel, or taste. *Dogs have a good **sense** of smell.*
2 knowing what is the right thing to do. *She had the **sense** to call an ambulance.*

sensible *adjective*
If you are sensible, you think carefully about something and do the right thing.
Word Building: sensibly

sensitive *adjective*
easily hurt.

sent *verb* see send

sentence *noun* sentences
a group of words that express a complete thought. A written sentence begins with a capital letter and ends with a full stop, a question mark, or an exclamation mark.

separate (sep-a-rate) *adjective*
not joined to anything.
Word Building: separately

separate (sep-a-rate) *verb* separates, separating, separated
1 to put or keep things apart. *The boys toilets are **separate** from the girls.*
2 to stop living together as a married couple.

September *noun*
the ninth month of the year.

sequel (see-kwel) *noun* sequels
a book or movie which continues the story of an earlier book or movie.

sergeant (sar-jent) *noun* sergeants
a policeman or soldier in charge of other policemen or soldiers.

series *noun* series
1 a number of things that come one after another. *We had a **series** of accidents.*
2 a number of television programs about the same people or subject. *What's your favourite TV **series**?*

serious *adjective*
1 thoughtful, not smiling. *a **serious** person.*
2 important. *a **serious** decision.*
3 very bad. *a **serious** accident.*
Word Building: seriously

sermon *noun* sermons
a talk given in church.

serpent *noun* serpents
a large snake.

servant *noun* servants
someone whose job is to work in someone else's house.

serve *verb* serves, serving, served
1 to sell things in a shop. *Are you being **served**, sir?*
2 to give food out at a meal. *Breakfast is **served** from 7.00 to 9.00 a.m.*

service *noun* services
1 a business that does useful work for people. *a bus **service**, the postal **service**.*
2 serving people in a shop, hotel, or restaurant.
3 work that must be done regularly to keep a car or machine in good condition.
4 a meeting in church with prayers and singing.

serviette *noun* serviettes
a square of cloth or paper for keeping you clean while you eat.

session (sesh-un) *noun* sessions
a length of time spent doing one thing. *After a **session** with the coach, Yawi was better at kicking a football.*

set *noun* sets
a group of people or things that belong together.

set *verb* sets, setting, set
1 to become solid or hard. *Has the jelly **set** yet?*
2 to put things ready to use. *The teacher helped me **set** up my science experiment.*
3 to give someone work to do. *Our teacher **set** us a lot of homework.*
to set off to start.

settle *verb* settles, settling, settled
1 to get comfortable in a place and stay there. *The cat **settled** on my lap.*
2 to decide. *We've **settled** who goes first by tossing a coin.*

settlement *noun* settlements
a community of people from another place living inside or on the edge of a town or city.

settler *noun* settlers
a person who goes to live in a new country. *The **settlers** enjoyed their new life in PNG.*

seven *noun* sevens
the number 7.
Word Building: seventh

seventeen *noun*
the number 17.
Word Building: seventeenth

seventy *noun*
the number 70.
Word Building: seventieth

several *adjective*
more than a few but not a lot. *I've read this story **several** times.*

severe (se-veer) *adjective* severer, severest
1 not gentle or kind. *a **severe** punishment.*
2 very bad. *a **severe** illness.*
Word Building: severely

sew (so) *verb* sews, sewing, sewed, sewn
to use a needle and cotton to join pieces of cloth together.
Word Building: sewing machine, sewing machines

sex *noun* sexes
one of the two groups, either male or female, that all people and animals belong to.

shabby *adjective* shabbier, shabbiest
looking old and nearly worn out. ***shabby** clothes.*

shack *noun* shacks
a small house, hut, or shed, usually made from old wood.

shade *noun* shades
1 a place that is darker than other places, because the light of the sun cannot get to it. *We sat under the **shade** of the tree.*
2 how light or dark a colour is. *Do you like this **shade** of blue?*

shade *verb* shades, shading, shaded
1 to keep strong light away from something.
2 to make part of a drawing darker than the rest.

shadow *noun* shadows
the dark shape that you see near someone or something that is in front of the light.

shady *adjective* shadier, shadiest
out of the strong light of the sun. *We sat in a **shady** part of the garden.*

shaft *noun* shafts
1 a long, thin pole.
2 a deep, narrow hole. *a mine **shaft**.*

shaggy *adjective* shaggier, shaggiest
with long, untidy hair.

shake *verb* shakes, shaking, shook, shaken
to move or make something move quickly up and down or from side to side. ***Shake** the bottle before opening it.*

shaky *adjective*
shaking, weak.

shall *verb*
this word is used in sentences about the future: *We **shall** go home soon. I **shall** see you tomorrow.*

shallow *adjective*
not deep. ***shallow** water.*

shame *noun*
the feeling you have when you are unhappy because you have done wrong.

shameful *adjective*
so bad that it brings you shame. *It's **shameful** to lose 12–0!*
Word Building: shamefully

shampoo *noun* shampoos
liquid soap that you use to wash your hair.

shape *noun* shapes
the pattern that a line drawn around the outside of something makes. *The bottom of this jar has a round **shape**.*

share *verb* shares, sharing, shared
1 to divide something into parts and give them out to other people. *Mum **shared** out the cake.*
2 to use something that someone else is also using. *Can I **share** your book?*

shark *noun* sharks
a large sea fish with sharp teeth.

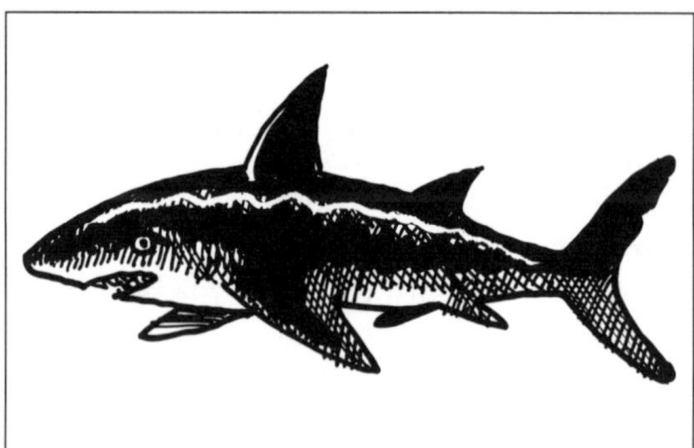

sharp *adjective* sharper, sharpest
1 with an edge or point that can cut or make holes. *a **sharp** knife.*
2 sudden. *a **sharp** bend in the road.*
3 quick to see or hear things. ***sharp** eyes, **sharp** ears.*
Word Building: sharply

sharpen *verb* sharpens, sharpening, sharpened
to make something sharp. ***sharpen** a pencil.*

shatter *verb* shatters, shattering, shattered
to break or make something break into tiny pieces. *A stone hit the window and **shattered** the glass.*

shave *verb* shaves, shaving, shaved
to cut hair from the skin to make it smooth.

shawl *noun* shawls
a piece of cloth or knitting worn around the shoulders or wrapped around a baby.

she *pronoun*
the female person or animal being talked about.
Word Building: she'd (she + had or would); she'll (she + will); she's (she + is or has)

shear *verb* shears, shearing, shorn
to cut the hair or wool off an animal.
Word Building: shearer, shearers

shears *noun*
a tool like a very large pair of scissors for cutting plants or for clipping wool from sheep.

shed *noun* sheds
a small wooden building. *a garden **shed**.*

shed *verb* sheds, shedding, shed
to let something fall. *Clara **shed** tears when the puppy died.*

sheep *noun* sheep
an animal kept by farmers for its wool and meat.

sheep-dip *noun* sheep-dips
1 the place where sheep are washed.
2 the liquid used to wash the sheep.

sheer *adjective*
1 very steep. *There is a **sheer** drop from the edge of the cliff.*
2 very thin so that you can partly see through it. *The curtain is **sheer**.*

sheet *noun* sheets
1 a large piece of light cloth you put on a bed.
2 a thin, flat piece of something. *a **sheet** of plastic, a **sheet** of paper.*

shelf *noun* shelves
a long piece of wood fastened to a wall, for putting things on.

shell *noun* shells
1 the thin, hard part around the outside of an egg, a nut, and some kinds of animals, such as snails.
2 a large bullet that explodes when it hits something.

shelter *noun* shelters
a place that protects people from wind, rain, heat, cold, or danger. *a bus **shelter**. Your plants need **shelter** from very hot sun.*

shelter *verb* shelters, sheltering, sheltered
to make someone or something safe from bad weather or danger. *The tree **sheltered** us from the rain.*

shield *noun* shields
a flat or curved sheet of wood, metal, plastic, or leather used to protect a person in a battle or in a riot.

shift *verb* shift, shifting, shifted
to move something. *Help me **shift** the table.*

shimmer *verb* shimmers, shimmering, shimmered
to shine with a light that comes and goes, like the light of sun on water.

shin *noun* shins
the front of the leg between the knee and ankle.

shine *verb* shines, shining, shone
1 to give out light. *The sun **shone** all day.*
2 to look very bright. *He will polish the silver plate until it **shines** brightly.*

shiny *adjective* shinier, shiniest
with a surface that shines. *a **shiny** new bike.*

ship *noun* ships
a large boat that takes people or things on the sea.

shipwreck *noun* shipwrecks
a bad accident that destroys or sinks a ship while it is at sea.

shirt *noun* shirts
a piece of clothing for the top half of the body with sleeves, a collar, and buttons down the front.

shiver *verb* shivers, shivering, shivered
to shake because you are cold or frightened.

shock *noun* shocks
a big surprise that is not pleasant.

shock *verb* shocks, shocking, shocked
to give someone a nasty surprise, or to upset them.

shoe (shoo) *noun* shoes
a covering that you wear on your foot.

shoot *noun* shoots
a part of a plant that has just grown.

shoot *verb* shoots, shooting, shot
1 to use a gun or a bow and arrow.
2 to hurt or kill by shooting.
3 to kick, hit, or throw a ball at a goal or net.

shop *noun* shops
a place that people go into to buy things.

shop *verb* shops, shopping, shopped
to go to a shop to buy something.
Word Building: shopper, shoppers

shore *noun* shores
the land along the edge of the sea.

shore, shorn *verb* see **shear**

short *adjective* shorter, shortest
1 not long. *a **short** visit.*
2 not tall. *a **short** person.*
short for a short way of saying or writing something. *PNG is **short for** Papua New Guinea.*

shortly *adverb*
soon, in a little while.

shorts *plural noun*
trousers that only cover the top part of the legs.

shot *noun* shots
1 the firing of a gun.
2 a photograph. *That's a good **shot** of you.*
3 the act of kicking or hitting a ball in games like soccer, tennis, or golf.

shot *verb* see **shoot**

should (shood) *verb*
ought to. *I **should** go home now.*

shoulder (shole-der) *noun* shoulders
the part of the body between the neck and arm.

shout *verb* shouts, shouting, shouted
to speak very loudly.

shove *verb* shoves, shoving, shoved
to push hard.

shovel *noun* shovels
a kind of curved spade for lifting things such as coal or sand.

show *noun* shows
1 something that you watch at the theatre or on television.
2 things organised for people to look at. *a flower **show**.*

show *verb* shows, showing, showed, shown
1 to let people see something. ***Show** me your new bike.*
2 to make something clear to someone. *He's **shown** me how to use the computer.*

shower (rhymes with *flower*) *noun* showers
1 a short fall of rain.
2 a piece of equipment that gives out water. You stand under it and wash yourself.
to have a shower to stand under a spray of water and wash yourself.

shown *verb* see **show**

shrank *verb* see **shrink**

shred *noun* shreds
a tiny strip or piece that has been cut, broken, or torn off something. *She tore the paper into **shreds**.*

shriek (shreek) ***noun*** shrieks
a short scream.

shrill ***adjective*** shriller, shrillest
sounding very high and loud.

shrimp ***noun*** shrimps
a small sea animal that you can eat.

shrink ***verb*** shrinks, shrinking, shrank, shrunk
to become smaller. *These jeans have **shrunk**.*

shrivel (shriv-l) ***verb*** shrivels, shrivelling, shrivelled
to get very dry and curl up at the edges like a dead leaf.

shrub ***noun*** shrubs
a bush.

shrug ***verb*** shrugs, shrugging, shrugged
to lift your shoulders to show that you do not know something or care about it.

shrunk ***verb*** see **shrink**

shudder ***verb*** shudders, shuddering, shuddered
to shake because you are cold or frightened.

shuffle ***verb*** shuffles, shuffling, shuffled
to drag your feet along the ground as you walk. *He **shuffled** around the room in his slippers.*

shut ***verb*** shuts, shutting, shut
to move a cover, lid, or door to close an opening.
to shut up to stop talking.

shutter ***noun*** shutters
1 a wooden cover that fits over a window.
2 the part inside a camera that opens to let in light as you take a photograph.

shy ***adjective*** shyer, shyest
1 if you are shy, you do not like meeting people you do not know.
2 easily frightened. *Mice are very **shy** animals.*
Word Building: shyly

sick ***adjective*** sicker, sickest
ill.
to be sick to bring food back up from the stomach through the mouth.
to be sick of to be tired of.

side ***noun*** sides
1 one of the outer parts between the front and back of a person, animal, or thing.
2 a flat surface. *A cube has six **sides**.*
3 an edge. *A triangle has three **sides**.*
4 a group playing or fighting against another group. *Whose **side** are you on?*

sideways ***adverb***
1 with the side first. *The table will fit through the door if you carry it **sideways**.*
2 to one side. *He moved **sideways** to avoid the puddle.*

siege (seej) ***noun*** sieges
a time when an army surrounds a town so that people and things cannot get in or out.

sigh (rhymes with *eye*) ***verb*** sighs, sighing, sighed
to breathe out heavily to show you are feeling sad, tired, or happy.

sight ***noun***
1 the power to see. *You are lucky to have good **sight**.*
2 something that you see. *He was a funny **sight** in that hat.*

sightseeing ***noun***
going to look at places or things of interest.

sign (rhymes with *line*) ***noun*** signs
anything written, drawn, or done to tell or show people something. *road **signs**.*

sign ***verb*** signs, signing, signed
to write your name in your own writing.

signal ***noun*** signals
a light, sound, or movement that tells people something. *A red light is a **signal** for cars to stop.*

signal *verb* signals, signalling, signalled
to give a signal. *The driver put out his right arm to **signal** he was turning right.*

signature *noun* signatures
your name written by yourself in your own writing.

silence *noun*
a time when there is no sound at all.

silent *adjective*
without any sound.
Word Building: silently

silk *noun*
fine, shiny cloth made from threads spun by insects called silkworms.

silky *adjective* silkier, silkiest smooth
smooth like silk.

sill *noun* sills
a ledge underneath a window.

silly *adjective* sillier, silliest
stupid, not clever.

silo *noun* silos
a pit or tower used to store grain or cement.

silver *noun*
a valuable, shiny white metal.

silverbeet *noun*
a vegetable with large green leaves.

similar *adjective*
of the same kind, like another person or thing. *The twins wore **similar** dresses.*
Word Building: similarly

simple *adjective* simpler, simplest
1 easy. *a **simple** question.*
2 plain. *a **simple** dress.*
Word Building: simply

sin *noun* sins
something that your religion says you should not do because it is very bad.

sinabada *noun*
an important lady; used to refer to a white woman during colonial times. [from Motu: *bada* = big, *sina* = mother]

since *adverb, conjunction, preposition*
1 from that time. *We have been friends **since** last year. The dog jumped out of the truck and I haven't seen it **since**.*
2 because. *We couldn't play outside **since** it was raining.*

sincere (sin-seer) *adjective*
truly meant. ***sincere** good wishes.*
Word Building: sincerely

sing *verb* sings, singing, sang, sung
to use your voice to make music.
Word Building: singer, singers

singe (sinj) *verb* singes, singeing, singed
to burn something slightly.

single *adjective*
1 only one. *The tree has a **single** avocado.*
2 not married.

singlet *noun* singlets
a top without sleeves that you wear under or instead of a shirt.

sing-sing *noun*
1 any festival where people sing and dance.
2 a song.
Word building: sing-sing ground. *Each year a big sing-sing is held on the **sing-sing ground** in the town.* [from Tok Pisin *singsing*]

singular *adjective*
the form of a word you use when you are talking about only one person or thing. *The word 'child' is **singular**, but 'children' is plural.*

sink *noun* sinks
a place that you can fill with water from the taps.

sink *verb* sinks, sinking, sank, sunk
1 to go under water. *The ship **sank** in the storm.*
2 to go down. *The sun **sank** behind the mountains.*

sip *verb* sips, sipping, sipped
to drink a very small amount at a time.

sipora *noun*
a lime or lemon. [from Motu *sipora*]

sir *noun*
a word used when speaking politely to a man, instead of his name.

siren (sy-ren) *noun* sirens
a machine that makes a loud sound to warn people about something. *Police cars and fire engines have **sirens**.*

sister *noun* sisters
a girl or woman who has the same parents as another person.

sister-in-law *noun* sisters-in-law
the sister of your husband or wife.

sit *verb* sits, sitting, sat
to rest on your bottom, as you do when you are on a chair.

site *noun* sites
the ground that is or was used for something. *a mine **site**.*

situation (sich-yoo-**ay**-shun) *noun* situations
the things that are happening to you. *I was in a difficult **situation** when I lost my money.*

six *noun* sixes
the number 6.
Word Building: sixth

sixteen *noun*
the number 16.
Word Building: sixteenth

sixty *noun*
the number 60.
Word Building: sixtieth

size *noun* sizes
1 how big or small something is. *My room is the same **size** as yours.*
2 the measurement something is made in. ***size** ten shoes.*

sizzle *verb* sizzles, sizzling, sizzled
to make a hissing and crackling sound. *food **sizzling** in the frying pan.*

skeleton (**skel**-e-tun) *noun* skeletons
all the bones inside the body of a person or animal.

sketch *verb* sketches, sketching, sketched
to draw quickly.

skid *verb* skids, skidding, skidded
to slide without meaning to. *The car **skidded** on the wet road.*

skill *noun* skills
the ability to do something well.
Word Building: skilful, skilfully

skim *verb* skims, skimming, skimmed
1 to take the cream off the top of the milk.
2 to move quickly over the surface of something and only just touch it.

skin *noun* skins
1 the outer covering of your body.
2 the outer covering of some fruits and vegetables. *banana **skin**.*

skinny *adjective* skinnier, skinniest
very thin.

skip *verb* skips, skipping, skipped
1 to move lightly and quickly by jumping from one foot to the other.
2 to leave out. ***Skip** the next page.*

skipper *noun* skippers
the person in charge of a ship or a team.

skirt *noun* skirts
a piece of clothing for women and girls that hangs down from the waist.

skull *noun* skulls
the bones in the head of a person or animal.

sky *noun* skies
the space above the earth where you can see the sun, moon, and stars.

skydiving *noun*
the sport of leaping from a plane, doing tricks, and free falling before opening a parachute.
Word Building: skydiver

skyscraper *noun* skyscrapers
a very tall building.

slab *noun* slabs
a flat, thick piece. *a **slab** of rock.*

slack *adjective* slacker, slackest
1 not tight. *a **slack** rope.*
2 careless. ***slack** work.*
3 not busy. *a **slack** day.*

slain *verb* see slay

slam *verb* slams, slamming, slammed
to close something loudly. *She **slammed** the door.*

slang *noun*
words you sometimes use in talking but which you don't normally use in writing or on important occasions.

slant *verb* slants, slanting, slanted
to have one part higher than the other; to be not straight. *My writing **slants** backwards.*

slap *verb* slaps, slapping, slapped
to hit with the flat part of your hand.

slash *verb* slashes, slashing, slashed
to make long cuts in something.

slaughter (slaw-ter) *verb* slaughters, slaughtering, slaughtered
1 to kill an animal for food.
2 to kill many people or animals.

slave *noun* slaves
someone who belongs to another person and has to work without wages.

slay *verb* slays, slaying, slew, slain
to kill.

sleek *adjective* sleeker, sleekest
neat, smooth, and shiny. ***sleek** fur.*

sleep *verb* sleeps, sleeping, slept
to close your eyes and rest completely, as you do every night.

sleepy *adjective* sleepier, sleepiest
ready to go to sleep.

sleet *noun*
a mixture of rain and snow.

sleeve *noun* sleeves
the part of a coat, shirt, blouse, or jersey, that covers your arm.

slender adjective
thin, graceful. *a **slender** girl.*

slept *verb* see sleep

slice *noun* slices
a thin piece cut off something. *a **slice** of bread.*

slide *noun* slides
1 a long, sloping piece of shiny metal that people can slide on.
2 a small photograph that you show on a screen using a projector.

slide *verb* slides, sliding, slid
to move smoothly and quickly over something. *We **slid** on the wet ground.*

slight *adjective* slighter, slightest
small, not important. *a **slight** cold.*

slim *adjective* slimmer, slimmest
thin, but not too thin.

slime *noun*
nasty wet, slippery stuff.

slimy *adjective* slimier, slimiest
covered with slime.

sling *noun* slings
1 a piece of cloth that goes round your arm and is tied around your neck. You wear a sling to support your arm if you have broken or hurt it.
2 a short leather strap used for throwing stones.

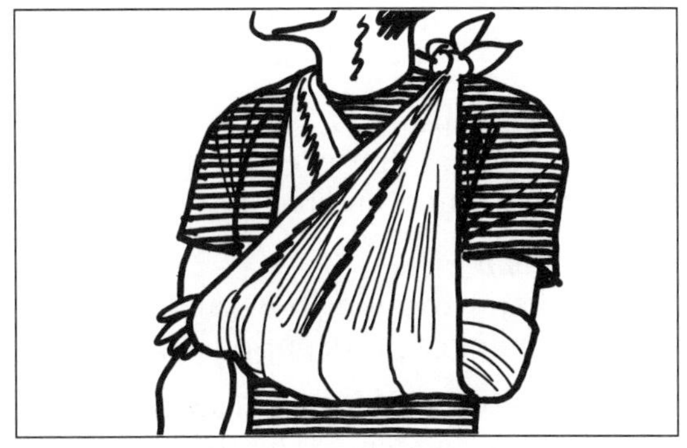

slink *verb* slinks, slinking, slunk
to move in a secret way because you are afraid or feel guilty about something. *The dog saw me and **slunk** away.*

slip *verb* slips, slipping, slipped
1 to slide accidentally. *Aisi **slipped** and fell over.*
2 to go away quickly and quietly. *She **slipped** out of the room.*

slipper *noun* slippers
a soft, comfortable kind of shoe that you wear indoors.

slippery *adjective*
with a smooth surface so that it is difficult to get hold of or walk on.

slit *noun* slits
a long cut or a narrow opening in something.

slope *noun* slopes
ground that is like the side of a hill.

slope *verb* slopes, sloping, sloped
to be not level, to have one part higher than the other. *a **sloping** roof.*

slot *noun* slots
a narrow opening for something like a coin or card to fit into.

slow *adjective* slower, slowest
1 a person or thing that is slow does not move or do something quickly. *You are **slow** this morning!*
2 showing a time that is earlier than the right time. *I'm sorry I'm late, but my watch is **slow**.*
Word Building: slowly

slug *noun* slugs
a small creature like a snail without its shell.

slum *noun* slums
a dirty, crowded place where many poor people live.

slumber *verb* slumbers, slumbering, slumbered
to sleep.

slunk *verb* see **slink**

sly *adjective* slyer, slyest
clever at tricking people secretly.
Word Building: slyly

smack *verb* smacks, smacking, smacked
to hit with the flat part of the hand.

small *adjective* smaller, smallest
not big or as big as usual. *The dress is too **small** for me. A mouse is much **smaller** than an elephant.*

smart *adjective* smarter, smartest
1 clever. *What a **smart** dog!*
2 neat and tidy. *You look very **smart** in your new clothes.*
Word Building: smartly

smart *verb* smarts, smarting, smarted
to feel a stinging pain. *The smoke made my eyes **smart**.*

smash *verb* smashes, smashing, smashed
to break into pieces with a loud noise. *The firefighter had to **smash** the windows to get into the house.*

smear *verb* smears, smearing, smeared
to spread a sticky or dirty substance over something.

smell *noun* smells
something that you find out about with your nose. *Many flowers have a nice smell.*

smell *verb* smells, smelling, smelled or smelt
to use your nose to find out about something. *Can you **smell** something burning?*

smelly *adjective* smellier, smelliest
having a bad smell.

smile *verb* smiles, smiling, smiled
to move your mouth to show that you are happy.

smoke *noun*
blue or grey gas that floats up from a fire and looks like a cloud.

smoke *verb* smokes, smoking, smoked
1 to give off smoke. ***smoking** chimneys.*
2 to breathe in smoke from cigarettes or tobacco.

smooth *adjective* smoother, smoothest
1 without any lumps or rough parts. *a **smooth** surface.*
2 without any bumps or jerks. *a **smooth** ride.*

smother *verb* smothers, smothering, smothered
to cover someone's mouth and nose so that they cannot breathe.

smoulder *verb* smoulders, smouldering, smouldered
to burn slowly with a lot of smoke.

smudge *noun* smudges
a mark made by rubbing against something wet or dirty.

smudge *verb* smudges, smudging, smudged
to make something dirty by touching it. *Leave the painting to dry or you'll **smudge** it.*

smuggle *verb* smuggles, smuggling, smuggled
to take something into or out of a country secretly when it is against the law.
Word Building: smuggler, smugglers

snack *noun* snacks
something you can eat quickly instead of a meal.

snail *noun* snails
a small animal that lives inside a shell. Snails are found on land and in water.

snake *noun* snakes
an animal with a long body and no legs. Some snakes can give poisonous bites.

snap *verb* snaps, snapping, snapped
1 to break suddenly. *The rope **snapped**.*
2 to try to bite. *The dog **snapped** at the stranger.*

snapper *noun* snapper
a pink sea fish that can be eaten.

snare *noun* snares
a trap for catching animals.

snarl *verb* snarls, snarling, snarled
to make the sound a dog makes when it is angry.

snatch *verb* snatches, snatching, snatched
to take something quickly.

sneak *verb* sneaks, sneaking, sneaked
to move trying not to be seen or heard. *She **sneaked** up behind me and made me jump.*

sneer *verb* sneers, sneering, sneered
to speak or smile in an unkind way.

sneeze *verb* sneezes, sneezing, sneezed
to make a sudden noise as air rushes out of the nose. *I can't stop **sneezing** in this dusty room.*

sniff *verb* sniffs, sniffing, sniffed
to make a noise by suddenly taking in air through the nose. *People **sniff** when they have a cold.*

snip *verb* snips, snipping, snipped
to cut a little bit off something.

snob *noun* snobs
someone who only associates with people who are rich, famous, or clever.
Word Building: snobbish, snobbery

snooze *verb* snoozes, snoozing, snoozed
to have a short sleep.

snore *verb* snores, snoring, snored
to breathe very noisily while sleeping.

snort *verb* snorts, snorting, snorted
to make a short, loud noise by forcing air through the nose.

snout *noun* snouts
an animal's nose and mouth sticking out from the rest of its face. Pigs have snouts.

snow *noun*
small, thin, white pieces of frozen water. Snow floats down from the sky when the weather is very cold.

snowflake *noun* snowflakes
one piece of falling snow.

snub *verb* snubs, snubbing, snubbed
to show someone who is trying to be friendly that you don't want to be their friend.

snug *adjective* snugger, snuggest
cosy, warm, and comfortable.
Word Building: snugly

snuggle *verb* snuggles, snuggling, snuggled
to curl up in a warm, comfortable place.

so *adverb, conjunction*
this word has several uses. Here are some of the ways you can use it: *Why are you **so** late? 'I like this colour.' '**So** do I.' Speak up **so** we can all hear you.*

soak *verb* soaks, soaking, soaked
to make something very wet.

soap *noun* soaps
stuff you use with water for washing.

soar *verb* soars, soaring, soared
to move high into the air.

sob *verb* sobs, sobbing, sobbed
to cry noisily, making gasping sounds.

soccer *noun*
a game played by two teams who kick a round ball and try to score goals.

society (so-sy-e-tee) *noun* societies
people living together in a group or nation. *People of many tribes make up PNG **society**.*

sock *noun* socks
a covering for the foot and part of the leg.

socket *noun* sockets
the part that an electric light bulb or plug fits into.

sofa *noun* sofas
a long, comfortable seat with a back.

soft *adjective* softer, softest
1 not hard, easy to cut or to change into another shape. ***soft** butter, a **soft** bed.*
2 not loud. ***soft** music.*
Word Building: softly

softball *noun*
a game like baseball which uses a larger and softer ball that is thrown underhand to the batter.

soggy *adjective* soggier, soggiest
very wet. ***soggy** grass.*

soil *noun*
earth, the brown stuff on the ground that plants grow in.

solar (sole-ar) *adjective*
anything to do with the sun. ***solar** energy, the **solar** system.*

sold *verb* see **sell**

soldier (sole-jer) *noun* soldiers
a person in an army.

sole *noun* soles
the flat part underneath a foot or shoe.

solemn (sol-em) *adjective*
serious.
Word Building: solemnly

solid (sol-id) *adjective*
1 without a space inside. *Basket balls are hollow but cricket balls are **solid**.*
2 hard, not like a liquid or gas. *Water becomes **solid** when it freezes.*

solitary (sol-i-tair-ee) *adjective*
alone or lonely.

solo *noun* solos
something sung, played, danced, or done by one person.

solution (so-loo-shun) *noun* solutions
the answer to a puzzle or problem.

solve *verb* solves, solving, solved
to find the answer to a puzzle.

some *adjective, pronoun*
1 a few but not all. ***Some** of us can swim, but the others can't.*
2 a number or amount of something. *Would you like **some** cake?*
3 a, an, or one. ***Some** insect has just bitten me.*

somebody *pronoun*
a person.

somehow *adverb*
in some way that you do not know. *We must find him **somehow**.*

someone *pronoun*
a person.

somersault (sum-er-solt) *noun* somersaults
a movement in which you turn head over heels and finish on your feet.

something *pronoun*
a thing that you do not know or do not say what it is. *I have forgotten **something**.*

sometimes *pronoun*
at some times. ***Sometimes** I catch a PMV to school and **sometimes** I walk.*

somewhere *adverb*
in some place or to some place. *I put the book **somewhere** but I've forgotten where.*

son *noun* sons
someone's male child.

song *noun* songs
a short piece of music with words for singing.

soon *adverb*
in a very short time from now. *Jo will be home **soon**.*

soot *noun*
the black powder left behind by smoke.

soothe (sooth) *verb* soothes, soothing, soothed
to make someone who is upset feel calm. ***soothing** words.*

sorcerer *noun* sorcerers
a man who makes magic.
Word building: sorceress, a woman who makes magic.

sore *adjective* sorer, sorest
painful when it is touched.

sorrow *noun* sorrows
a very sad feeling.

sorry *adjective* sorrier, sorriest
1 sad about something that you wish you had not done.
2 sad because of something that has happened to another person.
3 a word you use when you feel bad about something. ***Sorry** I'm late!*

sort *noun* sorts
a kind. *Which **sorts** of cordial do you like?*

sort *verb* sorts, sorting, sorted
to put things into different groups. *The apples are **sorted** into different sizes.*

sought (sawt) *verb* see seek

soul *noun* souls
the part of a person that cannot be seen but some people believe goes on living after they have died.

sound *adjective* sounder, soundest
1 healthy, strong, in good condition. *a **sound** building.*
2 right and good. ***sound** work.*
Word Building: soundly

sound *noun* sounds
anything that you can hear.

sound *verb* sounds, sounding, sounded
to make a certain kind of sound; to appear to be a certain way. *That voice **sounds** like your brother's.*

soup *noun* soups
a hot liquid made from meat or vegetables.

sour *adjective* sourer, sourest
1 with the kind of taste lemons have, not sweet.
2 not fresh. ***sour** milk.*

source *noun* sources
the place something has come from. *The **source** of the river is up in the hills.*

soursop *noun*
1 an evergreen tropical tree which has large, delicious, juicy fruits.
2 the fruit of this tree.

south *noun, adjective*
the direction to your right when you face east.

Southern Cross *noun*
a group of stars in the southern part of the sky that make a cross pattern. The Southern Cross is also found on the Australian flag.

souvenir (soo-ve-**neer**) *noun* souvenirs
something that you keep because it makes you think about a person or place. *He brought back **souvenirs** from his holiday.*

sovereign (**sov**-ren) *noun* sovereigns
a ruler who is a king, queen, emperor, or empress.

sow (rhymes with *cow*) *noun*
a female pig.

sow (rhymes with *low*) *verb* sows, sowing, sowed, sown
to put seeds in the ground so that they will grow into plants.

space *noun* spaces
1 the area or distance between things.
2 a place with nothing in it. *There is a **space** here for you to write your name.*
3 all the places beyond the Earth, where the stars and planets are.

spacecraft *noun* spacecraft
any kind of vehicle that can travel in space.

spaceship *noun* spaceships
a machine that can travel in space.

spacious (**spay**-shus) *adjective*
with plenty of space. *a **spacious** room.*

spade *noun* spades
1 a tool with a long handle and a wide blade that you use for digging.
2 a small, black spade printed on some playing cards.

spaghetti (spa-**get**-tee) *noun*
a thin, long kind of pasta, similar to a noodle.

spak *adjective*
drunk.
Word building: spakman, a drunk man.
[from Tok Pisin *spak*]

spank *verb* spanks, spanking, spanked
to smack someone on the bottom.

spanner *noun* spanners
a tool that fits around a nut so that you can turn it.

spare *adjective*
not used but kept in case it is needed. *a **spare** tyre.*

spare *verb* spares, sparing, spared
to give up something so that someone else can have it. *Could you **spare** one of your pencils?*

spark *noun* sparks
1 a tiny piece of burning material that shoots out from a fire.
2 a tiny flash. *There was a **spark** as the wires touched.*

sparkle *verb* sparkles, sparkling, sparkled
to shine with a lot of tiny flashes of bright light. *The sea **sparkled** in the sunlight.*

spat *verb* see spit

speak *verb* speaks, speaking, spoke, spoken
to say something.
Word Building: speaker, speakers

speaker *noun* speakers
the part of a stereo, radio, or television that the sound comes from.

spear *noun* spears
a long pole or stick with a sharp point, used as a weapon.

special (spesh-al) *adjective*
1 different from any other kind. *Your birthday is a **special** day.*
2 for one person or thing. *Stefanie has her tea in her own **special** mug.*

specialist (spesh-a-list) *noun* specialists
a person who is an expert in something, such as a doctor who is an expert in certain illnesses.

specimen *noun* specimens
1 a small amount of something that shows what the rest is like. *a **specimen** of rock.*
2 an example of one kind of plant or animal. *She showed them a **specimen** of a fern.*

speck *noun* specks
a tiny bit. *a **speck** of dust.*

speckled *adjective*
covered with small spots.

spectacles *noun*
a pair of glasses.

spectacular (spek-tak-yoo-lar) *adjective*
very exciting or impressive to watch. *a **spectacular** fireworks display.*

spectator (spek-tay-tor) *noun* spectators
someone watching a game or show. *football **spectators**.*

speech *noun* speeches
1 the power of speaking.
2 a talk given to a group of people.

speed *noun* speeds
how quickly something moves or happens.

speed *verb* speeds, speeding, sped
to go or move very fast. *He **sped** past me in his car.*

spell *noun* spells
magic words that are supposed to make things happen.

spell *verb* spells, spelling, spelled or spelt
to put the right letters in the right order to make a word.

spend *verb* spends, spending, spent
1 to use money to pay for things. *How much have you **spent** so far?*
2 to pass time. *I **spent** all morning tidying my room.*

sphere (sfeer) *noun* spheres
the shape of a ball or the earth.

spice *noun* spices
part of a plant that is dried and used to flavour food. Ginger and pepper are spices.
Word Building: spicy *__spicy__ food.*

spider *noun* spiders
a small creature with eight legs that spins webs.

spike *noun* spikes
a thin piece of metal with a sharp point. *The fence has **spikes** along the top.*

spill *verb* spills, spilling, spilled or spilt
to let something fall out of a container. *Dorcas **spilled** her drink on the floor.*

spin *verb* spins, spinning, spun
1 to turn round and round quickly, to make something turn quickly. *I **spun** until I was dizzy.*
2 to make thread by twisting long, thin pieces of wool or cotton together.
3 to make a web. *The spider **spun** a web.*

spinach (spin-ich) *noun*
a vegetable with a lot of green leaves, which you cook to eat.

spine *noun* spines
1 the long bone down the centre of your back.
2 one of the long sharp points on some plants and animals. *Echidnas have **spines**.*

spiral *noun* spirals
the shape of a line that keeps going around the same point in smaller and smaller or bigger and bigger curves.

spire *noun* spires
a tall, pointed part on top of a church tower.

spirit *noun* spirits
1 the part of a person that you cannot see but some people believe goes on living after they have died.
2 a ghost.
3 something that makes a person very brave and lively.

spit *verb* spits, spitting, spat
to send drops of liquid out of the mouth. *The baby **spat** out the nasty medicine.*

spite *noun*
a wish to hurt someone by what you say or do.
Word Building: spiteful, spitefully

splash *verb* splashes, splashing, splashed
to make water fly about noisily.

splendid *adjective*
very good. *We had a **splendid** holiday.*

splint *noun* splints
a straight piece of wood or metal that is tied to a broken arm or leg to hold it firm.

splinter *noun* splinters
a sharp bit of wood, glass, or metal.

split *verb* splits, splitting, split
1 to break or make something break into parts. *He **split** the log with an axe.*
2 to share something. *We **split** the money between us.*

spoil *verb* spoils, spoiling, spoiled or spoilt
1 to make something less good than it was.
2 to be too kind to someone so that they think they can always have what they want.

spoke *noun* spokes
one of the wires or rods that go from the centre of a wheel to the edge.

spoke, spoken *verb* see speak

sponge (spunj) *noun* sponges
something thick and soft with a lot of holes in it. Sponges soak up water and are used for washing.

sponsor *verb* sponsors, sponsoring, sponsored
to support a person or a group of people by giving them money. *a **sponsored** swim.*

spool *noun* spools
a round piece of wood or metal that cotton, string, or film is wound around.

spoon *noun* spoons
what you use for eating soup and ice cream.
Word Building: spoonful, spoonfuls

sport *noun* sports
a game that you do that is usually done outside and exercises your body. Swimming, football, and netball are sports.

spot *noun* spots
1 a round mark.
2 a small red swelling on the skin.
3 a place. *This is a good **spot** for a picnic.*

spot *verb* spots, spotting, spotted
to notice something. *Edoa **spotted** Vaai's mistake at once.*

spotless *adjective*
perfectly clean.

spotlight *noun* spotlights
a strong light that can shine on one small area.

spout *noun* spouts
the part of a container that is made like a pipe so that you can pour liquid out of it easily. *the **spout** of a teapot.*

sprain *verb* sprains, spraining, sprained
to twist your wrist or ankle so that it swells and is painful.

sprang *verb* see **spring** *verb*

sprawl *verb* sprawls, sprawling, sprawled
to sit or lie with your arms and legs spread out.

spray *verb* sprays, spraying, sprayed
to make tiny drops of liquid fall all over something.

spread (spred) *verb* spreads, spreading, spread
1 to stretch something out to its full size. *The bird **spread** its wings.*
2 to make something cover a surface. *She **spread** the cloth on the table.*

spring *noun* springs
1 the part of the year when plants start to grow and the days are getting lighter and warmer.
2 a place where water comes out of the ground.
3 a piece of metal wound into rings so that it jumps back into shape after it has been pressed or stretched.

spring *verb* springs, springing, sprang, sprung
1 to jump suddenly. *Nora **sprang** up to catch the ball.*
2 to grow quickly. *Weeds had **sprung** up all over the garden.*

sprinkle *verb* sprinkles, sprinkling, sprinkled
to make a few tiny pieces or drops fall on something. *to **sprinkle** sugar on top of a cake.*

sprint *verb* sprints, sprinting, sprinted
to run a short distance very quickly.
Word Building: sprinter

sprout *verb* sprouts, sprouting, sprouted
to start to grow, to send out shoots.

sprung *verb* see **spring** *verb*

spun *verb* see **spin**

spurt *verb* spurts, spurting, spurted
to shoot out or upwards quickly. *Blood **spurted** out of the wound.*

spy *noun* spies
someone who works secretly to find out things about another person or country.

spy *verb* spies, spying, spied
to see, to notice.

squabble *verb* squabbles, squabbling, squabbled
to quarrel about something that is not important.

squad (skwod) *noun* squads
a small group of people working together or training together.
Word Building: squadron
*A **squadron** is a group in the army, navy, or air force.*

square *noun* squares
1 a flat shape with four straight sides that are all the same length.
2 an open space in a town with buildings round it.

squash *noun*
1 a game played indoors with racquets and a small rubber ball.
2 a drink made from fruit. *orange squash.*

squash *verb* squashes, squashing, squashed
1 to press something hard so that it goes out of shape. *One of the sandwiches got **squashed**.*
2 to push a lot of things or people into a small space.

squat *verb* squats, squatting, squatted
to sit on the ground with your knees bent and your bottom resting on your heels.

squawk *verb* squawks, squawking, squawked
to make a loud, harsh cry like a large bird.

squeak *verb* squeaks, squeaking, squeaked
to make the tiny, high sound a mouse makes.
Word Building: squeaky

squeal *verb* squeals, squealing, squealed
to make a long, loud sound that a pig makes.

squeeze *verb* squeezes, squeezing, squeezed
1 to press something between your hands or two other things.
2 to go or push too much into a small space. ***Squeeze** another person in.*

squid *noun* squids
a soft-bodied sea animal with tentacles joined to its head.

squirt *verb* squirts, squirting, squirted
to send or come out with a jet of liquid. *He **squirted** his friend with a water pistol.*

stab *verb* stabs, stabbing, stabbed
to push a knife or other sharp thing into a person or thing.

stable (stay-bl) *noun* stables
a building in which horses are kept.

stack *noun* stacks
a neat pile. *a **stack** of books.*

stadium (stay-dee-um) *noun* stadiums
a large place where people can watch sports and games. *a football **stadium**.*

staff *noun*
a group of people who work together in an office, shop, or school.

stag *noun* stags
a male deer.

stage *noun* stages
1 a raised floor in a hall or theatre, on which people act, sing, or dance to entertain other people.
2 the point someone has reached in doing something. *The baby is at the crawling **stage**.*

stagger *verb* staggers, staggering, staggered
to try to stand or walk but find it difficult to stay upright.

stagnant *adjective*
not flowing or fresh. *a pool of **stagnant** water.*

stain *noun* stains
a dirty mark made on something by a liquid.

stair *noun* stairs
one of a set of steps for going up or down inside a building.

staircase *noun* staircases
a set of stairs with a rail to hold on to.

stake *noun* stakes
a thick, pointed stick. ***Stakes** are often used to support young trees.*

stale *adjective* staler, stalest
not fresh. ***stale** bread.*

stalk *noun* stalks
a thin stem that flowers and fruit grow on.

stall *noun* stalls
1 a small shop or a table that things are sold on. *Some markets have **stalls**.*
2 a place for one animal in a stable or shed.

stallion (stal-yon) *noun* stallions
a male horse.

stammer *verb* stammers, stammering, stammered
to keep repeating the sounds at the beginning of words when you speak.

stamp *noun* stamps
a piece of sticky paper with a picture on it. People put stamps on letters and parcels to show that they have paid to post them.

stamp *verb* stamps, stamping, stamped
to bang your foot heavily on the ground.

stand *noun* stands
something to put things on. *a music **stand**.*

stand *verb* stands, standing, stood
to get on your feet, or to be on your feet without moving. *He **stood** by the door. The teacher asked us all to **stand**.*

standard *noun* standards
1 how good something is. *a high **standard** of work.*
2 a flag.

stank *verb* see stink

stap isi *verb*
to behave; to settle down. [from Tok Pisin *stap isi*]

staple *noun* staples
a small piece of metal used to hold pieces of paper together.

staple *verb* staples, stapling, stapled
to fasten pieces of paper together with a staple.
Word Building: stapler

star *noun* stars
1 one of the tiny, bright lights you see in the sky at night.
2 a famous singer or actor. *a movie **star**.*

starch *noun*
a substance which is in many foods, such as potatoes and rice.

stare *verb* stares, staring, stared
to look at someone or something for a long time, without moving your eyes.

starry *adjective*
full of stars. *a **starry** night.*

start *verb* starts, starting, started
1 to begin to do something. *We **started** to paint the room.*
2 to get something going. *Gena **started** the car.*

startle *verb* startles, startling, startled
to suddenly surprise or frighten someone. *You **startled** me when you shouted.*

starve *verb* starves, starving, starved
to be ill or to die because you do not have enough food.
Word Building: starvation

state *noun* states
1 how someone or something is. *Your room is in a very untidy **state**.*
2 a country or part of a country with its own government. *the United **States** of America.*

state *verb* states, stating, stated
to say or write something clearly. *Please **state** your name and address.*
Word Building: statement, statements *All of her **statements** to the police were true.*

station (stay-shun) *noun* stations
1 a place where people get on or off trains or buses. *a railway **station**.*
2 a building for police or firefighters.
3 a place that radio or television programs come from.
4 a large sheep or cattle farm in Australia.

statue (stat-choo) *noun* statues
a model of a person made in stone or metal.

stay *verb* stays, staying, stayed
1 to be in the same place.
2 to live somewhere as a visitor.

steady *adjective* steadier, steadiest
firm, not shaking.
Word Building: steadily

steak *noun* steaks
a thick slice of meat or fish.

steal *verb* steals, stealing, stole, stolen
to take something that does not belong to you and keep it.

steam *noun*
the gas that water turns into when it gets very hot.

steel *noun*
a strong, shiny metal made from iron. *Knives and forks are usually made of **steel**.*

steep *adjective* steeper, steepest
sloping sharply. *a **steep** hill.*

steeple *noun* steeples
a tall, pointed tower on top of a church.

steer *verb* steers, steering, steered
to make a ship, car, or canoe go in the direction you want.

stem *noun* stems
1 the main part of a plant above the ground.
2 the thin part that joins a leaf, flower, or fruit to the rest of the plant.

step *noun* steps
1 the movement you make with your foot when you are walking, running, or dancing.
2 a flat place where you can put your foot when you are going up or down something.

stereo (stair-ee-o) *noun* stereos
a machine for playing music.

stereo (stair-ee-o) *adjective*
with the sound coming from two sources or speakers. *a **stereo** cassette player.*

stern *adjective* sterner, sternest
serious, strict. *The teacher had a **stern** expression on her face.*
Word Building: sternly

stew *noun* stews
meat or vegetables cooked in gravy or sauce.

stew *verb* stews, stewing, stewed
to cook food slowly in liquid.

stick *noun* sticks
1 a long, thin piece of wood.
2 a long, thin piece of anything. *a **stick** of dynamite.*

stick *verb* sticks, sticking, stuck
1 to become fixed. *The door has **stuck**.*
2 to fasten one thing to another. *He **stuck** a stamp on the envelope.*
3 to press a sharp point into something. *She **stuck** a pin in me!*
4 (*informal*) to put. *She **stuck** her tongue out at her brother.*

sticker *noun* stickers
a label or sign that you can stick on something.

sticky *adjective* stickier, stickiest
able to stick to things. *Glue, gum and honey are all **sticky**.*

stiff *adjective* stiffer, stiffest
not easily bent. ***stiff** card.*
Word Building: stiffly

still *adjective* stiller, stillest
without moving. *The injured man lay **still**.*

still *adverb*
1 not moving. *Stand **still**!*
2 the same now as before. *He's **still** asleep.*

sting *verb* stings, stinging, stung
to hurt someone with a sting. *A bee **stung** me yesterday.*

stingy (stin-jee) *adjective* stingier, stingiest
not wanting to spend money or share things with other people.

stink *verb* stinks, stinking, stank or stunk
to have a strong smell.

stir *verb* stirs, stirring, stirred
1 to move a liquid or a soft mixture around with a spoon.
2 to start to move. *After a long sleep the baby **stirred**.*

stitch *noun* stitches
1 a loop of thread made by the needle in sewing or knitting.
2 a sudden pain in your side.

stock *noun* stocks
1 a lot of things kept ready to be sold or used.
2 farm animals, livestock.

stocking *noun* stockings
a covering for the foot and leg worn next to the skin.

stockman *noun* stockmen
a person in the bush who looks after cattle.

stole, stolen *verb* see steal

stomach (stum-ik) *noun* stomachs
the part in the middle of the body, where food goes when it is eaten.

stone *noun* stones
1 rock. *The castle was built of **stone**.*
2 a small piece of rock. *He threw a **stone** into the water.*

stone-fish *noun*
a deadly, poisonous fish found on coral reefs.

stood *verb* see **stand**

stool *noun* stools
a small seat without a back.

stoop *verb* stoops, stooping, stooped
to bend the body forwards.

stop *verb* stops, stopping, stopped
1 to make someone or something stay still. *The policeman **stopped** the traffic.*
2 to become still. *The bus **stopped**.*
3 to finish. *The baby **stopped** crying.*

store *noun* stores
a shop, tradestore.

store *verb* stores, storing, stored
to keep things until you need them.

storey *noun* storeys
all the rooms on the same floor in a building. *He lived in a three-**storey** building.*

storm *noun* storms
a very strong wind with a lot of rain or snow.
Word Building: stormy

story *noun* stories
words that tell you about something that has happened or about something that someone has made up. *adventure **stories**.*

stove *noun* stoves
something that gives out heat for warming a room or for cooking.

stow (rhymes with *go*) ***verb*** stows, stowing, stowed
to stack or store something away.
Word Building: stowaway
*A **stowaway** is someone who hides on a ship or aeroplane.*

straight (strate) ***adjective*** straighter, straightest
not bending, going the shortest way from one place to another. *a **straight** road, **straight** hair.*
straight away now, immediately.

straighten (stray-ten) ***verb*** straightens, straightening, straightened
1 to make something straight. ***Straighten** your back.*
2 to become straight. *The road bends, then **straightens** out again.*

strain ***verb*** strains, straining, strained
1 to stretch, push, or try too hard.
2 to hurt part of yourself by stretching or pushing too hard.
3 to separate a liquid from lumps or other things floating in it.

strait ***noun*** straits
a narrow passage of water joining two large areas of water.

strange ***adjective*** stranger, strangest
1 not known or seen before. *a **strange** place.*
2 unusual and surprising. *a **strange** story.*
Word Building: strangely

stranger (strain-jer) ***noun*** strangers
1 a person you do not know.
2 a person in a place he or she does not know. *Please show me the way, because I am a **stranger** here.*

strangle (strang-gl) ***verb*** strangles, strangling, strangled
to kill someone by pressing their throat until they cannot breathe.

strap ***noun*** straps
a flat strip of leather or another strong material. *a watch **strap**.*

straw ***noun*** straws
1 dry stalks of wheat.
2 a very thin tube for drinking through.

strawberry ***noun*** strawberries
a small, red, juicy fruit.

stray ***verb*** strays, straying, strayed
to wander, to get lost. *The children had **strayed** off the track.*

streak ***noun*** streaks
a long, narrow line. *a **streak** of lightning.*

streak ***verb*** streaks, streaking, streaked
1 to mark something with streaks.
2 (*informal*) to move very quickly. *The car **streaked** past.*

stream ***noun*** streams
1 a small river.
2 anything else which moves in a line like a stream of water. *a **stream** of cars.*

streamer ***noun*** streamers
a long strip of paper or ribbon used to decorate something.

street ***noun*** streets
a road with houses along each side.

strength ***noun***
1 how strong someone or something is.
2 something that makes a person or thing better. *Her greatest **strength** is her good memory.*

strengthen ***verb*** strengthens, strengthening, strengthened
to make something stronger.

stretch ***verb*** stretches, stretching, stretched
1 to pull something to make it longer, wider, or tighter. *You can **stretch** a piece of elastic.*
2 to push your arms and legs as far as you can. *Julius got out of bed and **stretched**.*

A B C D E F G H I J K L M N O P Q R S T U V W X Y Z

stretcher *noun* stretchers
a pair of poles with canvas stretched across them for carrying a person who is hurt or ill.

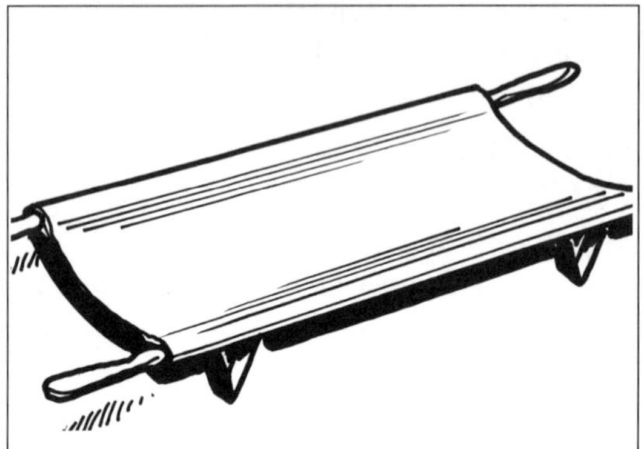

strict *adjective* stricter, strictest
demanding certain behaviour. *The new teacher is very **strict**.*

stride *verb* strides, striding, strode
to walk with long steps.

strike *verb* strikes, striking, struck
1 to hit. *The tree was **struck** by lightning.*
2 to stop working because you want more money or are angry about something.
to strike a match to rub a match along something rough until it bursts into flame.

string *noun* strings
very thin rope.

string band *noun* string bands
a group of musicians playing music, mostly with guitars.

strip *noun* strips
a long, narrow piece of something.

strip *verb* strips, stripping, stripped
to take off clothes or a covering.

stripe *noun* stripes
a coloured band across or down something. *a shirt with blue and white **stripes**.*
Word Building: striped
*a **striped** dress.*

strode *verb* see **stride**

stroke *verb* strokes, stroking, stroked
to move the hand gently along something. *Cats like being **stroked**.*

stroll *verb* strolls, strolling, strolled
to walk slowly.

strong *adjective* stronger, strongest
1 healthy and able to do things that need a lot of energy. *a **strong** man.*
2 not easily broken. ***strong** rope.*
3 with a lot of flavour. ***strong** tea.*
Word Building: strongly

struck *verb* see **strike**

structure *noun* structures
1 anything that has been built. *Schools, houses, and fences are **structures**.*
2 the way something has been made or built. *We are studying the **structure** of a leaf.*

struggle *verb* struggles, struggling, struggled
1 to use your arms and legs in fighting or trying to get free.
2 to try hard to do something you find difficult. *Soi **struggled** with his homework.*

stubborn *adjective*
not wanting to change your ideas even though they might be wrong.

stuck *verb* see **stick** *verb*

student *noun* students
someone who studies at a school or university.

studio *noun* studios
a place where an artist works, or where people make films or radio or television programs.

study *noun* studies
a room where someone studies.

study *verb* studies, studying, studied
1 to spend time learning about something. *We are **studying** rivers in science.*
2 to look at something very carefully. *He **studied** the map looking for the place.*

stuff *noun*
any kind of substance or material. *What's that **stuff** in the corner?*

stuff *verb* stuffs, stuffing, stuffed
1 to fill something tightly.
2 to put soft material into such things as cushions and soft toys.

stuffy *adjective* stuffier, stuffiest
without fresh air. *a **stuffy** room.*

stumble *verb* stumbles, stumbling, stumbled
to fall over something.

stump *noun* stumps
1 the part of a broken tree, tooth, or pencil that is left.
2 one of the set of three upright sticks put at each end of the pitch in cricket.

stun *verb* stuns, stunning, stunned
1 to hit or hurt someone so much that they cannot think properly.
2 to make someone very surprised. *She was **stunned** to receive so many presents.*

stung *verb* see **sting**

stunk *verb* see **stink**

stunt *noun* stunts
something difficult or dangerous done as part of a movie or to attract people's attention.

stupid *adjective*
1 very silly. *a **stupid** idea.*
2 slow to learn and understand. *a **stupid** person.*
Word Building: stupidly

sturdy *adjective* sturdier, sturdiest
strong; not easily broken. ***sturdy** shoes.*

stutter *verb* stutters, stuttering, stuttered
to keep repeating the sounds at the beginning of words when you speak.

sty *noun* sties
1 a sore swelling on the edge of an eyelid.
2 a place where pigs are kept.

style *noun* styles
the way something is done or made. *a neat **style** of writing, a hair**style**.*

subject *noun* subjects
1 the person or thing that you are writing about or learning about.
2 the subject of a sentence is the person or thing that does the action of the verb. In the sentence *Kari threw the ball, Kari* is the ***subject**.*
3 someone who is ruled by a king, queen, or government.

submarine *noun* submarines
a ship that can travel under water.

submit (sub-**mit**) *verb* submits, submitting, submitted
1 to surrender.
2 to give something in to someone. *We must **submit** our work tomorrow.*

subscription *noun* subscriptions
money you pay regularly—for example, to belong to a club, or to get the same magazine each month.

substance *noun* substances
anything that you can see, touch, or use for making things. *Glue is a sticky **substance**.*

substitute (**sub**-sti-tute) *noun* substitutes
a person or thing used instead of the proper person or thing. *Margarine is a **substitute** for butter.*

subtract *verb* subtracts, subtracting, subtracted
to take away. *If you **subtract** 6 from 9 you get 3.*
Word Building: subtraction, subtractions

suburb *noun* suburbs
an area of houses and other buildings that is part of a large city. *Waigani is a **suburb** of Port Moresby.*
Word Building: suburban

succeed (suk-seed) *verb* succeeds, succeeding, succeeded
to do or get what you wanted to do or get. *Con **succeeded** in winning the race.*

success (suk-sess) *noun* successes
a person or thing that does well or that people like a lot. *The party was a great **success**.*

successful (suk-sess-ful) *adjective*
able to do or get what you wanted to do or get.
Word Building: successfully

such *adjective*
1 of the same kind. *I like games **such** as Aussie Rules and Rugby.*
2 so great. *It was **such** a surprise!*

suck *verb* sucks, sucking, sucked
1 to take in air or liquid from something. *I **sucked** the iceblock.*
2 to keep moving something around inside your mouth without chewing it. *He was **sucking** a lolly.*

sudden *adjective*
happening quickly without any warning. *a **sudden** scream.*
Word Building: suddenly

suffer *verb* suffers, suffering, suffered
to have to put up with pain or something else that is not pleasant.

sufficient (suf-fish-ent) *adjective*
enough. *Have you got **sufficient** money for your trip?*
Word Building: sufficiently

suffocate *verb* suffocates, suffocating, suffocated
to die because there isn't enough air to breathe.
Word Building: suffocation

sugar (shoog-ar) *noun*
a sweet food that is put in drinks and other foods to make them taste sweet.

suggest (sug-jest) *verb* suggests, suggesting, suggested
to give someone an idea that you think is useful.
Word Building: suggestion, suggestions

suicide (soo-i-side) *noun* suicides
the act of killing yourself.
Word Building: suicidal

suit (soot) *noun* suits
a jacket and trousers or skirt that are meant to be worn together.

suit (soot) *verb* suits, suiting, suited
1 to fit in with someone's plans. *Does it **suit** you if we start at once?*
2 to look good on someone. *That colour **suits** you.*

suitable (soot-a-bl) *adjective*
just right for something. ***suitable** shoes for running.*

suitcase (soot-kase) *noun* suitcases
a kind of box with a lid and a handle for carrying clothes and other things on journeys.

sulk *verb* sulks, sulking, sulked
to stop speaking to someone, because you are angry about something.

sulky *adjective* sulkier, sulkiest
silent and bad tempered, sulking.

sullen *adjective*
sulky.

sultana (sul-tan-a) *noun* sultanas
a dried grape.

sum *noun* sums
1 a problem to be solved in arithmetic.
2 an amount. *a **sum** of money.*

summer *noun* summers
the hottest part of the year.

summit *noun* summits
the top of a mountain.

Sun *noun*
the star that shines in the sky and gives the Earth heat and light.

Sunday *noun* Sundays
the second day of the weekend.

sundial *noun* sundials
a kind of clock that uses a shadow made by the sun to show what time it is.

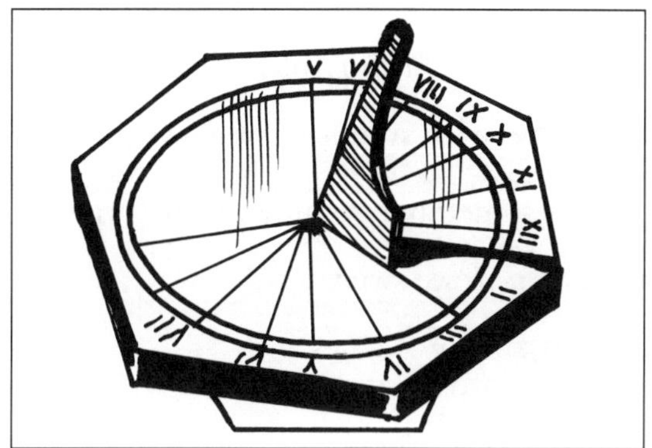

sung *verb* see **sing**

sunk *verb* see **sink** *verb*

sunscreen *noun*
a cream which protects the skin from the sun's harmful rays.

sunny *adjective* sunnier, sunniest
the sun shining. *a* ***sunny*** *day.*

sunrise *noun* sunrises
the time when the sun rises.

sunset *noun* sunsets
the time when the sun goes down.

sunshine *noun*
the light and heat that come from the sun when it is shining.

superior (soo-**peer**-ee-or) *adjective*
better than something or someone else. *The* ***superior*** *mangoes were juicier than the others.*

supermarket *noun* supermarkets
a large shop where people help themselves to things as they go around and pay for them all on the way out.

supernatural *adjective*
not natural; to do with gods, ghosts, spirits or other strange beings.

supersonic *adjective*
travelling faster than sound travels. *The pilot liked to fly* ***supersonic*** *jets.*

superstitious (soo-per-**stish**-us) *adjective*
believing that certain things will bring you good luck, and other things will bring you bad luck.

supply (sup-**ply**) *noun* supplies
things kept ready to be used when you need them. ***supplies*** *of food.*

supply *verb* supplies, supplying, supplied
to give or sell you what you need. *The school* ***supplies*** *me with paper to write on.*

support *verb* supports, supporting, supported
1 to hold up something so that it does not fall. *These pieces of wood* ***support*** *the roof.*
2 to help or encourage someone. *Which team do you* ***support****?*
Word Building: supporter, supporters

suppose *verb* supposes, supposing, supposed
to think something is true although it might not be.

sure (shoor) *adjective*
knowing something is true or right. *I'm* ***sure*** *her name is Papi.*

surf *noun*
big, white, foaming waves.

surf *verb* surfs, surfing, surfed
to ride a long, narrow board on the waves as they come in to shore.
Word Building: surfer, surfie

surface *noun* surfaces
the outside or top of something. *This leaf has a shiny **surface**. She dived below the **surface**.*

surgeon (**sur**-jen) *noun* surgeons
a doctor who is trained to do operations.

surgery (**sur**-je-ree) *noun* surgeries
the room you go in to see a doctor or dentist.

surname *noun* surnames
your last name that is the same as your family's name.

surprise *noun* surprises
1 the feeling you have when something suddenly happens that you were not expecting. *She looked at me in **surprise** when I said I don't like ice cream.*
2 something that happens and was not expected. *We arranged the party as a **surprise**.*

surprise *verb* surprises, surprising, surprised
to give someone a surprise. *I came early to **surprise** you.*
Word Building: surprised, surprising

surrender *verb* surrenders, surrendering, surrendered
to stop fighting and agree to obey the enemy.

surround *verb* surrounds, surrounding, surrounded
to be all around someone or something. *The lake is **surrounded** by trees.*

surroundings *plural noun*
the things and places that surround you.

survey (**sur**-vay) *noun* surveys
1 a careful look at something.
2 a set of questions to find out what people think about something.

survive *verb* survives, surviving, survived
to carry on living after an accident or some other event.
Word Building: survivor, survivors

suspect (sus-**pekt**) *verb* suspects, suspecting, suspected
to have a feeling that there might be something wrong. *We **suspect** he has stolen some money.*

suspense *noun*
the feeling of being uncertain and worried that something may happen.

suspicious (sus-**pish**-us) *adjective*
feeling that there might be something wrong.
Word Building: suspiciously

susu *noun*
milk; breast. [from Tok Pisin *susu*]

swallow *verb* swallows, swallowing, swallowed
to let something go down your throat.

swam *verb* see **swim**

swamp *noun* swamps
an area of very wet ground.

swap (swop) *verb* swaps, swapping, swapped
to change one thing for another.

swarm *noun* swarms
a large number of insects together. *a **swarm** of bees.*

sway *verb* sways, swaying, swayed
to move from side to side. *The trees were **swaying** in the wind.*

swear (swair) *verb* swears, swearing, swore, sworn
1 to make a serious promise. *He **swore** to tell the truth.*
2 to use bad words. *He **swore** when he hit his finger.*

sweat *verb* sweats, sweating, sweated
to lose liquid through your skin, because you are ill or very hot.

sweep *verb* sweeps, sweeping, swept
to use a brush to clear away dust and litter from something.

sweet *adjective* sweeter, sweetest
1 with the taste of sugar or honey.
2 very pleasant. *a **sweet** smell.*

sweet potato *noun*
a tropical plant with a root which is eaten as a vegetable; kaukau.

swell *verb* swells, swelling, swelled, swollen
to get bigger than it usually is. *I twisted my ankle and now it's **swollen**.*

swelling *noun* swellings
a lump on the body that is not usually there.

swept *verb* see sweep

swerve *verb* swerves, swerving, swerved
to move suddenly to one side. *The driver **swerved** when she saw the child run onto the road.*

swift *adjective* swifter, swiftest
quick.
Word Building: swiftly

swim *verb* swims, swimming, swam, swum
to move yourself through water without touching the bottom.
Word Building: swimmer, swimmers

swindle *verb* swindles, swindling, swindled
to cheat someone.
Word Building: swindler, swindlers

swing *noun* swings
a seat hung from a tree or metal frame so that you can move backwards and forwards on it.

swing *verb* swings, swinging, swung
to move or make something move backwards and forwards, from side to side, or in a curve. *The bilum was **swinging** from a tree.*

swirl *verb* swirls, swirling, swirled
to move around quickly in circles.

switch *noun* switches
anything that is turned or pressed to make something work or stop working. *an electric light **switch**.*

switch *verb* switches, switching, switched
to change from one thing to another.
to switch on, to switch off to use a switch to make something work or stop working. *Yaking **switched on** the television.*

swollen *verb* see swell

swoop *verb* swoops, swooping, swooped
to fly down suddenly to attack something. *The bird **swooped** down onto the mouse.*

sword (sord) *noun* swords
a weapon like a knife with a long blade.

swore, sworn *verb* see swear

swum *verb* see swim

swung *verb* see swing *verb*

syllable (sil-a-bl) *noun* syllables
any word or part of a word that has one separate sound when you say it. *Tre-men-dous* has three syllables and *big* has one syllable.

syllabus (sil-a-bus) *noun* syllabuses
a list of the things students have to study.

symbol (sim-bl) *noun* symbols
a sign which shows or means something. *The + **symbol** means you add numbers together.*

symmetrical (sim-met-trik-l) *adjective*
with two halves that are exactly alike but the opposite way round.

sympathy (sim-pa-thee) *noun*
the feeling you have when you are sorry for someone who is sad, ill, or in trouble.
Word Building: sympathetic
*Everyone was very **sympathetic** when I hurt myself.*

symptom (simp-tum) *noun* symptoms
one of the things you notice is wrong with you when you are ill. *A sore throat is a **symptom** of a cold.*

synonym (sin-o-nim) *noun* synonyms
a word which has nearly the same meaning as another word. *Beautiful and lovely are **synonyms**.*

syrup (sir-rup) *noun* syrups
a very sweet, sticky liquid.

system (sis-tem) *noun* systems
a set of parts, things, or ideas that work together. *a road **system**, a computer **system**.*

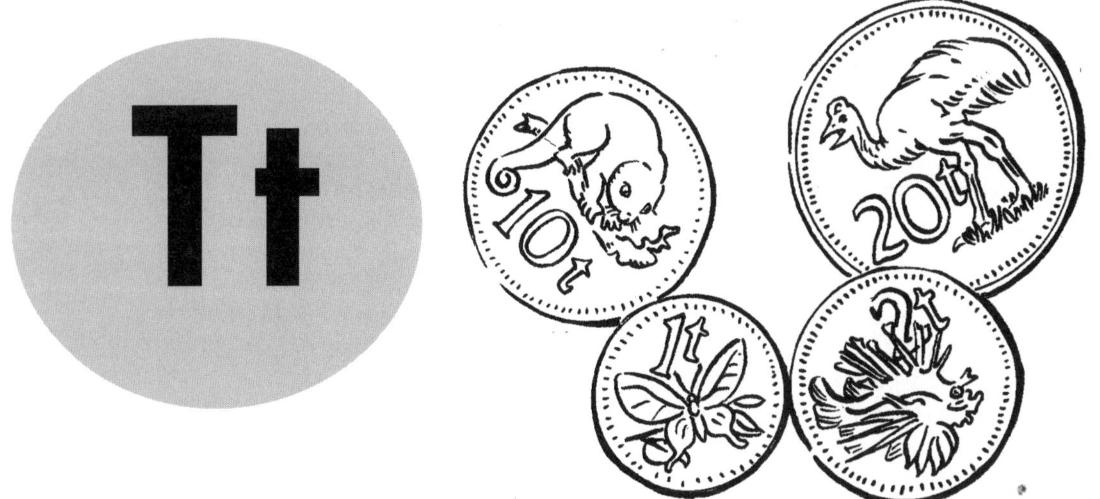

table *noun* tables
1 a piece of furniture with a flat top and legs.
2 a list of facts or numbers arranged in order.

tabby *noun* tabbies
a cat with grey or brown streaks in its fur.

tablet *noun* tablets
a small, hard piece of medicine.

tackle *verb* tackles, tackling, tackled
1 to start to do a difficult job.
2 to grab someone to make them stop running.

tactful *adjective*
careful not to upset people.
Word Building: tactfully

tadpole *noun* tadpoles
a tiny animal that lives in water and will turn into a frog, toad, or newt. Tadpoles have long tails.

tai chi (tie chee) *noun*
a Chinese martial art that uses a set of slow, smooth movements and balance.

tail *noun* tails
1 the part at the end of the body of an animal, bird, or fish. *The dog wagged its **tail**.*
2 the part at the back of something. *the **tail** of an aeroplane.*

tailor *noun* tailors
someone whose job is to make suits and coats.

taipan (tie pan) *noun* taipans
a long-fanged, poisonous snake of Papua New Guinea and northern Australia.

take *verb* takes, taking, took, taken
1 to get hold of something. *He **took** his prize and smiled.*
2 to move something or go with someone to another place. *Uncle **took** us fishing.*

takeaway *noun* takeaways
1 a meal you buy at a shop or tucker box to eat at home.
2 the place where takeaway food is sold.

take-off *noun* take-offs
the action of an aeroplane leaving the ground and flying into the air.

tale *noun* tales
a story.

talent *noun* talents
the ability to do something very well. *Aisi has a **talent** for singing.*

talented *adjective*
very good at something.

talk *verb* talks, talking, talked
to use words to speak to other people.

talkback *noun* talkbacks
a radio program in which people ring the station to give their opinions.

tall *adjective* taller, tallest
1 measuring more than usual from top to bottom. *a **tall** person, a **tall** tree.*
2 how high a person or thing is. *She's 1.42 metres **tall**.*

tambourine (tam-ba-reen) *noun* tambourines
a musical instrument that you shake or hit with your fingers.

tambu *noun*
1 something forbidden or not allowed.
2 a brother-in-law or sister-in-law.
3 all of your in-laws.
4 a small shell used as money. [from Tok Pisin *tambu*]

tame *adjective* tamer, tamest
not wild or afraid of people.

tamper *verb* tampers, tampering, tampered
to make changes in something so that it will not work properly. *Who's been **tampering** with the computer?*

tangerine (tan-je-reen) *noun* tangerines
a kind of small orange.

tangket *noun*
a plant with brightly coloured leaves used as clothing and to mark boundaries. [from Tok Pisin *tanget* or *tangket*]

tangle *noun* tangles
a mass of things like hair, string, or branches that are twisted together in an untidy way so that it is difficult to separate them.

tangled *adjective*
twisted up in knots. ***tangled** hair.*

tank *noun* tanks
1 a large container for liquid. *an oil **tank**, a fish **tank**.*
2 a strong, heavy car used in war. It has a big gun on top and can move over very rough ground.

tanker *noun* tankers
1 a large ship for carrying oil.
2 a large truck for carrying milk or petrol.

tantrum *noun* tantrums
a sudden bad temper. *My little brother is having a **tantrum** because he doesn't want to sleep yet.*

tap *noun* taps
a thing you can turn on and off to control water or gas in a pipe.

tap *verb* taps, tapping, tapped
to hit or touch someone or something quickly and lightly. *She **tapped** me on the shoulder.*

tapa *noun*
cloth made from beaten bark, usually covered in red or black patterns.

tape *noun* tapes
1 a narrow strip of special material that you can record sound or pictures on.
2 a narrow strip of material used for sticking things together. *Put a piece of **tape** on the torn page.*

tape *verb* tapes, taping, taped
1 to fix, cover or surround something with tape.
2 to record sound or pictures.

tape deck, tape recorder *noun* tape decks, tape recorders
a machine for recording music on tape and playing it back.

tapioca *noun*
a starchy food from the root of the cassava plant; tapiok.

tar *noun*
a thick, black, sticky liquid made from coal or wood and used for making roads.

target *noun* targets
something that people aim at and try to hit. *The bullet hit the* ***target****.*

taro *noun*
a tropical plant with a thick root which is good to eat. [from Tok Pisin *taro*]

tart *noun* tarts
pastry with jam or fruit on it. *apple* ***tart****.*

task *noun* tasks
a piece of work that must be done. *I had the* ***task*** *of cleaning the floor.*

taste *noun* tastes
the feeling you get through your tongue when you eat something. *Sugar has a sweet* ***taste****. Lemons have a sour* ***taste****.*

taste *verb* tastes, tasting, tasted
1 to eat a little bit of food or sip a drink to see what it is like.
2 to have a particular taste. *Honey* ***tastes*** *sweet.*

tasty *adjective* tastier, tastiest
with a strong, pleasant taste.

tattered *adjective*
badly torn.

tattoo *noun* tattoos
a picture or pattern made on someone's skin with a needle and some colour.

taubada *noun*
an important man; used to refer to a white man during colonial times. [from Motu: *bada* = big, *tau* = man]

taught *verb* see **teach**

tax *noun* taxes
money that people have to give to the government.

taxi *noun* taxis
a vehicle that you can travel in if you pay the driver.

tea *noun* teas
1 a hot drink made with boiling water and the dried leaves of a tea plant.
2 a meal eaten in the evening.

teach *verb* teaches, teaching, taught
to tell or show someone how to do something. *She* ***taught*** *me to swim last year.*
Word Building: teacher, teachers

team *noun* teams
a group of people who work together or play together on the same side in a game. *a netball* ***team****.*

tear (teer) *noun* tears
a small drop of water that comes out of the eye when you cry.

tear (tair) *verb* tears, tearing, tore, torn
to pull something apart so that you damage it. *I* ***tore*** *the letter up and threw it away. Paper* ***tears*** *easily.*

tease (teez) *verb* teases, teasing, teased
to make fun of someone for fun. *People often* ***tease*** *me because I'm short.*

technical (tek-ni-kl) *adjective*
concerned with machines and how things work.

technology (tek-**nol**-o-jee) *noun*
an area of science which studies and uses practical ways of doing things.

teenager *noun* teenagers
someone who is older than twelve but younger than twenty years old.

teeth *noun* see **tooth**

teething (tee-*th*ing) *adjective*
beginning to grow teeth. *The baby is crying because she's* ***teething****.*

telegram *noun* telegrams
a short message sent along electric wires and delivered as a printed note.

telegraph *noun* telegraphs
a system for sending messages by electric signals sent along wires.

telephone (tel-e-fone) *noun* telephones
an instrument which you use to speak to another person a long way away.

telephone (tel-e-fone) *verb* telephones, telephoning, telephoned
to speak to someone on a telephone. *I **telephoned** Sayah to ask her to come to tea.*

telescope *noun* telescopes
a tube with lenses at each end. People look through telescopes to see things that are far away.

television *noun* televisions
a machine that picks up signals sent through the air and changes them into pictures and sound so that people can watch them.

tell *verb* tells, telling, told
to speak in order to pass on news, stories, or instructions. *Kati **told** me he would be home for tea.*
to tell someone off to say you are angry with them because of something they have done.

temper *noun* tempers
the mood someone is in. *He's shouting at everyone because he's in a bad temper.*
to lose your temper to get angry.

temperature (tem-pra-cher) *noun*
how hot or cold something is. *The **temperature** today is 28 degrees.*

temple *noun* temples
a place where people go to pray.

temporary *adjective*
not for ever, for a short time only. *When they dug up the road, they put up **temporary** traffic lights.*

tempt *verb* tempts, tempting, tempted
to try to make someone do wrong.

temptation *noun* temptations
something that makes you want to do wrong. *Don't leave money around, it's a **temptation** to thieves.*

ten *noun* tens
the number 10.
Word Building: tenth

tenant *noun* tenants
a person who pays money to live in or use a place.

tend *verb* tends, tending, tended
to be likely to do or be something. *Men **tend** to be stronger than women.*

tender *adjective* tenderer, tenderest
1 loving. *a **tender** smile.*
2 soft, easy to eat. ***tender** meat.*
3 sore, easily hurt. ***tender** skin.*
Word Building: tenderly

tendon *noun* tendons
a thick cord in the body which joins a muscle to a bone.

tent *noun* tents
a shelter made of waterproof nylon or canvas stretched over poles.

tentacle (ten-ta-kl) *noun* tentacles
a long, snake-like part of an animal's body. *An octopus has eight **tentacles**.*

tepid (tep-id) *adjective*
only slightly warm. ***tepid** water.*

term *noun* terms
1 a word or phrase. *We learned some technical* ***terms*** *to do with science.*
2 the time between holidays when you go to school.

termite *noun* termites
a small ant-like insect which eats wood.

terrace (tair-us) *noun* terraces
1 a level area on a hillside.
2 an area outside a house for sitting and relaxing.

terrible *adjective*
very bad.
Word Building: terribly

terrific (te-rif-ik) *adjective*
1 (*informal*) very good. *I had a* ***terrific*** *idea.*
2 (*informal*) very great. *There was a* ***terrific*** *storm.*

terrify (tair-i-fy) *verb* terrifies, terrifying, terrified
to make a person or animal very frightened.
Word Building: terrified, terrifying

territory (tair-i-tree) *noun* territories
land that belongs to one country or person or group.

terror *noun*
great fear.

terrorist *noun* terrorists
a person who frightens, hurts, or kills people to try to make the government or other people do what he or she wants.

test *noun* tests
a set of questions you have to answer or something you have to do to show what you have learned. *a spelling* ***test****, a driving* ***test****.*

test *verb* tests, testing, tested
1 to make someone do a test.
2 to use something in order to find out whether it works. *Gima* ***tested*** *his fishing net.*

tether (te*th*-er) *verb* tethers, tethering, tethered
to tie an animal up.

text *noun* texts
printed words. *This book has a lot of* ***text*** *and no pictures.*

texta *noun* textas
a thick, coloured, felt-tipped pen.

textbook *noun* textbooks
a book which gives you the facts about a subject. *a maths* ***textbook****.*

than *conjunction, preposition*
compared with another person or thing. *You are smaller* ***than*** *me.*

thank *verb* thanks, thanking, thanked
to tell someone you are pleased about something they have given you or done for you.

thankful *adjective*
pleased, grateful. *I was* ***thankful*** *it wasn't raining.*

that, those *adjective, pronoun*
the one there, the ones there. ***That*** *is mine, this is yours.* ***Those*** *books are yours.*

thaw *verb* thaws, thawing, thawed
to melt, to stop being frozen. *The frost* ***thawed*** *when the sun came out.*

theatre (thee-a-ter) *noun* theatres
a place where people go to see plays and shows.

theft *noun* thefts
stealing.

their *adjective*
belonging to them. ***their*** *bags.*

them *pronoun* see **they**

themselves *pronoun*
they and no one else. *They did not hurt* ***themselves****.*
by themselves on their own, without help. *They solved the puzzle* ***by themselves****.*

A B C D E F G H I J K L M N O P Q R S **T** U V W X Y Z

then *adverb*
1 after that. *I had breakfast and **then** I went to school.*
2 at that time. *We didn't know about it **then**.*

theory (theer-ee) *noun* theories
an idea someone suggests to explain something.

there *adverb*
in that place or to that place. *You can sit **there**.*

therefore *adverb*
for that reason. *Ali was ill and **therefore** he didn't go to school.*

thermometer (ther-mom-e-ter) *noun* thermometers
an instrument that measures temperature.

these *adjective, pronoun* see **this**

they, them *pronoun*
people or things you are talking about. ***They** were playing softball. Did you see **them**?*
Word Building: they're (they + are)

thick *adjective* thicker, thickest
1 not thin, measuring a lot from one side to the other or from top to bottom. *a **thick** slice of bread.*
2 not easy to see through or go through. ***thick** bush, **thick** fog.*
3 not easy to pour, not runny. ***thick** soup.*
Word Building: thickness

thicken *verb* thickens, thickening, thickened
1 to make something thicker. *Add flour to **thicken** the sauce.*
2 to become thicker. *Tonight the clouds will **thicken**.*

thief (theef) *noun* thieves
someone who steals things.

thigh (thy) *noun* thighs
the top part of the leg down to the knee.

thin *adjective* thinner, thinnest
1 not fat or thick. *He is tall and **thin**. Cut the bread into **thin** slices.*
2 easy to pour, with lots of water in it. ***thin** soup.*
Word Building: thinly

thing *noun* things
anything that you can see, touch, or think about. *A pen is a **thing** you use to write with. Have you got your **things** ready for school?*

think *verb* thinks, thinking, thought
1 to use your mind. ***Think** carefully before you answer the question.*
2 to believe something. *I **thought** you were older than me.*

third *adjective, adverb*
coming after the second. *I got **third** prize.*

third *noun* thirds
one of the three equal parts something can be divided into. It can also be written as $\frac{1}{3}$.

thirst *noun*
the feeling you have when you want a drink.
Word Building: thirsty

thirteen
the number 13.
Word Building: thirteenth

thirty
the number 30.
Word Building: thirtieth

this, these *adjective, pronoun*
the one here, the ones here. ***This** is mine, that is yours. **These** books are mine.*

thistle (this-sl) *noun* thistles
a wild plant with prickly leaves and purple flowers.

thongs *plural noun*
rubber sandals with a strap that fits between the first toe and the second toe.

thorn *noun* thorns
a sharp point that grows on a plant. *Bougainvillea have **thorns**.*

thorough (thur-a) *adjective*
1 done properly and carefully. *a **thorough** job.*
2 complete. *a **thorough** mess.*
Word Building: thoroughly

those *adjective, pronoun* see **that**

though (tho) *adverb*
however. *I like Otto. I don't like his brother **though**.*

though (tho) *conjunction*
and yet or although. *It was very cold **though** the fire kept us warm.*

thought (thort) *verb* see **think**

thought (thort) *noun* thoughts
something that you think.

thoughtful (thort-ful) *adjective*
1 thinking a lot.
2 thinking about others and what they want in a kind way.
Word Building: thoughtfully

thousand *noun* thousands
the number 1000.
Word Building: thousandth

thrash *verb* thrashes, thrashing, thrashed
to keep hitting something or someone with a stick.

thread (thred) *noun* threads
a long, thin piece of cotton, nylon, or wool used for sewing or weaving cloth.

thread (thred) *verb* threads, threading, threaded
to put a thread through the eye of a needle or the hole in a bead.

threat (thret) *noun* threats
a promise that you will do something bad if what you want does not happen.

threaten (thret-en) *verb* threatens, threatening, threatened
to make threats. *The rascal **threatened** the man.*

three *noun* threes
the number 3.

three-dimensional *adjective*
a three-dimensional object is solid rather than flat.

thrill *noun* thrills
a sudden excited feeling.

thrilling *adjective*
very exciting.

throat *noun* throats
the front of your neck and the tube inside it that takes foods, liquid, and air into your body.

throb *verb* throbs, throbbing, throbbed
to keep up a regular beat, like your heart pumping blood round your body.

throne *noun* thrones
a special chair for a king or queen.

through (threw) *adverb, preposition*
from one end or side to the other. *We went **through** the tunnel. We opened the gate and walked **through**.*

throughout (threw-out) *adverb, preposition*
all through. *They talked **throughout** the film.*

throw *verb* throws, throwing, threw, thrown
to make something move through the air.

thrust *verb* thrusts, thrusting, thrust
to push hard.

thud *verb* thuds, thudding, thudded
to make the low, dull sound something heavy and large makes when it hits the ground.

thumb (thum) *noun* thumbs
the short, thick finger at the side of each hand.

thump *verb* thumps, thumping, thumped
to hit hard. *He **thumped** on the door.*

thunder *noun*
the noise that you hear after a flash of lightning in a storm.

thunder *verb* thunders, thundering, thundered
to make the sound that thunder makes.

thunderstorm *noun* thunderstorms
a storm with thunder and lightning.

Thursday *noun* Thursdays
the day after Wednesday.

tick *noun* ticks
1 a small mark like this ✔ that shows that something is right.
2 an insect that sucks blood from animals.

tick *verb* ticks, ticking, ticked
1 to put a tick next to something.
2 to make regular sounds like the little clicks some clocks make.

ticket *noun* tickets
a piece of paper or card that you buy so that you can travel on an aeroplane or to get into places like theatres.

tickle *verb* tickles, tickling, tickled
to touch someone lightly with your fingers to make them laugh.

tide *noun* tides
the movement of the sea towards the land and away from the land.

tidy *adjective* tidier, tidiest
with everything in the right place. *Is your room **tidy**?*
Word Building: tidily

tidy *verb* tidies, tidying, tidied
to put things away in the right place.

tie *noun* ties
1 a long strip of material that you wear around your neck.
2 when two people or players have the same number of points at the end of a game. *The match ended in a **tie**.*

tie *verb* ties, tying, tied
to fasten something with a knot or a bow. *I **tied** my shoelaces.*

tiger *noun* tigers
a big wild cat found in Asia. It has orange fur with black stripes.

tight (tite) *adjective* tighter, tightest
1 fitting very closely. ***tight** trousers.*
2 fixed firmly so you cannot move it. *a **tight** knot.*
Word Building: tightly

tighten (tite-en) *verb* tightens, tightening, tightened
to make something tighter, or to get tighter.

tile *noun* tiles
a thin piece of baked clay, used in covering a roof, wall, or floor.

till *noun* tills
a drawer or box for money in a shop.

tilt *verb* tilts, tilting, tilted
to make something slope. *Don't **tilt** the table.*

timber *noun* timbers
wood used for building or making things.

time *noun* times
1 seconds, minutes, hours, days, weeks, months, and years.
2 a certain moment in the day. *'What **time** is it?' 'It's **time** for lunch.'*
3 the rhythm and speed of a piece of music.

times *preposition*
multiplied by. *Two **times** four equals eight.* $2 \times 4 = 8$

timetable *noun* timetables
a list of times when things such as lessons at school happen, or when buses or planes go.

timid *adjective*
not brave.
Word Building: timidly

tin *noun* tins
1 a metal container for food or other things. *a **tin** of beans.*
2 a silver-coloured metal.

tingle *verb* tingles, tingling, tingled
to sting a little bit. *Cold water makes your skin **tingle**.*

tinkle *verb* tinkles, tinkling, tinkled
to make the light, ringing sound a small bell makes.

tiny *adjective* tinier, tiniest
very small.

tip *noun* tips
1 the part at the end of something. *the **tip** of a pencil.*
2 a small amount of money given to someone for their help. *a **tip** for the waiter.*

tip *verb* tips, tipping, tipped
1 to move something so that it is not straight. *Don't **tip** your chair back.*
2 to turn a container over so that something falls out. *I **tipped** the rubbish into the bin.*

tiptoe *verb* tiptoes, tiptoeing, tiptoed
to walk on your toes without making a sound.

tire *verb* tires, tiring, tired
to make or become sleepy, worn-out or bored. *Do you **tire** after a long walk?*
Word Building: tireless, tirelessly, tiresome

tired *adjective*
1 needing to rest or sleep.
2 bored with something. ***tired** of waiting.*

tissue (tish-oo) *noun* tissues
1 very thin, soft paper that you use for wrapping things like glass or china.
2 a paper handkerchief.

title *noun* titles
1 the name of a book, film, picture, or piece of music.
2 a word like Dr, Mr, and Ms that is put in front of a person's name.

to *preposition*
this word has several uses. Here are some of the ways you can use it: *a trip **to** Rabaul; give it **to** me; from one o'clock **to** four o'clock; she wants **to** go out.*

toad *noun* toads
an animal like a big frog. It has rough, dry skin and lives on land.

toast *noun*
bread cooked until it is crisp and brown.

tobacco (ta-bak-o) *noun*
a plant with leaves that are dried and smoked in pipes or used to make cigarettes.

today *noun*
this day.

toe *noun* toes
one of the five separate parts at the end of each foot.

toea *noun*
a unit of currency in PNG. *100 toea equals one kina.*

toffee *noun* toffees
butter and sugar cooked together and made into sticky sweets.

together (to-ge*th*-er) *adverb*
1 with another. *I stuck two pieces of paper* ***together.***
2 at the same time as another. *They sang* ***together.***

toil *verb* toils, toiling, toiled
to do hard work. *The women* ***toiled*** *all day in the garden.*

toilet *noun* toilets
1 a large bowl with a seat that you use to empty waste from your body.
2 a room where the toilet is.

token *noun* tokens
a piece of plastic, paper, or material that you can use instead of money to pay for something. *a book* ***token.***

Tok Pisin *noun*
the type of pidjin spoken in PNG.

tok ples *noun*
the mother tongue; the local language. [from Tok Pisin *tok ples*]

tok save *noun*
information; news. [from Tok Pisin *tok save*]

told *verb* see tell

tomato *noun* tomatoes
a soft, round, red fruit with seeds inside it. *You can eat* ***tomatoes*** *uncooked.*

tomb (toom) *noun* tombs
a place where a dead person's body is buried.

tomorrow *noun*
the day after today.

tone *noun* tones
how something sounds. *He spoke in an angry* ***tone*** *of voice.*

tongs *plural noun*
a tool that looks like a pair of scissors and is used for getting hold of something and picking it up.

tongue (rhymes with *sung*) *noun* tongues
the long, soft, pink part that moves about inside your mouth.

tonight *noun*
this evening or night.

tonne *noun* tonnes
a measure for weight.
1 tonne = 1000 kilograms.

tonsils *plural noun*
two soft organs in your throat.

tonsillitis *noun*
an infection of the tonsils.

too *adverb*
1 as well. *Can I come* ***too****?*
2 more than is needed. ***too*** *much.*

took *verb* see take

tool *noun* tools
something that you use to help you to do a job. *Hammers and saws are* ***tools.***

tooth *noun* teeth
1 one of the hard, white parts in the mouth which grow in rows and which you use for biting and chewing.
2 one of the sharp parts of a comb or saw.

toothache *noun*
a pain in a tooth.

toothbrush *noun* toothbrushes
a small brush with a long handle, for cleaning your teeth.

toothpaste *noun*
a thick paste that you put on a toothbrush and use for cleaning teeth.

top *noun* tops
1 the highest part of something. *the* ***top*** *of a hill.*
2 a cover that you put on something. *a bottle* ***top.***

top *adjective*
highest. *the **top** shelf.*

topic *noun* topics
something interesting that you are writing or talking about.

topple *verb* topples, toppling, toppled
to fall over because there is too much on top. *The pile of books **toppled** over.*

torch *noun* torches
a light that you can carry about with you, usually operated by batteries.

torment *verb* torments, tormenting, tormented
to be deliberately cruel to someone or something.

tore, torn *verb* see tear *verb*

torrent *noun* torrents
a very fast stream of water.

tortoise *noun* tortoises
a slow-moving, cold-blooded animal that has four legs and a hard shell over its body.

torture *verb* tortures, torturing, tortured
to deliberately to make someone or something feel great pain.
Word Building: torturer, torturers

toss *verb* tosses, tossing, tossed
1 to throw something. *They **tossed** the ball to each other.*
2 to move quickly up and down or from side to side. *The boat was **tossing** around on the waves.*

total *adjective*
complete. ***total** silence.*
Word Building: totally

total *noun* totals
the amount when you have added everything up.

touch *verb* touches, touching, touched
1 to feel something with part of your body. *Don't **touch** the plate—it's hot!*
2 to be so close to something else that there is no space in between. *The two wires were **touching**.*

tough (tuf) *adjective* tougher, toughest
1 strong. ***tough** shoes, a **tough** fighter.*
2 hard to chew. ***tough** meat.*

tour *noun* tours
a journey you make to visit different places.

tour *verb* tours, touring, toured
1 to travel about on holiday.
2 to go around a place looking at things. *We **toured** the museum before we had our picnic.*

tourist *noun* tourists
a person on holiday who goes around looking at interesting places.

tournament (ter-na-ment) *noun* tournaments
a series of contests between a number of players or teams.

tow (rhymes with *low*) *verb* tows, towing, towed
to pull along. *The car was **towing** a boat.*

toward, towards *preposition*
in the direction of something.
*He walked **towards** the school.*

towel *noun* towels
a piece of cloth for drying things that are wet.

tower *noun* towers
a tall, narrow building, or a tall part of a building. *a church **tower**.*

town *noun* towns
a place with schools, shops, offices, factories, and a lot of houses built near each other.

toy *noun* toys
something you play with.

trace *noun* traces
a mark left by something.

trace *verb* traces, tracing, traced
to copy a picture using thin paper that you can see through.

track *noun* tracks
1 a path.
2 a railway line.

track *verb* tracks, tracking, tracked
to follow the marks left by a person or animal.

tractor *noun* tractors
a vehicle used to pull farm machines and other heavy things.

trade *noun*
buying and selling. *The shops do a lot of **trade** at Christmas.*

trade store *noun* trade stores
A small shop selling many different types of goods. *The **trade store** in our village sells tinned meat and rice.*

tradition (tra-**dish**-on) *noun* traditions
something that people have done or believed in for a long time.
Word Building: traditional

traffic *noun*
cars, buses, bicycles, trucks, and other things travelling on the road.
traffic jam a long line of traffic that cannot move.
traffic lights lights that change colour to tell traffic when to stop and go.

tragedy (**traj**-e-dee) *noun* tragedies
1 something very sad that happened.
2 a play with a very sad ending.

trail *noun* trails
1 a rough path.
2 smells or marks left behind by something. *The dog was on the **trail** of a bandicoot.*

trail *verb* trails, trailing, trailed
1 to follow a trail.
2 to be dragged along the ground. *Mirou's dress is so long that it **trails** in the mud.*

trailer *noun* trailers
something that is pulled along by a car or truck.

train *noun* trains
the vehicle which carries goods or passengers on a railway.

train *verb* trains, training, trained
1 to teach a person or animal how to do something.
2 to practise for a competition or game.
Word Building: trainer, trainers

traitor *noun* traitors
someone who gives away secret or private information to the enemy.

tramp *noun* tramps
someone without a home or job who walks from place to place.

tramp *verb* tramps, tramping, tramped
to walk with heavy footsteps.

trample *verb* tramples, trampling, trampled
to spoil something by walking heavily on it. *Don't **trample** on the flowers!*

transfer *verb* transfers, transferring, transferred
to move someone or something to another place. *He was **transferred** to a different team.*

transform *verb* transforms, transforming, transformed
to change someone or something so that they are completely different.

translate *verb* translates, translating, translated
to put something into another language.

transparent *adjective*
so clear that you can see through it.

transplant *noun* transplants
an operation to move part of the body from one person to another. *a heart **transplant**.*

transport *noun*
vehicles used to take people, animals, or things from one place to another.

trap *noun* traps
a device for catching animals or people.

trap *verb* traps, trapping, trapped
to catch a person or animal by using a trap or a clever trick.

trapdoor *noun* trapdoors
a door in the floor or ceiling.

travel *verb* travels, travelling, travelled
to go from one place to another.

trawler *noun* trawlers
a fishing boat that pulls a large net along the sea bottom.

tray *noun* trays
a flat piece of wood, metal, or plastic used for carrying cups, plates, and other things.

treacherous (trech-er-us) *adjective*
1 not to be trusted.
2 dangerous. *a **treacherous** sea.*

tread (tred) *verb* treads, treading, trod, trodden
to walk on something.

treason (tree-zun) *noun*
giving away your country's secrets to the enemy.

treasure (trezh-er) *noun*
gold, silver, jewels, or other valuable things.

treat *noun* treats
something special that you enjoy.

treat *verb* treats, treating, treated
1 to behave towards someone or something in a certain way. *The horse had been badly **treated**.*
2 to try to make a sick person well again.
3 to pay for another person's food or drink. *My uncle **treated** us to lunch in a hotel.*

treaty *noun* treaties
a paper that is signed when two countries or races agree to live together in peace.

tree *noun* trees
a tall plant with leaves, branches, and a thick stem of wood. *a rain **tree**.*

tree-kangaroo *noun* tree-kangaroos
a wallaby-like animal which lives in trees in PNG and northern Australia.

tremble *verb* trembles, trembling, trembled
to shake because you are cold or frightened.

tremendous *adjective*
very large or great.

trench *noun* trenches
a long, narrow hole dug in the ground.

trespass *verb* trespasses, trespassing, trespassed
to go on someone else's land, without asking them if you can.

trial *noun* trials
1 trying something out to see how well it works.
2 the time when a prisoner is in court. The people there decide whether or not he or she has done wrong.

triangle *noun* triangles
a flat shape with three straight edges and three corners.
Word Building: triangular

tribe *noun* tribes
a group of families who live together and are ruled by a chief.

trick *noun* tricks
1 something you do to cheat someone or to make someone look silly.
2 something clever that you have learned to do. *card **tricks**.*

trick *verb* tricks, tricking, tricked
to cheat someone with a trick.

trickle *verb* trickles, trickling, trickled
to move like a very small stream.

tricky *adjective* trickier, trickiest
cunning, sly, sneaky. *The **tricky** players on the other team had to be watched very closely.*

trigger *noun* triggers
the part of a gun that you pull with your finger to fire it.

trim *verb* trim, trimming, trimmed
1 to cut something to make it neat and tidy. *She **trimmed** my hair.*
2 to decorate a piece of clothing. *a collar **trimmed** with shells.*

trio (tree-o) *noun* trios
a set of three people or things.

trip *noun* trips
a journey or outing. *a school **trip**.*

trip *verb* trips, tripping, tripped
to catch your foot on something so that you stumble or fall.

tripod (try-pod) *noun* tripods
a stand with three legs. *He put the camera on a **tripod** to hold it steady.*

triumph (try-umf) *noun* triumphs
a great success. *Our school concert was a **triumph**.*
Word Building: triumphant, triumphantly

trod *verb* see tread

trolley *noun* trolleys
a large container on wheels that you carry things in. *a supermarket **trolley**.*

troop *noun* troops
a group of soldiers or scouts.

troops *noun*
soldiers.

tropical *adjective*
belonging to the very hot countries and regions such as PNG, Africa, Asia, Australia, and South America. *tropical rainforests.*

tropical ulcer
a large open sore which is often on the leg.

trot *verb* trots, trotting, trotted
to move quickly with high short steps.

trouble (trub-l) *noun* troubles
something that upsets, worries, or bothers you.
to be in trouble to be in a difficult situation because you have done something wrong or something bad has happened.

trouble *verb* troubles, troubling, troubled
to worry, to bother someone.

trough (trof) *noun* troughs
a long, narrow container that holds food or water for farm animals.

trousers (trow-zerz) *noun*
a piece of clothing that covers the body from the waist to the ankles and has separate parts for the legs.

trout (trowt) *noun* trout
a fish found in rivers and lakes.

truck *noun* trucks
a large vehicle for carrying heavy things on the road.

trudge *verb* trudges, trudging, trudged
to walk slowly and heavily in a tired way.

true *adjective* truer, truest
correct or real. *a **true** story, a **true** friend.*
Word Building: truly

trumpet *noun* trumpets
a brass musical instrument that you blow into.

trunk *noun* trunks
1 a tree's thick stem.
2 an elephant's long nose.
3 a large box with a lid and handle for carrying things on a journey or storing things.

trust *verb* trusts, trusting, trusted
to believe that someone is good and honest and would not hurt you.

truth *noun*
something that is true. *Is he telling the truth?*
Word Building: truthful, truthfully

try *verb* tries, trying, tried
1 to work hard at something you want to be able to do. *I **tried** to climb that tree, but I couldn't.*
2 to use or test something to see what it is like. ***Try** the brakes before you drive the car.*

try *noun* tries
putting the ball down over the other team's goal line to score points in rugby.

T-shirt *noun*
a short sleeved casual shirt without buttons or a front opening.

tub *noun* tubs
a round or square container. *a **tub** of ice cream.*

tube *noun* tubes
1 a long, thin, round container. *a **tube** of toothpaste.*
2 a long, thin, hollow piece of plastic, rubber, glass, or metal.

tuck *verb* tucks, tucking, tucked
to push the ends of something into or under something else. *Maria **tucked** her shirt into her jeans.*

tucker box *noun*
a small trade store which can usually be moved from place to place.

tuck shop *noun* tuck shops
a shop in a school, selling snacks, lunches, and drinks.

Tuesday *noun* Tuesdays
the day after Monday.

tuft *noun* tufts
a number of feathers, hairs, or blades of grass growing together.

tug *verb* tugs, tugging, tugged
to pull hard.

tulip *noun* tulips
a spring flower that grows from a bulb and is shaped like a cup.

tumble *verb* tumbles, tumbling, tumbled
to fall.

tuna *noun* tuna
a large sea fish.

tune *noun* tunes
a group of musical notes which make a pleasant sound.

tunic (tew-nik) *noun* tunics
a dress or long shirt without sleeves.

tunnel *noun* tunnels
a long hole that has been made under the ground or through a hill.

tura *noun*
a friend. [from Motu *tura*]

turkey *noun* turkeys
a large bird that is kept on a farm for its meat.

turn *noun* turns
the proper time for someone in a group to do something. *your **turn** next.*

turn *verb* turns, turning, turned
1 to move around. *I* ***turned*** *round to see who was behind me.*
2 to move something round. *He* ***turned*** *the key in the lock.*
3 to become. *She* ***turned*** *pale.*
to turn into to change into something different. *Tadpoles* ***turn into*** *frogs.*

turtle *noun* turtles
a sea creature with a hard shell on its body.

tusk *noun* tusks
one of the two long, pointed teeth an elephant has.

tweezers *plural noun*
a tool for getting hold of very small things.

twelve
the number 12.
Word Building: twelfth

twenty
the number 20.
Word Building: twentieth

twice *adverb*
two times.

twig *noun* twigs
a small, thin branch of a tree.

twilight *noun*
the dim light at the end of the day before it gets completely dark.

twin *noun* twins
one of two children born to the same mother at the same time.

twinkle *verb* twinkles, twinkling, twinkled
to shine with a lot of tiny flashes of bright light.

twirl *verb* twirls, twirling, twirled
to turn round and round quickly.

twist *verb* twists, twisting, twisted
1 to turn or bend. *The path* ***twisted*** *and turned through the bush.*
2 to turn things round each other. *We* ***twisted*** *the wires together.*

twitch *verb* twitches, twitching, twitched
to make little, quick movements with part of the body.

twitter *verb* twitters, twittering, twittered
to keep making quick, light sounds like a bird.

two *noun* twos
the number 2.

two-dimensional *adjective*
a two-dimensional object is flat rather than solid.

type *noun* types
a kind or sort.

type *verb* types, typing, typed
to write with a typewriter.

typewriter *noun* typewriters
a machine with keys that you press in order to print letters and numbers.

typical (tip-i-kl) *adjective*
normal, usual.
Word Building: typically

tyre *noun* tyres
a circle of rubber round the rim of a wheel.

ugly *adjective* uglier, ugliest
not beautiful to look at.

umbrella *noun* umbrellas
a round piece of cloth stretched over a frame that can be opened and shut. You hold an umbrella over your head to keep off the rain.

umpire *noun* umpires
someone who makes sure that the rules are kept in games such as soccer and netball.

unable *adjective*
not able to do something. *Vagi was **unable** to go to the party.*

unaware *adjective*
not knowing about something. *I was **unaware** that someone was watching me.*

uncertain *adjective*
not sure, not decided. *She was **uncertain** what to do next.*

uncle *noun* uncles
the brother of your mother or father or the husband of your aunt.

unclear *adjective*
not clear.

uncomfortable (un-**kumf**-tra-bl) *adjective*
not comfortable.

uncommon *adjective*
not common, unusual.

unconscious (un-**kon**-shus) *adjective*
not aware of anything, in a very deep sleep. *Tau hit his head and was **unconscious** for several minutes.*

under *adverb, preposition*
1 below or lower than something. *The dog is **under** the table.*
2 less than something. *If you are **under** 18 you are not allowed to drive a car.*
3 covered by something. *I'm wearing a singlet **under** my shirt.*

underground *adjective, adverb*
under the ground.

undergrowth *noun*
shrubs and other plants growing under tall trees.

underline *verb* underlines, underlining, underlined
to draw a straight line underneath a word.

underneath *adverb, preposition*
below; in a place under something. *The snake lay **underneath** the tree. She wore a blue jacket with a white T-shirt **underneath**.*

underpants *plural noun*
underwear worn on the bottom half of the body.

understand *verb* understands, understanding, understood
to know what something means or how it works.

underwear *noun*
clothes that you wear next to your skin, under your other clothes.

undo *verb* undoes, undoing, undid, undone
to open something that has been tied or fixed. *She **undid** the string and opened the parcel. I can't **undo** these buttons.*

undress *verb* undresses, undressing, undressed
to take clothes off.

unemployed *adjective*
without a job, not working.

uneven *adjective*
not smooth or flat. *an **uneven** road.*

unexpected *adjective*
surprising because you did not expect it. *an **unexpected** visit.*
Word Building: unexpectedly

unfair *adjective*
not fair, not right or just.
Word Building: unfairly

unfortunate *adjective*
unlucky, unhappy.
Word Building: unfortunately

unfriendly *adjective*
hostile, nasty, rude. ***Unfriendly** children are not liked by their classmates.*

ungrateful *adjective*
not showing or saying thanks when someone helps you or gives you something. *The **ungrateful** child never thanked them for the present.*

unhappy *adjective*
not happy.
Word Building: unhappily, unhappiness

unhealthy *adjective*
1 not well, not healthy. *an **unhealthy** diet.*
2 that can make you ill. ***unhealthy** food.*

unicorn *noun* unicorns
in stories, an animal like a horse with a long, straight horn growing from the front of its head.

uniform *noun* uniforms
the special clothes that everyone in the same school, job, or club wears.
*a school **uniform**.*

union (**yoon**-yun) *noun* unions
a group of workers who have joined together to talk to their employer about things like pay and the way they work.

unique (yoo-**neek**) *adjective*
not like anyone or anything else.
*Every person in the world is **unique**.*

unit *noun* units
1 a single thing; one part of some larger thing.
2 an amount used in measuring or counting. *Centimetres are **units** of length.*
3 an amount of one. *The sum 254 is made up of two hundreds, five tens, and four **units**.*

unite *verb* unites, uniting, united
to join together to make one.

universe *noun*
all the worlds that there are and everyone and everything in them.

university *noun* universities
a place where some people go to study when they have left school.

unkind *adjective* unkinder, unkindest
not kind, cruel.
Word Building: unkindly

unknown *adjective*
not known.

unleaded *adjective*
not containing lead. ***unleaded** petrol.*

unless *conjunction*
if not. *You'll be late **unless** you leave now.*

unlike *adjective*
not like, different.

unlikely *adjective*
not likely, not what you expect. *It's **unlikely** to rain today.*

unload *verb* unloads, unloading, unloaded
to take off the things that an animal, boat, car, or truck is carrying.

unlock *verb* unlocks, unlocking, unlocked
to open a door or box with a key.

unlucky *adjective* unluckier, unluckiest
not lucky; good things do not happen to you.
Word Building: unluckily

unnatural *adjective*
not natural, not normal.
Word Building: unnaturally

unnecessary *adjective*
not necessary, not needed.

unpleasant *adjective*
not nice, not pleasant.

unpopular *adjective*
not liked by many people.

unsafe *adjective*
not safe; dangerous.

unselfish *adjective*
not selfish, thinking of others.

unsuccessful *adjective*
not able to do or get what you wanted to do or get.

unsuitable *adjective*
not suitable.

untidy *adjective* untidier, untidiest
not tidy.

untie *verb* unties, untying, untied
to undo a knot.

until *conjunction, preposition*
up to a certain time. *I stayed up **until** midnight.*

untrue *adjective*
false; not true or correct.

unusual *adjective*
not usual, strange.
Word Building: unusually

unwell *adjective*
ill.

unwrap (un-**rap**) *verb* unwraps, unwrapping, unwrapped
to take something out of the covering it is wrapped in.

up *adverb, preposition*
to somewhere higher. *Run **up** the hill.*

uphill *adverb*
up, towards the top of the hill.

upon *preposition*
on or on top of.

upper *adjective*
higher. *the **upper** floors of a building.*

upright *adjective*
1 standing straight up. *an **upright** post.*
2 honest. *an **upright** person.*

uproar *noun*
loud noise made by people who are angry or excited.

upset *verb* upsets, upsetting, upset
1 to make someone unhappy.
2 to knock over. *He **upset** a glass of cordial all over the table.*

upside down *adjective, adverb*
turned over so that the bottom is at the top. *That picture is **upside down**.*

upstairs *adjective, adverb*
the part of a house that you get to by climbing the stairs.

up-to-date *adjective*
modern.

upwards *adverb*
moving to somewhere higher, up.

urge (erj) *noun* urges
a strong feeling that you want to do something. *I had a sudden **urge** to laugh.*

urge (erj) *verb* urges, urging, urged
to try to make someone do something. *I **urged** him to hurry up.*

urgent (er-jent) *adjective*
so important that you must do it or answer it at once. *an **urgent** message, an **urgent** telephone call.*
Word Building: urgently

urn *noun* urns
a large, metal container.

us *pronoun*
me and others. *Bring **us** some drinks, please.*

use (rhymes with *lose*) *verb* uses, using, used
to do a job with something. *I **used** paper and glue to make it. Don't **use** all the milk!*
used to be or do was or did something in the past. *She **used to be** my friend.*
to be used to something doing something as a habit. *I **am used to** getting up early.*

use (rhymes with *loose*) *noun* uses
what you do with something. *Paper has a lot of **uses**.*

used *adjective*
second-hand. ***used** clothing.*

useful *adjective*
good and helpful. *a **useful** bag to put things in, **useful** information.*

useless *adjective*
not useful, cannot be used. *A car is **useless** without petrol.*

user-friendly *adjective*
easy to understand and use. *a **user-friendly** computer.*

usual *adjective*
normal, happening most often. *Today, I got up earlier than **usual**.*
Word Building: usually

ute *noun* utes
(*informal*) a small truck. This word is a shortened form of utility vehicle.

utensil (yoo-ten-sil) *noun* utensils
a tool or piece of equipment, usually used in the kitchen.

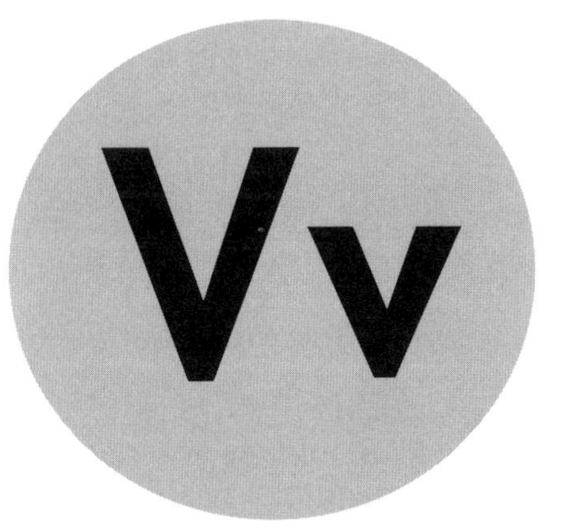

vacant *adjective*
with nobody in it. *a **vacant** room.*

vaccination (vak-si-**nay**-shun) ***noun*** vaccinations
an injection that stops you getting an illness.

vacation ***noun*** vacations
a holiday. *We went to Madang for our Christmas **vacation**.*

vacuum (**vak**-yoom) ***noun***
a space with no air or anything inside it.

vacuum cleaner ***noun*** vacuum cleaners
a machine that sucks up dust and dirt from floors and carpets.

vague (vayg) ***adjective*** vaguer, vaguest
not clear or certain.
Word Building: vaguely

vain ***adjective*** vainer, vainest
too proud of what you can do or how you look. *The **vain** children kept looking at themselves in the mirror.*
in vain without success.

valley ***noun*** valleys
low land between hills. ***Valleys** often have rivers running through them.*

valuable ***adjective***
1 worth a lot of money. *a **valuable** painting.*
2 useful. ***valuable** advice.*

value ***noun*** values
1 the amount of money something could be sold for.
2 how important or useful something is.

vampire ***noun*** vampires
in stories, a creature that is supposed to suck blood.

van ***noun*** vans
a vehicle with a roof, for carrying goods.

vandal ***noun*** vandals
a person who deliberately breaks things that belong to other people.
Word Building: vandalism

vanilla ***noun***
1 a climbing plant that produces sweet-smelling seed pods.
2 the seed pods of this plant which are used to flavour food.

vanish ***verb*** vanishes, vanishing, vanished
to go away suddenly and not be seen any more.

vapour or **vapor** ***noun*** vapours
steam, mist, or fog.

variety ***noun*** varieties
1 a lot of different kinds of things. *a **variety** of flavours.*
2 a certain sort. *rare **varieties** of butterflies.*

various *adjective*
different. *boxes of* ***various*** *shapes and sizes.*

varnish *noun* varnishes
a clear liquid painted on to wood or metal to make it shiny.

vary *verb* varies, varing, varied
1 to be different, to change. *The date of Easter* ***varies*** *each year.*
2 to make something different.

vase *verb* vases
a jar for holding flowers.

vast *adjective*
very big. *The Whagi is a* ***vast*** *valley.*

veal *noun*
meat from a calf.

vegetable (vej-ta-bl) *noun* vegetables
part of a plant used as food. *Potatoes, carrots, and beans are* ***vegetables.***

vegetarian (vej-e-**tair**-ee-an) *noun* vegetarians
a person who does not eat meat.

vegetation (vej-e-**tay**-shun) *noun*
plants and trees.

vehicle (vee-hik-l) *noun* vehicles
anything that takes people or things from one place to another on land. *Cars, vans, buses, PMVs, and trucks are* ***vehicles.***

veil (vail) *noun* veils
a piece of thin material used to cover the face or head.

vein (vain) *noun* veins
one of the narrow tubes inside the body, that carry blood to the heart.

velvet *noun*
thick material that is smooth and soft on one side. ***velvet*** *curtains.*

venom (ven-um) *noun*
the poison of snakes and spiders.
Word Building: venomous
The python is not a ***venomous*** *snake.*

ventriloquist *noun* ventriloquists
an entertainer who seems to make a dummy speak.

verb *noun* verbs
any of the words that tell you what someone or something is doing. *Come, go, sit, take, and think are all* ***verbs.***

verdict *noun* verdicts
what is decided about a person accused of a crime at the end of a trial in a law court.

verse *noun* verses
part of a poem or song.

version (ver-zhun) *noun* versions
1 a particular way of telling a story. *Papi's* ***version*** *of the accident is different from Samuel's.*
2 a particular way of doing or making something. *This is a new* ***version*** *of the book.*

vertebra (ver-te-bra) *noun* vertebrae
a bone in your spine.

vertebrate (ver-te-bret) *noun* vertebrates
an animal with a backbone.

vertical *adjective*
standing or pointing straight up, the opposite of horizontal.

very *adverb*
You use 'very' before another word to make it stronger: *I'm* ***very*** *hungry. OK Tedi is a* ***very*** *big mine. He is* ***very*** *tall.*

vessel *noun* vessels
1 any container for liquid.
2 any kind of ship or boat.

veterinarian (vet-re-**nair**-ee-an) *noun* veterinarians
someone whose job is to help animals that are ill or hurt to get better.
Word Building: veterinary
We took our dog to the ***veterinary*** *hospital when he hurt his paw.*

vibrate *verb* vibrates, vibrating, vibrated
to move very quickly to and fro. *The whole house **vibrates** when a truck goes past.*

vicious (vish-us) *adjective*
bad and cruel.

victim *noun* victims
someone who has been hurt, robbed, or killed.

victory *noun* victories
the winning of a fight or game.

video *noun* videos
1 a machine that records and plays back television programs on videotape.
2 a videotape with a movie or television programs on it.

videotape *noun* videotapes
a special tape for recording television programs.

view *noun* views
1 everything that you can see from one place. *a beautiful **view** of the sea.*
2 what a person thinks about something. *My **view** is that school holidays are too short.*

view *verb* views, viewing, viewed
to look at something, to watch. *We **viewed** the stars through a telescope.*
Word Building: viewer, viewers
*television **viewers**.*

vigour or **vigor** *noun*
strength, liveliness or energy. *The young children are full of **vigour**.*
Word Building: vigorous, vigorously

vigorous *adjective*
1 active, energetic. ***vigorous** exercise.*
2 strong and healthy. ***vigorous** plants.*
Word Building: vigorously

vile *adjective*
very nasty. *Burning rubber has a **vile** smell.*

village *noun* villages
a place where a small community lives.

villain *noun* villains
a bad person.

vine *noun* vines
a plant that grapes grow on.

vinegar (vin-ee-gar) *noun*
a sour liquid which you can put on some foods.

vinyl (vi-nil) *noun*
a kind of plastic.

violence (vie-o-lens) *noun*
a force that causes harm or danger. *The **violence** of the storm caused the roof to blow off.*
Word Building: violent, violently
*My sister has a **violent** temper.*

violin *noun* violins
a musical instrument made of wood with strings across it. You play the violin with a bow.

virus *noun* viruses
a tiny living thing that can cause diseases. *a flu **virus**.*

visible *adjective*
that you can see. *Stars are only **visible** at night.*

vision (vizh-un) *noun*
1 the power to see. *Glasses will improve your **vision**.*
2 a kind of dream.

visit *verb* visits, visiting, visited
to go to see a person or a place.
Word Building: visitor, visitors

A B C D E F G H I J K L M N O P Q R S T U V W X Y Z

vitamin (vi-ta-min) *noun* vitamins
one of the things in food that you need to keep you healthy. *Green vegetables are full of **vitamins**.*

vivid *adjective*
1 bright. ***vivid** colours.*
2 so clear it seems real. *a **vivid** dream.*
Word Building: vividly

vocabulary (vo-**kab**-yoo-lair-ee) *noun*
1 all the words in a language or that someone knows.
2 a list of words in a book that you must learn.

voice *noun* voices
the sound you make with your mouth when you are speaking or singing.

volcano *noun* volcanoes
a mountain that contains hot liquid, gases, and ash that sometimes burst out of it.

volleyball *noun*
a game in which two teams hit a large ball to and fro over a net with their hands.

volt *noun* volts
a unit for measuring the strength of an electric current.
Word Building: voltage

volume *noun* volumes
1 the amount of space filled by something. *We measured the **volume** of liquid in the bottle.*
2 one of a set of books. *The encyclopedia has ten **volumes**.*
3 how loud a sound is. *Turn down the **volume** on your radio.*

voluntary (vol-un-tree) *adjective*
done without being paid and without being forced.
Word Building: voluntarily

volunteer *noun* volunteers
someone who offers to do something without being paid.

volunteer *verb* volunteers, volunteering, volunteered
to offer to do something you do not have to do.

vote *verb* votes, voting, voted
to say which person or idea you think should be chosen, by putting up your hand or by making a mark on a piece of paper.

voucher *noun* vouchers
a printed paper you can use instead of money.

vow *verb* vows, vowing, vowed
to make a serious promise.

vowel *noun* vowels
any one of the letters, a, e, i, o, u, and sometimes y.

voyage *noun* voyages
a long journey by boat or in space.

vulgar *adjective*
rude, bad-mannered.

vulnerable (vul-ner-a-bl) *adjective*
easily hurt or harmed. *Elderly people are **vulnerable** to influenza during cold, wet weather.*
Word Building: vulnerability

vulture *noun* vultures
a large bird that eats dead animals.

waddle *verb* waddles, waddling, waddled
to walk like a duck.

wade *verb* wades, wading, waded
to walk through water.

wafer *noun* wafers
a very thin biscuit.

wag *verb* wags, wagging, wagged
to move quickly from side to side.
*The dog **wagged** its tail.*

wages *noun*
the money paid to someone for the job they do.

wagon *noun* wagons
1 a cart with four wheels that is pulled by horses and used for moving heavy things.
2 an open part of a train where things like coal are carried.

wail *verb* wails, wailing, wailed
to make a long, sad cry.

waist *noun* waists
the narrow part in the middle of the body.

wait *verb* waits, waiting, waited
to stay until someone comes or until something happens.

waiter *noun* waiters
someone who brings food to people in cafés, hotels, and restaurants.

wake *verb* wakes, waking, woke, woken
1 to stop sleeping. *I **woke** at six.*
2 to make someone stop sleeping.
*I asked Mum to **wake** me early.*

walk *verb* walks, walking, walked
to move along on your feet.
Word Building: walker, walkers

wall *noun* walls
1 a thing made of bricks or stone around a garden or field.
2 one of the sides of a building or room.

wallaby *noun* wallabies
an animal that is like a kangaroo, but smaller.

wallet *noun* wallets
a small, flat case for paper money that you can carry in your pocket.

walnut *noun* walnuts
a nut with a hard shell.

walrus *noun* walruses
an animal with long tusks that lives in the Arctic.

waltz *noun* waltzes
a kind of dance done with a partner.

wand *noun* wands
a thin stick used for casting magic spells.

wander *verb* wanders, wandering, wandered
to move about without trying to get anywhere in particular.

want *verb* wants, wanting, wanted
1 to feel that you would like to have something. *I **want** a new shirt.*
2 to need. *That car **wants** washing.*

wantok *noun*
1 a person who speaks the same mother tongue.
2 a friend.
Word building: wantok system, making use of friends and relatives to get what you want. [from Tok Pisin *wantok*]

war *noun* wars
a fight between countries.

ward *noun* wards
a room in a hospital where several patients stay.

wardrobe *noun* wardrobes
a cupboard where you hang clothes.

warehouse *noun* warehouses
a large building where things can be stored.

warm *adjective* warmer, warmest
fairly hot. *a **warm** bath.*

warn *verb* warns, warning, warned
to tell someone that they are in danger.

warrior *noun* warriors
someone fighting in a battle.

wart *noun* warts
a dry, hard spot on the skin.

was *verb* see be

wash *verb* washes, washing, washed
to clean something with water.
to wash up to clean the plates, knives, and forks.

washing *noun*
clothes that need washing or are being washed.

wasp *noun* wasps
a black and yellow striped insect that flies and can sting.

waste *noun*
1 things that you get rid of because you do not need them any more.
2 not using things in a careful way. *It's a **waste** to throw away all this food.*

waste *verb* wastes, wasting, wasted
1 to use more of something than you need to. *Write on both sides so that you don't **waste** paper.*
2 to throw something away that you could use. *Don't **waste** this food—we can have it tomorrow.*

watch *noun* watches
a small clock that you wear on your wrist.

watch *verb* watches, watching, watched
to look at.

water *noun*
the clear liquid in rivers and seas.

water *verb* waters, watering, watered
1 to put water on the soil to help seeds or plants to grow.
2 to fill with water. *The smoke made my eyes **water**.*

waterfall *noun* waterfalls
a stream of water falling from a high place to a low place.

waterlogged *adjective*
soaked or filled with water.

waterproof *adjective*
made of material that does not let water through. *a **waterproof** coat.*

watertight *adjective*
closed tightly so that no water can get through. *a **watertight** lid.*

watt *noun* watts
a measure for electric power.

wattle *noun* wattles
a tree with flowers ranging in colour from white to deep gold.

wave *noun* waves
a raised line of water, like those that move across the top of the sea.

wave *verb* waves, waving, waved
1 to raise your hand and move it from side to side, as people do when they say goodbye.
2 to move backwards and forwards or from side to side. *The branches were* ***waving*** *in the wind.*

wavy *adjective*
with curves in it. ***wavy*** *hair.*

wax *noun*
stuff that melts easily, used to make such things as candles and polish.

way *noun* ways
1 a road or path that takes you to a place. *This is the* ***way*** *to the station.*
2 how you do something. *This is the* ***way*** *to weave a bilum.*

we *pronoun*
a word used by someone to talk about himself or herself and another person or other people. *Maria, Regan and I decided that* ***we*** *would go to the beach.*
Word Building: we'd (we + did or had); we'll (we + will); we're (we + are); we've (we + have)

weak *adjective* weaker, weakest
not strong.

weaken *verb* weakens, weakening, weakened
to get weaker or to make weaker.

wealth (welth) *noun*
a lot of money or treasure.

wealthy (wel-thee) *adjective* wealthier, wealthiest
rich.

weapon (wep-on) *noun* weapons
something used to hurt another person in a fight, such as a gun or a knife.

wear *verb* wears, wearing, wore, worn
to be dressed in something. *I* ***wore*** *my jeans.*
to wear out to become useless because it has been used so much. *My sweater was* ***wearing out*** *at the elbows.*
to wear someone out to make someone very tired. *The children were* ***worn out*** *from their trip to the river.*

weary *adjective* wearier, weariest
very tired.

weather (we*th*-er) *noun*
the sun, wind, rain, temperature, and other conditions that you notice when you go out of doors.

weave *verb* weaves, weaving, wove, woven
to make cloth by pushing a thread under and over other threads.

web *noun* webs
a thin net spun by a spider to trap insects.

web-footed *adjective*
having feet with toes joined together by skin, as ducks have.

wedding *noun* weddings
the time when a man and a woman get married.

Wednesday *noun* Wednesdays
the day after Tuesday.

weed *noun* weeds
a wild plant growing where you don't want it.

week *noun* weeks
1 the seven days from Monday to Sunday.
2 any period of seven days. *My cold will be better in a* ***week****.*

weekend *noun* weekends
Saturday and Sunday.

weep *verb* weeps, weeping, wept
to cry.

weigh (way) *verb* weighs, weighing, weighed
1 to find out how heavy something is. *The shop assistant **weighed** the fish.*
2 to have a certain weight. *How much do you **weigh**?*

weight (wait) *noun* weights
1 how heavy something is. *Do you know the **weight** of the parcel?*
2 a piece of metal that you use to measure how heavy something is.

weird *adjective* weirder, weirdest
very strange.

welcome *verb* welcomes, welcoming, welcomed
to show someone you are pleased when they arrive.

well *adjective*
healthy, not ill. *I hope you are **well**.*

well *adverb* better, best
1 in a good way. *Gima plays the piano **well**.*
2 very much. *Shake the bottle **well** before you open it.*
as well also. *Can I come **as well**?*

well *noun* wells
a hole dug to get water or oil out of the ground.

well-known *adjective*
known to many people.

wept *verb* see weep

went *verb* see go

west *noun, adjective*
the direction where the sun goes down in the evening.

wet *adjective* wetter, wettest
1 covered or soaked in water or some other liquid, not dry. *a **wet** towel, **wet** paint.*
2 with a lot of rain. *a **wet** day.*

whack *verb* whacks, whacking, whacked
to hit hard. *Hekere **whacked** the ball with the cricket bat.*

whale *noun* whales
the largest sea animal there is.

wharf *noun* wharves
a place where ships are loaded and unloaded.

what *adjective, pronoun*
this word has several uses. Here are some of the ways you can use it: ***What** is your name? I don't know **what** this word means. **What** a beautiful picture!*

whatever *adjective, pronoun*
1 any or every. *These animals eat **whatever** food they can find.*
2 no matter what. ***Whatever** happens, I'll help you.*

wheat *noun*
a plant grown by farmers. It has seeds called grains that are used to make flour.

wheel *noun* wheels
a circular object that turns on an axle through the middle. Cars, bicycles, and buses have wheels.

wheelbarrow *noun* wheelbarrows
a small cart with one wheel at the front and handles at the back.

wheelchair *noun* wheelchairs
a chair on wheels for a person who can't walk.

when *adverb, conjunction*
1 at what time. ***When** are you coming?*
2 at the time that. ***When** I moved, the bird flew away.*

whenever *conjunction*
at any time. *Come to play **whenever** you like.*

where *adverb, conjunction*
1 in what place. ***Where** are you? Tell me **where** you are.*
2 in the place that. *Leave it **where** it is.*

wherever *adverb, conjunction*
no matter where. *I'll find you, **wherever** you are.*

whether *conjunction*
if. *He asked **whether** I was ready.*

which *adjective, pronoun*
this word has several uses. Here are some of the ways you can use it: ***Which** way did he go? I like the book **which** you gave me best. I don't know **which** to choose.*

whichever *adjective, pronoun*
any person or thing. *You can choose **whichever** book you want.*

while *conjunction*
during the time that something else is happening. *I'll slice the bread **while** you make the tea.*

whimper *verb* whimpers, whimpering, whimpered
to make a weak, crying sound when you are frightened or hurt.

whine *verb* whines, whining, whined
to make a long, high sound because you are hurt or unhappy.

whip *noun* whips
a piece of rope or strip of leather fixed to a handle.

whip *verb* whips, whipping, whipped
to hit someone or something with a whip.

whirl *verb* whirls, whirling, whirled
to turn round and round very fast.

whisk *verb* whisks, whisking, whisked
1 to stir something round and round very fast.
2 to move very quickly. *He **whisked** the book away before I could look at it.*

whiskers *noun*
hairs or bristles growing on the face of a man or an animal.

whisky *noun* whiskies
a strong alcoholic drink.

whisper *verb* whispers, whispering, whispered
to speak very quietly.

whistle (whis-l) *noun* whistles
something that makes a high sound when you blow it.

whistle (whis-l) *verb* whistles, whistling, whistled
to make a high sound by blowing air through a whistle or your lips.

white *adjective* whiter, whitest
1 having the colour of snow.
2 very pale.

whitebait *noun* whitebait
a tiny fish that is caught in nets at river mouths.

whiteboard *noun* whiteboards
a board made from white plastic and written on with felt-tip pens.

who (hoo) *pronoun*
which person. ***Who** broke my mug?*

whoever (hoo-ev-er) *pronoun*
no matter what person. ***Whoever** did it should own up.*

whole (hole) *adjective*
1 with nothing missing or left out. *We ate the **whole** chicken.*
2 in one piece, not broken. *The bird swallowed the fish **whole**.*

whose (hooz) *adjective, pronoun*
belonging to what person. ***Whose** cup is this?*

why *adverb*
because of what, for what reason. ***Why** are you late?*

wick *noun* wicks
the string through the middle of a candle, which you light.

wicked *adjective*
very bad, evil.

wicket *noun* wickets
the set of three stumps in cricket.

wide *adjective* wider, widest
measuring a lot from one side to the other. *a **wide** river.*

widow *noun* widows
a woman whose husband has died.

widower *noun* widowers
a man whose wife has died.

width *noun* widths
how wide something is. *We measured the **width** of the room.*

wife *noun* wives
a woman married to someone.

wig *noun* wigs
a covering of false hair that you wear on the head.

wild *adjective* wilder, wildest
1 not tame; not looked after by people. *The **wild** dogs attacked the sheep.*
2 not grown by people. ***Wild** plants grow in the bush.*
3 not controlled; violent. *Their behaviour was **wild**.*

wilderness *noun* wildernesses
wild land where no one lives.

wildlife *noun*
wild animals.

will *noun* wills
1 instructions left by a person who has died telling people what he or she wants to be done with his or her money and things.
2 the power to choose what you want to do.

will *verb*
this word is used in sentences about the future: *Vaitania will be ten next birthday.*

willing *adjective*
ready and happy to do what someone wants. *Geua is **willing** to help in the garden.*

willow *noun* willows
a tree that grows near water and has thin branches that bend easily.

wily *adjective* wilier, wiliest
crafty. ***wily** fox.*

win *verb* wins, winning, won
to beat all the others in a game, fight, or competition.
Word Building: winner, winners

wind (rhymes with *tinned*) *noun* winds
air moving along quickly. *leaves blowing in the **wind**.*

wind (rhymes with *find*) *verb* winds, winding, wound
1 to turn a key to make a machine work. *The clock started when she **wound** it up.*
2 to wrap cloth, thread, tape, or string tightly round something.

windmill *noun* windmills
a mill that uses wind to make its machinery work.

window *noun* windows
an opening filled with glass to let the light in.

windscreen *noun* windscreens
the window at the front of a car.

windy *adjective* windier, windiest
with a lot of wind.

wine *noun* wines
an alcoholic drink made from grapes.

wing *noun* wings
1 one of the parts a bird or insect flaps when it is flying.
2 one of the flat parts which stick out on each side of an aeroplane.

wink *verb* winks, winking, winked
to close and open one eye quickly.

winter *noun* winters
the coldest part of the year.

wipe *verb* wipes, wiping, wiped
to rub something with a cloth to dry it or clean it.

wire *noun* wires
a long, thin strip of metal that can be bent into different shapes. *Electricity passes along **wires**.*

wise *adjective* wiser, wisest
able to understand things and make good decisions.

wish *verb* wishes, wishing, wished
to say or think what you would like to happen. *I **wish** I had lots of money.*

wisp *noun* wisps
a little bit of straw, hair, or smoke.

witch *noun* witches
a woman who uses magic.

with *preposition*
this word has several uses. Here are some of the ways you can use it: *I play football **with** Igo. We saw a bird **with** a blue breast. I filled the jug **with** water.*

wither (with-er) *verb* withers, withering, withered
to dry up and get paler and smaller. ***withered** flowers.*

without *preposition*
not having. ***without** any money.*

witness *noun* witnesses
someone who sees something important happen. *There were two **witnesses** to the accident.*

witty *adjective* wittier, wittiest
clever and funny.

wizard *noun* wizards
a man in fairy stories who can do magic things.

wobble *verb* wobbles, wobbling, wobbled
to shake or rock. *Jelly **wobbles**.*

wok *noun* woks
a large, shallow, metal pan used for cooking foods quickly at high temperatures.

woke *verb* see wake

wolf *noun* wolves
a wild animal like a big dog.

woman *noun* women
a grown up female human being.

wombat *noun* wombats
a large, burrowing marsupial with a heavy body and short legs.

won *verb* see win

wonder *verb* wonders, wondering, wondered
to ask yourself about something.

wonderful *adjective*
very good.

wood *noun*
the branches and trunks of trees cut up so that they can be used for making things or burnt on fires.

wooden *adjective*
made of wood.

wool *noun*
the thick, soft hair that covers sheep. It is used for making cloth and for knitting.

woollen *adjective*
made of wool.

woolly *adjective*
made of wool, or like wool.

woolshed *noun* woolsheds
a farm building where sheep are shorn.

word *noun* words
a sound or group of sounds that means something when you write it, or read it. In writing there are spaces between words.

wore *verb* see wear

work *noun*
a job or something else that you have to do.

work *verb* works, working, worked
1 to do or make something, to be busy. *We **worked** hard at school today.*
2 to do something as a job and get paid for it. *He **works** in a shop.*
3 to do or make something do what it is supposed to do. *How does this computer **work**?*
Word Building: worker, workers

workshop *noun* workshops
a place where things are made or mended.

world *noun*
the Earth with all its countries and people.

worm (werm) *noun* worms
a long, thin creature that wriggles about in the soil.

worn *verb* see wear

worry *verb* worries, worrying, worried
to be upset because you think something bad might happen.

worse *adjective*
less good. *He's a **worse** swimmer than I am.*

worship *verb* worships, worshipping, worshipped
to love and praise.

worst *adjective*
least good. *He's the **worst** in the class at swimming.*

worth *adjective*
1 with a certain value. *This old stamp is **worth** K100.*
2 if something is worth doing or having, it is good or useful.

worthless *adjective*
not worth anything.

would (wood) *verb*
this word has several uses. Here are some of the ways you can use it:
*He said he **would** come. '**Would** you pass the salt, please?' I **would** like some coffee.*

wound (rhymes with *spooned*) *noun* wounds
a cut or hole in your body, often made by a weapon.

wound *verb* wounds, wounding, wounded
to hurt someone with a weapon or by cutting or hitting them.

wound (rhymes with *found*) *verb* see wind *verb*

wove *verb* see weave

woven *verb* see weave

wrap (rap) *verb* wraps, wrapping, wrapped
to put cloth or paper round something. ***wrap** a birthday present.*

wreath (reeth) ***noun*** wreaths
flowers or leaves twisted together into a ring. *a funeral **wreath**.*

wreck (rek) ***noun*** wrecks
a wrecked ship or car.

wreck (rek) ***verb*** wrecks, wrecking, wrecked
to break or destroy something so that you cannot use it.

wren (ren) ***noun*** wrens
a very small bird.

wrestle (res-sl) ***verb*** wrestles, wrestling, wrestled
to fight with someone by trying to throw them on the ground.

wretched (retch-ed) *adjective*
unhappy or ill.

wriggle (rig-gl) ***verb*** wriggles, wriggling, wriggled
to twist and turn about like a worm.

wring (ring) ***verb*** wrings, wringing, wrung
to squeeze and twist something wet to get the water out of it.

wrinkle (ring-kl) ***noun*** wrinkles
a small line in the skin that often appears when you get old.
Word Building: wrinkled

wrist (rist) ***noun*** wrists
the thin part of the arm where it is joined to the hand.

write (rite) ***verb*** writes, writing, wrote, written
to put words or signs on paper so that people can read them. *to **write** a poem, to **write** a letter.*
Word Building: writer, writers

writing (rite-ing) ***noun***
1 something that you have written. *a piece of **writing**.*
2 the way you write. *neat **writing**.*

wrong (rong) *adjective*
1 not right. *He gave the **wrong** answer.*
2 bad. *Stealing is **wrong**.*
Word Building: wrongly

wrote *verb* see write

wrung *verb* see wring

Xx

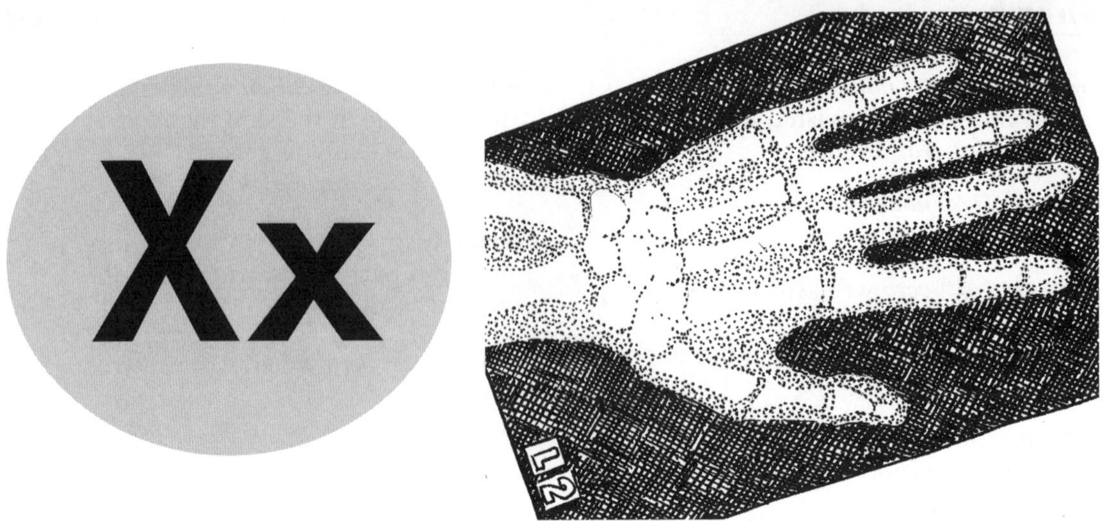

X-ray *noun* X-rays
a photograph that shows the inside of a body so that doctors can see if there is anything wrong.

xylophone (zy-la-fone) *noun* xylophones
a musical instrument with a row of wooden or metal bars that you hit with small hammers.

yabby *noun* yabbies
a small, edible freshwater crayfish.
Word Building: yabbying
*The children went **yabbying** near the river.*

yacht (yot) *noun* yachts
a boat with sails, often used for racing.

yap *verb* yaps, yapping, yapped
to make short, barking sounds.

yard *noun* yards
ground that is next to a building and has a wall or fence around it.

yawn *verb* yawns, yawning, yawned
to open your mouth wide because you are tired.

year *noun* years
1 a measure for time. A year is twelve months, or three hundred and sixty-five days.
2 one of the classes in a school.

yeast (yeest) *noun*
a substance used in bread that makes the dough get bigger. It is also used in making beer and wine.

yell *verb* yells, yelling, yelled
to shout.

yellow *noun, adjective*
the colour of a lemon.

yelp *verb* yelps, yelping, yelped
to make a shrill, sharp bark or cry, like a dog in pain.

yesterday *noun*
the day before today.

yet *adverb, conjunction*
this word has several uses. Here are some of the ways you can use it:
*Are you ready **yet**? He hurt his knee, **yet** he still plays football. Ila is late **yet** again!*

yield (yeeld) *verb* yields, yielding, yielded
to give in, to surrender.

yoghurt (yo-gert) *noun*
a thick liquid made from milk. You eat it with a spoon.

yoke *noun* yokes
a curved, wooden frame put across the necks of animals to help them pull a cart or wagon.

yolk (yoke) *noun* yolks
the yellow part of an egg.

you *pronoun*
the person or people you are speaking to.

young *adjective* younger, youngest
not old, born not long ago. *My brother is **younger** than me.*

your *adjective*
belonging to you. *Is this **your** bag?*

yourself, yourselves *pronoun*
you and no one else. *Did you hurt yourself?*
by yourself on your own.

youth *noun* youths
1 a boy or young man.
2 the time in your life when you are young.

zebra (zeb-ra) *noun* zebras
an animal like a horse with black and white stripes.

zero (zee-ro) *noun* zeros
nothing, the number 0.

zigzag *noun* zigzags
a line with sudden turns in it like this ΛΛΛ.

zip, zipper *noun* zips, zippers
a fastener for joining two edges of material together. *Some dresses, trousers, and bags have **zips**.*

zoo *noun* zoos
a place where different kinds of wild animals are kept so that people can go and see them.

zucchini (zoo-kee-nee) *noun*
a long, thin, green vegetable.

APPENDICES

Headwords and word origins

Days of the week

Monday *(p. 135)* Monday is from Old English *Mondaeg* meaning 'day of the moon'.

Tuesday *(p. 235)* Tuesday is an Anglo-Saxon name honouring the god of war called *Tiw* (pronounced tue).

Wednesday *(p.247)* Wednesday is an Anglo-Saxon name honouring the god Odin or Woden.

Thursday *(p. 228)* Thursday is an Anglo-Saxon name meaning 'day of thunder'.

Friday *(p. 83)* Friday is from Old English *Frigedaeg*, and is named after the Norse goddess Frigg, wife of Odin.

Saturday *(p. 188)* Saturday is named after the Roman god *Saturn.*

Sunday *(p. 217)* Sunday is an Anglo-Saxon name meaning 'day of the sun'.

Months of the year

January *(p. 110)* The word January comes from the name of the Roman god *Janus*, who was the patron of doors and beginnings. January is the first month of the year, so it is the gateway into the year.

February *(p. 76)* The word February comes from a Latin word *februum* meaning 'purification' because a Roman festival of purification was held about this time.

March *(p. 128)* The word March comes from the Roman month *Martius*, named after the god Mars.

April *(p. 9)* The word April probably comes from a Latin word *aperio* 'to open' because flowers open in spring.

May *(p. 129)* The word May comes from the Roman month *Maius*, named after the goddess Maia.

June *(p. 112)* The word June comes from the Roman month *Junius*, named after the goddess Juno.

July *(p. 112)* The word July comes from the Roman month *Julius*, named after the Roman Emperor Julius Caesar.

August *(p. 11)* The word August comes from the name of the Roman Emperor *Augustus*. It became the name of the Roman month in 8 BC because that month was thought to be his lucky month.

September *(p. 192)* The word September comes from the Latin word *septem* meaning 'seven', because it was the seventh month in the Roman calendar.

October *(p. 146)* The word October comes from the Latin word *octo* meaning 'eight', because October was the eighth month in the Roman calendar.

November *(p. 143)* The word November comes from the Latin word *novem* meaning 'nine', because November was the ninth month in the Roman calendar.

December *(p. 54)* The word December comes from the Latin word *decem* meaning 'ten' because it was the tenth month in the Roman calendar.

month *(p. 136)* The word month is from an Old English word *monath*, which is related to the word for moon, because time used to be measured by the appearance of the moon.

Words that come from people's names

atlas *(p. 11)* *Atlas* was the name of a person in Greek mythology who had to hold the universe on his shoulders. A picture of him was often put at the beginning of old books of maps, and this is how they got their name.

braille *(p. 24)* This word is from the name of Louis Braille, a Frenchman who was blind from the age of three and invented this system. He died in 1852.

cardigan *(p. 31)* Cardigan is named after the 7th Earl of Cardigan, James Thomas Brudenel. He was a soldier and his men were the first to wear this kind of short jacket with buttons. He died in 1868.

sandwich *(p. 187)* The sandwich is named for John Montagu, the 4th Earl of Sandwich, who ate food in this convenient form so as to avoid having to leave the table where games and gambling took place. He died in 1792.

volt *(p. 244)* Volt is named after an Italian scientist called Alessandro Volta, who invented the electric battery.

watt *(p. 246)* Watt is named after a Scottish engineer called James Watt, who studied energy. The energy of lightbulbs or machines is measured in watts.

Shapes

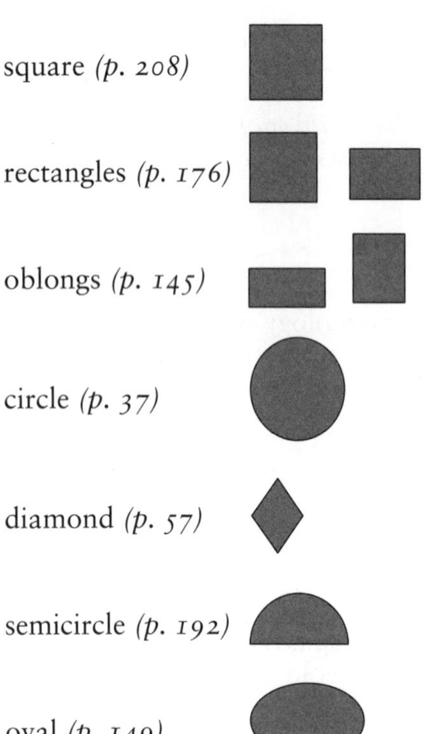

square *(p. 208)*

rectangles *(p. 176)*

oblongs *(p. 145)*

circle *(p. 37)*

diamond *(p. 57)*

semicircle *(p. 192)*

oval *(p. 149)*

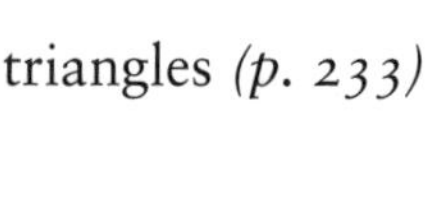

triangles *(p. 233)*

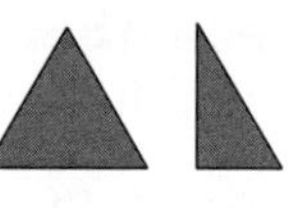

quadrilaterals *(p. 171)*

pentagon *(p. 155)*

heptagon *(p. 98)*

hexagon *(p. 98)*

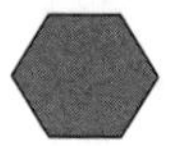

octagon *(p. 146)*

spiral *(p. 207)*

Solid shapes

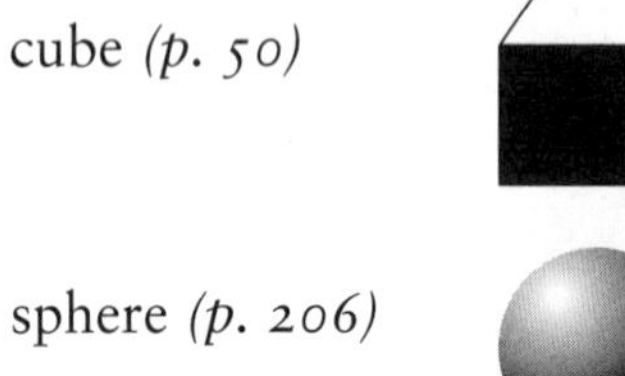

cube *(p. 50)*

sphere *(p. 206)*

hemisphere *(p. 98)*

cylinder *(p. 51)*

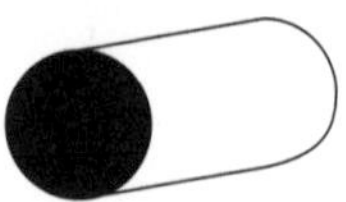

pyramid *(p. 170)*

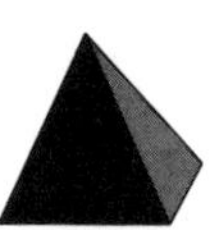

prism *(p. 166)*

cone *(p. 43)*

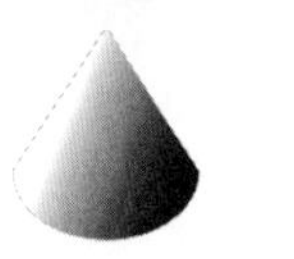

spiral *(p. 207)*

Machines, science and technology

antenna *(p. 8)*
astronaut *(p. 11)*
ATM *(p. 11)*
atmosphere *(p. 11)*
atom *(p. 11)*
battery *(p. 16)*
calculator *(p. 29)*
camera *(p. 30)*
cartridge *(p. 32)*
cassette *(p. 32)*
catamaran *(p. 32)*
CD *(p. 33)*
Celsius *(p. 33)*
compact disc *(p. 41)*
compost *(p. 42)*
computer *(p. 42)*
container ship *(p. 44)*
data *(p. 53)*
diesel *(p. 57)*
disc *(p. 59)*
eclipse *(p. 66)*
electronic *(p. 67)*
elevator *(p. 67)*
Fahrenheit *(p. 74)*
fax *(p. 76)*
gas *(p. 86)*
helicopter *(p. 97)*
incubate *(p. 105)*
Internet *(p. 108)*
jeep *(p. 110)*
keyboard *(p. 114)*
laboratory *(p. 117)*
lever *(p. 121)*
liquid *(p. 122)*
loom *(p. 123)*
machine *(p. 126)*
machine-gun *(p. 126)*
machinery *(p. 126)*
mechanical *(p. 130)*
metal *(p. 132)*
microphone *(p. 132)*
microscope *(p. 132)*
microscopic *(p. 132)*
mineral *(p. 133)*
monitor *(p. 135)*
motor *(p. 136)*
motorbike, motorcycle *(p. 136)*
mouse *(p. 137)*
movie *(p. 137)*
orbit *(p. 148)*
password *(p. 153)*
photocopier *(p. 157)*
PIN *(p. 158)*
prism *(p. 166)*
propeller *(p. 167)*
pulley *(p. 169)*
pump *(p. 169)*
radiator *(p. 173)*
recycle *(p. 176)*
refrigerator *(p. 177)*
satellite *(p. 187)*
science *(p. 189)*
scientific *(p. 189)*
scientist *(p. 189)*
scooter *(p. 189)*
solar *(p. 203)*
solid *(p. 204)*
spacecraft *(p. 205)*
stereo *(p. 211)*
submarine *(p. 215)*
telescope *(p. 224)*
television *(p. 224)*
temperature *(p. 224)*
thermometer *(p. 226)*
torch *(p. 231)*
train *(p. 232)*
trawler *(p. 233)*
tripod *(p. 234)*
truck *(p. 234)*
typewriter *(p. 236)*
vacuum cleaner *(p. 241)*
wagon *(p. 245)*
watch *(p. 246)*
watt *(p. 246)*
wheelbarrow *(p. 248)*
wheelchair *(p. 248)*
yacht *(p. 255)*

Papua New Guinea

aibika [from Tok Pisin *aibika*] *(p. 4)*
aid post *(p. 4)*
Air Nuigini *(p. 5)*
aupa *(p. 12)*
bagarap [from Tok Pisin *bagarap*] *(p. 13)*
baret [from Tok Pisin *baret*] *(p. 14)*
betel nut *(p. 18)*
bighead [from Tok Pisin *bikhet*] *(p. 19)*
big man [from Tok Pisin *bikpela man*] *(p. 19)*
bilas [from Tok Pisin *bilas*] *(p. 19)*
binatang [from Tok Pisin *binatang*] *(p. 19)*
blakbokis [from Tok Pisin *blakbokis*] *(p. 20)*
boi haus (or **boy house**) [from Tok Pisin *haus boi*] *(p. 22)*
bubu *(p. 26)*
cousin-brother *(p. 47)*
cousin-sister *(p. 47)*
cuscus [from Tok Pisin *cuscus*] *(p. 51)*
daka [from Tok Pisin *daka*] *(p. 52)*
didiman [from Tok Pisin *didiman*] *(p. 57)*
digging stick *(p. 58)*
dimdim [from Milne Bay language *dimdim*] *(p. 58)*
dukduk [from Tok Pisin *dukduk*] *(p. 63)*
elementary school *(p. 67)*
em inap [from Tok Pisin *em inap*] *(p. 67)*
em nau [from Tok Pisin *em nau*] *(p. 68)*
em tasol [from Tok Pisin *em tasol*] *(p. 68)*
five-corner [from Tok Pisin *faivkona*] *(p. 79)*
galip [from Tok Pisin *galip*] *(p. 85)*
garamut [from Tok Pisin *garamut*] *(p. 85)*
go finish [from Tok Pisin *go pinis*] *(p. 88)*
grille [from Tok Pisin *grile*] *(p. 91)*
gumi [from Tok Pisin *gumi*] *(p. 92)*
guria [from Tok Pisin *guria*] *(p. 93)*
hamamas [from Tok Pisin *hammas*] *(p. 94)*
hausboi (house boy) [from Tok Pisin *hausboi*] *(p. 96)*

hausmeri (house meri) [from Tok Pisin *hausmeri*] *(p. 96)*
haus tambaran [from Tok Pisin *haus tambaran*] *(p. 96)*
haus win [from Tok Pisin *haus win*] *(p. 96)*
Highlands *(p. 99)*
hiri *(p. 99)*
Hiri Motu *(p. 99)*
ice block *(p. 103)*
kai or kaikai [from Tok Pisin *kaikai*] *(p. 113)*
kalabus [from Tok Pisin *kalabus*] *(p. 113)*
kalang *(p. 113)*
kalapua [from Tok Pisin *kalapua*] *(p. 113)*
kambang [from Tok Pisin *kambang*] *(p. 113)*
kanaka [from Tok Pisin *kanaka*] *(p. 113)*
kapkap *(p. 113)*
kapul [from Tok Pisin *kapul*] *(p. 113)*
kaukau [from Tok Pisin *kaukau*] *(p. 113)*
kiap [from Tok Pisin *kiap*] *(p. 114)*
kina [from Tok Pisin *kina*] *(p. 114)*
kindam [from Tok Pisin *kindam*] *(p. 114)*
kuka [from Tok Pisin *kuka*] *(p. 115)*
kula *(p. 115)*
kulau [from Tok Pisin *kulau*] *(p. 115)*
kumu [from Tok Pisin *kumu*] *(p. 116)*
kumul [from Tok Pisin *kumul*] *(p. 116)*
kunai [from Tok Pisin *kunai*] *(p. 116)*
kundu [from Tok Pisin *kundu*] *(p. 116)*
kuru *(p. 116)*
lagatoi or lakatoi [from Motu *lakatoi*] *(p. 117)*
Lahara *(p. 117)*
laplap [from Tok Pisin *laplap*] *(p. 118)*
lapun [from Tok Pisin *lapun*] *(p. 118)*
laulau [from Tok Pisin *laulau*] *(p. 118)*
Laurabada *(p. 119)*
lime pot *(p. 122)*
long house *(p. 123)*
longlong [from Tok Pisin *longlong*] *(p. 123)*
luluai [from Tok Pisin *luluai*] *(p. 124)*
magani [from Motu *magani*] *(p. 126)*
makau [from Tok Pisin *makau*] *(p. 127)*
manioc [from Tok Pisin *manioc*] *(p. 127)*
marita [from Tok Pisin *marita*] *(p. 128)*
maski [from Tok Pisin *maski*] *(p. 129)*
masta [from Tok Pisin *masta*] *(p. 129)*
mauswara [from Tok Pisin *mauswara*] *(p. 129)*
meri [from Tok Pisin *meri*] *(p. 131)*
meri blaus [from Topk Pisin *meri blaus*] *(p. 131)*
missis [from Tok Pisin *misis*] *(p. 134)*
Moka *(p. 135)*
Motu *(p. 136)*
Mud man *(p. 137)*
muli [from Tok Pisin *muli*] *(p. 137)*
muli water *(p. 137)*
mumu [from Tok Pisin *mumu*] *(p. 137)*
muruk [from Tok Pisin *muruk*] *(p. 137)*
nambawan [from Tok Pisin *nambawan*] *(p. 139)*
national *(p. 139)*
national high school *(p. 139)*
natnat [from Tok Pisin *natnat*] *(p. 140)*
nogat [from Tok Pisin *nogat*] *(p. 142)*
Nuigini [from Tok Pisin *Nu Gini* or *Nui Gini*] *(p. 143)*
okari nut [from Tok Pisin *okari*] *(p. 147)*
Papuan black *(p. 152)*
patrol box *(p. 154)*
patrol officer *(p. 154)*
pay-back *(p. 154)*
Pay Friday *(p. 154)*
pekpek [from Tok Pisin *pekpek*] *(p. 155)*
pidgin *(p. 157)*
pigbel *(p. 158)*
pikinnini [from Tok Pisin *pikinini*] *(p. 158)*
pitpit [from Tok Pisin *pitpit*] *(p. 159)*
poisin [from Tok Pisin *poisin*] *(p. 161)*
pokies *(p. 161)*
Police Motu *(p. 161)*
primary school *(p. 166)*
provincial high school *(p. 168)*
pukpuk [from Tok Pisin *pukpuk*] *(p. 169)*
pumpkin tips *(p. 169)*
puripuri [from Tok Pisin *puripuri*] *(p. 169)*
saksak [from Tok Pisin *saksak*] *(p. 186)*
sanguma [from Tok Pisin *sanguma*] *(p. 187)*
sarep or saref [from Tok Pisin *sarip, sarep*] *(p. 187)*
secondary school *(p. 191)*
sinabada *(p. 198)*
sing-sing [from Tok Pisin *singsing*] *(p. 198)*
sipora [from Motu *sipora*] *(p. 199)*
spak [from Tok Pisin *spak*] *(p. 205)*
stap isi [from Tok Pisin *stap isi*] *(p. 210)*
string band *(p. 214)*
susu [from Tok Pisin *susu*] *(p. 218)*
tambu [from Tok Pisin *tambu*] *(p. 222)*

tangket [from Tok Pisin *tanget* or *tangket*] *(p. 222)*
tapa *(p. 222)*
taro [from Tok Pisin *taro*] *(p. 223)*
taubada [from Motu: *bada* = big, *tau* = man] *(p. 223)*
toea *(p. 230)*
Tok Pisin *(p. 230)*
tok ples [from Tok Pisin *tok ples*] *(p. 230)*
tok save [from Tok Pisin *tok save*] *(p. 230)*
trade store *(p. 232)*
tucker box *(p. 235)*
tura [from Motu *tura*] *(p. 235)*
wantok [from tok Pisin *wantok*] *(p. 246)*

Biological classification words

amphibian *(p. 7)*
animal *(p. 7)*
bacteria *(p. 13)*
bird *(p. 19)*
fish *(p. 78)*
fruit *(p. 83)*
insect *(p. 107)*
invertebrate *(p. 108)*
living *(p. 122)*
mammal *(p. 127)*
marsupial *(p. 128)*
nocturnal *(p. 142)*
plant *(p. 159)*
reptile *(p. 180)*
vegetable *(p. 242)*
vertebrate *(p. 242)*

My body: inside and out

artery *(p. 10)*
bone *(p. 22)*
ear *(p. 65)*
eye *(p. 74)*
eyebrow *(p. 73)*
eyelash *(p. 73)*
face *(p. 74)*
finger *(p. 78)*
fingernail *(p. 78)*
fingerprint *(p. 78)*
heart *(p. 97)*
joint *(p. 111)*
lung *(p. 124)*
muscle *(p. 135)*
nose *(p. 139)*
nostril *(p. 142)*
pimple *(p. 158)*
pupil *(p. 169)*
skeleton *(p. 199)*
skin *(p. 199)*
spine *(p. 207)*
tendon *(p. 224)*
tonsils *(p. 230)*
tooth *(p. 230)*
vein *(p. 242)*
vertebra *(p. 242)*

Abbreviations

EHP Short for Eastern Highlands Province.
Elcom Short for the PNG electricity commission.
ENB Short for East New Britain.
ESP Short for East Sepik Province.
NBC Short for National Broadcasting Commission.
NCD Short for National Capital District.
PMV Short for Public Motor Vehicle; a vehicle for paying passengers.
PNG Short for Papua New Guinea.
SHP Short for Southern Highlands Province.
St Short for saint or street. **St** John's Church is on Mary **St** in Port Moresby.
Telikom Short for telecommunications; the government department concerned with such communications, e.g. telephones.
TV Short for television.
Unitech Short for University of Technology.
UPNG Short for University of Papua New Guinea.
WHP Short for Western Highlands Province.
WNB Short for West New Britain.

MAP OF PAPUA NEW GUINEA

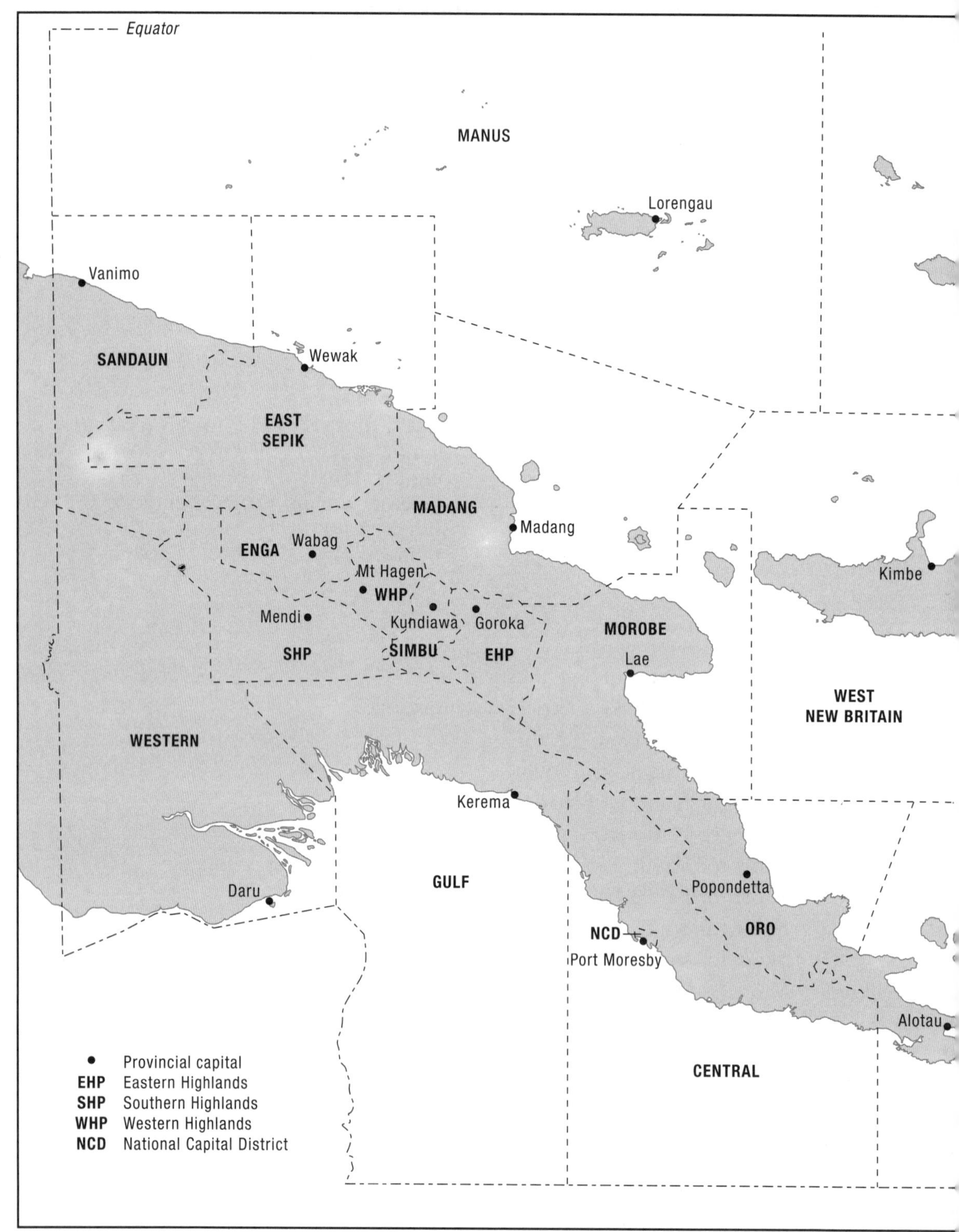

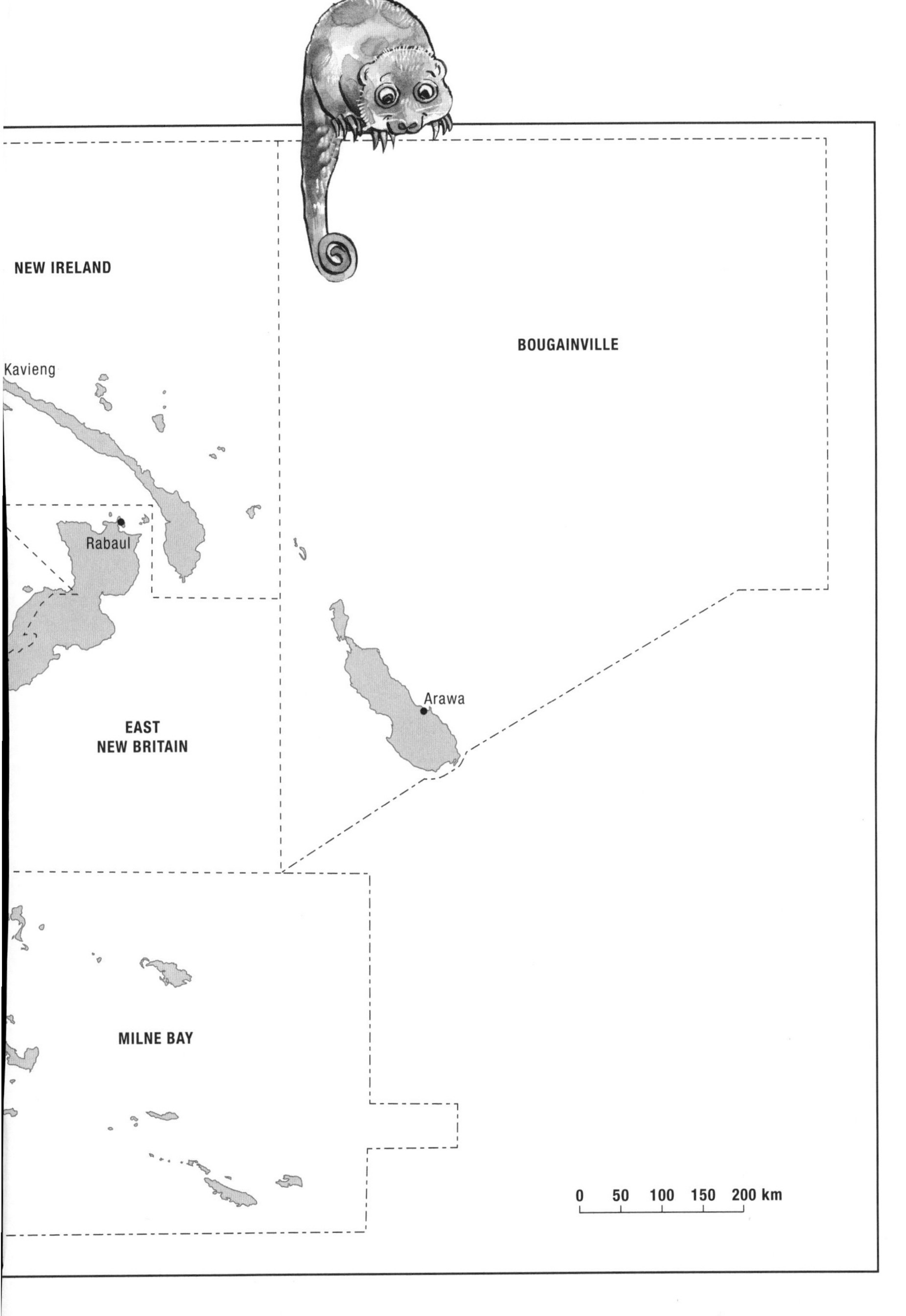
NEW IRELAND
BOUGAINVILLE
Kavieng
Rabaul
Arawa
EAST
NEW BRITAIN
MILNE BAY
0 50 100 150 200 km